Democracy in Nigeria

European University Studies
Europäische Hochschulschriften
Publications Universitaires Européennes

Series XXIII
Theology

Reihe XXIII Série XXIII
Theologie
Théologie

Vol./Bd. 608

PETER LANG
Frankfurt am Main · Berlin · Bern · New York · Paris · Wien

Uche Felix Onwukike

Democracy in Nigeria

Its Anthropological and Social Requirements

PETER LANG
Europäischer Verlag der Wissenschaften

Die Deutsche Bibliothek - CIP-Einheitsaufnahme

Onwukike, Uche Felix:

Democracy in Nigeria : its anthropological and social requirements / Uche Felix Onwukike. - Frankfurt am Main ; Berlin ; Bern ; New York ; Paris ; Wien : Lang, 1997
(European university studies : Ser. 23, Theology ; Vol. 608)
Zugl.: Augsburg, Univ., Diss., 1996
ISBN 3-631-32143-0

D 384
ISSN 0721-3409
ISBN 3-631-32143-0
US-ISBN 0-8204-3503-1

Printed in Germany 1 3 4 5 6 7

To

My parents, Matthias (of blessed memory) and Virginia Onwukike, whose immense love has sustained me and made me what I am today; all the members of Onwukike family, who have always been the source of inspiration and encouragement to me; and Ogom, whose unmitigated love and life-experiences have made me wiser and brought me much closer to God and to humanity.

Preface

Never before has a book been written on democracy in Nigeria with the human person as its base. By introducing the social teachings of the Church into the political, socio-economic and cultural life of Nigeria, this book elevates the worth and dignity of every Nigerian person and places him/her above everything else and at the centre of all systems, plans and structures. However, to what extent this book rightly assesses and meets a need, my readers must judge. That it has not the last word on democracy in Nigeria I am well aware. But if it succeeds in conveying to some readers (especially Nigerians) a little of what I have in mind, then it would not have fully failed and my efforts would have been rewarded.

The book is the fruit of my doctoral research. The dissertation was written under the supervision of Prof. Dr Anton Rauscher, SJ, Head of the Department of the Christian Social Sciences, University of Augsburg, Germany. It was submitted to the Catholic Theology Faculty of the University on 23 July 1996. And it was approved by the Faculty on 4 December 1996 and defended on Friday, 20 December 1996. Apart from the necessary minor corrections - the dedication and this preface - no fundamental changes have been effected in the original text.

Many hands were on deck, directly or indirectly, to bring this book to light. To each and everyone of them I am most grateful. However, some people need to be singled out for some special thanks. Top in the list are: my Bishop, Most Rev. Dr M. N. Okoro, who sent me for further studies; Missio Aachen, whose scholarship made my study possible; and the Catholic Diocese of Augsburg (under the late Archbishop Josef Stimpfle and Bishop Viktor Josef Dammertz), which offered me accommodation and took care of my insurance and of my some other needs. Others are Prof. Dr Anton Rauscher (SJ), my moderator, who was always there for me as a father, a brother, a friend, and a benefactor; Prof. Dr Klaus Kienzler, my second moderator; and Prof. Dr Joachim Piegsa, a member of the Examination Commission, whose good dispositions I enjoyed in the course of my studies.

Not to be forgotten are the members of staff and seminarians of the Priesterseminar St. Hieronymus Augsburg, where I spent my first two and a half years in Germany. They created the family atmosphere and provided every necessary assistance I needed during the initial and most difficult stage of my studies. Many thanks to the Rector, Fr. Rudolf Kopold and his sister, Rosa, as well as to the vice-Rector, Fr. Franz Götz and his sister, Barbara, for making this possible.

My indebtedness also goes to Messrs Michael Onwukike, Kenneth Mbah, Emeka and Stanislaus Onwukike, Julius and Emeka Igwilo, Peter Ohoma Ibekwe, Frs. Martin F. Asiegbu and Chukwudi G. Okafor, who helped me to gather materials in Nigeria for this work. It is also thanks to Deacon Bill and Pat Glover, as well as Carl Hamilton, for taking care of my subscriptions to the *Journal of Democracy*.

To Dr Peter Adams, Dr Bill Graham, and Fr. Benjamin A. Chima, who read through my scripts and offered me constructive criticisms and suggestions I am most grateful.

I will not fail to thank the members of staff of the American Library of Congress (where I did most of my research-work), for their immense services and help. My profound gratitude also goes to Ms Ogom B. Ezeanyaeche, Dr and Mrs Sunday-Chinwe Nwosuh, and St. Patrick's family, Newburgh, under the good leadership of Msgr. John Budwick, who took adequate care of me each time I was in the USA for research.

Last but not the least, I sincerely thank Fr. Cyprian I. Aginah with whom I shared all my sadness and joy in the course of writing this book, Ms Christa Manusch (the secrtary to Prof. Rauscher) who took care of all official correspondences concerning my studies, and Dietmar Mozet who took care of my computer problems. The same thanks goes to Sr. Janet N. Ayim, Dave and Etta McArthur, Dr Manfred and Hannelore Marz, Daniel and Monica van de Werf, Michael and Viktoria Popfinger, for their immense support and encouragement.

Uche F. Onwukike
(Augsburg, January 1997)

Table of Contents

Part Two

Democracy In Nigeria: Its anthropological and social requirements

GENERAL INTRODUCTION

1. Stating the Problem

There is a strong wind of change - a change from communism and autocracy to democracy - blowing all over the world. "Almost everywhere, command economies and overtly authoritarian politics are in retreat. Constitutional democracy and market capitalism now hold sway, at least as ideals, even in places where these concepts were anathema less than a decade ago. This is as true for Central and Eastern Europe as it is for Latin America, sub-Saharan Africa, and much of East Asia."[1] This is a good omen for democracy. However, the processes of building and sustaining democratisation and market-oriented economy are not at all easy. Many of the developing countries are finding it very difficult to cope with the stringent economic reform thought necessary for democratisation by the Western World. Africa, as a whole, in this regard, is in trouble.

One hears and reads nowadays many ugly and disheartening things from media reports about Africa. Such reports include: "Africa is a lost continent," "African continent is in a process of decay," "Africa is a continent on international periphery." Two reports are hereby quoted to buttress my point. In his article on "Economic Reform and Democracy: Crisis and Opportunity in Africa," Nicolas van de Walle observes that:

> A profound pessimism pervades much recent commentary on Africa. According to many observers, the region's increasing marginalization from international arena is being accompanied by - if not contributing to - the collapse of central states under the pressures of economic crisis and ethnoregional conflict. The most pessimistic analysts see a generalized return to the violent lawlessness of the immediate precolonial period. Others, like Thomas Callaghy, discount the worst scenarios but suggest that the 'specter of anarchy' will hunt the continent indefinitely, with many states ultimately succumbing to chaos. In view of many such observers, the wave of democratization that has washed over the continent since 1990 will only add to the burden of the beleaguered African state. Reforms are likely to be short-lived, overwhelmed by many severe problems that are devastating the region.
> Africa does indeed offer ample cause for pessimism. Some states are clearly in the process of collapsing.... The biggest threat to the consolidation of democracy in sub-Sahara Africa is likely to be the continent's continuing economic crisis. The dozen African nations in which power has been transferred thanks to multiparty elections in the last five years are all beset by daunting economic difficulties....[2]

In the same vein, Thomas Callaghy writes:

> Africa is a weak neighborhood in the international political economy. I use the term 'weak neighborhood' in two primary senses, one referring to the acceleration of the continent's economic crisis and its attendant marginilization from the international system, and a second referring to the internal weakness of African

> states. Africa has been experiencing both economic and politico-strategic marginalization, but the former is more significant. The continent no longer plays a substantial role in the international division of labor and is no longer very important to the major actors in the world economy - multinational corporations, international banks, the leading Western countries, and such newly industrialized countries as Korea, Taiwan, Chile, Brazil, and Mexico. Africa generates a declining share of world output. The main commodities it produces are becoming less valuable or are more effectively produced by other Third World countries. Trade is declining; no one wants to lend to African countries; and few want to invest in the area, with the exception of certain parts of the mineral sector....
> Africa's per-capita income levels and growth rates have declined since the first oil crisis in 1973, even though the continent's share of worldwide official development assistance rose from 17 percent in 1970 to about 38 percent in 1991. Since 1970, nominal GDP growth has risen more slowly than in developing countries elsewhere, while real GDP growth rates have dropped dramatically since 1965. Given this dismal economic performance, it is not surprising that world business leaders have taken an increasingly jaundiced view of Africa.[3]

Truly these two reports, and others like them, are very frightening. Yes, with economic crisis and marginalization on the one hand, and political weakness on the other - coupled with interrelated social, health, ecological, and infrastructural crisis - Africa's future, especially concerning democratisation, seems very bleak. It is even feared that given such a fragile base, democratisation may well intensify rather than ameliorate Africa's problems. This is already evident in some African countries, which have embarked on democratisation and economic reform and, where life has become very unbearable and worse than it was before their venture into democratisation and economic reform.

Nigeria, the choice of this thesis, being an African country, shares in the fate described above. Thirty-six years old as an independent nation, Nigeria has had ten years of democratic rule and twenty-six years of military dictatorship - and the military are still in power - indicating how politically weak Nigeria is. This situation is made worse by Nigeria's ethnic and religious divides. Nigeria suffers from economic crisis. It is plagued with huge external debt of about $32,245,000,000 (1991), high inflation rate of 64-80% (1995), very low per capita income of less than $250 (1996). Moreover, the country lacks social amenities and services, and is deeply immersed in bribery and corruption.

Surely Nigeria does not want the good wind of democracy to pass it by. Surely Nigeria does not want to remain forever the underdogs of the world. Therefore Nigeria must rise from its developmental slumber, get on its feet, and begin to do something to better its lot. But the problem is "how"? How can Nigeria get itself out of its political, socio-economic, and moral mess? How can Nigeria build an effective and responsible government: a government that will be accountable to the people - a government that will play the game of politics according to the democratic norms and principles - a government that will respect, safeguard, and promote the basic human rights and freedoms - a government that will work for equity and social justice - a government that will shun the self and sectionalism and work for the common good - a government that will raise the country above the poverty level - a government that will bring the nation back to the international forum? How can Nigeria groom a citizenry that will be very much aware of its rights and duties? How can Nigeria establish an independent and impartial judiciary for the maintenance of the rule of law and justice? How can Nigeria establish the mass media that will be conscious of its educating, informative and correcting roles? How can Nigeria cultivate and enforce a workable economic reform? In short, how can Nigeria build a stable and lasting democracy? These are the problems that this thesis is set to tackle.

2. Scope and Purpose of Work

This thesis is centred on Nigeria, though it could be very helpful to other developing countries, especially in Africa. I have chosen Nigeria, not necessarily because I am from Nigeria but also because of the important place Nigeria occupies and the eminent roles it plays in Africa in particular, especially in the sub-Saharan Africa, and in the world at large. Indeed, Nigeria is a major voice in virtually all African events and issues. This, not only because of its human and mineral resources, but also because of Nigeria' foreign policy based on the liberation and uplift of the black person, not only in Africa but in the whole world.[4] No wonder Nigeria has been variously called "the Giant of Africa," "the regional power of black Africa," "the symbol of African unity" and "the symbol of African democracy"! In his examination of the American policy toward Nigeria (from Kennedy to Reagan), Robert B. Shepard highlights the prominence of Nigeria in African affairs thus:

> The overarching goal of American foreign policy since the end of World War II has been the containment of the Soviet Union. But since the late 1960s and the early 1970s, the United States increasingly has been forced to deal with a broad range of states that occupy the intermediate position in the international hierarchy. Saudi Arabia, South Korea, Taiwan, and Nigeria have come to rank among America's trading partner.... Israel, Vietnam, and South Africa have come to occupy high positions on the American foreign-policy agenda because of their dominant military positions in their regions. Other 'regional powers,' such as Brazil, Mexico, India, Pakistan, and Nigeria, which in the 1960s had been relegated to the periphery of international relations, began in the 1970s and 1980s to exercise influence on a more occasional basis over their neighbors.
>
> ....
>
> Nigeria is black Africa's wealthiest and most populous state.... Since 1974, its gross domestic product (GDP), as well as its export earnings, has accounted for about one-half of black Africa's eonomic output.... It is about the size of California, Arizona, and Nevada put together or, alternatively, roughly the combined size of West Germany, France, Switzerland, and Austria....
>
> Nigeria has played an influential role in west African affairs, pan-African issues, and even, at times, global economic issues. It figured prominently in the creation of

> the Organization of African States (OAS) and the development of the trade regime that links Africa and Western Europe (the Lome Convention), and it was driving force in the creation of the Economic Community of West African States (ECOWAS). In the mid-1970s, Nigeria became one of the world's leading oil exporters, and for two years it was the major source of oil imports by the United States.
> Because of its size and influence, Nigeria has variously been charaterized as a 'regional power,' an 'emerging middle power,' 'the key to Africa,' and 'Africa's major power.'....[5]

It is true - and a pity - that Nigeria has fallen short of world expectations of it. The once "symbol of African democracy" is today many million miles away from democracy and from being democratic - due to the many years of military rule in Nigeria. The once one of the ten richest countries in the world ranks today among the poorest countries in the world - due to high rate of corruption, non-accountability, and bad administration, coupled with the global economic crunch. There is lack of security, equity and social justice. And there is a degradation in Nigeria's image and reputation at home and abroad. Nevertheless, its ailments notwithstanding, Nigeria remains a big force to be reckoned with in Africa. (Then Nigeria is "one eyed-man in a blind country.") Hence it is very necessary that Nigeria recovers very quickly from its "sickness" to be able to play well the leading role expected of it.

Therefore, it is the purpose of this thesis to draw the attention of Nigeria to its immense potentials and to its lacks and faults, and then to present it with certain guidelines which will help it to establish a stable and lasting democracy: a democracy with a human face, which makes for a disciplined, fair, just and humane Nigeiran society; a good and capable government that will place the well-being of the society and that of its citizens - thus, the common good - above every other thing else. Then when Nigeria has recovered - when it has become a democratically developed country - it will be able to help and strengthen other African states in the process of constructing stable democracies.

3. Method of Presentation

The thesis has been divided into two parts. Part one treats the general ideals of modern democracy. It is a very important introduction to the theme of the thesis (dealt with in part two). This is so because to be able to build or construct anything, it is very necessary to have a plan - an ideal or a model - to which one would look up, and from which one would copy. Firstly, one of the major problems any developing country meets with is the forceful impact from the developed countries: the developed countries force their ideologies on developing countries as part of their aid-packages to the latter. In accepting any of these ideologies under aid-package, a developing country wishing to build or in the process of building a democratic society should first weigh how democratic the proposed ideology is, because not all claimants on democracy are democratic. For this reason, chapter one is devoted to the problem of the claims on democracy. Secondly, to successfully build a democracy, a country should have before it the general ideals of modern democracy from which to model its democratic structures and institutions. These ideals of are discussed in chapter two (the universal principles of democracy) and in chapter three (the necessary institutions for democracy). And to encourage a developing country in the face of difficulties during its democratisation processes, chapter four considers the meaning, purpose, and way of democracy - showing democracy as the best available system, its weaknesses notwithstanding.

Part two deals with the theme of our thesis: the anthropological and social requirements of democracy in Nigeria. In treating this theme, attention is paid to the political development of Nigeria, from the colonial time to the present day up to the end of 1995 (chapter two); the problem of democracy in Nigeria - that is, the factors that constitute a hindrance to the growth of enduring democracy in Nigeria (chapter three); and the building of a stable and lasting democracy in Nigeria, with special emphasis on the development of the human person and on democracy as a way of life, concluding with a call to patriotism (chapter four).

NOTES

1 Leslie E. Armijo, Thomas J. Biersteker & Abraham F. Lowenthal, "The Problems of Simultaneous Transitions," in: L. Diamond and M. F. Plattner, eds., **Economic Reform and Democracy** (Baltimore and London: The Johns Hopkins University Press, 1995), p. 226.

2 Nicolas van de Walle, "Economic Reform and Democracy: Crisis and Opportunity in Africa," in: **Journal of Democracy**, vol. 6, no. 2, April 1995 (Baltimore: John Hopkins University Press), p. 128.

3 Thomas Callaghy, "Africa: Back to the Future," in: L. Diamond and M. F. Plattner, eds., **Economic Reform and Democracy** (Baltimore and London: The Johns Hopkins University Press, 1995), pp. 140-141.

4 See Robert B. Shepard, **Nigeria, Africa and the United States: From Kennedy to Reagan** (Bloomington and Indianapolis: Indiana University Press, 1991) and Peter Holmes, **Nigeria: Giant of Africa** (Lagos: National Oil and Chemical Marketing Co. of Nigeria, 1985).

5 Robert B. Shepard, op. cit., pp. 2-4.

PART ONE

THE IDEALS OF MODERN DEMOCRACY

1. THE PROBLEM OF THE CLAIMS ON DEMOCRACY

Democracy as an organisational system and as a way of life - like culture - is not static. It grows. It develops. It changes, with years, in form as well as in purpose.[1] So modern democracy has undergone many changes and developments.[2] Such changes and developments go from the classical Greek experience in Athens,[3] through the ideas and institutions of Medieval Europe (that is, the concept of divine, natural and customary law as a restraint on the exercise of power; and the community as the source of all political authority),[4] to the practices of European kings in the Middle Ages (that is, the consultations with the different "estates," or group of interests, in the approval of their policies).[5] They are also visible from the impacts of the Enlightenment period and of the American and French Revolutions (that is, the concepts of natural rights and political equality)[6] to the Evangelical Inspirations (that is, religious thoughts as the source of the fundamental principles upon which the democratic order is built).[7] Due to these changes and developments, the modern man might find it difficult to consider the Athenian democracy a democracy,[8] just like the Athenian citizen, if he were somehow to appear in our midst, "would surely contend that a modern democracy is not, after all, a democracy."[9] Thus, the saying: "everybody is a child of his age" holds much water here, even for the term democracy.

Moreover, the term "democracy" has rather become hackneyed through constant loose usage. It has become a domestic word - a commonplace word - indeed, a cliche´. Many people use the word without knowing its meaning and/or its implications. Some have come to think of it as something to which to give lip or mind service, without using their minds to re-examine the term. It can be said that since Herodotus coined the word, *demokratia*, some 2,400 years ago,[10] "democracy has acquired diverse meanings, referring, as it has, to very different historical settings as well as to very different ideals. Thus, with the passing of time, both its denotative and connotative uses have changed."[11] Today all are not agreed on the meaning of, form and substance of democracy. C. J. Friedrich laments that everybody is for democracy "the way he understands it."[12] H. Laufer writes that "the confusion about form and substance of democracy is great" that man must speak perhaps even from an "empty form."[13] And Keith Graham hints on this confusion more succinctly:

> Crudely speaking, up to the eighteenth century everyone had a very clear idea what democracy was and hardly anyone was in favour of it. Now that position is reversed. Everyone is in favour of it but no one has a clear idea any longer what it is. Republicans would claim to be as democratic as Democrats. Conservative and Communist parties claim to embrace democracy. In the West we speak of western democracy, in the East they speak of people's democracies. No wonder confusion reigns on the subject.[14]

This lack of "unanimity as to what should be understood as democracy"[15] is further evidenced in the markedly different political practices of the various institutions and regimes that claim to be democracies and/or democratic. David Held (a Senior Lecturer in Social Science at the Open University) calls this a historical fact and he writes:

> ... nearly everyone today says they are democrats no matter whether their views are on the left, center or right. Political regimes of all kinds in, for instance, Western Europe, the Eastern Block and Latin America claim to be democracies. Yet, what each of these regimes says and does is radically different.[16]

Thus, in appearance, autocracy may sometimes be difficult to distinguish from non-autocratic rule. Often, autocracies attempt to borrow legitimacy by adopting the language of the constitutions of non-autocratic regimes or by establishing similar institutions. It is a common practice, for example, in many modern totalitarian states to establish institutions - parliaments or assemblies, elections and parties, courts and legal codes - that differ little in appearance from the institutional structures of constitutional democracies. Similarly, the language of totalitarian constitutions is often couched in terms of doctrines of popular rule or democracy. That the democratic legitimacy could be, and would be, claimed by popular or constitutional dictatorships such as those of Napoleon III in France or Adolf Hitler in Germany only shows how central the double ideal of democracy and constitutional justification had become. The autocratic regimes often have similar goals as their democratic counterparts[17] - such as the attainment of a measure of economic security, the general social welfare of the people. According to Milburn Lincoln Wilson, "it is a fact so universally admitted that it is the very heart and center not only of the system of the democracies but the justification of Fascism, of Nazism and of Communism. Each one of those systems asserts that it is based upon social welfare of all."[18] Furthermore, it is not only democracy that has a claim on *the will of the people*. Any kind of government - be it oligarchy or monarchy or dictatorship or democracy - can claim to rest on *the will of the people*. R. M. MacIver (Professor Emeritus of Political Philosophy and Sociology at Columbia University) writes that " in Russia, at the time of writing (he wrote in 1947), a larger proportion of the people approves and supports its government than may be found in democratic countries to support their governments."[19] Similarly, Walter E. Boek argues that "the occurrence of elections by themselves do not make a country democratic. A 'populist' election may be a populist tyranny wherein the leader is sovereign."[20] The Germany's Hitler came to power with full support and with full consent and will of the German people. Also there is no successful military coup in Nigeria that was not greeted with great applause and welcomed by Nigerians.[21] All said and done, these examples of apparent similarities between democratic regimes and autocratic ones do not make the latter democracies or democratic. There is a world of difference between the two types of regimes - a type of difference between heaven and hell. Since "all that glitters are not gold," it is very necessary for us to make and to note this difference - to be able to "separate the sheep from the goats."

To be able to make this separation we must de-emphasise *the goal theory* of government and emphasise *the means theory*. It is obvious that "the end does not justify the means." Both democratic and autocratic regimes may have similar goals or ends but their means of achieving these goals or of attaining these ends are definitely not the same. In theory the former Soviet Union, for instance, is a democracy - if we go by the goal theory alone - since its leaders number efficiency and material progress among their primary goals, and boast of them as totalitarian achievements. In practice it was but a tyrannical oligarchy. Thus the difference democracy and autocracy is clear. On the one hand, in democracy people have a say on how they are governed and on who should govern them - that is, there is room for public opinion and discussion. On the other hand, in autocracy everything is dictated from above - that is, the people do not have the final say (if at all they have any say). Although totalitarian regimes often attempt to borrow legitimacy by adopting the language of the constitutions of non-autocratic regimes or by establishing similar institutions, neither the institutions nor the constitutional provisions act as effective checks on the power of the single centre. They are essentially facades for the exercise of power through hierarchical procedures that subject all the officials of the state to the commands of the ruling individual or group. The underlying realities of autocratic rule are always the concentration of power in a single center and the mobilisation of force to prevent the emergence of opposition. Using the words of J.A. Schumpeter, "it is the characteristic of almost every anti-democratic philosophy that it purports to serve the welfare of the people but refuses to trust the judgment of the people on questions affecting their welfare...."[22] Referring to the situation in the former Soviet Union, R. M. MacIver points out that "...there is no free exercise of opinion on matters of policy, nor any constitutional means by which the changing currents of opinion can find political expression. It would therefore be the sheerest confusion to classify the Soviet system as democratic."[23] In the same vein, Schumpeter emphasises that "a 'constitutional' monarchy does not qualify to be called democratic because electorates and parliaments, while having all the other rights that electorates and parliaments have in parliamentary monarchies, lack the power to impose their choice as to the governing committee: the cabinet ministers are in this case servants of the monarch, in substance as well as in name, and can in principle be dismissed as well as appointed by him...."[24] In contrast to these autocracies is the democratic society "in which policy slowly and uncertainly and hesitatingly emerges out of thousands of conferences and millions of conversations, out of pressure groups, out of the opinion of the press, and out of all the paraphernalia that a free country employs to make vocal the opinion of its citizens...."[25]

At this juncture, it has become very clear, using the words of Jesus Christ, that "it is not those who say to me, 'Lord, Lord,' who will enter the kingdom of heaven, but the person who does the will of my Father in heaven."[26] In other words, it is not all who lay claim on democracy are democratic.[27] A good many of them are just "wolves in sheep's clothing."[28] One is not democratic simply by wearing the tag "democracy". After all, what is in a name? To be democratic, therefore, one has to go according to the principles and methods of democracy - not only in theory but also, and much more so, in practice. Democracy is something you do; not just something you talk about. Walter Boek posits 39 criteria[29] which "may be used to obtain a score indicating how democratic a country is by judging how well the government meets the 39 criteria." He argues that "by utilizing these to rate governments, some nations claiming to be democratic or that have democratic sounding names will be found not to be democratic.... Other nations may be partially democratic because they have some of the characteristics." However, we shall not give here details of Walter's 39 criteria since they fall under our discussion of the principles, institutions, and methods of democracy. But then what are the principles, institutions, and methods - in short, the ways - of democracy?

It is the onus of this section to answer this question. Chapters two and three deal with the principles and institutions of modern democracy respectively; and chapter four concludes with the way of democracy - that is, with what democracy is all about.

NOTES

1 Cf. B. R. Ambedka, **Conditions Precedent For The Successful Working Of Democracy** (Nagpur: Y. M. Panchbhai, 1976), pp. 1-2.

2 For special reading, I recommend: George H. Sabine, **A History Of Political Theory**, 4th. ed., revised by Thomas L. Thorson (U.S.A.: Holt, Rinehart and Winston, Inc., 1973); and Garrett Ward Sheldon, **The History Of Political Theory: Ancient Greece To Modern America**, Series X, Political Science, Vol. 21 (New York-Bern-Frankfurt am Main- Paris: Peter Lang, 1988).

3 Cf. J. A. O. Larson, **Representative Government In Greek And Roman History** (Berkeley & Los Angeles: University of California Press, 1966); R. K. Sinclair, **Democracy and Participation in Athens** (G. Britain: Cambridge University Press, 1989); W. R. Connor, et al., **Aspects Of Athenian Democracy**, with a preface by J. Rufus Fears (Copenhagen: Museum Tusculanum Press, 1990); A. H. M. Jones, **Athenian Democracy** (Oxford: Basil Blackwell, 1975); M. I. Finley, ed., **Studies in Ancient Society** (London and Boston, 1974); Thucydides, *The History Of The Peloponesian War* (tr. by Richard Crawley and rev. by R. Feetham), bk. II, 37 & 40, in: **Great Books Of The Western World**, vol. 5, (Chicago: Encyclopaedia Britannica, Inc., 2nd. edition, 1990); Aristotle, *The Politics*, VI. ii. or 1317a(40) - 1318a(3), in: **Great Books Of The Western World**, vol. 8, (Chicago: Encyclopaedia Britannica, Inc., 2nd. edition, 1990); E. Barker (Sir), **Greek Political Theory, Plato And His Predecessors**, 5th. ed. (London: Metheien & Co. Ltd., 1977); M. H. Hansen, **The Athenian Ecclesia: A Collection of Articles, 1976-83** (Copenhagen: Museum Tusculum Press, 1983); L. B. Carter, **The**

Quiet Athenian (Oxford: Clarendon Press, 1986); J. Ober, "Public Speech and the Power of the People in Democratic Athens", in: **PS: Political Science & Politics**, vol. XXVI, no. 3 (September 1993), pp. 481-485; M. H. Hansen, **The Athenian Democracy in the Age of Demosthenes: Structure, Principles and Ideology** (Oxford: Blackwell, 1991); M. H. Hansen, **The Sovereignty of the People's Court in the Fourth Century B.C. and the Public Action against Unconstitutional Proposals** (Odense, 1974); J. Peter Euben, "Democracy Ancient and Modern", in: **PS: Political Science & Politics**, vol. XXVI, no. 3 (Sept. 1993), pp. 478-480; Bernard Grofman, "Lessons of Athenian Democracy: Editor's Introduction", in: **PS: Political Science & Politics**, vol. XXVI, no. 3 (Sept. 1993), pp. 471-474; T. Hobbes, **Thucydides' History**, ed. by Richard Schlatter (New Bruswick: Rutgers University Press, (1627) 1975); W. Mitford, **The History of Greece** (London: t. Cadell, Strand, (1829) 1838); A. W. Saxonhouse, "Athenian Democracy: Modern Mythmakers and Ancient Theorists," in: **PS: Political Science & Politcs**, vol. XXVI, no. 3 (Sept. 1993), pp. 486-490; D. Webster, **Writings and Speeches**, national ed. (Boston: Little, Brown & Co., 1903); Garry Wills, **Lincoln at Gettysburg: The Words that Remade America** (New York: Simon and Schuster, 1992); A. Zimmern, **The Greek Commonwealth** (Oxford: At the Clarendon Press, 1914); F. Turner, **The Greek Heritage in Victorian Britain** (New Haven: Yale University Press, 1981); H. Arendt, **On The Human Condition** (Chicago: University of Chicago Press, 1958); M. I. Finley, **Democracy: Ancient and Modern** (New Bruswick: Rutgers University Press, (1973) 1985); C. Farrar, **The Origins of Democratic Thinking: The Invention of Politics in Classical Athens** (Cambridge: Cambridge University Press, 1988); D. Kagan, **Pericles of Athens and the Birth of Democracy** (New York: The Free Press, 1991); M. T. Clark "Realism Ancient and Modern: Thucydides and International Relations," in: **PS: Political Science & Politics**, vol. XXVI, no. 3 (Sept. 1993), pp. 491-494; Irwin Edman, "Classical Origins," in: **Foundations of Democracy**, by Institute for Religious and Social Studies, Jewish Theological Seminary of America (New York: Cooper Square Publishers, 1964, c 1947), pp. 18-26.

4 Cf. R. W. Carlyle and A. J. Carlyle, **A Hisory of Medieval Political Theory In The West** (Edinburgh & London: William Blackwood & Sons Ltd., 1928), esp. vols. 5 & 6; George N. Shuster, "Mediaeval Sources," in: **Foundations of Democracy**, by Institute for Religious and Social Studies, Jewish Theological Seminary of America (New York: Cooper Square Publishers, 1964, c 1947), pp. 35-43; Irwin Edman, "Classical Origins," in: **Foundations of Democracy**, by Institute for Religious and Social Studies, Jewish Theological Seminary of America (New York: Cooper Square Publishers, 1964, c 1947), pp. 18-26; Marcus T. Cicero, *Republic*, III, 22. - trans. by G. H. Sabine and S. B. Smith. See their work: **On the Commonwealth: Marcus Tullius Cicero** (Columbus, Ohio, 1929. Introduction); Munroe Smith, **The Development of European Law** (New York, 1928); Henry II's Assize of Woodstock, 1184, Stubbs, *Select Charters*, 9th. ed. (1913), p. 188; trans. in: Adams and Stephens, **Select Documents of English Constitutional History** (1901), No. 18.

5 Cf. R. W. Carlyle and A. J. Carlyle, **A Hisory of Medieval Political Theory In The West** (Edinburgh & London: William Blackwood & Sons Ltd., 1928), esp. vols. 5 & 6; **Summa Theologica**, 1. 2, 105, 1, in: Carlyle, op. cit., vol. V, p. 94; **Selected Chapters**, "Summons to a Great Council," A.D. 1213, in: Carlyle, op. cit., vol. V, p.130; **Selected Chapters**, "Writ of Summons for Two Knights," A. D. 1254, in: Carlyle, id.; **Collecion de Cortes De Los Reinos de Leon et de Castilla**, vii, in: Carlyle, op.cit., vol. V, p.134; M. G. H., **Constitution**, vol. III, 67, in: Carlyle, op. cit., vol. V, p. 135;

Asculta Fili and **Unam Sanctam** of Nov. 1302, in: Carlyle, op. cit., vol. V, p. 139; **Statutes of the Realm**, vol. i, p. 189 (Edward II, 1322), in: Carlyle, op. cit., vol. VI, p. 108; Stubbs, **Constitutional History**, vol. ii (ed. 1877), pp. 387-391, in: Carlyle, op. cit., vol. VI, p. 109; Nicolas of Cusa, **De Concordantia Catholica**, iii. 25, in: Carlyle, op. cit., vol. VI, pp. 215 f.; Sir John Fortescue, **De Natura Legis**, i. 16, in: Carlyle, op. cit., vol. VI, p. 217; Sir John Fortescue, **De Laudibus Legis Angliae**, XVIII, in: Carlyle, op. cit., vol. VI, p. 217.

6 Cf. John Locke, *Concerning Civil Government, Second Essay*, Chap. II. 4, in: **Great Books Of the Western World**, vol. 33, ed. by Mortimer J. Adler, et al. (Chicago, et al.: Encyclopaedia Britannica, Inc., 1991); J. J. Rousseau, *On The Origin Of Inequality*, in: **Great Books Of the Western World**, vol. 35, ed. by Mortimer J. Adler, et al. (Chicago, et al.: Encyclopaedia Britannica, Inc., 1991); J. J. Rousseau, *The Social Contract*, Bk. I, Chap. 8, in: **Great Books Of the Western World**, vol. 35 (1991); James Madison, *The Federalist Papers*, no. 10, in: **Great Books Of The Modern World**, vol. 40 (1991), pp. 49-53; A. N. Wilder, "Literary Sources," in: **Foundations of Democracy**, by Institute for Religious and Social Studies, Jewish Theological Seminary of America (New York: Cooper Square Publishers, 1964, c 1947), pp. 87-108; H. M. Kallen, "Humanistic Sources," in: **Foundations of Democracy**, by Inst. for Rel. and Soc. Studies, Jewish Theol. Seminary of America (New York: Cooper Square Publishers, 1964), pp. 62-86; H. C. Mansfield, Jr., "Thomas Jefferson," in: **American Political Thought**, ed. by M. J. Frisch and R. G. Stevens (New York: Charles Scribner's Sons, 1971); Thomas Jefferson, *The Declaration of Independence*, in: **The Great Books of the Western World**, vol. 40 (1991); P. Corbett, **Ideologies** (London: Hutchinson & Co. (Publishers) Ltd., 1970).

7 Cf. J. Maritain, **Christianity And Democracy & The Right of Man And Natural Law**, trans. by Doris C. Anson (San Fracisco: Ignatius Press, 1986); Theodore Roosevelt, **Letter to American Bishops**, in: **Catholic News** (Jan. 17, 1942); Henry A. Wallace, **The Price of Free World Victory**: Speech dilivered on May 8, 1942, before the Free World Association; A. E. Holt, **Christian Roots of Democracy in America** (New York: Friendship Press, 1941); L. Finkelstein, "Hebrew Sources: Scipture and Talmud," in: **Foundations of Democracy**, by Inst. for Rel. and Soc. Studies, Jewish Theol. Seminary of America (New York: Cooper Square Publishers, 1964), pp. 27-34; J. T. McNeil, "Reformation Sources," in: **Foundations of Democracy**, by Inst. for Rel. and Soc. Studies, Jewish Theol. Seminary of America (N. Y.: Cooper Square Publishers, 1964), pp. 44-61.

8 David Held writes: "Thus, whether we can legitimately refer to Athens as a democracy at all is a question that at least has to be posed. Unquestionably, the politics of ancient Athens rested on a highly undemocratic base. But it is worth stressing, as Finley has done, that the choice between 'rule by the few' or 'rule by the many' was 'a meaningful choice', and that the 'rights' that various groups claimed for themselves, and bitterly fought for, were of the greatest significance, even though "'the many' were a minority of the population" (Finley, 1983, p. 9). Both the remarkable achievements and the strict limits of Athenian democracy need to be appreciated." (See his **Models Of Democracy** (UK: Polity Press, 1987), pp. 23f..)

9 R. A. Dahl, **Democracy And Its Critics** (New Haven & London: Yale University Press, 1989), p. 20.

10 1992 - 1993 was the 2,500th anniversary of the birth of democracy. See **PS: Political Science & Politics,** vol. XXVI, no.3, Sept. 1993, pp. 471-494, for some papers

delivered by some eminent scholars to mark this anniversary in America. Note that Herodotus is often held to have been the first to say "democracy." (See **History**, bk. III, 80-83).

11 G. Sartori, **The Theory Of Democracy Revisited** (Chatham, New Jersey: Chatham House Publishers, Inc., 1987), p. 278.

12 C. J. Friedrich, **Der Verfassungsstaat der Neuzeit** (Berlin-Göttingen-Heidelberg, 1953), p. 1.

13 H. Laufer, **Die demokratische Ordnung** (Stuttgart-Berlin-Köln--Mainz, 1966), p. 9.

14 K. Graham, **The Battle of Democracy: Conflict, Consensus and Individual** (Great Britain: Wheatsheaf Books, 1986), p.1.

15 M. Hättich, **Demokratie als Herrschaftsordnung** (Köln-Opladen, 1967), p. 12.

16 D. Held, **Models Of Democracy** (UK: Polity Press, 1987), p. 1.

17 Cf. M. L. Wilson, **Democracy Has Roots** (New York: Carrick & Evans, inc., c. 1939), pp. 91-110; also, Henry S. Commager, "In Defense of Majority Rule," in: **Basic Issues of American Democracy: A Book of Readings**, selected and edited by H. M. Bishop and S. Hendel, 6th. ed., (New York: Appleton-Century Crofts, 1970), p. 79; R. M. MacIver, "The role of People," in: H. M. Bishop, et al., eds., op. cit., pp. 17-18; J. A. Schumpeter, "Competition for Political Leadership," in: H. M. Bishop, et al., eds., op. cit., pp. 22f.; and J. R. Lewis, **Democracy: The Theory and Practice** (London: Allman, 1966), p. 15.

18 M. L. Wilson, op. cit., p. 106.

19 R. M. MacIver, op. cit., p. 18.

20 Walter E. Boek, **How to Establish a Democracy or Improve the One You Now Have - A Practical Guide for Developing Essential Government and Business Structures and Personal Systems of Values** (Arlington, Va.: College of Democracy of National Graduate University, 1993), p. 16.

21 See Dan Agbese's "In Their Custody," in: **Newswatch** (Nigeria's Weekly Newsmagazine), July 12, 1993, p. 6.

22 J. A. Schumpeter, op. cit., p. 79.

23 R. M. MacIver, op. cit., p.18.

24 J.A. Schumpeter, op. cit., p. 22f.

25 M. L. Wilson, op. cit., p. 109.

26 Mtt. 7: 21.

27 It is very worth reading Sartori Giovani's "What Democracy Is Not," in his book, **The Theory of Democracy Revisited** (New Jersey: Chatham House Publishers, Inc., 1987), pp. 182-213.

28 Cf. S. K. Padover: 'The current fashion in many parts of the world of referring to dictatorships as "people's democracy," "basic democracy," or "guided democracy" is a libel on democracy. It is a fraud perpetrated by dictators to mislead the people' (sic, **Sources of Democracy; Voices of freedom, hope and justice** (New York: McGraw-Hill Book Co., 1973), p. xxxiii).

29 Cf. Walter E. Boek, op. cit., pp. 6-15.

2. THE UNIVERSAL PRINCIPLES OF DEMOCRACY

By the term "universal principles of democracy," we mean the prerequisite for a sustainable democracy - the necessary conditions of democracy - the basis of democracy. The term "universal" implies that these principles apply to every democracy, no matter where it may be found. The terms "prerequisite", "necessary", and "basis" imply that every democracy, worthy of its name, cannot but possess these principles. In other words, without these principles "democracy could not for long continue to exist."[1] These universal principles of democracy are basically two: equality and freedom. However, they also include popular sovereignty, majority rule and minority rights, the rule of law and constitutional safeguards which are corollaries of equality and freedom.[2]

2.1. Equality

Some authors, like Tocqueville[3] and Ambedkar,[4] consider equality the first and the most important condition precedent for the successful working of democracy. Tocqueville, writing on "Why democratic nations show a more ardent and enduring love for equality than for liberty," argues that equality, not liberty, lies at the heart of democracy. He maintains that "Political liberty occasionally gives sublime pleasure to a few. Equality daily gives each man in the crowd a host of small enjoyments. The charms of equality are felt the whole time and are within the reach of all; the noblest spirits appreciate them, and the commonest minds exult in them. The passion engendered by equality is therefore both strong and general.... Democratic people always like equality, but there are times when their passion for it turns to delirium."[5] And he concludes that if given the choice between liberty and equality, democratic people would always choose the latter.[6]

From the nature of things, from everyday experience, no two individuals are alike. "Individuals are different in everything: health, longevity, beauty, intelligence, talents, charm, tastes, preferences, and more."[7] Inequality then seems more natural than equality. No wonder G. Sartori, in his "A Protest Ideal,"[8] writes, inter alia, that "to have inequality, all that is demanded of us is to let things follow their course. But if we are to seek equality, we can never afford to relax. ... Inequality can be attributed to acts of God; equality can result only from the acts of men. Inequality is 'nature'; equality is denaturalization.... When equality is sought, differences in power, wealth, status, and life chances, as they are 'naturally' found to exist, cease to be routinely accepted differences."[9] In its face value Sartori's protest ideal sounds plausible and convincing. However, it fails to realise that if inequality "be attributed to the acts of God," then no amount of human effort - no "acts of men" - can bring about equality. No person can surely swim against the current of nature or of God. It also fails to realise that since "inequality" is a negation of "equality," the latter precedes the former, for it is the absence of equality that gives rise to inequality. Hence his protest ideal is on the realm of equality as "sameness" - equality in the physical sense - and not on the realm of equality as a moral principle - of, for instance, justice[10] - which is the object of democracy and our concern here.

The democratic idea of equality stems from the Judaeo-Christian belief in the value of the individual - that all men are equal before God, all being equally God's children.[11] It was on this belief that "the thinkers of the Reformation and the seventeenth century produced that mighty heave of the will which translated otherworldly ideals into aims for earthly community. And modern democracy began when people fought to establish conditions of equality and of freedom"[12] - based on natural law, self-government, natural rights or human rights or individual liberty. For instance, it was on this belief that J. Locke based his assertion of the natural equality of all persons in a state of nature:

> Though I have said above ... 'That all men by nature are equal,' I cannot be supposed to understand all sorts of equality. Age or virtue may give men a just precedency. Excellency of parts or of merit may place others above the common level. Birth may subject some, and alliance or benefits others, to pay an observance to those whom Nature, gratitude, or other respects, may have made it due; and yet all this consists with the equality which all men are in respect of jurisdiction or dominion one over another, which was the equality I there spoke of as the business in hand, being that equal right that every man hath to his natural freedom, without being subject to the will or authority of any other man.[13]

Locke's is an assertion that all men are equal in their right to participate in government and to be protected from the action of government in the exercise of some forms of individual freedom. This is what R. A. Dahl terms "the idea of intrinsic equality"[14]: "all human beings are of equal intrinsic worth, ... no person is intrinsically superior to another."[15] From this follows the principle of equal consideration of interests: "the good or interest of each person must be given equal consideration."[16]

This Lockean idea is further developed in the Declaration of American Independence, July 4, 1776:

> We hold these truths to be self-evident: that all men are created equal; that they are endowed by their Creator with certain unalienable rights; that among these are life, liberty, and the pursuit of happiness; that to secure these rights government are instituted among men, deriving their just powers from the consent of the governed....[17]

In his many memorable interpretations of the Declaration, Lincoln pointed out that the authors of the Declaration "did not mean to say all were equal in color, size, intellect, moral development, or social capacity. They defined with tolerable distinctness in what respects they did consider all men created equal -

equal in certain inalienable rights, among which are life, liberty, and the pursuit of happiness."[18] H. M. Kallen agrees: "the men and women who wrote and signed the Declaration and the men and women who fought and suffered and died for it did not intend by this proposition either to abolish or to penalize differences. They intended to vindicate differences, to acknowledge and to defend their equal right to life, liberty, and the pursuit of happiness. They affirmed the right to be different and the parity of the different as different. They did not look on any hidden metaphysical equality; they looked to the overt experience that people who are different from each other can and do live together with each other on the basis of equal title of each to the rights of life, liberty, and pursuit of happiness inherent and unalienable in each.... They meant 'unalienabe' to be a synonym for 'inherent,' for 'constitutive.' They meant that the nature of any and every human being, whatever his color, sex, race, faith, occupation, or social status, is constituted by these rights as a triangle is constituted by three sides and three angles; that life, liberty, and the pursuit of happiness make up the substance of human nature as the angles and sides of a triangle make up the being of the triangle...."[19]

To the above could be added the various French Declarations of Rights of Man. The Declaration of 1789, article 6, reads: "All citizens being equal (in the eyes of the Law), they are equally entitled to all the emoluments and positions of public office in accord with their capabilities and under the sole distinction of their virtue and intelligence."[20] The Declaration of August 1791 gives the ground for the equality of all men: "All men are born Equal, with an equal right to the pursuit of happiness. That each man may secure this right and preserve his liberty as a member of a community, he must have an equal share in its government, that government being created and maintained by the consent of the community. Equality is the guarantee of independence. These axioms, being delivered as self-evident truths, antecedent and independent of experience, require no proof. They are propounded as parts of the universal Law of Nature, written on men's hearts, and therefore true always and everywhere."[21] The Declaration of May 29, 1793, article 2, puts it succinctly: "Equality consists of everybody being entitled to the same rights."[22] And the Constitution of August 1795, article 3, says: "Equality consists of this, that the law is equal for all, regardless of whether it protects or punishes. Equality admits of no distinction of birth, no inheritance of power."[23] Thus equality for the French revolutionaries tantamounts to equal rights and equal laws.

From the above considerations we arrive at the following three conclusions. One, the notion of equality of all men, though undemonstrable, is self-evident, a postulate of natural law. Two, equality is not uniformity[24] - a type of egalitarianism, which knows no superioity[25] - a mere leveling or an anonymous average.[26] Equality is not standardisation[27] nor is it unrestricted behaviour.[28] Three, equality is linked with freedom and self-government. Hence it is a political concept[29] which implies "the 'natural' right to *equal participation* in the government and to *equal opportunity* in public affairs."[30]

Therefore, as a political concept, equality implies "the demand that the system of power be erected upon the similarities and not the differences between men"[31] - that is, erected upon "the 'essential human qualities' - those that are possessed by all human beings and which can be discerned beneath 'all the undeniable differences among men'."[32] Carl Cohen puts it well: "What is the sense of the principle of human equality upon which the justification of democracy in the body politic depends? It is, simply, that beneath all the undeniable differences among men there is in every human being an element, or aspect, or essential quality which justifies our treating him as the equal of every other in the largest sphere of human life."[33] In this regard, "one's membership in his polity has no ground other than that he is a man. The origin and foundation of his membership is - equally with all others - the simple fact that he was born or lives there, just as the others do."[34] Political equality then is "an idea of universal membership in humanity which attaches value to the life of each individual"[35] - "a community of interests, a responsibility of each one to consider others as equal participants in that community."[36] Thus a democratic state is a community of equals in which "all have an essentially equal stake in its affairs"[37] and in which there is "an equal voice for each in the making of its directive decisions."[38] This is *the principle of equal opportunity.*

"Equal opportunity"[39] means that any man has roughly as good a chance as any other in the society: of leading the kind of life he wants to lead - of developing his personality - of working and earning his livelihood - of making a decision as to who should rule him and on how he should be ruled - of equal treatment under the laws of the land, and so on, the peculiarities of each man not withstanding. It signifies that no distinction should be made between human beings because of their race, colour, sex, or any other characteristic beyond the control of the individual. Three quotations from Aristotle, J. F. Kennedy and Adolf Kreisberg will help make this point clearer. Aristotle writes:

> When a number of flute-players are equal in their art, there is no reason why those of them who are better born should have better flutes given to them; for they will not play any better upon the flute.... For if there were a superior flute-player who was far inferior in birth and beauty ... still he ought to have the best given to him, unless the advantages of health and birth contribute to excellence in flute-playing, which they do not. Moreover upon this principle any good may be compared with any other.[40]

This shows that the existence of superiority does not hinder the practice of equal opportunity. As L. Stapleton rightly points out, "If we think that certain qualities are truly superior, we must be willing to allow any individual, of any race or nation, to demonstrate that he has them,"[41] because "true superiority consists in the possession of talent or skill which is potentially beneficial to everyone."[42]

J. F. Kennedy, speaking of education for all children, in his radio address on June 11, 1963, says the same thing with regard to differences in talents:

> Not every child has an equal talent or an equal ability or equal motivation. But they should have the equal right to develop their talent and their ability and their motivation to make something of themselves.[43]

Lastly, but not the least, A. Kreisberg considers democracy a school of experience in which everybody has equal opportunity to develop his/her natural aptitudes, to make mistakes and to prove his/her worth, because all are equal before the law. His text is worth quoting in full:

> In a democracy, as an apt school of experience, people have an equal opportunity to grade themselves in accordance with their natural aptitudes and potential qualifications. In this school of democracy, as in no other, the people are free to make mistakes. They are ... free to learn from and benefit from their experiences. While all are entitled to equal respect, no one is or should be looked up to expect to be emulated if he is outstanding and worth while. No one should be condemned for unintentional mistakes, nor for the wrongs committed by others - not even when committed by his kin. In a democracy, human beings, in spite of their shortcomings, are on the upgrade of progress.
> Credit goes where credit belongs. All are free and equal before the law. They are also entitled to equal protection under the law. They are ... subject to equal punishment for intentional violation thereof. As a system of government democracy exists for the collective benefit of all the people living under it....
> In a democracy, such as the U. S., all men, women and children, irrespective of their race, color or creed, are entitled as a matter of right and not as a favour, to equal treatment under the law of the land. They are thus afforded equal opportunity to develop their latent talents and to make the most of their respective qualifications. The strong and too wilful, if wrongly minded, are restrained under the law. The weak and timid are encouraged. The rule of reasons prevails, and not the rule of force. No law ex post facto, or after the act, may be enacted, to operate retroactively.
> No one, even if he is right, may force another to follow him, if that other is unwilling to do so. Everyone has or should have an equal opportunity to work and to earn his livelihood, whether he belongs to a union or not. No one has or should have the right to deprive anyone else of an equal opportunity to seek and to find work, or to hinder him in his work, by lack of his union membership. In a democracy, under the laws and constitution, the government is obligated to protect the constitutional right of everyone alike, irrespective of whether he belongs to a union or not....
> In a democracy, no one is above the law. No one is outside the law....[44]

To end this discussion, it is important to point out that equality as equal opportunity should not be restricted to the political sphere alone (as many writers and political thinkers do). Equal opportunity also holds water in all spheres of human life, including social and economic spheres.[45] Seen in the light of equal opportunity, social equality then means equal respect for all regardless of rank and status. It is, as G. Sartori would have it: "to everyone the same social importance, that is, the power to resist social discrimination."[46] Coming to economic equality, this should not be taken to mean "identity of income" (since equality does not mean identity or uniformity). Instead it means that everybody should have equal opportunity in the economic life and pursuit of his state, and that, since "great disparity of wealth creates barriers among men and negates human equality ... we must abolish great disparity in income" - that is, we must "lessen the effect and reduce the range of economic inequality."[47] The successful working of democracy demands that there must be no glaring inequalities in the society; there must not be an oppressed or a suppressed class; and there must not be a class which has got all the privileges and a class which has got all the burdens to carry. Therefore, equality demands justice and fairness: "do unto others what you want others do unto you" - "giving each person his due." It also demands love for and mutual respect to other people. These are great virtues without which democracy becomes a child's play. However, equality can never stand alone. For example, there cannot be equality in a society where freedom is lacking. Hence equality needs freedom and must fight for "the removal of the heaviest constraints on freedom ... throughout the society,"[48] in order to be meaningful.

2.2. Freedom

Here the words "freedom" and "liberty" are used interchangeably.

Nobody denies the importance of freedom or liberty in his life or in the life of any given society. Everybody wants and cherishes freedom, even though some would like to deny - and/or do deny - it to others theirs. Isaac Penington, in his "The Right, Safety and Liberty of the People" (1651), remarks that "Freedom is of more worth than your estates, yea than your lives and therefore deserves to be higher prized." C. Bay says that a "society is as free as its underdogs are."[49] This is so because "without the liberty of the individual and of the group man cannot attain the goals he is capable of reaching. As a person he can reach a higher stage of human development if he is free from the regimentation imposed by an authority above him."[50] Hence man fights tooth and nail to preserve his freedom. As Rousseau rightly puts it, "To renounce one's freedom is to renounce one's status as a man, the rights of humanity and even its duties.... Such a renunciation is incompatible with the nature of man...."[51] And L. Stapleton agrees: "All democratic behavior depends upon freedom.... Our valuing of equality, for example, led straight to freedom as a condition of its understanding or fulfilment. Any meaning we ascribe to human existence, any apprehension that is not mechanical, presupposes freedom."[52] But what is freedom? What are the different kinds of freedom? Has freedom any limit? These are the questions that demand now our attention.

What is freedom and on what is it predicated? J. R. Lewis observes that "liberty, as a concept, is a changing thing, a shifting kaleidoscope showing different hues, different forms as time passes.... This can only lead to the impossibility of arriving at an accurate and acceptable definition of what precisely constitutes 'liberty'."[53] But this does not stop us from delving into the meaning of liberty. For John Stuart Mill, liberty means "protection against the tyranny of the political rulers."[54] For J. Locke, "natural freedom" means that a person is not to be "subjected to the will or authority of any other man."[55] Not preoccupied with the problem of slavery (like Locke and Mill), Christian Bay defines freedom as "self-expression, or the individual's capacity, opportunity, and incentive to express whatever he is or can be motivated to express."[56] But it is L. Stapleton who gives us a more comprehensive definition of freedom. He writes:

> Freedom is more than the ability to make a choice or to act; it is a state of feeling ... (which) might be described as a sense of manifold possibilities and a relationship to them which is not striving, but is an equipoise.... In other words, freedom expresses faith in the determinable elements of life as well as in the quality of newness, surprise, freshness, delight in what may come to be.... Freedom, then, belongs not merely to man and to political life; it is somehow a constituent of all that happens. Nor is freedom merely chance.... By the principle of freedom is meant the belief that this state of being is desirable both in itself and as an atmosphere that permits the realization of other forms of good - an atmosphere without which, truly, other forms of good cannot be identified....[57]

Freedom then means a power of self-determination experienced by individuals. Hence freedom, like equality, is predicated on the worth of the individual - a value accruing to him from the law of Nature.[58] This implies that the individual has a natural right of self-determination: to live under the laws of his choosing.[59] This means that the individual "is not to be subjected to the will or authority of any other man"[60] (which denotes an absence of certain kinds of constraint, for example freedom "from governmental arbitrariness"[61]) and that "the individual has the freedom to establish and control his own government."[62] At this juncture it becomes clear that freedom in a democracy means "political freedom"[63] - what G. Sartori calls "freedom **from**, not freedom **to**," "a defensive or protective freedom"[64] and "participation in (the affairs of the polity)."[65] Sartori introduces the idea of "complete freedom (which) may be said to imply the following five traits: independence, privacy, capacity, opportunity, and power,"[66] and thereby cautions about "the temptation to treat political freedom ... as if it were, in itself, a complete freedom." According to him, "Political liberty (independence from) protects and permits the individual to choose; and the successive freedoms all add sustaining conditions to greater and more effective choice. Privacy is to choose without being pressured, by looking quietly into oneself; capacity is, among other things, a broadening of available choices; opportunity is the coming within reach of alternatives among which to choose; and power is, in the context of freedom, the equalizing condition, the condition that makes for equal freedom to choose.... Political freedom is ... a relational freedom; it occurs among actors whose freedoms must coexist in reciprocity."[67] To "coexist in reciprocity" some restraint is required. This brings in the necessity of law vis-a-vis freedom, which shall be treated after considering the kinds of freedom in a democracy.

Certain freedoms are necessary in a democracy. They include:

1) **Freedom of the person**. This means "security from arbitrary seizure, imprisonment, or punishment"[68] - call it "freedom from fear,"[69] "freedom from coercion" and "the right to stay alive and healthy."[70] Freedom of the person is considered "the most basic of all human rights,"[71] "the most fundamental of all civil liberties"[72] and "the first pillar of self-government,"[73] because it is the right to life itself. Freedom of the person includes body freedom, freedom of movement, livelihood freedom, right of privacy, and the right of trial by jury. **Body freedom** forbids chattel slavery because "each member of a democratic community must own himself."[74] **Freedom of movement** demands that people should be free to "move from place to place, subject only to traffic rules which are the same for all."[75] **Livelihood freedom** demands that one should have "choices between various means of making a living (free enterprise) or a voice in determining economic policy (industrial democracy)."[76] **The right to privacy** entails that everybody is entitled to his/her privacy in the home and in correspondence. **The right of trial by jury** means that nobody is to be considered guilty until proven so by an independent judiciary under well known and impartial laws.

2) **Freedom of speech**. This is "the right to think and believe after one's own mind and heart, the right to express one's opinions and to organize for their furtherance, the right to vote according to one's opinions, and so forth."[77] It concerns individual autonomy and self-expression: that a person be able to think for himself, that whatever his "outer" condition he be not intellectually or psychologically subjugated to another person's will.[78] "A person cannot think freely," writes Judith Lichtenberg, "if he cannot speak; and he cannot think freely if others cannot speak, for it is in hearing the thoughts of others and being able to communicate with them that we develop our thoughts."[79] The freedom of speech could be broken down into: **freedom of thought**, "including an equal opportunity to learn, and to seek truth, and a choice in the matter of belief and faith;"[80] **freedom of expression** - "in speech, writing, drama, the pictorial arts, music;"[81] and **freedom of investigation** - "inquiry, invention and discovery."[82] Freedom of speech is based on the belief in the equality of men and the value of the individual, with the result that nobody has the right to interfere with another person's free expression of opinion. Freedom of speech is very important that without it, in the words of L. Stapleton, "the other major aspects of freedom would be meaningless. Obviously, freedom of religion is contingent on (it) ... (and) freedom of assembly presupposes (it)."[83] In the same vein MacIver writes: "The importance of the creative role assigned to public opinion under democracy lies primarily in the fact that if opinion is free then the whole cultural life of man is free. If opinion is free, then belief is free and science is free and art and philosophy and all the variant styles and modes in which men manifest and develop their values and tastes and ways of living - always up to the limit where they endeavor by oppression or violence to deprive their fellowmen of these same prerogatives."[84] John Milton and J. S. Mill are perhaps the best writers in defence of freedom of speech: the former, in

his *Areopagitica*,[85] argues against censorship, and the latter, in his *On Liberty* (*Of Thought and Discussion*),[86] argues against repression of opinion.

3) **Freedom of religion or worship**. This means that "neither government nor any church shall impose upon an individual the observance of religious rites, but that each person shall be free to worship God according to his own understanding."[87] The arguments in favour of freedom of religion stem from the nature of faith itself: faith demands belief and nobody forced into a religion could be said to have faith. This is so because "faith compelled is a contradiction in terms, and the person who mechanically follows religious rites or who mumbles the words of a creed is a hypocrite."[88] Pope John Paul II agrees: "*Man cannot be forced to accept the truth*. He can be drawn toward the truth only by his own nature, that is, by his own freedom, which commits him to search sincerely for truth and, when he finds it, to adhere to it both in his convictions and in his behavior."[89] Hence it is of paramount importance to uphold and defend freedom in the exercise of worship, provided it is peaceful. L. Stapleton rightly observes that "the best protection of religious liberty is a negative one - the absence of laws concerning it. The separation of church and state, the exemption from religious tests as a qualification for voting or office, freedom from compulsory religious education, or from any legal obligation for financial support of religious institutions, all these are the concrete embodiments of freedom of religion."[90]

4) **Freedom of assembly**. This is the "freedom of association in private or public meetings and in private or public organizations,"[91] provided such meetings are peaceful and convoked for some public aim. The importance of the freedom of assembly rests upon the fact that "private associations or meetings ... are a most necessary channel of thought and action for citizens; they serve as an unofficial but often direct mode of representation for groups whose views might otherwise be unknown or unheeded. Without freedom of assembly and petition, freedom of speech would be incomplete; for there might be no other effective means of producing simultaneous consideration of the same question by a large number of citizens.... The right of citizens to meet peacefully, to bring their common affairs, and to bring a petition ... before the government implies as well a basic right of association and of peaceful political action."[92]

These freedoms are very important in any given society, much more so in a democratic polity. But they do not mean "licence" to do whatever one likes - at the expense or detriment of another and of the common good. Freedom does not mean that one is a law unto himself. Hence one's right or liberty is not without a limit. It is not unrestrained, because "the individual cannot be perfectly free, for although he can be said to possess rights, he possesses duties also, duties towards the society in which he lives,"[93] and because "no society tolerates absolute freedom even of conscience and of speech, and no society reduces that sphere to zero."[94] One's right, therefore, ends where the right of another begins. Prof. Mikat (a CDU member of the West German Parliament - 'Bundestag'), on the argument that women have the right of 'self-determination' which allows them the sole decission either to kill their unborn baby or to bring it to birth, retorted that the right of self-determination of man should not be without limit: it stops at its boundary, where it meets another; for it should not be at the cost of another person's right of life, otherwise humanity is bound to perish.[95] This is understandable, because each citizen is equally entitled to the protection of his basic "human rights." Since man is neither an island nor self-sufficient but a social being who lives in relationship and in association with others and in dependence upon the government to protect and preserve the individual's rights and freedoms and the basic norms of the society from being violated laws are introduced.[96] Thus Burke, after a profound study of the fundamental conditions of free institutions, remarks that "liberty to be enjoyed must be limited by law: for where law ends there tyranny begins."[97] J. Locke agrees: "law, in its true notion, is not so much the limitation as the direction of a free and intelligent agent to his proper interest, and prescribes no farther than is for the general good of those under that law.... So that however it may be mistaken, the end of law is not to abolish or restrain, but to preserve and enlarge freedom. For liberty is to be free from restraint and violence from others, which cannot be where there is no law; and is not ... 'a liberty for every man to do what he lists.'... But a liberty to dispose and order freely as he lists his person, actions, possessions, and his whole property within the allowance of those laws under which he is, therein not to be subject to the arbitrary will of another, but freely follow his own."[98] It is then clear that "law" here does not mean any arbitrary law but "the rules, precepts, statutes, body of legal decisions, based upon consent and custom, deciding where the external sanctions of society will be applied to ensure just human relations."[99]

Let us give some examples of laudable restraints on freedom. First, freedom of speech is very desirable; but the restraint imposed by the law relating to defamation or to the endangering of the existence of government or public order is necessary also. Justice Holmes, in his judgement on the suit 'Schenck v. US', said, inter alia: "The most stringent protection of free speech would not protect a man in falsely shouting fire in a theater, and causing a panic. It does not even protect a man from an injunction against uttering words that may have all the effect of force."[100] Zechariah Chafee, commenting on Justice Holmes' decision, explains that "The principle on which free speech is classified as lawful or unlawful involves the balancing against each other of two very important social interests, in public safety and in the search for truth. Every reasonable effort should be made to maintain both interests unimpaired, and the great interest in free speech should be sacrificed only when the interest in public safety is really imperiled, and not ... when it is barely conceivable that it might be slightly affected.... Thus our problem of locating the boundary line of free speech is solved. It is located close to the point where words will give rise to unlawful acts."[101] Second, freedom of religion is very desirable; but "laws protecting public safety would rightly prohibit a religion based on human sacrifice or on physical danger to human beings."[102] Third, freedom of assembly is very desirable; but "an individual could not expect freedom of assembly to protect his activities in a secret society.... Such societies may be regulated by law without infringement of freedom of assembly.... Nor could freedom of assembly be invoked to protect a group organized for military drill, or for criminal conspiracy of any sort."[103]

Clearly, from the above, what is asked of political freedom is protection, and that this protection is enjoyed only by obeying laws and not masters. This fact is attested to by the sayings of Aristotle, Cicero, J. Locke and T. Paine. According to Aristotle, "men should not think it slavery to live according to the constitution; for it is their salvation."[104] For Cicero: "we are servants of the laws in order that we might be free" (*legum servi sumus ut liberi esse possimus*).[105] For J. Locke: "Where there is no law there is no freedom."[106] T. Paine holds that "the government of a free country ... is not in the persons but in the laws."[107] Therefore, it is of paramount importance, in a democratic society, that there be adequate laws to protect the fundamental rights and basic freedoms of man, and that everybody be subject to these laws, so that these rights and freedoms are enjoyed and exercised by all without unnecessary and unlawful restraints. Freedoms measure the extent to which democratic practices are present in any community. The more freedom there is in a community, the more democratic such a community becomes. But, if some of the necessary freedoms are lacking, then the social processes fail in that degree to be democratic.

Freedom and equality go hand-in-hand. They are not only proclaimed but are part of the daily life of man. Because they are values accruing to man from nature, man (wherever he find himself) enjoys and exercises them always for self-determination or self-government. Hence freedom and equality confer on man "sovereignty." Thus the saying, "power belongs to the people." This brings us to the next necessary condition for the existence of democracy, "popular sovereignty."

2.3. Popular Sovereignty

A democratic government is one that is responsive to the people. This responsibility to the people is due to the simple fact that government has its origin from the people. Hence the saying: "power belongs to the people." Popular sovereignty then implies that the authority (or power) of a state resides in the people or is vested in the people and not in any particular class or classes, ethnic, religious or interest groups within the society. Or as Scott Nearing would put it, "popular sovereignty signifies the participation of the individual citizen in the decision of public questions. This participation may be direct, as in a town meeting, or it may be through representatives. Neither one all-powerful ruler nor a minority may make final decisions in a political democracy. The voice of final authority must be that of the people, speaking directly or through representatives."[108] According to J. R. Lewis, "when a question of major importance arises within the democratic state, the democratic principle demands that such a question should be put for decision to the people of the state, or at the very least to as large a number of the people as can be arranged.... The individual democratic states do not all use the same methods of dealing with the fundamental issues that arise, but they all deal with them nevertheless on the basis that the people should decide. The minor matters will be left to the elected government itself to deal with ... and will not demand a majority vote from the electorate for decision to be reached."[109] Therefore, the decisions of government must derive from the express wishes of the people (who ultimately have the final say or authority in how they are governed). In other words, a democratic government must consult the people on policy issues - that is, it must at all times find out the popular desire and proceed to pursue it. This is the principle of *popular consultation.*

How do the people have the final say in how they are governed? How do the people express their wishes in governmental matters? In other words, what is the role of the public in a democratic state? All agree that the citizen must be involved in the *decision-making* of the state. Let us call this *participation* of the citizen in deciding public questions *public opinion*. The importance of participation is such that Barry Holden sees it "as a logically necessary condition for democracy - perhaps even a defining feature,"[110] and Almond and Verba say that "citizen competence and participation are at the heart of the definition of democracy."[111] But all are not agreed on what "citizen participation" or "public opinion" entails.

For J. A. Schumpeter, the only means of participation open to the citizen are voting and discussion. And he rules out such acceptable activity as "bombarding" representatives with letters as a negation of the whole concept of leadership. So he writes:

> Our chief troubles about classical theory (of democracy) center in the proposition that 'the people' hold a definite and rational opinion about every individual question and that they give effect to this opinion - in a democracy - by choosing 'representatives' who will see to it that that opinion is carried out. Thus the selection of the representatives is made secondary to the primary purpose of the democratic arrangement which is to vest the power of deciding political issues in the electorate. Suppose we reverse the role of these two elements and make the deciding of issues by the electorate secondary to the election of the men who are to do the deciding. To put it differently, we now take the view that the role of the people is to produce a government, or else an intermediate body which in turn will produce a national executive or government. And we define: *the democratic method is that institutional arrangement for arriving at political decisions in which individuals acquire the power to decide by means of competitive struggle for the people's vote.*[112]

To "the primary function of the electorate to produce a government (directly or through an intermediate body)," Schumpeter adds "the function of evicting it. The one means simply the acceptance of a leader or a group of leaders, the other means simply the withdrawal of this acceptance."[113]

On his part, Walter Lippmann (a Newspaper columnist) does not consider an election an expression of public opinion since the general public is both inattentive to political issues and lacks clear information about them. He writes:

> It may be objected at once that an election which turns one set of men out of office and installs another is an expression of public opinion which is neither secondary nor direct. But what in fact is an election? We call it an expression of the popular will. But is it? We go into a polling booth and mark a cross on a piece of paper for one or two, or perhaps three or four names. Have we expressed our thoughts on the public policy of the United States?... It would take us hours to express our thoughts, and calling a vote the expression of our mind is an empty fiction.... A vote is a promise of support. It is a way of saying: I am lined up with these men, on this side.... The public does not select the candidate, write the platform, outline the policy any more than it builds the automobile or acts a play. It aligns itself for or against somebody who has offered himself, has made a promise, has produced a play, is selling an automobile.... If that theory is accepted, we must abandon the notion that democratic government can be the direct expression of the will of the people. We must abandon the notion that the people govern. Instead we must adopt the theory that, by their occasional mobilizations as a majority, people support or oppose the individuals who actually govern. We must say that the popular will does not direct continuously but that it intervenes occasionally....[114]

Writing on *The Role of the Public*,[115] Lippmann does not set great store on what can be done by public opinion and the action of the masses, because he believes that "the public does not know in most cases what specifically is the truth or the justice of the case, and men are not agreed on what is beautiful and good;" that public opinion "is a reserve of force brought into action during a crises in public affairs.... In this theory, public opinion does not make the law. But by canceling lawless power it may establish the condition under which law can be made. It does not reason, investigate, invent, persuade, bargain or settle.... In this theory the public intervenes only when there is crises of maladjustment, and then not to deal with the substance of the problem but to neutralize the arbitrary force which prevents adjustment."[116] Thus he conceives public opinion to be, "not the voice of God, nor the voice of society, but the voice of the interested spectators of action" whose opinions and actions "must be essentially different from those of the actors."[117]

Unlike Lippmann, Robert M. MacIver (Prof. Emeritus of Political Philosophy and Sociology at Columbia University), in his *The Role of the People*,[118] sees democracy not as "the rule of the majority or the rule of the masses," not as "a way of governing, whether majority or otherwise," but as "primarily a way of determining who shall govern and, broadly, to what ends." For him, "the only way in which the people, *all the people*, can determine who shall govern is by referring the question to public opinion and accepting on each occasion the verdict of the polls." Going further, in his *The Function of the Public*,[119] MacIver rightly considers Lippmann's *The Phantom Public* as the work of one who "was disillusioned about democracy," and reiterates that "the people ... do not and cannot govern; they control the government. In every live democracy they decide the broad march of politics.... They decide these issues, not one at a time but by voting for an administration favorable to one or another 'platform.' They decide them partly - and in the last resort - at the polls."

But public opinion is more than just casting of votes. The citizen has a power not limited only to the election of representatives. In the words of J. R. Lewis, "he does much more and can do much more than simply cast his vote at the election. It is quite possible that he will do no more than just this, but it is always open to him to do more, to call for public enquiries in certain situations, lobby his elected representative, write letters, join pressure groups, commence campaigns and show the type of civic resentment to which elected representatives are always particularly pervious."[120] Thus at the base of public opinion is, to use the expression of M. L. Wilson, *due process of policy-making* which "occurs in those communities where a perennial argument about national policy is carried on among responsible citizens representing a cross section of the community's life, an argument begun with facts and reliable opinion about them, and carried forward until generally acceptable conclusions have been reached."[121] For Wilson, this "due process of policy-making is more important than elections - Hitler was elected in Germany. It is even more important than the deliberations of Congress because it gives Congress something to deliberate about: if the representative assembly is to be wise in its formulation of national policy, there must be a local soil out of which national policy can grow."[122] Here we see the importance of *contacting* - what Sidney Verba (of Harvard University) refers to as "that kind of public activity when citizens speak up; when they take pen (or word processor) in hand, or make a phone call, or go downtown to speak to someone, or send a FAX, or an e-mail message to a government official or to newspaper - or when they call a talk show about a public issue."[123] This implies that the citizens of a democracy - not necessarily as individuals deciding for themselves the successive problems of politics, each in speculative detachment registering his opinion on every issue; not merely as units casting their separate votes every few years as election time comes round, but also as the men and women who make the opinion of their various communities, as a voluntary group, not an organ of government, and not so large a number as the electorate, as responsible persons concerned about the public welfare, and thinking in terms of the interest of the community and of the part of the community they represent as labour leaders, farm leaders, factory managers, professional men and women - are continuously engaged in a massive give-and-take of creative opinion-making. This brings to naught Lippmann's view that it is not the business of the public to decide the substantive policies of government but merely to see that the government abides by the rules, like a referee who watches the players but takes no part in the game.

The effects of public opinion in any given society, especially in this modern age of technology and communication, is very enormous. For R. M. MacIver, "this incessant activity of popular opinion is the dynamic of democracy. It decides between the larger alternatives of policy-making and in that way has an impact on a thousand issues.... The great changes in the socio-economic policies of Western European countries in the nineteenth and twentieth centuries - the whole trend toward social legislation and the control of economic power - were due to the swelling currents of public opinion, responsive to changing conditions."[124] Sidney Verba, in his already cited work, has many examples of the impact public opinion has on the American society. He writes:

> Americans are activists and have been in touch with the government for a long time. One estimate is that members of Congress received about 50 letters a week from constituents in the age of Grant. In recent surveys, about a fifth to a quarter of the public report contacting an official.... Lots of this is to national officials, more is to local officials.... Of particular interest are reactions to specific events that generate a good deal of excitement and communications. In recent times, we need only to think of Robert Bork, several of Clinton appointments, gays in the military, the Clinton budget. These outbursts are not new. David McCullough describes the reaction to Truman's firing of MacArthur as 'stupendous, the outcry from the American people shattering'.... But the likelihood of such massive outbursts seems much greater. By now we have reached the stage of an almost constant referendum. Any major event can trigger a flood of letters, telephone calls, and faxes.... Contacting makes a difference.... Those who contact on personal matter report receiving a response, report satisfaction, and often say that their call or letter made a great deal of difference.... Looked at from the perspective of target of the communications, it is clear that members of Congress and the administration monitor and heed the flood of electronic communications. Congressional offices tally and pay attention.... Zoe Baird was shot down certainly in large part because of the outburst - no one seemed deeply concerned before. Alan Simpson described the Baird hearings: 'Staff members were coming in, putting little tallies in front of people's desks, said 160 calls this hour, or 200 or 300 or 800, and putting that in front of the Senator.' ... Outbursts of citizen messages had an impact on such issues as gays in the military, the congressional salary raise of 1989, and many other things. It is not that these communications make policy, but it would be hard to argue they are irrelevant. And it is not merely an echo of what elites would have the public ask them for."[125]

At this juncture, it should be noted that popular sovereignty has got its puzzle or paradox - its problems and benefits. We begin with the problems. Firstly, there is the problem of size. J. Madison, though a great supporter of the extended republic where many voices would be heard, realised the problem that size created of describing what the public wanted. According to him, "public opinion ... is the real sovereign in every free (government).... (But) the larger a country, the less easy for its real opinion to be ascertained, and the less difficult (for it) to be counterfeited...."[126] Secondly, but a follow up from the first, there is what S. Verba calls "the problem of organizing and making sense out of the cacophony of voices,"[127] because, among other things, as R. Dahl rightly points out, "it just takes too much time to listen - or to read letters. There are too many voices and they vary too much in what they say and how they say it."[128] Thirdly, it can be argued that popular sovereignty "limits government, it makes it responsive to a small and loud number of unthinking individuals, it disrupts the continuity of governing."[129] (This point could also be used in favour of popular sovereignty, as S. Nearing has it: "Popular movements are as dangerous to ruling minorities as they are advantageous to the people, since each advance in popular rights imposes a limitation upon social privilege. Popular movements are therefore opposed by the privileged few with every means at their disposal."[130])

However, the benefits of popular sovereignty outweigh its problems. Firstly, it is a type of adult education. According to S. Nearing: "The people discuss and decide questions of public policy. Then, in the working out of their policies, they are benefited or harmed in proportion to the wisdom or folly of their decisions. All life is a school of experience, and popular participation in shaping public policy is perhaps the most important single division of the life school."[131] And S. Verba adds: "An open and reasoned system of political discussion is one in which individuals exchange information about themselves, their life circumstances, their preferences. They also exchange reasons why they prefer some course of action over another. They discuss the consequences of various courses of action. And in the process we hope that they learn from each other."[132] Secondly, it is for the community good and development. "Popular government," S. Nearing maintains, "arouses in the largest number of people a sense of social responsibility and a will to community betterment because under a popular regime the responsibility for policy and achievement rests squarely upon the citizens. Their hope for advancing individual well-being lies in community improvement."[133] To this could be added Verba's view that "people care about what is going on in their community or in the nation; they act to affect the collective decisions made in the name of the community or the nation; sometimes they seek a selective benefit, but usually not; sometimes the collective outcome they seek can be construed as in their own self-interest, oftentimes not. They do it because they think about and care about the public good."[134] Lastly, popular sovereignty is a mark of "self-government" which ultimately makes for "self-improvement" since it affords man the opportunity to improve his lot - socially, intellectually, morally, spiritually, rationally.[135] Therefore, until popular opinion is given heed to by the government of a nation, that nation cannot be said to be really democratic. However, popular opinion does not imply non-tolerance of minor opinion. If anything, majority rule must respect the rights of the minority.

2.4. Majority Rule and Minority Rights

The terms "majority" and "minority" are very relative. It is always "majority" or "minority" in relation to whom? It is a well known fact that in some countries, like the former apartheid South Africa, the non dominant group constitute the majority of the population while the dominant group form the minority of the population. Take the Security Council of the United Nations for another example: it "is essentially rule by the minority"[136] because "the right of veto possessed by the great powers makes impossible the functioning of true law"[137] and hence "the demand for unanimity is really a demand that the smaller number shall have the power to block decision."[138] These two examples indicate that "majority" or "minority" "is a matter of recognition and influence, not of numbers."[139]

The two terms are also temporary. It is possible that the today's minority could become the tomorrow's majority, just as the today's majority could become the tomorrow's minority. According to L. Stapleton,

> A majority is not permanent or fixed. Members of a majority counted with respect to one question may be in the minority on another. The same individuals think differently at different times even on the same question; at one time their opinion may coincide with that of a majority, at another time with that of a minority.[140]

Though such terms as "majority rule," "minority rule," "tyranny of the majority," "tyranny of the minority," and so on, are common place, democracy concerns itself with majority, and not minority, rule[141] and abhors all tyrannies,[142] whether of majority or minority, thereby guaranteeing the rights and equality of all. It is the purpose of this section to highlight the importance of the presence of both the majority and the minority in a democratic decision-making process, based on the principle of equality and liberty.[143]

It is a fact that "democracy necessarily involves the application and utilization of both the principle of majority rule and the principle of minority rights."[144] In other words, a democratic government must base its actions and decisions on majority opinion.[145] However, while the decisions of the majority is implemented, the minority has the rights to be listened to and protected; or, put in another way, while the majority will have its way, the minority will have its say. It is also a fact that under such a democratic governmental structure "the right of the majority to rule will come into conflict with the right of individuals and minorities to assert and register in a formal way their political preferences,"[146] either by "majority action that deprives a minority of its legitimate role in the democratic decision-making process"[147] or by "action on the part of a minority that deprives a majority of legitimate right to rule."[148] Thus a problem arises as to how to check the excesses of the majority and/or the minority.[149] This problem will be overlooked here while attention is paid to the possible ways in which the majority and the minority can work together in a democratic decision-making process.

From the above, it is clear that the "why" of the principle of majority rule is for decision-making, or as Ulrich Scheuner would have it, it is a normal means of arriving at a common decision amidst dissenting opinions.[150] Since, as shown above, the majority and the minority are very often in opposition to each other (with dissenting opinions), what should they do so as to arrive at concord or unanimity?[151] In dealing with this question, the thought pattern of Professor Lothar

Roos in his article in Vol. 9 of "Mönchengladbacher Gespräche"[152] will be adopted.

Firstly, Prof. Roos deals with the possible options when decision is necessary for the accomplishment of certain goals of the society but there is insurmountable dissent among the decision makers.[153] He posits four options: 1) omission or delay of decision[154] (when serious doubt exists); 2) amicable understanding - requiring a compromise from all concerned - in order to arrive at a consensus.[155] The principle of compromise implies majority-minority discussion (for, surely, "the effect of a discussion modifies the views of many of the members"[156]) and their willingness to co-operate and to concede, their differences notwithstanding. "Men do not have to agree on fundamental beliefs in order to cooperate in necessary techniques"[157] and they "do not have to believe the same thing in order to pool thier resources in practice,"[158] because "the democratic way (is) the marvelous social technique which maintains maximum competition in ideas alongside a modicum of cooperation in action;"[159] 3) reducing or limiting the state-goals - that is, reducing the number of the important decisions being sought - for example, the exclusion of religious faith from the state-goals;[160] and 4) the restriction of "interests" - regarding the status of every citizen to be one.[161]

Secondly, Prof. Roos considers the possible options of setting the majority on equal footing with everybody else.[162] This is a demand for equality of participation which, in the words of Berg Elias, "implies a demand for non-discriminatory rules for decision-making."[163] Prof. Roos again gives four options: 1) construction of the "Common will"[164] - there must be the presence of common interest or of group solidarity, and all, the majority and the minority, should be involved in the decision on and execution of the common will, because "it is the recognition of the common needs and the willingness to make a joint decision about them which provides the occasion to apply majority rule;"[165] 2) the constitutional distribution of authority[166]: this option is to enable as many people of different ranks and file as possible, through the representative organs, take part in the formulation of the common will, because, in the words of Karl Löwenstein, "the constitutional state is founded on the division of power;"[167] 3) the generality and openness of the political process[168]: "the most important means of broadening and making lighter the acceptance by the entire people of the majority decisions," writes Roos, "is through openness of the political process, through common access of all to the corresponding information, and through possibilities of co-operation;"[169] 4) protection of the minority[170]: this is meant to prevent the tyranny of the majority over the minority, because the minority (just like the majority) has got its important role in a democratic polity.[171] L. Stapleton explains the matter succinctly:

> True majority rule includes the protection of minorities. For no true majority, of whatever body, can be formed unless each person enjoys the right to be heard, with all the accompanying freedoms. All adult literate people in a given community form the body of citizens, without distinction of origin or function. When any decision is

> to be taken by them, the vote of the largest number is to prevail, but the votes of any smaller group do not expose them to any disabilities on account of their difference. If this is not so, there is in fact no real majority vote. For before the vote is taken, no one can predict its outcome, hence if there is to result an honest majority, all without exception must be free and uncoerced. And this condition must prevail at all times; both individuals and groups must be uncoerced; they must have access to information and to means of communication with others and the right to consult and to assemble. *In short, the conditions that allow a true majority to form are the same as those to which minorities owe protection.* Where minorities are coerced, we cannot truly speak of the will of the majority.[172]

S. Nearing agrees: "While minorities must submit to majority will in order to expedite the carrying out of community decisions, the majority must guarantee to each minority an opportunity to spread its propaganda and build its organization with the object of becoming, in its turn, the majority. The principle of majority is meaningless unless it includes the tolerance of minorities."[173] Hence "the minority must always feel safe that although the majority is carrying on the Government, the minority is not being hurt, or the minority is not being hit below the belt."[174] Moreover, since "a majority is not permanent or fixed - members of a majority counted with respect to one question may be in the minority on another"[175] - then "every majority must look at its own majority in such a way, and reckon from it, that it can any time become the minority."[176]

Lastly, Prof. Roos treats the options of trusting in the fundamental worth of consensus.[177] The point here is that the practice of the majority principle is possible only within the framework of fundamental worth of consensus which, on its part, does not indicate the disposition of the majority. This fundamental worth of consensus depicts the basis of confidence or trust of all political business in a democracy. The problem is how to arrive at, and how to protect, this basic trust. Roos has the following options: 1) timely control of power[178]: a popular maxim has it that "trust is good, but control is better," thus the need for checks and balances; 2) trustworthiness of the majority[179]: the majority must so comport itself so as to win the people's trust; and 3) widening of non-votable area,[180] so that the points at issue will become better understood by all

2.5. The Rule of Law and the Constitutional Safeguards

One may wonder how law - with its many limiting functions - could be regarded as a necessary condition for democracy. True enough, democracy is not attained through law; but without respect for the process of law democracy cannot even begin to exist. A. M. Bingham agrees: "Even if constitutional safeguards do not themselves equal democracy they are indispensable techniques of democracy. More than anything else they serve to distinguish democracy from totalitarianism. Their function is to protect the individual - whether he is alone or a member of a minority group or in the numerical majority - from the abuse of power."[181] Hence the rule of law is a necessary condition for the existence of democracy. This accepted, some questions arise for consideration: What is the rule of law? Why the rule of law in a democracy? And how does the rule of law help to maintain and further a democracy?

What is the rule of law? A good summary of the meaning of the rule of law is given by the Staff of the Centre for Democratic Studies (CDS), Abuja (Federal Capital Territory of Nigeria):

> The rule of law implies equality before the law, due process of the law and absence of arbitrary rule. The rule of law also implies that an accused person cannot be deemed guilty without being given a chance to defend himself.[182]

The German "Rechtsstaat"[183] - meaning the state in which the power of government is limited through the process of law and in which the right place of the citizen is secured; or, as Mathilde Berghofer-Weicher precisely put it, "the state in which the law is supreme;"[184] and so on[185] - brings out the import of the principle of the rule of law. This principle is well-expressed in the saying of Frederick the Great (during the second half of the 18th century): "In court the laws must speak and the ruler must keep quiet." Thus we hear of such phrase as "a government of laws and not of men" which is, literally taken, an absurdity, but which, like the phrase "due process of the law," expresses the craving men have for regularity, order and impersonality in the rules by which they are governed. For L. Stapleton, "impartial judgment ... according to known standards and without respect to persons may be called a rule of law, and any person who has the right to appeal for such judgment may benefit from it, but it has not the character of law for him unless he participates in the making of the standards or otherwise voluntarily accepts them."[186] This brings out the fact that the rule of law derives from the people, because "a rule is law only for people who participate in the making of the laws or consent to them, and who are protected by basic rights, evinced in procedural safeguards, making their consent voluntary. For all others, even if they submit to the compulsion, the norms are not law but plain force."[187] And Stapleton goes on: "In a democracy, all persons of mature age take part in the political process by which the law is made, amended, or reformed, and the judicial order derives its authority from the fundamental law set forth by the majority as the basis of government."[188] Not only that law derives from the people, "but the process as a whole must be satisfactory to the citizens, or they have the power to change it."[189]

Moreover, the rule of law must be founded on a *constitution* - hence the term, "constitutional safeguards of democracy." It does not matter whether the constitution is written (like the American Constitution) or unwritten (like the British Constitution), whether it is crystallised in a dependable tradition or drafted at a particular time, so long as a fundamental law may be counted upon. The essence of a constitution is that it formalises a set of fundamental norms governing the political community and determining the relations between rulers and the people and the interaction among the centres of power. "The constitution," writes Stapleton, "must show the derivation of legal authority from the people, must define the manner of their participation in the making and amending of law, must show the accountability of officials to them, and give scope to rights."[190] In most constitutional democracies, there is a constitutional document providing for fixed limitations on the exercise of power - declaring what the government and its various officials may or may not do. These provisions usually include (at least) the following three major elements[191]: 1) an assignment of certain specified state functions to different state organs or offices (call it *separation of powers*), the delimitation of the powers of each organ or office, and the establishment of arrangements for the co-operative interaction (call it *checks and balances*); 2) a list of individual rights or liberties (call these *fundamental or unalienable rights*) that are protected against the exercise of state power; and 3) a statement of the methods by which the constitution may be amended. These elements shall be considered in detail later.

Why the rule of law? Why are constitutional safeguards necessary? Madison gives us a ready answer:

> But what is government itself, but the greatest of all reflections on human nature? If men were angels, no government would be necessary. If angels were to govern men, neither external nor internal controls on government would be necessary. In framing a government which is to be administered by men over men, the great difficulty lies in this: you must first enable the government to control the governed; and in the next place oblige it to control itself. A dependence on the people is, no doubt, the primary control on the government; but experience has taught mankind the necessity of auxiliary precautions.[192]

The rule of law then is, to use Stapleton's terminology, "an emblame of man's imperfection."[193] Since men are not angels (they are imperfect), then men need government (that is, law) to control them; and since angels do not govern men (but government, made up of men who are imperfect, do), then government needs law to control it and its actions. "The safeguards," writes A. M. Bingham, "against encroachment of government beyond proper limits are only safeguards against certain human weaknesses, ambition and love of power. The tyrant whom men hate is not much the dictator who gathers all power to himself as the despot who rules by personal caprice. Institutions of government are mainly human beings in special relation to each other and to the rest of the world. Power can be exercised only by human beings. Their weaknesses must be taken into account."[194] Or as Walter Lippmann would have it: "Constitutional restraints and bills of rights, the whole apparatus of responsible government and of an independent judiciary, the conception of due process of law in courts, in legislatures, among executives, are but the rough approximations by which men have sought to exorcise the devil of arbitrariness in human relations."[195] Hence the rule of law is meant to define the structure of government and to protect fundamental rights.[196]

How are these tasks of the rule of the law achieved? First, with regard to defining the structure of government: in most modern constitutional democracies, there is a constitutional document providing for limitations on the exercise of power - declaring what the government and its various officials may or may not do. There are mainly two provisions to this effect, namely, *the separation of powers* and *the system of checks and balances*.[197]

By *separation of powers* is meant the assignment of certain specified state functions to different state organs or offices - that is, the distribution of power among such functionally differentiated agencies of government as the legislature, the executive, and the judiciary. The reason is to prevent any one branch of government from becoming supreme. Madison warns that "the accumulation of all powers, legislative, executive, and judiciary, in the hands, whether of one, a few, or many, and whether hereditary, self-appointed, or elected, may justly be pronounced the very definition of tyranny."[198] What Montesquieu wrote on this is worth quoting in detail:

> The political liberty of the subject is a tranquility of mind arising from the opinion each person has of his safety. In order to have this liberty, it is requisite the government be so constituted as one man need not be afraid of another.
> When the legislative and executive powers are united in the same person, or in the same body of magistrates, there can be no liberty; because apprehensions may arise, lest the same monarch or senate should enact tyrannical laws, to execute them in a tyrannical manner.
> Again, there is no liberty, if the judiciary power be not separated from the legislative and executive. Were it joined with the legislative, the life and liberty of the subject would be exposed to arbitrary control; for the judge would be then the legislator. Were it joined to the executive power, the judge might behave with violence and oppression.
> There would be an end of everything, were the same man or the same body, whether of the nobles or of the people, to exercise those three powers, that of enacting laws, that of executing the public resolutions, and of trying the causes of individuals.[199]

Thus the aim of the principle of separation of powers is to prevent the misuse of power and, through mutual control of state powers, to secure, above all, the freedom of the individual. But how separate should the various powers be from each other? Is it a complete separation - total independence (as Hamilton would want it - "a strong executive , who could be independent of Congress"[200])? Or is it a separation with overlapping of function (as Madison strongly believed and propagated[201])? Complete separation is not it. The several departments of power should not be kept absolutely separate and distinct. Although there should be dispersal of power - although government agencies should be broken down functionally and territorially - to make government agencies stick to their own fields of action and to make them act independent of each other, there should still be much overlapping of functions between them. Take, for example, the US Constitution: "the President, and in effect also the Supreme Court, may veto legislation; Congress acts judicially in cases of impeachment, and can control executive power by withholding appropriations; the President has the judicial power to grant pardons."[202] This overlapping of functions helps the different organs of government to act as checks on each other.

By *checks and balances* is meant the system whereby the several constituent parts of government, by their mutual relations, become the means of keeping each other in their proper places[203] - that is, "the legislative, executive and judicial departments each enjoying certain delegated powers and each acting as a balance to prevent the usurpation of power by other departments. The governmental apparatus thus represented a balance of power designed to prevent any department from running away with the machinery of government."[204] This does not mean an encroachment of one department on another. Of course, those who administer each department should be given what Madison calls "the necessary constitutional means and personal motives to resist encroachments of others," for "ambition must be made to counteract ambition,"[205]and appeal to independent courts should be assured. But it does mean the keeping of watch on each other, to make sure that no department acts outside the law. In this way due process of the law is maintained in all government actions - leading to a democratic polity in which law is supreme and fundamental rights are respected and protected. With this we come to the second part of the tasks of the rule of law, namely the protection of fundamental rights.

Second, with regard to fundamental rights, the constitution should provide the list of individual rights or liberties (called *the Bill of Rights*) that are protected against the exercise of state power. The Bill of Rights contains certain "unalienable rights" - the civil rights or civil liberties which protect the citadel of man's individualism, such as the freedom of speech, of assemblage and of the press; religious freedom; freedom of unauthorised search and seizure, the right of trial by jury - never to be encroached upon without mortal danger to democracy. "The safeguards of the Bill of Rights," Bingham observes, "rest on the assumption that no man is to be merely a means to some other man's end, even if the other man be a government official. The criminal himself is a citizen with inviolable rights, till the formalities of trial, sentence and execution are complied with. The writ of *habeas corpus*, by which even the enemy of society is assured his day in court, was the first foundation stone of modern democracy."[206] This highlights the equality of all before the law and the fact that an accused person cannot be deemed guilty without being given a chance to defend himself. According to Stapleton, "if persons have equality of standing in their opportunity to resort to the judicial order as a protection from the arbitrary use of force by anyone, including government officials, a degree of law exists, a degree of right exists, even a rudimentary beginning of self-government exists. But where a person has no right to appeal for judgment to be guided by a general standard rather than by a caprice or by a *parti pris* in favor of his opponent, then neither law nor the beginning of self-government exists."[207] The point is that the state is a means, not an end. It exists for the sake of the individuals of which it is composed, not vice versa. Hence it is bound to defend the civil liberties. Such a defence is the essence of democracy, for it is an assertion of the dignity and worth of the individual.

This discussion could not be concluded without mentioning the moral obligations accrueing from the rule of law, namely the obligation to obey the law or what Ambedkar calls "the observance of constitutional morality."[208] Stapleton rightly says that "it is by no means a sign of profundity to maintain that rights are conditioned upon duties.... Of course right and duty are related concepts. It is our duty to extend to others the safeguards we claim for ourselves. To maintain them, we must take an intelligent interest in government and co-operate in necessary social tasks. All this is true, but does not change the crucial fact that fundamental rights belong to individuals."[209] Political obligation and respect for law pertains to all, the governed as well as the government. Thus the sayings: "Equality under the law" and "The law is no respecter of person."

On the part of the governed, the citizen must be law conscious[210] and must "cherish and inbreed a strong respect for law."[211] However, his obligation to obey the law is based on his "consent to the method of its making or agreement with the direction it gives, or both."[212] Thus it could be said with Stapleton that "in a democracy, the citizen has a moral obligation to obey the law, whether or not he considers it wise, because he has consented to the method of its making. If, however, the law directs him to perform an action that would cause serious injustice, he cannot be considered obligated to obey it. To take any other view robs conscience of all integrity. But this principle holds only in cases where obedience to the law would cause real injury to a vital principle."[213]

On the part of the government, it must abide by the rule of law (the constitution). It must never introduce any law arbitrarily or act arbitrarily. Thus the state business must be open, measurable, foreseeable and calculable. To this belong the prohibition of retrospective laws (especially when these would be injurious to the citizens) and the "law of protection of trust."[214] The government must guarantee the legal process: which guarantees the autonomy and independence of the judiciary (because an independent judiciary is the principal guard against arbitrary exercise of power), not only in view of the protection of the individual but also in view of the commitment of the state power to the constitution and the law.[215] And its agents and agencies must respect and obey the spirit and letters of the law. George Washington of the USA serves as a good example of what is meant here:

> To the American people, Washington was God. If you read his life and history, he was made the first President of the United States after the constitution was drafted. After his term was over, what happened? He refused to stand for a second time. I have no doubt that if Washington had stood ten times one after another for the Presidentship, he would have been elected unanimously without a rival. But he

stepped down for the second time. When he was asked why, he said, '*My dear people, you have forgotten the purpose for which we made this constitution. We made this constitution because we did not want a hereditary monarchy and we did not want a hereditary ruler or a dictator. If after abandoning and swerving away from the allegiance of the English king , you come to this country and seek to worshipping me year after year and term after term what happens to your principles? Can you say that you have rightly rebelled against the authority of the English king when you are substituting me in his place? Even if your loyalty and fidelity to me compels you to plead that I should stand a second time, I as one who enunciated that principle that we should not have hereditary authority, must not fall a prey to your emotion.*'[216]

Thus, when both the government and the governed observe "constitutional morality," justice and peace become the order of the day, and the stability and growth of the democratic polity is assured. A quotation from J. F. Kennedy will buttress as well as summarise these points:

Our nation is founded on the principle that observance of the law is the eternal safeguard of liberty and defiance of the law is the surest road to tyranny.
The laws which we obey includes the final rulings of the courts as well as the enactments of our legislative bodies. Even among law-abiding men few laws are universally loved.
But they are uniformly respected and not resisted.
Americans are free, in short, to disagree with the law, but not to disobey it. For in a government of laws and not of men, no man, however prominent or powerful, and no mob, however unruly or boisterous, is entitled to defy a court of law.
If this country should reach the point where any man or group of men, by force or threat of force, could long deny the demands of our court and our Constitution, then no law would stand, no judge would be sure of his writ and no citizen would be safe from his neighbors....[217]

To conclude the discussion, it is necessary to point out that although law has its limiting effects on the government as well as on the citizens - for instance, "through a high tide of laws and rulings," according to Gerhard Merkl, there obtains "a nearly complete over-legitimisation of our life," making "the knowledge of law no longer possible," so that "the law is looked at as a restriction of personal freedom"[218] - it is very healthy for the democratic process. As Stapelton has it, "law cannot give anyone a good life. It can at best create an area of freedom in which the individual ventures on the pursuit of happiness and of accomplishment."[219] Hence with the provisions of the constitution (limiting the exercise of power), a concentration of power in the hands of a single ruler is prevented, certain areas of political and social life are made immune to governmental intervention (thereby protecting the fundamental rights of the individual), and peaceful change in the political order is made possible. Therefore, without the rule of law and the constitutional safeguards, all the essential elements of democracy - equality, freedom, popular sovereignty, majority rule and minority rights - and, in short, democracy itself will be in jeopardy.

2.6. Conclusion

These principles of democracy are no mere classroom or textbook affair. They pertain to and touch the life of the people. They are meant to be cultivated and lived. Unless a given nation has integrated these principles into its way of life, democracy can never thrive in it.[220] However, the principles alone are not enough to build a democratic state. These principles need democratic structures or institutions for their actualisation. The treatment of these democratic institutions is the object of the next chapter.

NOTES

1 Barry Holden, writing on "The Necessary Conditions of Democracy," treats the question of the meaning of "necessary conditions" thus: "To say that 'x' is a necessary condition for 'y' is to say that without 'x' there will be no 'y'. (A necessary condition differs from a sufficient condition: if 'x' is a sufficient condition for 'y', then the presence of 'x' would guarantee the presence of 'y'.) In statements of necessary condition for democracy, there is some variation in 'the meaning given' to 'y'. The most obvious meaning is 'the existence of democracy'. And, indeed, 'a necessary condition of democracy' is very often taken to mean 'that without which democracy could not exist'. But this is not always so. Quite frequently 'the *continued* existence of democracy' appears in the place of simply 'the existence of democracy'. A necessary condition of democracy then becomes that without which democracy could not for long continue to exist...." (Sic, **The Nature of Democracy** (London: Nelson, 1974), pp. 183 f.)

2 Walter E. Boek breaks down these principles of democracy into 39 charateristics or criteria with which "a score indicating how democratic a country is judging by how well the government meets the 39 criteria" is obtained. (Sic, op. cit., pp. 6-15.)

3 A. de Tocqueville, **Democracy in America**, bk. 2, pt. 2, chap. 1, tr. by George Lawrence, in: **Great Books of the Western World** (Encyclopaedia Britannica, Inc., 1991 edition), vol. 44, pp. 269-271. He also wrote, in the Introduction to bk. 1, that "no novelty in the United States struck me more vividly during my stay there than the equality of conditions" - "Great Books of the Western World," ibid., p. 1.

4 B. R. Ambedkar, op. cit., pp. 3-4.

5 A. de Tocqueville, op. cit., p. 270.

6 For J. S. Mill, this choice does not need to occur since the democratic ideal provides liberty and equality for all. (See **Great Books of the Western World**, vol. 1, pp. 240f.) G. Sartori, writing on how equality relates to freedom, observes that "the more equality is sameness, the more an equality so conceived feeds a distaste for variety, self-asser-

tion and eminence, and thereby, in the final analysis, for freedom" and "that freedom signifies, when it meaningfully exists, equal freedom, the same freedom for each and all. Freedoms are also manifestations of equality." (Sic, op. cit., pp. 340 & 342.) This is further supported by J. Plamenatz, "Equality of Opportunity," in: **Aspects of Human Equality**, ed. by Bryson et al. (New York: Harper, 1956): "The equality that matters in this world is equality of freedom, all other kinds of worldly equality being important only as a means to it. There is equality of opportunity wherever any man has roughly as good a chance as any other of leading the kind of life he wants to lead" (p. 84) and thus, "Our equality is rooted in freedom and is not to be understood apart from it. It is not equality of status but equality of opportunity, and the opportunity is to 'be oneself'" (p. 94).

7 G. Sartori, op. cit., pp. 347f..

8 Ibid., pp. 337-338.

9 Ibid., p. 337.

10 G. Sartori made this distinction himself in his treatment of equality under "Justice and Sameness." (Ibid., pp. 338-341.)

11 Note that the Sophists were the first to state the issue in its secular, rational manner: "Our natural endowment is the same for us all on all points, whether we be Greek or Barbarian." In the same vein, the Stoics argued, in opposition to Plato and Aristotle, that all men are alike by nature because they all have reason and the ability to know and do good. For the historical development of the idea of equality as belief in the value of the individual, see L. Stapleton, **The Design of Democracy** (New York: Oxford University Press, 1949), pp.14-24.

12 L. Stapleton, op. cit., p. 18.

13 J. Locke, *Second Treatise of Government*, chap. 6, para. 54, in: **Great Books of the Western World**, vol. 33, p. 36.

14 Cf. R. A. Dahl, op. cit., pp. 84-88.

15 Ibid., p. 85. Among the protagonists of this view is Major William Rainborough who, in the *Putney Debates*, Oct. 29 1647, said: "For really I think that the poorest he that is in England hath a life to live, as the greatest he; and therefore truly, sir, I think it is clear, that every man that is to live under a government ought first by his own consent to put himself under that government." (Woodhouse 1938, p. 53).

16 Ibid.

17 T. Jefferson, *The Declaration of Independence*, in: **Great Books of the Western World**, (1991), vol. 40, p. 1. Cf. H. M. Kallen, op. cit., p. 67, and P. Corbett, op. cit., p. 40.

18 Quoted in: L. Stapleton, op. cit., p. 19.

19 H. M. Kallen, op. cit., pp. 69f..

20 Quoted in: G. Sartori, op. cit., p. 342.

21 Quoted in: B. Holden, op. cit., pp. 208f.; Cf. J. Bryce, **Modern Democracies**, vol. 1, p. 49.

22 G. Sartori, op. cit., pp. 342f..

23 Ibid., p. 343.

24 Cf. L. Stapleton, op. cit., p. 13.

25 Ibid., p. 25

26 Ibid., p. 27.

27 Ibid., p. 28.

28 Ibid., p. 22.

29 J. R. Lewis believes that "any other attempts to bring about equality, in fields outside the political, are virtually doomed from the start in that such equality is impossible. The inherent characteristics of the individual prevent this, so that any 'equality' in such fields can only result in grading down to the lowest common factor, the mass of the people who will be endowed with none of the qualities that might otherwise be recognized and lauded in the state" - sic, op. cit., p. 25. Cf. S. K. Padover, **Sources of Democracy - Voices of Freedom, Hope and Justice** (New York: McGraw-Hill Book Company, 1973), p. xxxiii. But, as we shall see later in this discussion, democracy today demands more than "a political equality;" it demands also "economic or social equality" without "a grading down to the lowest common factor."

30 S. K. Padover, ibid..

31 H. J. Laski, **Equality and Democracy**, in: H. M. Bishop et al., op. cit., p. 15.

32 B. Holden, op. cit., p. 208.

33 C. Cohen, *The Justification of Democracy*, in the philosophical journal **The Monist**, vol. 55, No. 1 (Jan. 1971), p. 12.

34 Ibid., p. 18.

35 L. Stapleton, op. cit., p. 29.

36 Ibid.

37 C. Cohen, op. cit., p. 8.

38 Ibid.

39 G. Sartori's division of equal opportunity into "Equal access" and "Equal start" is worth noting. He writes: "**Equal access** amounts, in essence, to non-discrimination in entry or promotion; the access is made equal to equal abilities (not to all).... Equal access implies that what is recognized and rewarded is **actual performance** and thereby leads to equality in merit, capacity, or talent. The notion of **equal start** addresses ... how equally to develop **individual potentialities**.... Once each person is given the fairest possible start (by allowing all his potentialities to blossom), it can cogently follow that from this point onward individuals should be left to ascend via their merits and abilities." (Sic, op. cit., pp. 346-347.) Cf. S. Nearing, op. cit., p. 88.

40 Quoted in L. Stapleton, op. cit., p. 26.

41 Ibid.

42 Ibid.

43 Quoted in S. K. Padover, op. cit., p. xxxiii.

44 A. Kreisberg, **The ABC of Democracy** (New York: Philosophical Library Inc., 1943), pp. 69-72.

45 My contention here is not to make a distinction between "political democracy" and "economic democracy" and/or to enthrone the supremacy of economic equality over political equality as some authors, like Harold J. Laski (late Prof. of Political Science at London School of Economic and Political Science), have done. For example, Prof. Laski writes that "It is because political equality, however profound, does not permit

the full affirmation of the common man's essence that the idea of democracy has spread to other spheres. The discovery that men may be politically equal without attaining a genuine realization of their personalities was seen by not a few during the Puritan revolution, and the demand for economic equality was loudly and ably voiced then by Winstanley and his followers. It was only, however, with the French Revolution that economic equality may be said to have become a permanent part of the democratic creed. From that time, particularly in the context of socialist principles, it has been increasingly insisted that in the absence of economic equality no political mechanisms will of themselves enable the common man to realize his wishes and interests. Economic power is regarded as the parent of political power.... To divide a people into rich and poor is to make impossible the attainment of a common interest by state action...." (Sic, "Equality and Democracy," in: H. M. Bishop et al., op. cit., pp. 15-16.) Hence I agree with R. M. MacIver that "'the economic sphere' can never be separated from 'the political sphere'." (Cf. R. M. MacIver, "The Role of the People," in: H. M. Bishop et al., op. cit., pp. 21-22.)

46 G. Sartori, op. cit., p. 345.

47 L. Stapleton, op. cit., pp. 28-29.

48 C. Bay, "Human Rights and Majority Rule," in: Berg Elias, **Democracy and the Majority Principle** (Goteborg, Sweden: Akademiforlaget, 1965), p. 105. And John Plamenatz holds that "the equality that matters in this world is equality of freedom, all other kinds of worldly equality being important only as means to it." (See his "Equality of Opportunity" in: L. Bryson et al., eds., op. cit., p. 84; Cf. this chap., note 5.) However, days are gone when, as G. Sartori observes, "liberty implied 'equality in liberty' and that equality in itself ... obtained little salience.... Today liberty and equality command separate recognition - and along this path equality may not only implement freedom but also destroys freedom." (G. Sartori, op. cit., p. 357.)

49 C. Bay, op. cit., p. 7 - in B. Elias, op. cit., p. 102.

50 J. R. Lewis, op. cit., pp. 16f..

51 Rousseau's justification for moral autonomy during his discussion of slavery - see his "Social Contract," bk. 1, chap. 4.

52 L. Stapleton, op. cit., pp. 33ff. This supports the many arguments that freedom - and not equality, as some authors like Tocqueville and Ambedkar believe (see the discussion on equality, par. 1) - is primary in a democracy. S. K. Padover considers freedom as "perhaps the most fundamental to all 'natural' rights" (sic, op. cit., p. xxxiii).

53 J. R. Lewis, op. cit., pp. 19f.

54 J. S. Mill, "On Liberty" (chap. 1), in his **Three Essays**, with an introduction by Richard Wollheim (Oxford/New York: Oxford University Press, 1989 ed.), p. 5; and in: **Great Books of the Western World**, vol. 40, p. 267.

55 J. Locke, "Of Slavery," - chap. 4 of his **Second Essay Concerning Civil Government**, in: **Great Books of the Western World**, vol. 33, pp. 29-30.

56 C. Bay, **The Structure of Freedom** (1958, p. 83), in: B. Elias, op. cit., p. 100.

57 L. Stapleton, op. cit., pp. 33-34.

58 This is a tradition of thought, stemming from Locke and Paine, in which areas of individual liberty are sanctified as an individual's natural right. This thought is evident in the Bill of Rights of some countries (like the USA and France) and Organizations (like the UNO). The American Declaration of Independence (July 4, 1776): "We hold these

truths to be self-evident, that all men are created equal, that they are endowed by their Creator with certain unalienable Rights, that among these are Life, Liberty and the pursuit of Happiness...." The French Declaration of the Rights of Man and of the Citizen (August, 1789): "Men are born, and always continue, free and equal in respect of their rights...." And the United Nations Universal Declaration of Human Rights (adopted by the UN General Assembly, Dec. 6, 1948): "All human beings are born free and equal in dignity and rights...." (Cf. S. K. Padover's "Declarations And Documents - Milestones On The Road To Freedom" in his already quoted work, especially pp. 304f., 325f., and 341-343.

59 See R. A. Dahl's treatment of "Freedom of Self-determination" as one of the three ways in which democracy is instrumental to maximum feasible freedom. (Sic, op. cit., pp. 89-91.)

60 See note 55 above. This implies "absence of external impediments, removal of external constraints, lessening of coercive bonds" (G. Sartori, op. cit., p. 301). Cf. Hobbes' **Leviathan**, pt. I, chap. 14: "By liberty is understood ... the absence of external impediments; which impediments may oft take away part of man's power to do what he would...." and pt. II, chap. 21: "Liberty, or freedom, signifieth, properly, the absence of ... external impediments of motion." (All these are found in: **Great Books of the Western World**, vol. 21, pp. 86-90 and pp. 112-117).

61 S. K. Padover, op. cit., p. xxxiii.

62 Ibid.

63 Just like political equality, political freedom does not work in isolation. It presupposes other freedoms like psychological freedom, intellectual freedom, moral freedom, social freedom, economic freedom, legal freedom, and so on, and promotes them - for a healthy democratic state. G. Sartori writes: "Political freedom is by no means the only freedom, nor is it by any necessity the one that should rank highest in value. It is, however, the primary liberty on procedural grounds, for it is the sine qua non of all other freedoms" (sic, op. cit., p. 304).

64 Ibid., p. 301.

65 Ibid., p. 304.

66 Ibid., p. 303.

67 Ibid., pp. 305-306.

68 S. Nearing, op. cit., p. 48.

69 The necessity of this freedom is brought out by Winston Churchill's vivid description of the gruesome violation of the freedom of the person by the state agency. He writes: "At present a family might be gathered around the fire side enjoying the fruits of their toil when suddenly there is a knock at the door and heavily armed policemen appear. It may be that the father, son or friend sitting in that cottage is called out, taken into the dark and no one knows whether he will ever come back again or what is his fate. All they know is that they had better not inquire.... President Roosevelt laid down Four Freedoms.... Freedom of fear ... has been interpreted as if it were only freedom from the fear of invasion by a foreign country. That is not the fear of ordinary families in Europe tonight. Their fear is of the policemen knocking at the door" (Quoted in: L. Stapleton, op. cit., p. 49).

70 C. Bay, "The Structure of Freedom" (1958), p. 92, in: B. Elias, op. cit., p. 101

71 Ibid., p. 102, in: B. Elias, op. cit., p. 101.

72 S. Nearing, op. cit., p. 48.

73 Ibid., p. 51.

74 Ibid., p. 7; cf. H. M. Kallen, op. cit., p. 76.

75 S. Nearing , op. cit., p. 8; cf. L. Stapleton, op. cit., p. 51.

76 S. Nearing, ibid..

77 R. M. MacIver, "The Function of the Public," with the subtitle "Democracy and Free Expression," in: H. M. Bishop et al., op. cit., p. 20. Cf. L. Stapleton, op. cit., pp. 51-54; J. Macdonald, **The Corner Stone of Democracy** (Toronto: The Ryerson Press, 1939), pp. 4-5.

78 For a view of autonomy as the pre-eminent value in freedom of expression, see Thomas Scanlon, "A Theory of Freedom of Expression," in: **Philosophy & Public Affairs 1** (1972).

79 J. Lichtenberg, "Foundations and limits of freedom of the press," in: **Democracy and the Mass Media - A collection of essays**, ed. by J. Lichtenberg herself (New York: Cambridge University Press, 1990), p. 108.

80 S. Nearing, op. cit., p. 8.

81 Ibid..

82 Ibid..

83 L. Stapleton, op. cit., pp. 51-52. (My Brackets)

84 R. M. MacIver, op. cit., p. 21. And here the four arguments of J. Macdonald in favour of free speech are worthy of mention: 1) "the effects of repression on the individual are a considerable importance. It is good for him to feel free, bad for him to feel repressed...." 2) "it is best to allow free expression of opinion always because, even though the opinion appear to be dangerous, a) you do not get rid of them by repressing them: you drive them underground; and b) you can depend on the good sense of the people as a whole to discount them if they are really dangerous to society in general and not simply to a particular group which has reasons of its own for not liking them.... (R)epression is not the best way to fight a bad idea; the best way to fight a bad idea is to produce a better one...." 3) "by repressing opinions which run counter to the feelings of the community as a whole, you may be repressing something really valuable - something that the world needs. History has only too many examples of the man who was ahead of his time, was persecuted and eventually proved right...." 4) "there is the 'thin end of the wedge' argument.... If we allow any repression at all, it is hard to know where we shall end.... It creates a spirit which is highly infectious and will destroy freedom in the end. It is best to 'play safe'...." (sic, op. cit., pp.7-10).

85 This is J. Milton's "speech for the liberty of unlicensed printing, to the Parliament of England (1644)" - see **Great Books of the Western World**, vol. 29, pp. 381-412.

86 Cf. J. S. Mill, op. cit., pp. 22-68. He writes, inter alia: "If all mankind minus one, were of one opinion, and only one person were of the contrary opinion, mankind would be no more justified in silencing that one person, than he, if he had the power, would be justified in silencing mankind" (p. 23) and "But the peculiar evil of silencing the expression of an opinion is, that it is robbing the human race, posterity as well as the existing generation, those who dissent from the opinion, still more than those who hold it" (p. 24).

87 L. Stapleton, op. cit., p. 59.

88 Ibid., p. 60. This agrees with St. Thomas' teaching that it is wrong for one to make an act of faith in Christ if in one's conscience one is convinced, however absurdly, that it is wrong to carry out such an act (cf. **Summa Theologiae** 1-2. 19. 5). On the same note, Jefferson, in his **Notes on Virginia**, remarks that "Almighty God hath created the mind free" to the clear enunciation that "our civil rights have no dependence on our religious opinions" (ibid.) and that "No man has power to let another prescribe his faith. Faith is not faith without belief" (quoted in H. M. Kallen, op. cit., p. 74).

89 John Paul II, **Crossing the Threshold of Hope**, ed. by Vittorio Messori (New York: Alfred A. Knopf, 1994), p. 190; cf. "Declaration on Religious Liberty" (**Dignitatis Humanae**) of Vatican Council II, ed. by Austin Flannery, O. P. (Northport, New York: Costello Publishing Company, 1988 revised edition), esp. Nos. 1 & 2.

90 L. Stapleton, op. cit., p. 60.

91 S. Nearing, op. cit., p. 8.

92 L. Stapleton, op. cit., p. 62-63.

93 J. R. Lewis, op. cit., p. 17.

94 J. A. Schumpeter, op. cit., in: H. M. Bishop et al., op. cit., p. 24.

95 Prof. Mika's exact words are: "Das Selbstbestimmungsrecht des Menchen sei nicht uneingeschränkt, sondern stoße da an seine Grenze, wo es auf einen anderen treffe. Selbstbestimmungsrecht dürfe nicht zum Fremdbstimmungsrecht werden: 'Aber Recht auf Kosten anderer Rechte? Selbstbestimmungsrecht auf Kosten des Lebensrechtes? - Nein, das ist nicht Humanität, sondern das hebt die Humanität auf'." (Quoted in: M. Gante, **§ 218 in der Diskussion: Meinungs- und Willensbilding 1945-1976** (Düsseldorf: Droste Verlag GmbH, 1991), p. 338.)

96 This is well put by L Stapleton thus: "No one has ever seriously argued that freedom means an absence of all restraint upon the actions of the individual. Political freedom assumes the dependence of people upon society and organized government. It assumes dependence upon society, because the aspects of freedom that democracy ensures take the individual as a being and give him freedom in relation to social situations. It assumes dependence upon government, because no guarantee of freedom could exist without government. Political freedom depends upon the existence of law. It is an aim for law, a demand that government should secure certain spheres of life from invasion by its own activity." (Sic, op. cit., pp. 46f.)

97 Quoted by John Murray Clark, K.C. (President of the Royal Canadian Institute) in his work, **The Reign of Law** (Toronto: University of Toronto Press, 1918), p. 14. Cf. J. Locke, op. cit., chap. XVIII, par. 202.

98 J. Locke, op. cit., chap. VI, par. 57 - in: **Great Books of the Western World**, vol. 3, pp. 36-37.

99 L. Stapleton, op. cit., p. 47

100 Quoted in: L. Stapleton, op. cit., p. 56.

101 Quoted in: L. Stapleton, op. cit., p. 57.

102 L. Stapleton, op. cit., pp. 60f.

103 Ibid., pp. 63-64.

104 See Aristotle's **Politics**, 1310a.

105 See Cicero's **Oratio pro Cluentio**, 53.

106 J. Locke, op. cit., chap. VI, para. 57.

107 T. Paine, **Rights of Man** (1792), pt. II, chap. 3, last paragraph.

108 S. Nearing, op. cit., p. 89.

109 J. R. Lewis, op. cit., p. 21. He based this assertion on Aristotle's view that "for the many, of whom each individual is but an ordinary person, when they meet together may very likely be better than the few good, if regarded not individually but collectively, just as a feast to which many contribute is better than a dinner provided out of a single wallet. For each individual among the many has a share of virtue and prudence, and when they meet together they become in a manner one man."

110 B. Holden, op. cit., p. 185.

111 Quoted in: B. Holden, op. cit., p. 185 (from "The Civic Culture" written by Almond and Verba, p. 230).

112 J. A. Schumpeter, "Competition for Political Leadership" - from his **Capitalism, Socialism and Democracy**, 3rd. ed. (New York: Harper & Brothers, 1950), pp. 269-273; quoted in: H. M. Bishop et al., op. cit., p. 22.

113 Ibid., p. 24.

114 W. Lippmann, **The Phantom Public** (New York: The Macmillan Co., 1927), quoted in: H. M. Bishop et al., op. cit., pp. 9-11.

115 Ibid., pp. 13-14.

116 Ibid..

117 Ibid..

118 R. M. MacIver, "The Role of the People" - from his **The Web of Government** (New York: The Macmillan Co., 1947), pp. 198-199 - in: H. M. Bishop, et al., op. cit., 17f.

119 R. M. MacIver, "The Function of the Public" - from his **The Ramparts We Guard** (New York: The Macmillan Co., 1950), pp. 27-30, 49-51, in: H. M. Bishop et al., op. cit., pp 18-20.

120 J. R. Lewis, op. cit., pp. 42ff.

121 M. L. Wilson, op. cit., p. 111.

122 Ibid., pp. 111f.

123 Sidney Verba, **The 1993 James Madison Award Lecture: The Voice of the People**, published in: **PS: Political Science & Politics**, vol. XXVI, No. 4, Dec. 1993, p. 677.

124 R. M. MacIver, op. cit., p. 19.

125 Sidney Verba, op. cit., pp. 679-684.

126 See **The Complete Madison**, ed. by Saul K. Padover (New York: Harper, 1953), p. 284. (My Brackets)

127 S. Verba, op. cit., p. 678.

128 Ibid..

129 Ibid., p. 685.

130 S. Nearing, op. cit., p. 109.

131 Ibid., p. 91.

132 S. Verba, op. cit., p. 685.

133 S. Nearing, op. cit., p. 109.

134 S. Verba, op. cit., pp. 682-684.

135 Cf. J. R. Lewis, op. cit., pp. 22-23.

136 L. Stapleton, op. cit., p. 73.

137 Ibid., p. 72.

138 Ibid., p. 73.

139 Prof. James Fawcett, DSC, (President of the European Commission of Human Rights 1972-81 and Professor of International Law at King's College, London, 1976-80), "Intervention to Protect Minorities," in: Ben Whitaker, ed., **Minorities: A Question of Human Rights?** (Oxford, New York: Pergmon Press, 1984), pp. 76f.

140 L. Stapleton, op. cit., p. 75.

141 S. Nearing writes that "majority rule is an indispensable element in popular government" (sic, op. cit., p. 91). T. V. Smith agrees: a majority is "indispensable for democracy because since government cannot be of all (though it may be for all), it is better for it to be of as many as possible;" hence "democracy ... is the operation of the majority will" (sic, **The Democratic Way of Life**, 1951, p. 11, in: Berg Elias, op. cit., p. 43). Lincoln reminds us that "(a) majority ... is the only true sovereign of a free people. Whoever rejects it does, of necessity, fly into anarchy or to despotism. Unanimity is impossible; the rule of a minority, as a permanent arrangement, is wholly inadmissible; so that, rejecting the majority principle, anarchy or despotism in some form is all that is left" (see Henry S. Commager, **Majority Rule and Minority Rights** (New York: P. Smith, 1950, c.1943), p. 8). Prof. Ralf Dahrendorf (the Director of London School of Economics and previously a EEC Commissioner and Parliamentary Secretary of State for Foreign Affairs in West Germany), in his **Minority Rights and Minority Rule**, laments the rise in minority rules and the difficulty in curbing them, and points out that "Minority rule is ... immoral; majority rule is more nearly moral...." (see Ben Whitaker, ed., op. cit., pp. 82-83 & 90). And the position of Austin Ranney and Willmoore Kendall shows that the case for majority rule is developed wholly from the case against minority: "A policy or procedure, obviously, does not gain in rightness by picking up enough support to justify the claim that it represents the wishes of a majority, or lose in rightness by losing support. But that is not the point at issue, since what the majoritarean asserts is not the superior intelligence or wisdom or even morality of popular majorities, but the wrongness, from the democratic point of view, of a state of affairs where the few are in a position to have their way over the wishes of the many" (sic, **Democracy and the American Party System** (New York: Harcourt, Brace & World, Inc., 1956), p. 32).

142 On the fear of the tyranny of the majority: see H. S. Commager, op. cit., pp. 10-14; A. de Tocqueville, "Tyranny of the Majority" - taken from his "Democracy in America," Henry Reeve's trans., 1835, vol. I, Chaps. XIII-XV - in: H. M. Bishop et al., op. cit., p. 81. And on the tyranny of the minority: see T. Roosevelt, **The Right of the People to Rule** (Washington: Government Printing Office, 1919), p. 3; B. Whitaker, op. cit., pp. 82-91; Thomas Landon Thorson (a Political Scientist; Editor of "Plato: Totalitarian or Democrat"), in his **The Logic of Democracy** (New York: Holt, Rinehart & Winston, Inc., 1962), says that what is wrong with minority rule is that "it violates political equality and popular sovereignty" (see H. M. Bishop et al., op. cit., pp. 86-87).

143 See L. Stapleton's assertions that "The need for self-government is inherent in the concept of equality and freedom, for they imply individual responsibility, and that can-

not be exercised without choice" (sic, op. cit., p. 66); that "Both majorities and minorities are made up of individuals. Unless individuals are free, no such thing as a choice of majority can exist.... The least important aspect of a majority is its manifestation of numbers; its meaning lies in its being a sign of voluntary agreement" (ibid., p. 75); and that "the will of the majority alone is not equivalent to democracy, although without the consent of the majority democracy cannot be achieved. It has been only when the majority choose to live according to the concepts of freedom, equality, and self-government - these three, but the greatest of these is freedom. For having freedom, the rest can be won" (ibid., p. 76).

144 T. L. Thorson, "The Logic of Democracy," in: H. M. Bishop et al., op. cit., p. 82.

145 S. Nearing insists that "since unanimity on public policies is unlikely in a complex community, if decisions are to be reached, policies determined, plans made and steps taken toward their fulfilment, it follows that means must be devised to determine the will of the majority and when that will is determined, to put it into effect" (sic, op. cit., p. 91).

146 T. L. Thorson, "The Logic of Democracy," in: H. M. Bishop et al., op. cit., p. 82.

147 Ibid.

148 Ibid.

149 Cf. ibid., pp 83-87. Here Thorson categorises the various solutions to the problem of majority rule and minority rights into two camps: one, "the natural rights democrats" (like James Madison, in some measure Thomas Jefferson, and John C. Calhoun) "who see democracy essentially as an instrument for limiting the powers of government officials," for whom "the widest possible freedom for individuals consistent with stable government is the highest value," and whose greatest fear is that of tyranny, especially tyranny of the majority, hence the urgent need to limit or check governmental activity; and two, "the majority rule democrats" (like Felix Frankfurter and Learned Hand (jurists) and Austin Ranney and Willmoore Kendall (political scientists)) who "see democracy as the method of popular government" (with stress "upon popular sovereignty, political equality, and therefore upon majority rule"), and for whom "the test of whether a government act is democratic or not is not so much a matter of how it affects individuals as it is of whether the policy has been decided by a majority of the citizenry;" hence "less emphasis upon limiting the governmental activity and more emphasis upon allowing the majority to do what it wants" (p. 83). Then Thorson goes on to consider two questions which arise from the above, viz.: "(A) should there be constitutional checks at all? (B) Given that constitutional checks exist, how should they be applied?" (pp 84-87). Cf. R. A. Dahl's view on the problem at hand: "... so far as I am aware, no one has ever advocated, and no one except its enemies has ever defined democracy to mean, that a majority would or should do anything it felt an impulse to do. Every advocate of democracy of whom I am aware, and every friendly definition of it, includes the idea of restraints on majorities. But one central issue is whether these restraints are, or should be, (1) primarily internalized restraints in the individual behavior system, such as the conscience and other products of social indoctrination, (2) primarily social checks and balances of several kinds, or (3) primarily prescribed constitutional checks. Among political systems to which the term 'democracy' is commonly applied in the Western world, one important difference is between those which rely primarily on the first two checks, and those like the United States which also employ constitutional checks" (sic, **A Preface to Democratic Theory** (Chicago: University of Chicago Press, c. 1956), p. 36).

150 See Ulrich Scheuner, **Das Mehrheitsprinzip in der Demokratie** (Opladen 1973), p. 13: Das Mehrheitsprinzip is "ein normales Mittel, um bei Dissens zu einer gemeinsamen Entscheidung zu gelangen." Cf. L. Stapleton: "Majority rule is a convention, the best known, whereby a community of free men may make decisions when they are not all in agreement" (sic, op. cit., p. 68).

151 It is very interesting how the Quakers - the Society of Friends - of the seventeenth century dealt with this problem in their business meetings. An insight into their proceedings, I hope, will be of some help to modern democrats: "A clark of the meeting presides over the meeting. Debating is discouraged. There is an attempt for the group to be attentive to the inward voice in the course of the meeting. All kinds of secular affairs are discussed, but there is an attempt on the part of the clark to draw together the various creative combinations of all the group and finally to phrase it and put it back to the group and say, 'Is this what Friends now have arrived at?' ... Votes are not taken. The resolution of the issue is put back to Friends, reformulated, phrased by the clark, and members speak up and say, 'Yes, I am satisfied with that' and the word of approval goes around, or someone says, 'No, I can't be satisfied with that,' and the process goes on. Considerable patience is often necessary to arrive at decisions where real conflicts ... are there. But when a decision is arrived at after that patience, the minority of the Quakers' own group are given their opportunity to make a suggestion that may alter or modify ... that thing which would have been accepted had perhaps the majority opinion at it came into the meeting been immediately recorded by a vote. Therefore the minority, although they may not be completely convinced of this, are convinced sufficiently that they have been heard and had a fair opportunity to influence the other group so that they do not stand in the way of the final decision being taken." (Quoted in: L. Stapleton, op. cit., p. 71.)

152 Prof. Dr Lothar Roos (Professor for the Catholic Social Teachings and Pastoral Sociology in the University of Bonn, Germany), "Mehrheitsregel im Entscheidungsprozeß. Zur Geschichte eines demokratischen Strukturelements und seiner Bedingungen," in: **Mönchengladbacher Gespräche** (a publication by K.S.Z. Mönchengladbach), vol. 9, entitled **Mehrheitsprinzip und Minderheitenrecht**, edited by Anton Rauscher (Köln: J. P. Bachem Verlag, 988), pp. 9-53.

153 See L. Roos, op. cit., in: Anton Rauscher, ed., **Mehrheitsprinzip und Minderheitenrecht** (Köln: J. P. Bachem Verlag, 1988), pp. 15-27.

154 Cf. Ibid., pp. 18-20.

155 Cf. Ibid., pp. 20-23.

156 L. Stapleton, op. cit., pp. 68f..

157 T. V. Smith, **The Democratic Way of Life** (1951), p. 22 - see his "Majority Rule and Compromise" in: B. Elias, op. cit., p. 43.

158 Ibid., pp. 80 & 106; cf. B. Elias, op. cit., p. 43.

159 Ibid., p. 22; cf. B. Elias, op. cit., p. 43. Cf. Ernest Barker's **Reflections on Government** (1942). Mr Barker says that "the thought, the will, and the general capacity of every member" must be elicited and enlisted by the form of government; such a government must depend on "mutual interchange of ideas, on mutual criticism of ideas interchanged, and on the common and agreed choice of the idea which emerges triumphant from the ordeal of interchange and criticism" (p. 36). This is because, Barker goes on, the "essence of democracy" is discussion (p. 19); democracy is a "system of govern-

ment by discussion" (pp. 37, 39); cf. "The Demand for Procedural Prior Consensus - Ernest Barker: Government by Discussion," in: B. Elias, op. cit., pp. 48-57.

160 Cf. L. Roos, in: A. Rauscher, ed., op. cit., pp. 23-24.

161 Cf. ibid., pp. 24-27.

162 Cf. ibid., pp. 15-40. Commenting on Ulrich Scheuner's view that the majority rule has meaning only "where the possibility of different opinions is admitted and considered" (see U. Scheuner, op. cit., p. 14), Prof. Roos says that "All must fundamentally, in freedom and equal competence, within a recognised room of discretion, be qualified for decision-making. It is only on these conditions that the setting of the majority on the same platform with all is understandable and the minority tolerable" (see A. Rauscher, ed., op. cit., p. 16).

163 B. Elias, "The Majority Principle and Equality of Participation," in sic, op. cit., p. 130. However, Mr Elias points out that "while equality of participation implies the use of majority principle, the reverse proposition is not true; the use of majority principle is also compatible with inequality of participation.... The majority principle does imply non-discrimination among persons and policies. Yet it is non-discriminatory only within its field of application. The majority principle can thus be applied to a particular governing (majority or minority) group instead of the whole people" (p. 132). Cf. his article "Democracy and the Majority Principle," op. cit., pp. 157ff.

164 Cf. L. Roos, in A. Rauscher, ed., op. cit., pp. 28-31.

165 L. Stapleton, op. cit., p. 68.

166 Cf. L. Roos, in A. Rauscher, ed., op. cit., pp. 31-34.

167 K. Löwenstein, **Verfassungslehre** (Tübingen, 1959), p. 27.

168 Cf. L. Roos, in: A. Rauscher, ed., op. cit., pp. 35-38.

169 Ibid., p. 35. Cf. Thomas Ellwein, **Politische Verhaltenslehre** (Stuttgart, 1964), p. 15. He says that the idea of democracy is based on "the initial natural belief that every citizen can take part in all important decisions."

170 Cf. L. Ross, in: A. Rauscher, ed., op. cit., pp. 38-40.

171 On the entrepreneurial role of minorities in a democratic political system, Charles Frankel remarks that a democratic society should be an "open society," that works so as to encourage and protect individuals whose task is "to criticise what exists and to indicate other possibilities" (sic, **The Democratic Prospect** (New York, 1962), p. 35). For R. A. Dahl, an important result of democratic government has been, not to produce majority rule but greatly to increase "the size, number and variety of minorities whose preferences must be taken into account by leaders in making policy choices" (sic, **A Preface To Democratic Theory** (Chicago, 1956), p. 32). On his part, B. R. Ambedkar sees the importance of the minority in the fact that "a successful working of democracy requires ... the existence of opposition.... Democracy means a veto power.... Democracy means that at some stage somewhere there must be a veto on the authority of those who are ruling the country.... Democracy requires that not only that the Government should be subject to the veto, longterm veto of five years, at the hands of the people, but there must be an immediate veto. There must be people in the parliament immediately ready there and then to challenge the Government...." (Sic, op. cit., pp. 4-6.) Cf. M. L. Wilson, for whom "the British system reposes ultimately upon two simple concepts, that the Government must govern and that the Opposition must criticize" (sic, op. cit., pp. 95-96) and for whom "Wise use of the initiatory power by the executive is ... conditioned by two necessities, the availability of an alert civil service, and the funct-

ioning of an active opposition. It was Benjamin Disraeli who first said that the most important adjunct of any government is a vigorous opposition, and subsequent experience has shown that its lack is possibly the greatest liability that a government can suffer" (ibid., p. 103f.).

172 L. Stapleton, op. cit., pp. 74-75.

173 S. Nearing, op. cit., p. 92. Cf. T. V. Smith: "A forbearing attitude toward the minority on the part of the majority is indispensable for the democratic way;" and the minority, on the other hand, must "accept the majority as constituted until it can supplant it" and "obey the rules of the game, both in its opposing and in its aspiring" (sic, "The Democratic Way of Life" (p. 14), in: Berg Elias, op. cit., p. 43).

174 B. R. Ambedkar, op. cit., pp. 11-12.

175 L. Stapleton, op. cit., p. 75.

176 L. Roos, in: A. Rauscher, ed., op. cit., p. 38.

177 Cf. ibid., pp. 16-17, 40-50.

178 Cf. ibid., pp. 42-44.

179 Cf. ibid., pp. 44-46.

180 Cf. ibid., pp. 47-50.

181 A. M. Bingham, op. cit., p. 41.

182 The staff of the CDS had the onerous task of preparing the Nigerians - through its various training programmes - for the transition from the military rule to a democratic rule. Our quotation is taken from "Module 1" - "The Search for Democracy" - of its manual, **Training Programme for State and National Officials of NRC and SDP, Part 1, July - August 1990. Training Modules** (Benin City: Hima & Hima Ltd., 1990), pp. 10-11.

183 See "Politische-Theoretische Reihe, Band 2," ed. by Leo Schütze and Konrad Bonkosch: Johannes Messner, **Der Staat** (Bonn: R + S-Verlag, 1978), pp. 28-30.

184 Mathilde Berghofer-Weichner (Dr, MdL, Stateminister of Justice, München): "Der Rechts-Staat, der Staat, in dem das Recht oberste Maxime ist ..." - her article, "Einheit von Demokratie und Rechtsstaat - eine ständige Herausforderung," in: **Politische Studien**, Sonderheft 5/1993: Bürgersinn und Rechtsbewusstsein, Verantwortung für die Demokratie, herausg. von Hanns Seidel Stiftung eV (München: Atwerb-Verlag, 1993), p. 5.

185 See the many definitions of "Rechtsstaat" given by Friedhelm Hufen (Prof. Dr, Institut für Öffentliches Recht und Rechtsphilosophie, Regensburg) in: **Politische Studien**, Sonderheft 5/1993, pp. 38-39, among which are: 1) "Der Rechtsstaat ist ein Staat, in dem Friedenspflicht der Bürger besteht" - a state in which the duty of the citizens' freedom exists (p. 38); 2) "Der demokratische Rechtsstaat ist der Staat, in den Entscheidungen in Transparenz und klar zugeordneter Verantwortung fallen" - a state in which decisions are made in transparence and in clear classified responsibility (p. 38); 3) "Der soziale Rechtsstaat ist ein subsidiäer Staat. Primär ist die Selbstverantwortung des Bürgers" - a subsidiary state in which the self-responsibility of the citizen is primary (pp.38f.); 4) "Der Rechtsstaat ist ein Staat der Verhältnismäßigkeit. Der Staat darf in die Freiheit seiner Bürger nur soweit eingreifen, wie dies wirklich unabdingbar ist, um zentrale Sicherheitsgebote zu erfüllen" - a state of relativeness; the state is permited to interfere in the freedom of her citizens only when this is truly unavoibable in order to fulfil the central duties of security (p. 39).

186 L. Stapleton, op. cit., p. 78.

187 Ibid., p. 77.

188 Ibid., p. 78.

189 Ibid., p. 77.

190 Ibid., p. 79.

191 Mathilde Berghofer-Weicher has eight elements: a) Gewaltenteilung (separation of powers); b) Grundrechte (fundamental rights); c) Gesetzmäßigkeit der Verwaltung (legality of administration); d) Rechtsweggarantie (guarantee of legal processes); e) Bestimmtheitsgrundsatz (principle of decisiveness); f) die Gebote der Rechtssicherheit (the rules of the security of law); g) die Gebote der materielen Richtigkeit oder Gerechtigkeit (the rules of material rightness or justice); and h) das Recht auf ein faires Verfahren vor allem im Strafrecht (the right of fair proceedings especially in criminal law) - see **Politische Studien**, Sonderheft 5/1993, pp. 5-7.

192 **The Federalist**, No. 51 (Note that many editions of **The Federalist** credit **Hamilton** with the authorship of Nos. 47 & 51; but recent research has established that both were written by **Madison**); cf. Great Books of the Western World (1991 ed.), vol. 40, p. 163; also H. M. Bishop et al., ed., op. cit., p. 48.

193 L. Stapleton, op. cit., p. 76.

194 A. M. Bingham, op. cit., p. 43.

195 W. Lippmann, **The Good Society** (1937), p. 346 - quoted in: A. M. Bingham, op. cit., p. 43.

196 See Gerhard Merkl (Dr., MdL, a member of the Commission for Constitutional, Legal and Communal Questions, München) who writes that "the law has its function in three areas: - Protection of the citizen from the state - Relationship of the citizen with the state - Relationship of the citizens with each other" (sic, in: **Politische Studien**, Sonderheft 5/1993, p. 40).

197 The Separation of Powers and the system of checks and balances by which it was accomplished have great advocates in: 1) John Locke who started the idea but did not develop it fully - see his *Second Essay Concerning Civil Government*, chap. XII, no. 143, in: **Great Books of theWestern World** (1991), vol. 33, p. 58; 2) B de Montesquieu, receiving the idea from Locke, formulated such a doctrine in his treatment of the British Constitution - see his famous "De L'esprit des Loix" (1748; English trans., 'The Spirit of Laws,' 1750), Bk. XI, Chap. 6, in: **Great Books of the Western World** (1991), vol. 35, pp. 69-75; 3) Hamilton, Madison and Jay who, influenced by Locke and Montesquieu, gave the doctrine its classic embodiment in the US Constititution and its political justification in that brilliant apology for the Constitution, "Federalist" (1787-88) - see their *The Federalist*, esp. Nos. 47 & 51, in: **Great Books of the Western World** (1991), vol. 40, pp. 153-156, 162-165, and in: H. M. Bishop et al., op. cit., pp. 45-50.

198 **The Federalist**, No. 47. Cf. Mathilde Berghofer-Weicher's description of "Gewaltenteilung" (separation of powers): "Es geht also um die Trennung von Gestzgebung durch ein unabhängiges Parlament, Verwaltung durch an die Gesetze gebundene Beamte, und Rechtsprechung, die durch unabhängige Richter ausgeübt wird und unter anderem auch die Gesetzmäßigkeit der Verwaltung nachprüfen kann, wenn ein Bürger eine Benachteiligung durch staatliches Handeln behauptet" (- it is about the separation of legislation through independent parliament, of management through officials/civil

servants bound to the law, of jurisdiction which is practised by independent judges and under which the legality of administration can be checked when a citizen observes an unfair treatment by state action) - see **Politische Studien**, Sonderheft 5/1993, p. 6.

199 Montesquieu, op. cit., Bk. XI, Chap. 6 - in: **Great Books of the Western World** (1991), vol. 35, p. 70.

200 A. M. Bingham, op. cit., p. 45.

201 Cf. **The Federalist**, Nos. 37, 47, 71.

202 A. M. Bingham, op. cit., p. 45. Cf. J. R. Lewis: "Even so, the separation is not complete in that there is still some overlap, or even interference by one over the other: the President will send messages or recommendations to the legislative body, he may call special sessions or exercise in some cases a right of veto; the legislature, on the other hand, possesses a certain amount of power in the making of appointments, it supervises the treaty-making powers of the President ... and it has a general power of supervision of the administration" (sic, op. cit., p 74).

203 Cf. **The Federalist**, No. 51.

204 S. Nearing, op. cit., p. 90.

205 **The Federalist**, No. 51.

206 A. M. Bingham, op. cit., p. 44.

207 L. Stapleton, op. cit., pp. 77f.

208 Cf. B. R. Ambedkar, op. cit., pp. 9-11.

209 L. Stapleton, op. cit., p. 85. Cf. Thomas Würtenberger (Prof. Dr, Institute for Public Law, Freiburg in Breisgau): "Zu den unversichtbaren psychologischen Grundlagen des demokratischen Rechtsstaates gehört der Gehorsam gegenüber dem demokratisch legitimierten Recht. Ein rechtsstaatliches Rechtsbewußtsein anerkannt, daß das Recht des Nächstens ebenso schützenswert ist wie das eigene Recht (- to the indispensable psychological basis of democratic 'Rechtsstaat' belongs the obedience to the democratic legitimate law. A law-consciousness in a state established, it follows that the right of another is equally important as one's own right), in his article, "Beständigkeit im Wandel, Unser Rechtsstaat und der Zeitgeist" (- Permanence in change, Our 'Rechtsstaat' and the Zeitgeist), in: **Politische Studien**, Sonderheft 5/1993, p. 16.

210 See Günther Beckstein (Dr, MdL, Secretary in the Interior Ministry of the State of Bavaria, Munich): "Das Rechtsbewußtsein der Bürger ist eine wesentliche Voraussetzung für Existenz und Stabilität des demokratischen Rechtsstaats" (- the law-consciousness of the citizens is an essential requirement for the existence and stability of the democratic state in which law is supreme), in his article, "Rechtsbewußtsein contra Gewaltbereitschaft" (Law-consciousness against Violence-readiness), in: **Politische Studien**, Sonderheft 5/1993, p. 32.

211 L. Stapleton, op. cit., p. 96.

212 Ibid., pp. 95f.

213 Ibid., p. 96.

214 See Mathilde Berghofer-Weicher on "Bestimmtheitsgrundsatz" (principle of decisiveness), op. cit., p. 7.

215 Cf. ibid., on "Rechtsweggarantie" (guarantee of legal process), op. cit., pp. 6-7.

216 B. R. Ambedkar, op. cit., pp.9-10. Note that, "ultimately, they prevailed upon him to stand at least a second time. And he did. And the third time when they approached him, he spurned them away."

217 S. K. Padover, on "Presidential Statements On Law and Equality," op. cit., p. 13.

218 G. Merkl, op. cit., p. 11.

219 L. Stapleton, op. cit., p. 97.

220 This accounts for one of the main reasons why many new or developing states find it very difficult to establish a stable democracy: the democratic principles are not made part of their culture.

3. THE NECESSARY INSTITUTIONS FOR DEMOCRACY

Apart from the universal principles of democracy, there are also necessary institutions for democracy - what Padover calls "the irreducible ingredients that make up a democracy."[1] They are necessary, because "a democracy that lacks those ingredients is either flawed or no democracy at all."[2] H. V. Wiseman sort of summarizes what obtains in the democratic institutions thus:

> *Political Democracy* is the regime of civilian rule through representative institutions and public liberties. Its components are first, a legislative body periodically elected by universal ... suffrage, empowered to initiate legislation ... and to enact or repeal legislation initiated by the executive. The latter is subject to review and control.... The executive carries out its policies through a hierarchically organized non-political bureaucracy....
> Candidates for the legislature are normally members of contending political parties.... Executive and legislative action is subject to periodic review through free elections, as well as being continually scrutinized by free organs of public opinion. Within the legislature, opposition and minority rights are guaranteed, and governments can be changed by regularized procedures of action....[3]

It is the task of this chapter to consider the following necessary institutions for modern democracy: competitive party system; impartial electoral commission; representative institutions (representative assemblies and the executives); an independent judiciary; free press (newspaper, radio, television, book-publishing, etc.); periodic free elections (of policy-making officials).

3.1. Competitive Party System

To better treat this topic let us consider the following questions: What is a political party? What are its functions? What are the different party systems and which of them is good for a democratic state? And what is competitive party system and why is it necessary for democracy?

What is a political party? A political party in a constitutional democracy is neither a faction[4] (as defined by Madison[5] and feared by Washington[6]) nor a pressure group.[7] It is defined as "a group of persons organized to acquire and exercise political power through election or revolution,"[8] or "the agency through which the electorate is involved in both the exercise and transfer of power."[9] Put in another way, it is at once a means of representing a mass electorate in the exercise of power and device for allowing the peaceful replacement of one set of power holders with another. Hence a political party is, as realised by Thomas Jefferson, "a necessary instrument for self-government and an indispensable agency for the maintenance of freedom."[10] Unlike the centralised, autocratic direction of the totalitarian single-party organisation, with its emphasis on ideological conformity and restricted membership, a modern political party is decentralised and is concerned with the integration of many interests and beliefs, and open to public participation.

What are the functions of the modern political party? Their functions could be reduced to three. One, they provide an opportunity for like-minded people to express their needs and voice their demands. Two, they furnish the leadership, the candidates, the mechanism, and the programme - to be presented to the electorate - for the achievement of the wishes of its members. Three, they create room for the attainment of public consent and consensus by legitimate means, through discussion and persuasion. Padover summarizes these functions thus:

> The modern political party performs functions supremely essential to democracy. It regulates conflict, which exists in every dynamic society that contains numerous interest groups. It legalizes the operations of such competitive interests. It provides the electorate with an acceptable and stable instrument to express its views and attain its objectives. Finally, it furnishes society with an outlet for accumulated aggressions generated by the pressures and vicissitudes of life. Without the vent of a political party, the temptation to use violence might not be easily resisted.[11]

Hence the importance of party politics cannot be over-emphasised. As Bingham writes, "The ballot was supposed to enable the citizen to select those who should rule him; but only the party could name the candidates to make that choice effective. The legislature was supposed to make laws; but only the party could give it the organizational structure and the discipline without which it would have been a mob, and only the party could enable it to perform its modern function as mediator of conflicts."[12] In the same vein a New York politician, Edward J. Flynn, once explained the reasons for the necessity of party "machines" thus: "... suppose you do away with machines. Without them you ... would have to devise some alternative means of discovering, before each election, the men and women best qualified for public office. Could you, out of your present knowledge, choose a city-wide slate on which your neighbors could agree? Obviously you would have to talk things over with your neighbors. But since every New Yorker has eight million "neighbors" ... doesn't this suggest some system of representation?... Would you be willing to drop your business every two years to devote full time to attending meetings, canvassing potential candidates, canvassing voters from door to door, raising the indispensable campaign funds?... One evening of it would convince you that politics is a full-time job, not a hobby."[13] Flynn's argument may sound very common-place and simplistic, but it does portray the indispensable place the political party occupies in a democratic polity.

What are the different party systems and which of these is good for a democratic state? There are, broadly speaking, three types of party system:

1) **One-party system**. This is found in countries where revolutionary parties have come to power or where leaders believe that political conflict and criticism

of the government serve only to divide a society. There have been three historical models of the single-party system:

a) **the communist model** (found in communist countries, like the former Soviet Union and China), in which the party bureaucracy, chosen from a small elite, has in effect become the state, and in which power flows from up downward;

b) **the fascist model** (found in fascist regimes, like Italy between 1922 and 1943), where the party is even more of a closed corporation but is usually subordinated to a charismatic leader or to the army; and

c) **the model in developing countries** (like the former Arab Socialist Union in Egypt, the Neo-Destour Party in Tunisia), with many variations, most of which claimed to be more or less Socialist or at least progressive, while remaining far removed from Communism and, in some cases, ardent foes of Communism. There is what R. N. Spann calls **a modified one-party system** "with some room for manoeuvre within the party, and perhaps with minor opposition groups as small parties at elections or in parliament."[14] This was the case in India where there was "a single party of central government, but also a good deal of intra-party diversity, some minor parties outside the governing elite, a relatively 'unpoliticised' administration and judiciary, and limited aims, which include a genuine attachment to the democratic ideal."[15] Between the systems in China and India "there are a variety of **intermediate one-party system**" (like Mexico's PRI, Tanzania's TANU, Ghana's CPP, and so on), in which power flows from down upward, and some of which claim the notion of "government by discussion" (like Julius Nyerere of Tanzania referring to traditional African democracy as the elders sitting under a tree until agreement is reached) and whose "leaders claim for their single dominant party some of the advantages that used to be for the two-party system."[16] One thing common to all single-party system is that they have the propensity to totalitarianism and to abhorrence of opposition. This fact makes one-party system unfit for democracy.

2) **Two-party system**. This is the system found in such countries like the Great Britain, the United States of America, and New Zealand. Under this system, though there exist invariably some "third-party" movements, two major parties dominate political life. The use of *single-ballot system* (in an election) excludes parties that may gain substantial numbers of votes but not the majority of votes necessary to elect a representative within a constituency. However, there is a possibility that such small parties might prevent one of the two major parties from gaining a majority of seats in the legislature. The Liberal Party in Great Britain is a good example here. Normally the two dominant parties are - in their manifestoes - never very far apart from each other. When one wins the election and thus forms the government (being sure of a majority in the legislature), the other automatically forms the opposition. "When the two parties are roughly equal in strength," writes Bingham, "each acts as a check on the other; if the 'ins' become too arbitrary, too inefficient, too corrupt, they can be thrown out of office

by the 'outs'. So long as their principles and policies are not too far apart, shifts in control from one party to the other can be accomplished without dangerous passions being aroused, and without a general direction of national policy too sharply altered."[17] Because two-party system operates in situations in which genuine political conflict is tolerated and in which opposition is given due recognition, it is good for a democratic polity.

3) **Multi-party system**. This is the system found in almost all of Western Europe (like in Germany and Austria). Here, because there are many competing parties, it is very rare for one party to have a majority in the legislature and thus to govern alone. Hence governments must be founded on coalitions and alliances between parties.[18] Such coalitions are always more heterogeneous and more fragile than a single party. In an election *proportional representation* or *second ballot* is used to ensure representation in the legislature for even smaller parties. And in a place like Germany *banning method* is also used, whereby any party that fails to win a certain minimum set percentage of votes (that is, below 5%) is denied a seat in the parliament. Generally, under the multi-party system, there is room for competition and opposition. Therefore, the multi-party system is also good for a democratic polity.

From the above discussions of the different party systems, it is clear that the one-party system, because of its totalitarian inputs, has no place in a democracy; and that the two-party and multi-party systems, because they are open to public participation, competition and opposition, are ideal for democracy. (This is not to say that the two-party and multi-party systems do not have their shortcomings. No, each one of them has got its pros and cons,[19] the details of which shall not considered here.) Hence democracy is about competitive party system.

What is a competitive party system? And why is it necessary for democracy? A competitive party system is one in which two or more parties seek political power. The fact of there being more than one party makes room for choice - the electorate is enabled to choose among the competing parties - and for effective opposition (both of which are necessary for any democratic state).[20] J. Locke draws attention to the advantages of making political decisions in an atmosphere of public disagreement: when legislators hear "all sides" on a controversial question, they are more likely to make an intelligent decision. We elect our deputies so that they may "freely act and advise, as the necessity of the Commonwealth, and the Publick good should, upon examination, and mature debate, be judged to require. This, those who give their Votes before they hear the Debate, and have weighed the Reasons on all sides, are not capable of doing."[21] Moreover, there is always some measure of competition among two or more parties, each of which, if it can hope to form a future government, has some ability to influence the course of state action. Even when a party does not form the government, it still performs a vital function to the society: it serves as a critic of - a watchdog indeed to - the power that be, while working hard and looking forward to winning the next election. As Padover rightly points out,

> Even when the party ... is defeated in its bid for power, it still performs services vital to democratic process. For one thing, in defeat it canalizes potentially active discontent into rightful expectation. Where periodic elections are fixed by law, the defeated party holds out the promise of future victory, of which there is always a reasonable chance. In any well-functioning party government, the loser of today is likely to be the victor of tomorrow.
> For another thing, the party that is out of power expects, and is expected by its followers, to serve as critic of the actions and program of the party holding office.... Provided ... that the opposition's criticism is loyal and not aimed at the subversion of the whole established system of freedom, it promotes the vigor of self-government in at least two ways. It exposes, or threatens to expose, corrupt officials and inefficient practices, and thus helps to improve government. It also brings issues to sharp or sharper focus, and thus helps to educate public opinion in regard to the prevailing men and measures.[22]

Such political parties must be independent, free from governmental coercion, control, or intimidation. This is to prevent the government from high-jacking the parties - making them, in effect, look like different branches of the same party[23] - thus, leading to a form of one-party system that is obnoxious to democracy. The independence of the parties implies their autonomy and makes room for variety in the body politics, both of which are very healthy for democracy.

3.2. Impartial Electoral Commission

All the political parties in a given state, including the one(s) in power, prepare themselves, and present their candidates, for an election. "Since men are not angels" (as Madison would say), it would be unwise to let the members of any one, or any combination, of the parties to organise, or to be in-charge of, the election. Otherwise partiality cannot be ruled out, for such members will always do things in favour of their party. Hence the need to have a body - totally independent of all the parties - charged with the responsibility of conducting elections according to laid-down rules and regulations. This body is what we call an "Impartial Electoral Commission." The members of such Electoral Commission must have no party affiliation. Its role must be that of an "impartial umpire" in a contest. The presence of such a body "creates favourable conditions for citizens to exercise their voting rights without let or hindrance;"[24] and it gives confidence and encouragement to the various parties, especially to the minor parties, that each one of them will get what is its due.

3.3. Representative Institutions

Since it is impossible in a large state for the people to meet as a legitimate body, they normally choose representatives to do what they could not do themselves.[25] These representatives of the people are constituted into different bodies to carry out the people's business. Hence, we have representative institutions. These are divided into 1) the legislature, and 2) the executive.

1) **The Legislature** or the representative assembly. This - whether at the local government level, or at state and federal government levels - is an institution where citizens can always vote in their representatives to exercise power on their behalf. It is a unique institution of democracy. For "dictatorships have executives. Dictatorships have supreme courts. But dictatorships do not have representative assemblies with the right to give legal recognition to the policies of the people."[26] It could be *bicameral*[27] - that is, made up of two Houses or Chambers (as in Great Britain or as in the USA), or *unicameral*[28] - that is, made up of one House only (as in Germany). Bicameral system is the one most favoured by democratic states.

The importance of the legislative assembly cannot be overemphasised. As its name (the legislature) implies, its primary function is to legislate - that is, to make laws. But it performs other functions as well.[29] In Laski's words, it is "an organ of registeration, an instrument of criticism, a sounding board through which the voice of the nation can make itself heard."[30] Or as C. S Hyneman would have it: "There in the legislative assembly they (the legislators) make the basic policies of the country, constantly critcize those in the seats of government, and feed out to the people the knowledge about affairs of government which permits intelligent action by the electorate."[31]

2) **The Executive**. This has two interpretations: a) in a wider sense, it means the whole administration of government - the Ministers, the civil service, the police for instance; and b) in a narrower sense, it means the head of the executive department - named the "President" in some countries like the US or the "Prime Minister" in others like the Great Britain. Our use of the term here is in the second sense - the head of executive department. The Executive "is concerned with the administration of the laws of the state; it is concerned with the *governing* of the country as opposed to the purely legislative function; it possesses wide powers in relation to the conduct of foreign affairs, the organization of the armed forces, the drafting of the legislative programmes for action of the legislature, the granting of pardons and reprieves, etc."[32] The terms "President" and "Prime Minister" imply two kinds of executive. On the one hand, there is the *parliamentary executive*,[33] also called *cabinet government*, found, for example, in Great Britain - normally with "the nominal executive" (vested in the Crown - like the Queen of England, or President - like the President of Germany, for purposes purely ceremonial) and "the real executive" or the working executive (like the Prime Minister in Great Britain or the Chancellor in Germany), both of which are different. On the other hand, there is the *fixed executive*,[34] also called *presidential government*, found, for example, in the US - with the ceremonial and real executives vested in the same body or person, the Head of the Executive.

It is worthy of note here that in the presidential system of government the legislature and the executive are separate while in the parliamentary system they are fused. But the important thing is that in both systems the Executive is elected by the people - either through direct popular election, or through election by an electoral college, or through election by parliament - and is very much accountable to the people. Therefore the Executive must show itself to be responsible to be able to win the people's confidence and votes.

3.4. Independent Judiciary

As already noted, the principle of the separation of powers assigns the three tasks of government to three bodies: law-making to the legislature, administration of laws to the executive, and law-enforcement to the judiciary. Hence the judiciary can be defined as an institution that enforces the laws of the state, ensuring that both the ruler and the ruled act within the law. The judiciary acts as the guardian of the constitution: interpreting the laws and imposing sanctions or punishment when there is infringement. J. R. Lewis thus points out that "the basic role of the judiciary in a democratic state is the preservation of the liberties of the individual, the protection of the constitution, the upholding of legal rights against the encroachments of the state and the individual and the pressure group. The judiciary is the buttress that ensures that the law is applied without fear or favour, whether a man is black or white, Christian or Hindu, Conservative or Communist, lawyer, litigant or thief."[35] And Mr Padover writes that the courts of justice serve a triple function: "On the level of individual relationships they adjudicate differences with objectivity and impartiality.... A second function of an independent judiciary is that of clarification of the rules by which the communities live - it provides for a government of laws and not of capricious men. Third, such a judiciary imposes legal restraints on the arbitrary power. By defining the laws and defending the rule of law, independent courts can put a damper on willful personal power and overweening political ambition."[36]

Very important is the fact that the judiciary could be called upon to deal with legislative and executive actions. For example,

> In a state like Britain, which employs a common-law system, ... the judge is called upon to interpret a legislative provision and his interpretation will then, within certain limitations, be binding upon later judges in cases of similar nature. In this way a secondary system of law is built up, always capable of being overruled by an Act of Parliament, but nevertheless forming a guide to litigants and counsel, and binding law for the future.... In their relations with the executive body, the judiciary in the common-law states are able to rely on the firmly based doctrine of the Rule of Law which allows the judge to regard the Executive simply as another member of the community. It allows him to place the Executive on a footing of equality with the individual who is harmed by the executive action complained of. The result is that in such states the judges are regarded as the ultimate arbiters of the constitu-

> tion, the protectors of the individual's rights, his shield against power and privilege.... (So) by regarding all as equal before the law, the judiciary is in a position to exercise a controlling influence over the activity of the executive.[37]

The enormous and all-important function of the judiciary requires that it be independent (of both the legislature and the executive). Although there is no complete separation between the judiciary and the executive or the legislature, democracy fares better when the judiciary enjoys greater autonomy from the other branches of government, in order to maintain its very essential impartiality and to avoid being exposed to political influences and pressures. Thus one would prefer the practice in the US (where no judge sits in the legislative body nor is a member of the executive) to that in Britain (where the Lord Chancellor is both a member of the Cabinet, and also a member of the House of Lords, and where the Lords of Appeal, whose function is judicial, sit in the House of Lords). Therefore the judiciary should be no creature of any class or special interest. It must not only be free but must feel free from threat, intimidation or reprisal.

Certain devices are used in democratic states to ensure the independence of the judiciary. One is the permanency of the judge's position. A judge is usually appointed to hold office 'during good behaviour' and so he may not be removed from office by any vent of the wind. For instance, in the United States the Federal judges may be removed only by impeachment before Congress; and in Britain they may be removed only by an address of both Houses. Two, social prestige and adequate salaries for judges: these enable a judge to maintain a certain standard of living that is above par and which reduces the chances of greed and wanton pursuit of wealth. Third, a judge is rendered immune from action in relation to the decisions he may take within his jurisdiction. The fourth is non-political appointment of judges: this is meant to prevent any judge from being partisan, which would definitely mar his juridical impartiality.[38] Lastly, the quality and calibre of men to be appointed as judges must be taken into consideration. As Mr Lewis rightly points out, "the judge, after all, is not a being of Olympian detachment; he is a man, with all man's prejudices, failings, experiences and partiality. He will try to be impartial, and perhaps will succed as far as is humanly possible. But the qualification of 'humanly possible' must be noted. The judge is not a computer. There is always a human element in his decision, an element influenced by his education, his home background, his social surroundings, his personal experiences, his philosophies of life.... In order to be able to overcome the worst of his prejudices and ensure that justice is done, the judge must be an exceptional man. He must be honest, a man of integrity and wisdom; he must above all be impartial, allowing no emotional feelings personal to himself to sway his judgement. He must be well versed in the law, since he is called upon to apply it, and he should thus have a sound background of legal training and practical experience."[39] Hence it is very necessary to have the right kind of men behind the law, for, in the words of T. Roosevelt, "while good laws are necessary, while it is necessary to have the right kind of governmental machinery, yet the all-important matter is to have the right kind of man behind the law. A State cannot rise without proper laws, but the best laws that the wit of man can devise will amount to nothing if the State does not contain the right kind of man, the right kind of woman."[40]

3.5. Free Press

"Press" here refers to all media of mass communication, whether print or electronic media - such as newspaper, radio, television, even book-publishing, etc.. Democracy demands that the press be free - for instance, from government interference. Such freedom enables it to discharge and to fulfil its very important role in the political process as "a means to attaining truth or individual self-realization, a necessary element in a democratic society, a precondition of personal autonomy, a watchdog of government."[41] Since the press is an institution for the expression of ideas and opinions, the arguments for the freedom of the press stem from the arguments for the freedom of speech or expression. J. Lichtenberg[42] points out that "when we examine the most famous arguments for freedom of the press, we find nothing to distinguish them from those for freedom of speech or expression generally. Mill's discussion in *On Liberty* begins by asserting the need for 'liberty of the press' and proceeds to enumerate arguments for freedom of expression in general. Similarly, in 'What Is Enlightenment?' Kant defends freedom of the press with general arguments for the benefits of freedom of thought and discussion.... The press is treated as a voice, albeit a more powerful one, on a par with individual voices, and defending press freedom is then tantamount to a general defense of free speech." However, she remarks that though "the arguments for freedom of the press *are* arguments for a more general freedom of expression, ... it does not follow that whatever supports freedom of speech also supports freedom of the press." For one reason, "considerations internal to the theory of free speech theory itself may provide reasons for limiting freedom of the press." For another reason, "the modern press consists largely of vast and complex institutions that differ in essential respects both from individuals and from the early press, around which the concept of freedom of the press grew. Arguments that support freedom of the expression for individuals or for small publications do not necessarily support similar freedoms for mass media." And it is here worthwhile to consider John Macdonald's four arguments in favour of free speech - and so in favour of freedom of the press:

> First, the effects of repression on the individual are a consideration of importance. It is good for him to feel free, and bad for him to feel repressed. Hence ... we should avoid putting restraints on his freedom of speech.... Second, it is best to allow free expression of opinion always because, even though the opinions appear to be dangerous, a) you do not get rid of them by repressing them: you drive them underground; and b) you can depend on the good sense of the people as a whole to

> discount them if they are really dangerous to society in general and not simply to a particular group which has reasons of its own for not liking them. Taking the first point: it may be conceded that repression is not the best way to fight a bad idea; the best way to fight a bad idea is to produce a better one.... Third, by repressing opinions which run counter to the feelings of the community as a whole, you may be repressing something really valuable - something the world needs. History has only too many examples of the man who was ahead of his time, was persecuted and eventually proved right. To silence the voice crying in the wilderness is foolish because it may turn out to have been the voice of a prophet.... What is suggested by this argument for free speech is the desirability of giving everybody the right to 'expression'.... Fourth, there is the 'thin end of the wedge' argument, as we call it. If we allow any repression at all, it is hard to know where we shall end. Repression of any kind in any circumstances creates an atmosphere which is favourable to more of the same thing. It creates a spirit which is highly infectious and will destroy freedom in the end. It is best to 'play safe'....[43]

In a democracy, therefore, the individual should be free to say what he thinks and it is open to one group to influence another, provided that this is done by methods which do not themselves defeat the ends of democracy. In other words, in a democracy everybody should be free to hold opinions and to receive and impart ideas and information without interference; everybody should be entitled to own, establish and operate any medium for the dissemination of information, ideas and opinions; and nobody should be denied these rights.[44]

What is the role of a free press in a democratic process? Fundamentally, the press has an informative and opinion-building function. It informs the people of the happenings around them and helps them to make up their minds on the various issues affecting them. It is viewed as a neutral observer of the political scene. But "the press today - the mass media in particular - is one of the primary actors on the political scene, capable of making or breaking political careers and issues,"[45] and so its role has diversified.

The press is often described as having a special "watchdog function" or as being a kind of "fourth branch of government." As a watchdog the press monitors critically, and makes public, the activities of government and citizens, draws the attention of the public to wrong-doings, and sensitises office holders not only to act within their constitutional powers but also to discharge their responsibilities well. Hence the press could be viewed as a depressant as well as a stimulant.

As a depressant, the press is critical and has cleansing, inhibiting, and abuse-preventing functions. It serves as the people's watchdog, ensuring independent criticism and evaluation of the established power of government and other institutions that may usurp democratic power. The press prevents, in Kant's words, the "secretive system of politics"[46] by bringing the affairs of the power that be in the open. "Exposure to the light of day," observes Stephen Holmes (complementing Brandeis' consideration of the sunlight as the best disinfectant), "was extraordinarily effective for flushing out corruption and revealing abuses of office. Compelled to expose their activities to public scrutiny, political figures are more reluctant to swindle and steal."[47] Publicity then becomes "a cure for abuses of power," for accusations that are made publicly allow "the accused a civilized chance for explanation and rebuttal."[48] Cato puts it poetically thus, "Liberty of Speech ... drags (guilt) out of its lurking Holes, and exposes its Deformity and Horror to Day-light."[49] David Hume notes an intimiate connection between distrust of governemnt and freedom of the press, and points out that, as an open channel of communication, a free press can co-ordinate popular resistance. He writes:

> Arbitrary power would steal in upon us, were we not careful to prevent its progress, and were there not an easy method of conveying the alarm from one end of the kingdom to the other. The spirit of the people must frequently be rouzed, in order to curb the ambition of the court; and the dread of rouzing this spirit must be employed to prevent that ambition. Nothing so effectual to this purpose as the liberty of the press, by which all the learning, wit, and genius of the nation may be employed on the side of freedom, and everyone be animated to its defense.[50]

Therefore, "by threatening to bugle awake a drowsy public, newspapers can *curb* the ambition of rulers and *prevent* the worst excesses of arbitrary power."[51]

The free press also serves as a stimulant. It is often said with regard to press freedom that "public disagreement is a creative force." S. Holmes explains it thus:

> Those who quarrelled with the authorities were not merely adjunct 'checks and balances,' supplementary dikes raised against oppression. Rather, they nourished the government with counterarguments, unsettling information, novel suggestions, and fresh perspectives, even while highlighting inconsistencies and unnoticed side effects of current policy. Publicity, in other words, was not merely a paralyzing spotlight. It was also an arena for give-and-take, for mutual criticism and mutual stimulation, for acquiring new ideas and advancing proposals for reform.... An uncriticizable ruler hears only one side of the story and never learns about serious problems until they have gotten out of hand.[52]

In the same vein, D. Hume contends that a free press strengthens the government by making magistrates aware of "murmers or secret discontents" before they become unmanageable.[53] I. Kant agrees: "To try to deny the citizen this freedom means to withhold from the ruler all the knowledge of those matters which, if he knew about them, he would himself rectify, so that he is thereby put in a self-stultifying position."[54] Thus press freedom enables the government to correct its mistakes,[55] for "if policies are set publicly and public criticism is encouraged, a government can avoid self-contradictory legislation, nip crises in the bud, and remedy its own blunders."[56] Hence political actors are forced to shape their messages and their images to the contours of the contemporary press, and this affects the public's perceptions and the political process.

Furthermore, a free press performs the role of an opposition - a role very vital in a democracy. No doubt, there is a lot to be said for making political decisions in an atmosphere of public disagreement: when the legislators or the political advisers hear all sides of a question, they are better placed to make more intelligent decisions.[57] This brings out the fact that unanimity on political questions may be a sign of irrationality rather than of rational agreement, for "unanimity of opinion," in the words of Mill, "unless resulting from the fullest and freest comparison of opposite opinions, is not desirable."[58]

We must not forget the "agenda setting" function of the press. Bernard Cohen argues that the press "may not be successful much of the time in telling people what to think, but it is stunningly successful in telling its readers what to think *about*."[59] The free press, therefore, permits the flow of information necessary for citizens to make informed decisions and for leaders or public officers to stay abreast of the interests of their constituents.

Lastly, the press also has a moral function of diseminating the truth, and nothing but truth. This implies that the men and women of the media "have grave moral responsibility with respect to the truth of the information that they spread, the needs and the reactions that they generate, and the values which they put forward."[60]

Because of these vital functions of the press, any repression of the press is considered obnoxious and undemocratic. It is very true that the freedom of the press could be misused and abused. The press could be weak and manipulated.[61] There could be inhibition of the flow of ideas and information.[62] There could be cases of partiality and partisanship, "yellow journalism" and libel, and so on. All these call for some sorts of regulation[63] of the press but should never lead to the repression or suppression of press freedom. If anything, more emphasis should be laid on the use of functional ethics codes or press councils - to discipline defaulting and erring journalists and/or publishers and to keep the press on the right course. Members of the press themselves should live up to the expectations of the people, many of whom place a tremendous amount of faith and trust in the ability of the press to feed the public with the truth and nothing but the truth. (What a great betrayal any time the press fails to be an embodiment of truth and impartiality!) The shortcomings of the press notwithstanding, there is no denying the fact that the free press brings peace, stability, and justice to the people, and that its role strengthens and advances democracy.[64]

Allied to the press is the important role of **polls**[65] in modern democracy. It is true that in populous, highly organised societies, institutional channels of communication are not up to the task of keeping national leaders informed about the thoughts, feelings, and wishes of the general population. The people's representatives can today turn to the latest poll readings to find out what the public really wants. Gallup writes that with polls "legislators, educators, experts, and editors, as well as ordinary citizens ..., can have a more reliable measure of the pulse of democracy."[66] Polls then are the primary source of political intelligence - a type of "continuing elections" - a powerful "machinery" in influencing elected officeholders - indeed, the "pulse" of democracy. Hence it is of paramount importance that this medium be encouraged and promoted rather than be hindered and repressed.

3.6. Periodic Free Elections[67]

I decided to treat elections last because it is only when the above five considered institutions are in place that the ground could be said to be ready for any meaningful elections. Elections are meaningless unless there are competitive party system (to vie for the elections), impartial electoral Commission (to organise the elections), representative institutions (into which people elect their representatives), independent judiciary (to judge and settle any cases that may crop up during the elections), free press (through which the competing parties and the candidates vying for elections sell their programmes and manifestoes to the public, and through which the masses are informed of and educated on the "modus operandi" of the elections). This section is meant to consider the definition, form and substance of elections; the functions of elections; voting systems and practices; and participation in elections.

Elections are means of making political choices by voting - be it in the selection of leaders or in the determination of issues. The conception of elections implies that the voters are presented with *alternatives* - that they can choose among a number of proposals designed to settle an issue of public concern. This is a necessary condition without which elections are deemed "a child's play" and not genuine. Thus we must distinguish between the form and substance of elections. This is necessary because election forms may be present but the substance may be absent. While the form is just *any* choosing or selection of candidate(s) for an office by vote, the substance is that the voter has a free and genuine choice between at least two alternatives.[68]

For the growth and survival of democracy, there is a fundamental need for periodic and free elections. This is so because, "above all, electoral mechanism provides a peaceful solution to one of the key problems of political systems - an orderly succession of rulers."[69] Elections serve not only to select leaders acceptable to the voters but also to hold the leaders accountable for their performance in office. They serve as forums for the discussion of public issues, facilitate the expression of public opinion, and, more generally, permit an exchange of influence between governors and the governed. They serve to reinforce the stability and legitimacy of political community in which they take place, because they serve to link the members of a body politic to each other and lend authority and legitimacy to the acts of those who wield power on behalf of the people. Elections also confirm the worth and dignity of the individual citizen as a human being, because participation in an election serves to gratify the voter's sense of self-esteem and self-respect.

Democracy demands free and fair elections. For this to happen it is necessary that the system of *universal suffrage*[70] be adopted, that there be formalization and standardization of voting pratices[71] and of systems of counting votes[72] acceptable to both voters and leaders as legitimate prior to the election, and that the electoral rules and regulations be followed by all to the letter.[73] It is then, and only then, that any election can be considered *valid* (that is, that the collective choice in fact expresses the sense of the electorate), *reliable* (that is, that each vote is accurately recorded and effectively counted into the total), and *legitimate* (that is, that the criteria of validity and reliability have been met, so that the result of the voting is acceptable and provides authoritative guidelines in subsequent political conduct).

Lastly, the importance of participation in elections merits our attention. It is a fact that in one area the rate of participation in elections may be high and in another area it may be low. It is also true that even in the same area, the people may show more interest in one election than in another. Many factors determine the rate at which individuals participate in the electoral process: such as the type of electoral system, the social groupings to which voters belong, the voters' personality and beliefs, their place of residence. Since participation in elections serve to gratify the voter's sense of self-esteem and self-respect - because his vote is his voice, his right, his freedom, and even his conscience - then all avenues must be explored to encourage the citizen's participation in elections. One (and for me, the most important) of these avenues is political education of the electorate.[74] Once the electorate is politically aware and educated, there is a high probability that it will take deep interest and active part in elections, since it will consider doing so its basic civic obligation and duty, the neglect of which is harmful to itself in particular and to the society at large.

3.7. Conclusion: The Institutions alone are not enough

It is a common knowledge that many developing states - who, for many years, lived under dictatorship and, now want democracy - very often begin their journey toward democracy by establishing democratic institutions found in Europe and America without their corresponding principles. Political parties are formed but they are kept under the firm control of the power that be or they may not be competitive because only one party, the government's party, matters. The judiciary is established where there is little or no sense of justice and no rule of law. The press may exist but under strict rules and regulations - in an atmosphere where freedom and equality are mere "fairy tales". These developing states assume - erroneously - that the development of democratic institutions inevitably brings in its train the achievements of democracy. (No doubt, this forms part of the answer to the disappointing development of democratic government in parts of Africa, Asia, and Latin America.) In chapter one, it is observed that "nearly everyone today says they are democrats no matter whether their views are on the left, center or right," and that, often, autocracies attempt to borrow legitimacy by adopting the language of the constitutions of non-autocratic regimes or by establishing similar institutions (like parliaments or assemblies, elections and parties, courts and legal codes). It follows from this that an excessive emphasis on the institutions of democracy, at the expense of the principles of democracy, cannot make any society democratic. The institutions themselves cannot bring about a democratic state. As J. R. Lewis puts it,

> if an excessive emphasis is placed upon the institutions of democracy, so that they are regarded as ends in themselves, without regard being paid to the principles behind the system, democracy as a theory must founder. It must be seen that setting up a Parliamentary system is a pointless exercise if Parliament's will is to be overruled by one man; it is equally pointless to set up a democratic constitution which is to be disregarded by social practices.... (T)he theory of democracy does not demand an absolute sense of institutionalism. There are no irreplaceable institutions in the democratic state; ... It is easy enough to establish a state and set up in that state institutions based on the democratic devices obtaining in other countries. But this is no guarantee of democracy. This is paying attention only to the *form* of democracy - democracy in the strict sense of a governmental system; attention must be paid also to the democratic *principle*, the other side of the coin - the advancement of man and of human dignity.[75]

It is important to note that while the institutions themselves cannot bring about democratic principles, the democratic principles can bring in their train democratic institutions. This does not mean that the democratic institutions are not important. No, they are needed for the actualisation of the principles. Therefore, a democratic state must embody both the institutions and the principles. Both are in fact inseparable, because democracy is both a system of government and a way of life. This point leads to the object of the next chapter: the meaning and purpose of democracy.

NOTES

1 S. K. Padover, op. cit., p. xxxiii.

2 Ibid..

3 H. V. Wiseman, **Political Systems** (London: Routledge & Kegan Paul, 1966), p. 72.

4 Cf. S. K. Padover: "A political party differs from a faction in several respects. Unlike a faction, a political party is not built around the selfish or self-seeking interests of an ambitious few, but is, rather, in the words of Edmund Burke, an aggregation of men 'united for promoting by their joint endeavours the national interests, upon some particular principle in which they are all engaged'." (Sic, op. cit., p. xx.)

5 James Madison defined (and sharply rejected) political party as "a number of citizens ... who are united and actuated by some common impulse of passion, or of interest, adverse to the rights of other citizens, or to the permanent and aggregate interests of the community" - see S. K. Padover, op. cit., p. xx.

6 In his **Farewell Address**, George Washington warned his countrymen against the "danger of Parties" and their "baneful effects." He pointed out that even in self-governing republics, parties led to excesses, and hence were "not to be encouraged." For once a political party comes into existence, it becomes "a fire not to be quenched; it demands a uniform vigilance to prevent its bursting into a flame, lest, instead of warming, it should consume" - see S. K. Padover, op. cit., p. xx.

7 Cf. "Interest Group," in: **The New Encyclopaedia Britannica**, vol. 6 (15th Edition), p. 341: A political party differs from a pressure group in that a party has a structure and presents candidates for public office, whereas a pressure group seeks to influence both government and parties; cf. "Political Parties and Interest Groups," in: vol. 25 (same edition), p. 979.

8 **The New Encyclopaedia Britannica**, vol. 9 (15th Edition), p. 564; cf. vol. 25 (same edition), p. 979.

9 **The New Encyclopaedia Britannica**, vol. 25 (15th Edition), p. 1013; cf. ibid., p. 979.

10 S. K. Padover, op. cit., p. xx.

11 Ibid., p. xxi. Cf. E. Barker, "Reflections on Government" (pp. 38-39), in: B. Elias, op. cit., p. 49; and R. N. Spann, "The Democratic Political System," in: W. H. C. Eddy (ed.), **Studies in Democracy** (Melbourne, Canberra, etc.: Cheshire, 1966), p. 11.

12 A. M. Bingham, op. cit., p. 33.

13 Quoted in: S. K. Padover, op. cit., pp. xx-xxi.

14 R. N. Spann, op. cit., in: W. H. C. Eddy (ed.), op. cit., pp. 14f..

15 Ibid..

16 Ibid..

17 A. M. Bingham, op. cit., p. 38.

18 One of the major criticisms against the multi-party system is based on this fact that the leaders must negotiate to form a coalition, which the voters have not directly chosen, and for whose failure no clear responsibility can be assigned.

19 Note, however, that "defenders of multi-party systems argue that two parties do not adequately reflect the main divisions of opinion.... Two-party adherents reply that, in any practicable party system, parties represent coalitions of interests; and add that one of their major services is to force such interests to compromise their claims inside the party, and not become the vehicle of exclusive minority demands or ideologies." (See R. N. Spann, op.cit., in: W. H. C. Eddy, op. cit., pp. 11-13.)

20 See M. Rejai, ed., "The existence of effective opposition parties is frequently regarded as a crucial criterion of democratic government" (sic, **Democracy: The Contemporary Theories** (New York: Atherton Press, 1967), p. 192). Cf. Edward Shils who treats "practice and acceptance of opposition" as a major variable in distinguishing democratic and non-democratic systems (sic, **Political Development inNew States** (The Hague: Mouton & Co., 1962), p. 54); and R. A. Dahl: "one is inclined to regard the existence of an opposition party as very nearly the most distinctive characteristic of democracy itself; and we take the absence of an opposition as evidence, if not always conclusive

proof, for the absence of democracy" (sic, **Political Oppositions in Western Democracies**, p. xvi.).

21 J. Locke, **Two Treatises of Government** (New York: Mentor, 1965), pp. 461-2 (2, 222). Cf. Stephen Holmes, "Liberal Constraints on Private Power?," in: Judith Lichtenberg, ed., **Democracy And The Mas Media**, A Collection of Essays (Cambridge, New York: Cambridge University Press, 1990), pp. 29-30.

22 S. K. Padover, op. cit., p. xxi.

23 This was the situation in Nigeria (1990) when the then military government disbanded all the political parties on the ground that non of them met the registration requirements. The government then created two political parties for the country and produced a manifesto and modus operandi for each of them. Throughout the existence of these parties, the government never ceased to interfere in their affairs - allowing them no freedom - and making them appear like different organs of the same body, the government.

24 The Staff of the Centre for Democratic Studies (CDS), Abuja (Nigeria), op. cit., III. (2), p. 11.

25 Cf. J. S. Mill, "On Representative Government": "... it is evident, that the only government which can fully satisfy all the exigencies of a social state, is one in which the whole people participate; ... and that nothing else can be ultimately desirable, than the admission of all to share in the sovereign power of the state. But since all cannot, in a community exceeding a single small town, participate personally in any but very minor portions of the public business, it follows that the ideal type of a perfect government must be representative" - in his **Three Essays**, with an Introduction by R. Wollheim (Oxford, New York: Oxford University Press, 1979), p. 198.

26 M. N. Wilson, op. cit., p. 116.

27 See J. R. Lewis, op. cit., pp. 61-63.

28 Ibid., pp. 63-64.

29 See A. M. Bingham, op. cit., pp. 30-33; cf. J. R. Lewis, op. cit., pp. 66-70.

30 H. J. Laski, "The American Presidency" (1940), p. 246.

31 C. S. Hyneman, "Grassroots of Democracy," in: R. B. Heilman, op. cit., p. 22. (My brackets.)

32 J. R. Lewis, op. cit., p. 70; for more on the power of the executive, see ibid., pp. 77-79.

33 Cf. ibid., pp. 71-73.

34 Cf. ibid., pp. 73-76.

35 Ibid., p. 81.

36 S. K. Padover, op. cit., p. xix.

37 J. R. Lewis, op. cit., pp. 81-82. (My brackets.)

38 It is a pity that in many countries the appointment of judges is done on political considerations and loyalties. Let us cite the US and the Great Britain as examples. "While politics plays little or no part in the selection of Federal judges in the United States, this is not the case with the selection of state judges" (ibid., p. 85). In Britain, "though the judges are deemed to hold no political opinions in their official capacities, and should not allow political considerations to cloud their impartiality, the head of the judiciary in England is in fact the Lord Chancellor, a man who is appointed for his political lean-

ings, and a man who will become an ex-Lord Chancellor when his party loses office, to be superseded by another" (ibid.).

39 Ibid., pp. 83-84. Cf. T. L. Thorson, on the influence of environmental factors on the judges, in: H. M. Bishop et al., op. cit., pp. 87-88.

40 T. Roosevelt, **A Charter of Democracy** (Washington Govt. Print. Off., 1919), p. 19.

41 See J. Lichtenberg (ed.), op. cit., p. 15.

42 Ibid., pp. 105-106.

43 John Macdonald, **The Corner Stone of Democracy** (Toronto: The Ryerson Press, 1939), pp. 7-10.

44 "If free expression of opinion is denied in any particular case," writes J. Macdonald, "the people who deny it should be called upon to show that they have a case for denial. The burden of proof is on them, not on those who claim the right to say what they think." (Sic, ibid., p. 5.)

45 J. Lichtenberg, op. cit., p. 1.

46 I. Kant, "Perpetual Peace" (1795), in: **Kant's Political Writings**, ed. Hans Reiss (Cambridge: Cambridge University Press, 1970), pp. 126, 130.

47 S. Holmes (Prof. of Political Science at the University of Chicago), "Liberal Constraints On Private Power?: Reflections on the origins and rationale of access regulation," in: J. Lichtenberg (ed.), op. cit., p. 27.

48 Ibid..

49 John Trenchard and Thomas Gordon, "Of Freedom of Speech: That the same is inseparable from Publick Liberty" (1720), in: **Cato's Letters: Essays on Liberty, Civil and Religious, and Other Important Subjects** (New York: Da Capo, 1971), vol. 1, p. 98.

50 D. Hume, "Of the Liberty of the Press," in his **Essays: Moral, Political, and Literary** (Oxford: Oxford University Press, 1963), pp. 10-11.

51 S. Holmes, op. cit., p. 28.

52 Ibid., pp. 28-29.

53 See D. Hume, op. cit., p. 11.

54 I. Kant, "On the Common Saying: 'This May Be True in Theory, but It Does Not Apply in Practice'," in: **Kant's Political Writings**, p. 85.

55 Cf. John Milton, "Areopagitica (1644)," in his **Complete Prose Works** (New Haven, Conn.: Yale University Press, 1959), vol. 2, p. 487.

56 S. Holmes, op. cit., p. 29.

57 See J. Locke, op. cit., pp. 461-2.

58 J. S. Mill, "On Liberty," in his **Essays on Politics and Society** (Toronto: University of Toronto Press, 1977), p. 260.

59 B. Cohen, **The Press and Foreign Policy** (Princeton: Princeton University Press, 1963), p. 1. Cf. Maxwell McCombs and Donald Shaw, "The Agenda-Setting Function of the Press," in: **Public Opinion Quarterly** 39 (1972).

60 Paul VI, Pope, Encyclical **Octogesima Adveniens** ("A Call to Action on the Eightieth Anniversary of Rerum Novarum"), 1971, no. 20.

61 Cf. J. Lichtenberg (ed.), op. cit., p. 10

62 Ibid., pp. 102-105.

63 For detailed account of press regulation, see J. Lichtenberg, "Introduction," in: sic (ed.), op. cit., pp. 11-18; Henry Geller, "Mass communications policy: where we are and where we should be going," in: Lichtenberg (ed.), pp. 290-323; T. M. Scanlon, Jr., "Content regulation reconsidered," in: Lichtenberg (ed.), pp. 331-353; Lee C. Bollinger, "The rationale of public regulation of the media," in: Lichtenberg (ed.), pp. 355-367.

64 Sanford J. Ungar (Dean of the School of Communication at The American University and the former host of "All Things Considered" on National Public Radio) has a nice article, "The role of a free press in strengthening democracy," in: J. Lichtenberg (ed.), op. cit., pp. 368-396.

65 See Crespi Irving, **Public Opinion, Polls, and Democracy** (Boulder, Colo: Westview Press, 1989). Cf. R. N. Spann, "Public Opinion," in: sic, op. cit., pp. 49-51.

66 Crespi Irving, op. cit., pp. 3-5

67 For detailed account of "Electoral Processes," see **The New Encyclopaedia Britannica** (15th edition), vol. 25, pp. 1025-1031. See also Michael Riley, **Power, Politics and Voting Behaviour - An introduction to the Sociology of Politics** (London: Harvester . Wheatsheaf, 1988).

68 It is important to note that in a purely formal sense, the great majority of more than 150 contemporary nations have what are called "elections," only about one third of these have more or less competitive elections; perhaps a fifth have one-party elections; and in some others the electoral situation is highly ambiguous.

69 B. Holden, op. cit., p. 213.

70 Universal suffrage implies that all "eligible voters," irrespective of status, creed, sex and colour, should be allowed to vote. Generally, the requirements that appear in every democratic state are that of citizenship and the attainment of a certain age. However, children, aliens, criminals in prison, persons of unsound mind in mental institutions are usually denied the right to vote. Cf. J. R. Lewis, op. cit., pp. 48-51.

71 The electoral practices around the world differ a great deal, depending not just on formal institutional arrangements, but even more on a country's political culture. So each country chooses its own voting practices: whether its elections should be by a) **secret voting** (which allows for the secrecy of the vote, makes for equality in voting - "one man, one vote," reduces drastically the possibility of undue influence on the voter, permits voters to break away from their social moorings and gives them a considerable degree of independence, etc.), as against **open voting** (which is today no longer tolerable precisely because it could and often did involve undue influence, ranging from hidden persuasion and bribery to intimidation, coercion, and punishment, etc.); b) **balloting** (which differs widely: from marking the names of preferred candidates to crossing out those not preferred or writing in the names of persons who are not formal candidates; and according to the type of voting system employed), as against **raising of hands** (which is now out mode).

72 The systems of vote counting are 1) by **plurality and majority decisions:** a) *plurality voting*, which requires that, among three or more alternatives, the winner need have only the highest number of votes; b) *simple majority voting*, which requires that the winner receive more than 50 percent of the vote; c) *extraordinary majority voting*, which requires some higher proportion for the winner, such as a two-thirds vote; d) *unanimity*, where the winner has no opposition; 2) by **proportional representation**: which requires that the distribution of offices be proportional to the distribution of

popular vote among competing political parties or candidates. It could be the *single transferable vote formula* (called "Hare System") or the *list systems*, which is further divided into the *largest average formula* (called "d'Hondt formula") and the *greatest remainder formula*. (For more on proportional representation, see J. R. Lewis, op. cit., pp. 44-47; J. A. Schumpeter, "Competition for Political Leadership," in: H. M. Bishop et al., op. cit., p. 25; E. Barker, "Government by Discussion," in: B. Elias, op. cit., p. 49); and 3) by **geographical representation**: the country is divided geographically into a number of areas, each returning one or more representatives; the citizens of each area thus have the power to elect certain representatives from their area to the government - cf. J. R. Lewis, op. cit., pp. 43-44.

73 This is done a) by avoiding electoral abuses, such as corruption of electoral practices: bribery, intimidation of the individual voter, dissemination of scurrilous rumours about candidates, deliberately false campaign propaganda, tampering with the machinery by stuffing the ballot box with fraudulent returns, dishonest counting or reporting of the vote, total disregard of electoral outcomes by incumbent officeholders, etc.; and b) by maintaining the integrity of the electoral process through the following devices and practices: maintaining permanent and up-to-date registries of voters to guarantee easy identification of those eligible to participate in elections; holding elections on a single day rather than have them staggered; making polling hours in all localities the same, and seeing to it that opening and closing hours are fixed and announced, so that voters have an equal opportunity to participate; making sure that polling stations are manned by presumably disinterested government officials or polling clerks under government supervision; political party agents or party workers should be given an opportunity to observe the polling process, to enable them to challenge irregularities and prevent abuses; efforts should be made to maintain order in polling stations, directly through police protection or indirectly through such practices as closing bars and liquor stores; making sure that the act of voting itself takes place in voting booths that protect privacy; votes should be counted and recounted by tellers, watched by party workers to assure an honest count; transmission of voting results from local polling stations to central election headquarters should be safeguarded and checked, etc..

74 Cf. J. R. Lewis, op. cit., pp. 51-52.

75 Ibid., pp. 15-16.

4. CONCLUSION: DEMOCRACY AT WORK

We have seen that not all governments that lay claim on democracy are democratic - even when they put on the garb of democracy (chapter one). We have also seen that democracy has got its essential ingredients that mark it out from all other systems of government, namely its principles (chapter two) and its institutions (chapter three). It remains for this chapter to define democracy, to ascertain its purpose - elaborating how democracy functions in practice, and to pointing out how, despite its weaknesses, democracy remains the best of all forms of government.

4.1. Democracy Defined

Various people - writers of political science and philosophers, sociologists and so on - have differently defined democracy. But it is Abraham Lincoln's definition of democracy that is the most popular. In his famous Gettysburg speech (which he made after the conquest of the Southern States), Abraham Lincoln defined democracy as

> A government of the people, by the people, and for the people.

This definition agrees with the modern democratic ideology - derived 1) from the ancient theories of political power emanating from the people; 2) from the medieval doctrine of "what touches all must be approved by all," and of the limitation of political power by unchanging laws of God and of nature; and 3) from the modern theory of the determination of consent by the majority. However, it is not, like every other definition, without criticisms: its *by* and *for* the people raises some problems. For example, it could be asked: in a sense government is always *of* the people, could be *for* the people (think that a benevolent despot or oligarchy might claim to govern for the people), but is it *by* the people, the whole people? K. Graham answers: "If we consider democracy at the societal level, nowhere in practice, does 'the whole people' range over the entire population, but it is a matter of historical fact that in the modern period admission to the political decision-making process has gradually extended to include more and more categories...."[1] And T. V. Smith rejects the notion of democracy as government *for* the people - because the politicians constitute a "third party" that represents but is not identical with the people.[2] We shall not bother ourselves here with this problem of "government by and for the people." But suffice it to say that the definition should not be taken literally, otherwise democracy becomes a misleading notion. Surely modern democracy is "government by the people" - through the system of representation and principle of majority rule.

Next, the definition given by J. R. Pennock appeals to me, because it adds some flesh to that of Lincoln. For him democracy is

> government by the people, where liberty, equality, and fraternity are secured to the greatest possible degree and in which human capacities are developed to the utmost, by means including free and full discussion of common problems and interest.[3]

The above two definitions bring out the two aspects of the meaning of modern democracy: a) as a particular system, a form of government, or a method by which the people, or the majority of the people, exercise a political control; and b) as a way of life.[4] The first aspect is the meaning of democracy in the strict sense, and it is to this that the definition of democracy as "the rule of the many" refers. The second aspect is the meaning of democracy in the wider sense: under it material and spiritual values - culture, the standard of living, all social and economic relations - are taken into consideration. Thus in its original conceptions democracy was mainly of a political nature - denoting control over, and restrictions on, power. But today democracy is fast embracing "the totality of man's hope, including his sense of dignity and identity and purpose. Democracy is becoming a philosophy of life through which man seeks to achieve ... his highest aspirations. It shapes outlooks, institutions, and daily attitudes."[5] This way of looking at democracy raises it above the level of a mere governmental system and gives to it the power and the inspiration to seek for the individual in society the "good life" and the promotion of his well-being. Hence democracy has endless possibilities. It is creative. It is, in the words of John Dewey, "a way of life controlled by a working faith in the possibilities of human nature" as exhibited in every human being regardless of "race, color, sex, birth, and family, of material or cultural wealth."[6]

I contend that the two aspects of the meaning of democracy should go hand-in-hand. Democracy is basically "a form of government, but a form which exists to supply and maintain a better society, and to provide the maximum amount of liberty for the individual consistent with the attainment of order and security within the society."[7] Too much emphasis on democracy as a system of government (which is still in vogue today), at the expense of its way of life definition, has always done, and is still doing, a great disservice to democracy. More attention is paid on leadership, on being in authority than on service. More attention is paid on structures than on human being, the way he/she lives. This accounts for one of the major reasons why some people lose interest in the affairs of government, regarding anything government as "their business" and not "my or our business". This happens because the government is very often after itself and not after the people's well-being which should be its main task.

4.2. Purpose of Democracy

Democracy has a purpose: to maintain, promote and advance the well-being of the citizens, of every individual without drawing the race lines, colour lines or making any other distinctions between them. Fundamentally, governments are instituted for the good of the human person.[8] Thus Roosevelt remarks that "the ends of good government in our democracy are to secure by genuine popular rule a high average of moral and material well-being among our citizens."[9] Then the government is only a means of arriving at the purpose of democracy. Referring to one of the propositions of the American Declaration of Independence - namely "to secure these rights governments are instituted among men," Horace M. Kallen writes: "It declared the inherent and unalienable rights of man to be the end, the government only a means; it made the people the master, government the servant; it made life, liberty, and the pursuit of happiness the purpose, government an instrument to attain this purpose."[10]

4.3. The Way of Democracy

No doubt, the purpose of democracy is the same with the goal of any other system of government. As shown in chapter one,[11] even non-democratic regimes have the welfare of its citizens at heart. But what differentiates democracy from other types of government is the means of attaining the goal. Both democratic and non-democratic regimes may have similar goals or ends, but their means of achieving these goals or of attaining these ends are not the same. While in democracy the people have a big say on who governs them and on how they are governed - that is, democracy depends on majority decision - hence the existence of an atmosphere of equality (of opportunity), in non-democratic regimes everything is dictated from above - hence the existence of an atmosphere of inequality. As Schumpeter puts it, "it is charateristic of most every anti-democratic philosophy that it purports to serve the welfare of the people but refuses to trust the judgment of the people on questions affecting their welfare."[12] Furthermore, while democracy makes room for public opinion and discussion, and tolerates minority and opposition - hence the existence of an atmosphere of freedom, non-democratic regimes abhor and cramp all oppositions - hence the existence of an atmosphere of suppression or of lack of freedom.

How does democracy provide for the well-being of the citizens? First, by building an equitable and free society - a society in which justice and fairness reign - a society in which everybody feels at home and nobody feels himself or herself estranged and/or marginalized - a society in which there is law and order - a society in which there are basic amenities, work and just payment for all. Here the democratic principles should permeate the life and culture of the people, so that the people - be it at home, in the schools, in the places of work or leisure, at all gatherings - are said to have a democratic culture. This demands much education and enlightenment.

Second, by providing a government that is the people's choice - a government that is suitable for, and capable of doing, the people's business - a government that is accountable to the people. To establish a good government capable of maintaining a just society and of catering for the people's welfare, there is much need for good leadership and good management.

True enough, the democratic process does not of itself provide or produce leadership. It merely offers opportunity and incentive to the largest numbers of those who have the capacity and will to lead. However the place of leadership - good leadership - in a democracy is very primary that due consideration needs to be given to leadership here.

Leadership takes various forms in present-day society. Some examples[13] of the forms of leadership today include:

a) **leadership in public service**: the public servant is in-charge of public business, ranging from the ordinary activities of legislatures, judicial and executive officers to the administrative tasks connected with schools, health, highways, lighting, water supply, and many other public services that fall within the accepted scope of political government. This is the most obvious field of leadership in a democratic community.

b) **leadership in certain quasi-public institutions**, such as churches, privately endowed schools, private health agencies, privately owned newspapers, magazines and publishing houses, movie studios, radio stations, social work agencies and the like. The organizers or directors of these institutions play a vital part in shaping public opinion, and in raising the standards of public health and well-being.

c) **leadership in the organization and direction of pressure groups**, like trade unions, chambers of commerce, political parties, trade and professional associations. Officers of these groups take active part in shaping public policy and are a determining element in directing community life.

d) **leadership in business** (i.e., commerce and industry): this is very crucial because the business world controls the productive apparatus and thus the sources of income upon which a large section of the population directly depends. It is also crucial because the pursuit of profit by business leaders may sink the entire group into disastrous economic depression, plunge it into war, or lead it along a part of economic adventurism that will result in the invasion of the country, the overthrow of the government and the enslavement of the population.

e) **leadership in personal adventurism or careerism**: here we have business persons who are seeking to enrich themselves, political demagogues, military adventurers, inventors and discoverers, artists, writers, journalists and preachers. Many of these play important roles in directing social forces.

It is with leadership in public service - especially in politics - that we are concerned here. Since not everybody has got leadership quality, then not just anybody should aspire to a leadership position. Governing should be restricted to those who are qualified to govern. Then the question posed by Plato (in "The Republic") many centuries ago resurfaces: Who are the best qualified to govern? Without going into details on this question, I do agree with R. A. Dahl's Aristos[14] that to be qualified to govern, one should be *morally* and *instumentally competent*. Moral competence requires that one should posses *moral understanding* or *moral capacity* (that is, an adequate understanding of the proper ends, goals or objectives that the government should strive to reach) and *virtue* (that is, a strong disposition actually to seek good ends), since it is not enough to know what is best without actively attempting to bring it about. Instrumental competence requires that one should posses *adequate technical* or *instrumental knowledge* - that is, one should know the best, most efficient, and most appropriate means to achieve desirable ends. Aristos maintains that "no single one of these qualities, or even any pair, would be enough. All three are necessary. To be properly qualified to govern, I say, one should be both morally competent and instrumentally competent. In combination, then, the three qualities define political competence."[15]

Leadership therefore should be taken as a career. This calls for training[16] and specialisation. "In a well-orderd society," Dahl writes (again using Aristos), "just as some persons would receive the rigorous training and meritocratic selection essential to the art and science of the physician, so also others would be rigorously trained and selected to function well as rulers. Because rulership is so crucial - it has never been more so than today - nothing could be of greater importance than the education of our rulers...."[17] S. Nearing agrees: "Leadership must be looked upon as an important form of specialization. As such, it may be treated like any other specialty. Specialized fields such as medicine and accounting are hedged about with numerous restrictions involving preparations for the specialty, admission into the specialized group and the practice of the specialized activity. Leadership must be handled in the same way."[18] It is worth pointing out here that disgarding leadership as a career, coupled with lack of training and specialisation in the field of leadership, has been the bane of democracy in many developing countries, where many people "mount the throne" - not on merit but - simply because they have power and/or money.

Next to good leadership is good management or good public administration. A good and well-qualified leader will do better in the management of public affairs than a bad and ill-qualified one. As Bingham rightly points out, "the key to the future of democracy lies in management. Management is the organizing and directing of group activity.... (I)t is persons that are managed rather than things, and the most effective person is the one whose enthusiastic and voluntary cooperation is enlisted."[19] Management or public administration in a democracy requires, among other things,

a) **responsible executive** or **authority**. "Responsible" here means that authority can be brought to account, that it can be checked, that it can be forced to stay within its power limits. "He must have 'power with people rather than power over people' (since management is not merely giving orders from on top, but an intricate process of systematizing group action). He must have not only the general qualities of energy, intelligence and imagination, but he must like people, and have some of the special traits of the democratic politician: sympathy, tact, patience, a sense of humor. More than that, if he must be really effective, he must have an understanding of human nature, not only its weakness but its capacities and potentialities.... The best executive may never give an order or a command. Instead he is adept at winning mutual agreement on what is to be done."[20]

b) **the personnel department**, which must serve as a "custodian of personality": by having a full respect for the personality of the worker, because it thinks of workers "as human beings - not costs, commodities, cogs, or even pets;"[21] by seeking to place the worker where his ability will be put to most use; and by seeking to secure the full participation of the worker and to give him the opportunity to develop his personality to the full in his work.

c) **representation of interests**: different interests - communities, labour unions, trade unions, and so on - must be represented in the administration, otherwise management is said to be unbalanced or one-sided.

d) **public participation**: a good management must give individual human beings a chance to participate in what concerns them, if democracy is to be truly concerned with the happiness and dignity of individual human beings.

e) **decentralisation**: democratic administration must distribute power and responsibility. It must not only break down the administrative job to the stature of the administrator as an ordinary human being, but must bring it within the competence of the ordinary citizen to understand and share in it. Thus, it brings government close to the citizen.

f) **professional spirit**: public administration demands expertise. Unlike the technical expert who is sometimes more interested in statistics than in the people (and this is why he should be "on tap rather than on top"), the democratic expert is an expert in human relations, the only engineering he knows is human engineering. The democratic expert should consult and make use of outstanding specialists in other fields, through temporary or permanent councils or as individuals. However, he "must know his subject so well that he can be the leader of the groups he calls together.... He must be a student of human nature, the lover of people, with a faith in their ultimate ability to reach for themselves things which he might do for them with less effort in the first instance."[22]

Leadership and management in a democracy, therefore, must be seen as an outstanding form of social service. Democratic communities must seek out and use some of their finest talent in this connection. Those capable of leadership must eagerly devote themselves to pressing issues that threaten the very existence of democracy - what I term the "danger of poor leadership and mis-management": ranging from power intoxication, personal venality, corruption by special interests, incompetence, lack of vision, to violation of human dignity (especially on the economic level where devastating depressions, due mainly to mass unemployment, are the order of the day). One can, at this point, allude to the defects of democracy.

4.4. Defects In Modern Democracy

Like everything human, democracy is not a perfect system - a system without stains, faults or shortcomings. It has its weaknesses. There is no democratic country in the world - not even the USA and the Great Britain which are rated high as examples of modern democracies - which does not display something short of democratic principle and/or action. In the USA, for example, there is still colour discrimination. And in Great Britain, there is still religious discrimination ("constitutionally" recognised): members of the royal family are not permitted to marry Catholics, and the post of the Prime Minister is reserved only for the Anglicans. All over the world the story is the same: there are rampant violations of the democratic principles and ideals. The 15th of May, 1995, issue of TIME magazine reports of how, in South America (precisely in Venezuela, Peru, Bolivia and Argentina), "Democracies under strain are seeing their elected civilian Presidents turn to authoritarian measures."[23] There are many and frequent reports from "Amnesty International" of human rights violations among democratic countries all over the globe. I will not mention cases of corruption and abuse of office that is today, in almost every country (that is, if at all any exemption exists), draging democracy to the muds and thus making it a cesspool. (How repulsive and uncomfortable its smell!) Any wonder that some very fundamental and disquieting criticisms have been made, and are still being made, of democracy? Let me cite a few paragraphs from what James Bryce said in *Modern Democracies* (published in 1921 by Macmillan Co.) to buttress my point:

> What then has democracy failed to accomplish? It has brought no nearer friendly feeling and the sense of human brotherhood among the peoples of the world toward one another.
>
> Freedom has not been a reconciler.
>
> Neither has it created good will and a sense of unity and civic fellowship within reach of these peoples. Though in earlier days strife between classes has arisen, it is only in these later days that what is called class war has become recognized as a serious menace to the peace of states and in some countries the dominant factor in political and economic conflicts.
>
> Liberty and equality have not been followed by fraternity. Not even far off do we see her coming shine. Democracy has not enlisted in the service of the state nearly so much of the best practical capacity as each country possesses and every country needs for dealing with the domestic and international questions of the present age.
>
> In some states corruption has been rife and the tone of public life no better than it was under the monarchies and oligarchies of the eighteenth century.

> Lastly, democracy has not induced that satisfaction and contentment with itself as the best form of government which was expected and has not exorcised the spirit that seeks to attain its ends by revolution.[24]

Does this lack in democracy imply that democracy has failed? No! Compared to other forms of government, do these shortcomings make democracy cease to be the best form of government? No!

4.5. Democracy Is The Word

The defects we observe in modern democracy do not mean that democracy has failed. This is because such defects are not inherent in democracy but are only weaknesses of individual operators of democracy. R. M. MacIver puts it this way: "the defects and shortcomings it (democracy) exhibits are due not to any inherent weakness in its principle but to the greater responsibilities it imposes on those who carry it out. These responsibilities are in themselves reasonable and never excessive, but interest and pride and office are always at hand, to deflect, to distort, and to betray."[25] These weaknesses of the operators will also be there, even if other systems of government are adopted. Where the principles and institutions of these other systems of government are defective (as they indeed are), then things are bound to be worse than they are in a democracy. Yes, democracy has its weaknesses but it is still better than any other system of government. As Mr Laski once put it: "I can destroy any case you can build up for democracy. I am sure I can knock it over in ten minutes. But I don't know any other kind of government that will last five."[26]

It is a historical fact that no other system of government has fared better than democracy. It is in democracy, more than in any other system of government, that the existence of equality of all and of the individual liberty (the two highest political goods) is guaranteed.[27] It is only in democracy that the people partake fully in the government - that is, the people govern themselves (self-government).[28] Democracy, more than any other system of government, allows for discussion. In other words, democracy allows (within certain limits) for the expression of, and influence upon policy by, many different view points,[29] thus minimising conflict and avoiding dangerous frustrations. This rhymes with James Fitzjames Stephen's saying that "in Democracy we count heads to avoid breaking them." In the same vein Commager writes: "it might plausibly be argued that it is one of the major advantages of democracy over other forms of government that it alone can indulge in the luxury of tolerating minority and dissenting groups because it alone has developed the technique for dealing with them.... (O)nly in a democracy where there is free play of ideas, where issues are freely fought out in the public forum, - where, in short, the safety valves of public discussion and experimentation and reconsideration are always open - can there be assurance that both majority and minority rights will be served. It is the glory of democracy that it - and it alone - can tolerate dissent. It is the strength of democracy that dissent, where tolerated, is helpful rather than harmful."[30] Moreover, it is democracy, more than any other form of government, that provides for an orderly succession of rulers.

These arguments justifying democracy apart, it is a fact that all known systems of government that can be compared with democracy - monarchy, aristocracy, oligarchy, and even communism - have all crumbled. Today the wind of democracy is blowing everywhere, and the current of democracy is sweeping across every nation. Arend Lijphart has called the 1990s "the decade of world-wide democratization."[31] Today one witnesses - all over the world where there is still dictatorship or autocracy (be it military or civilian) - agitations, demonstrations, protests (and even uprisings): all clamouring for a change to a democratic polity. The people are no longer satisfied with being mere spectators in their own affairs, taking orders from their leaders who are insensitive to their plights. The era of "image-worship" of leaders is gone. The people are no longer afraid to stand the dictators in the face. They are willing to oppose and reject the totalitarian policies and actions of those "thin gods" who, in the words of Cassius,[32] "doth bestride the narrow world (their countries) like a Colossus, and (would have their citizens like) petty men walk under (their) huge legs and peep about to find (themselves) dishonourable graves." Hence the only word everywhere today, concerning what system of government the people want, is democracy.

Therefore, although democracy is not a thing of perfection - it has not yet realised its full promise, and the complexities of modern life place before it awe-inspiring problems to which answers must be given - it is still the best system of government the world has. As Sir Winston Churchill once put it, the alternatives to democracy are too horrible to contemplate. Pope Pius XII agrees: "If then we consider the extent of the sacrifices demanded of all citizens, especially in our day when the activity of the state is vast and decisive, the democratic form of government appears to many as a postulate of nature imposed by reason itself."[33] It then follows that every country should endeavour to embrace democracy, if it must grow and remain stable in this age of free market economy.

However, the democrats must not rest on their oars. There is much work to be done to keep democracy on course. The survival of democracy - its growth, its future - inflicts heavy responsibilities on all: deep faith in its workings, moral commitment to its principles, and eternal vigilance to curb in the bud any derailment. Mr Padover puts the matter nicely:

> Democracy is not a mechanical process. Institutionalized contrivances, no matter how ingenious or elaborate, will not, by themselves, guarantee its proper functioning, or even its survival. There must be faith in its workings and morality at its heart. For democracy is rooted in moral values: moderation, reason, justice, compassion, faith in man, human dignity - what Professor Harold D. Lasswell calls 'a commonwealth of mutual respect.'

> And always at the heart of democracy there must lie a feeling of obligation to the community. A citizen must give of himself to the community before he can make moral claims on it. Claims without appropriate duties corrupt the democratic fabric. As its founders, formulators, and champions have repeatedly reminded us, democracy requires not only constant vigilance but also active participation. Democracy can never afford to recognize 'rights' without concomitant responsibilities.[34]

Lastly, the moral obligations of democracy demand from both the ruler and the ruled an earnest commitment to the common good. When everybody is less concerned about himself or herself and more concerned about the general good - when everybody is asking "What can I do for my country?" instead of "What can my country do for me?" - and when everybody has the fear of God in him/her and the love of neighbour at heart and is prepared to do the right thing (no matter to whomever, no matter where, and no matter when), then democracy would take root and it would blossom and bear fruits, fruits that will endure.

NOTES

1 K. Graham, op. cit., pp. 13-18. This agrees with Prof. Ralf Dahrendorf's position that "democracy, taken literally, has always been a misleading notion. There is not, and never has been, a country in which the people in the sense of all the people were in fact ruling (and the same is true for organisations and their members). The best that can be achieved is an effective system for making sure that those who rule do not ignore or trample on the interests of the majority. Elections, parties, a free press, even opinion polls are all instruments for preventing such aberrations." (Sic, in: B. Whitaker, op. cit., p. 85.)

2 Cf. B. Elias, op. cit., p. 47.

3 J. R. Pennock, **Democratic Political Theory** (New Jersey: Princeton University Press, 1979), p. 6.

4 Prof. Dr Lothar Roos' book on democracy as a form of life is worth reading. See his, **Demokratie als Lebensform** (München . Paderborn . Wien: Verlag Ferdinand Schöningh, 1969).

5 S. K. Padover, op. cit., pp. xxxiiif..

6 Ibid., p. xxxiv.

7 J. R. Lewis, op. cit., p. 14.

8 St. Paul writes: "The state is there to serve God for your benefit" (Rom. 13: 4). And in the articles of the American Declaration of Independence we read, inter alia, "to secure these rights" - that is, the rights of life, liberty, and the pursuit of happiness - "governments are instituted among men."

9 T. Roosevelt, **A Charter of Democracy** (Washington: Government Printing Office, 1919), p. 6.

10 H. M. Kallen, "Humanistic Sources," in: **Foundations of democracy**, by Institute for Religious and Social Studies, Jewish Theological Seminary of America (New York: Cooper Square Publishers, 1964), p. 70.

11 See chapter one above, pp. 8-9.

12 J. A. Schumpeter, op. cit., p. 79.

13 These examples are taken from S. Nearing, op. cit., pp. 117-118.

14 See Dahl's treatment of "The Qualifications of the Qualified," in his **Democracy And Its Critics** (1989), pp. 57-59, cf. pp. 59-64.

15 Ibid., p. 58.

16 Cf. S. Nearing, op. cit., pp. 121-122: "... the democratic community will develop training courses for leadership that will be open to all comers.... Leadership qualities begin to show themselves in the nursery and on the playground. Where and as they appear it will be the task of the psychologists, pedagogues and sociologists to provide specialized training for the boys and girls who possess them. From the cradle to adult life the alert democratic community will be looking eagerly for leadership qualities and giving them every opportunity for unfoldment. Potential leaders in their early teens will be singled out and trained in leadership as potential musicians are trained in their specialized fields. Those who measure up to standard will be continued in special leadership courses and activities. Those who fall below standard will turn elsewhere for their special work.... Young men and women who seek positions involving policy making or technical leadership will be asked to present their credentials as candidates for any specialized position.... Leadership will thus become a career, open to young people as engineering and architecture are open today. And in the course of their lives those who qualify for leadership will be advanced from local positions to positions of regional, national and world scope...."

17 R. A. Dahl, op. cit., p. 63.

18 S. Nearing, op. cit., p. 120.

19 A. M. Bingham, op. cit., p. 111.

20 Ibid., pp. 117-118. (My brackets.)

21 Marshall Dimock and Howard K. Hyde, **Bureaucracy and Trusteeship in Large Corporations** (T.N.E.C. monograph, 1940), p. 98.

22 Jennie M. Turner, "Democracy in Administration," **American Political Science Review** (1923), p. 216.

23 **TIME**, May 15, 1995, pp. 34-35.

24 Quoted by Prof. F. E. Johnson in his "Introduction Depicting The Crisis In Modern Democracy" (1964), published by Institute for Religious and Social Studies, Jewish Theological Seminary of America, op. cit., pp. 4-5.

25 R. M. MacIver, "The Role of the People" (taken from his "The Ramparts We Guard"), in: H. M. Bishop and S. Hendel, op. cit,. p. 20.

26 Quoted by F. E. Johnson, in: Institute for Religious and Social Studies, Jewish Theological Seminary of America, op. cit., p. 10.

27 Cf. B. Holden: "There is important justification in terms of individual liberty: it can reasonably be contended that individuals are less liable to suffer from undesirable actions by the government in a liberal-democracy than they are in other kinds of political system. This is basically because first, the people as a whole are not normally likely

to sanction certain kinds of action by the government (such as arrests without trial); and secondly, it can be argued that the absence of certain kinds of action by the government (notably those excluded by the 'freedoms' implied by the idea of 'free elections') is a logically necessary condition for the existence of democracy." (Sic, op. cit., p. 209.) See also C. B. Macpherson who considers democracy a sytem that works "to provide the conditions for the free development of human capacities, and to do this equally for all members of the society." (Sic, **The Real World of Democracy** (Oxford: Clarendon Press, 1966), p. 58.)

28 See B. Holden: "The virtues of participation are not seen as arising at the individual level only. Individuals are conceived to benefit from participation, but, besides - or interconnected with - this, there are benefits which accrue to the community." This is the linking of the individual with the community: "because of his involvement in the governing of the community the individual identifies with it and comes to appreciate the claims of other individuals and of the community as a whole." He goes further: "the main aspect of the value of participation has been seen as its educative function - educative both in a narrower sense of leading to the acquiring of information, and in a broader sense of developing a responsible and moral personality.... Other aspects can be summerized as the part held to be played by participation in securing the acceptance by individuals of communal decisions, and the general integration of the collectivity and enhancement of its sense of community." (Sic, op. cit., p. 210.)

29 See Wollheim's argument that "under modern conditions (democracy) is the only working possibility. No member of an emancipated industrial society will put up with political tutelage. He insists on having a fair chance of influencing the government in accordance with his own desires and ideas; and by a 'fair' chance he means a chance 'as good as the next man's'" - in: B. Holden, op. cit., p. 214. Cf. A. D. Linsday: "When men who are serving a common purpose meet to pool their experience, to air their difficulties and even their discontents, there comes about a real process of collective thinking" (sic, **The Essentials of Democracy** (Philadelphia: University of Pennsylvania Press, 1929), p. 36.

30 H. S. Commager, "In Defence of Majority Rule," in: H. M. Bishop and S. Hendel, op. cit., p. 80.

31 Arend Lijphard, "Democracies: Forms, performance, and constitutional engineering," in: **European Journal of Political Research**, vol. 25, 1994, p. 1.

32 Cassius is a character in Shakespeare's play, "Julius Caesar." (My brackets.)

33 Pope Pius XII, **Benegnitas et Humanitas** (ActApS 37, 1945), p. 13.

34 S. K. Padover, op. cit., p. xxxiv.

PART TWO

DEMOCRACY IN NIGERIA:

Its Anthropological and Social Requirements

1. INTRODUCTION

This part of the work deals with democracy in Nigeria. It is, therefore, necessary to say something about the country, Nigeria, before we go into the treatment of our theme. The history of Nigeria is well known, and there are many literatures on it.[1] However, a general information about modern Nigeria is given here to enable anyone who is hearing of Nigeria for the first time have a gentleman's knowledge of the country.

Nigeria, officially called the Federal Republic of Nigeria and once a British colony (from 1861 to 1960 when it got its independence), has a well-known history stretching back nearly two thousand years.[2] A member of the Commonwealth, it is one of the largest states in Africa and the largest state in West Africa - because of its size and large population of 88.5 million.[3] Until recently,[4] Nigeria is considered "the giant of Africa". This is due to its wealth, and its foreign policy that is geared towards peacekeeping and towards the liberation of the black person all over the globe, beginning from Africa.[5] Nigeria lies on the Golf of Guinea (that is, between West and Equatorial Africa), on latitude 4°-14° north and on longitude 3°-15° east. Its land area is 923,768 km^2 (or 356,669 mi^2): almost three times the size of Germany or the size of Denmark, Iceland, Norway, Sweden and the Netherlands put together. The country borders on Benin Republic in the West, on Niger and Chad in the North, on Cameroon in the East, and on the Atlantic ocean in the South. It is divided into thirty States, plus the Federal Capital Territory, Abuja.

Economically, Nigeria is richly blessed with fertile land and with natural mineral resources. The country is divided into three belts or zones:

a) **The tropical rain forest zone**. This lies within the southern part of the country. It stretches from the Atlantic coast to about 9° north latitude. Its main agricultural products are timber, palm oil, cocoa, rubber, yams, kola-nuts, rice, fish, citrus, and other types of fruits and vegetables.

b) **The savannah zone**. This covers the rest of the country. In it are found such products as potatoes, tomatoes, onions, rice, groundnuts, cotton, soya beans, millet, tea, coffee, wheat, etc., and such livestock as cattle, sheep, goats, and so on.

c) **The middle belt**. This lies between the rain forest area and the savannah area (though it falls within the rain forest zone). The chief products here include yams, tomatoes, potatoes, rice, soya beans, carrots, onions, cabbage, and various types of fruits.

The mineral wealth of the country is spread throughout the three zones. In the rain forest area we have petroleum, coal, marble, clay, limestone, and salt. In the middle belt we have coal, tin, tantalite, uranium. In the savannah area we have gold. So endowed with agricultural and mineral wealth, Nigeria exports (by 1991 record[6]) crude petroleum (about 96.2% of the total export), cocoa beans (about

1.4% of the total export), rubber (about 0.8% of the total export), chemicals (about 0.1% of the total export). Other significant exports include cocoa products, textiles, and cashew nuts. (Note the country's major export destinations, by 1991 record[7]: USA 40.7%, Spain 12.6%, Germany 8.6%, Netherlands 5.0%, France 5.0%, Italy 4.0%.) Its currency is Naira (N) and Kobo (K); and one hundred kobo (100 K) equal one naira (N1).

Culturally, Nigeria is a pluralistic society. It has about 400 ethnic groups, each of which has its own language and customs (with rich arts and culture[8]) and has accepted one or more of the three main religions in the country, namely Christianity, Islam and traditional religions. The main ethnic composition, by 1983 record,[9] stands as follows: Hausa 21.3%; Yoruba 21.3%; Igbo or Ibo 18.0%; Fulani 11.2%; Ibibio 5.6%; Kanuri 4.2%; Edo 3.4%; Tiv 2.2%; Ijaw 1.8%; Bura 1.7%; Nupe 1.2%; other 8.1%. The country's religious affiliation is as follows: Christian 49.0%, Muslim 45.0% and traditional religions 6.0%. The pluralistic nature of the Nigerian society explains why the country has English as its official language and why it remains a secular state.

Politically, Nigerians believe in liberal democracy. The four years (1957-60) of 'colonial self-government' for the old three regions, the six years (1960-66) of the civil rule after independence, and the four years (1979-83) of civil rule during the Second Republic are conceived as situations of liberal democracy. Even the years of military rule (1966-79 and 1983 to date) were (and still are) excused by the political class and even scholars as temporary diversion - an aberration - from liberal democratic politics. This strong belief of Nigerians in liberal democracy is expressed in the speeches and actions of Nigerian leaders, civilian and military. Few examples will do. Dr Nnamdi Azikiwe, the former President of Nigeria, speaking in 1959, expressed the position of the ruling class. One, the government of Nigeria was established upon the "belief in democracy - government by discussion, based on the consent of the governed, whose will is collectively expressed by the majority of the duly accredited representatives of an electorate that is based on universal adult suffrage."[10] Two, there is belief in "the existence of Opposition as an essential ingredient of democracy." Three, there is belief in government according "to the rule of law and respect for human dignity; government that is prepared to support and enforce fundamental human rights, ensure freedom of speech, press, peaceful assembly, association and movement; protect the property of the citizen by ensuring and enforcing the right of the individual to private property, respects for free enterprise and provides social security."[11] On another occasion, in the post 1970 debate for the country's return from military to civil rule, Dr Azikiwe repeated the beliefs and basis of democratic politics: "... our multilingual peoples have trodden the path of democracy from time immemorial. Irrespective of our social origins, our indigenous institutions have been essentially democratic. Our contact with British administrators reinforced our faith in the democratic way of life...."[12] On his part, Chief Obafemi Awolowo (another prominent Nigerian political leader) - for whom "the best form of Government is democracy; ... any form of Government other than democracy is evil (because of its) utter disregard for the rights, welfare and happiness of the people"[13] - expressed his attachment and that of Nigerians to democracy thus: "After many centuries of experimentation, civilised man has come to accept the ballot box as the means through which the people's will, in the exercise of their sovereignty, can be expressed and ascertained. Without the enjoyment of the basic freedoms of conscience, of expression, of assembly and of association, among others, it is not possible for the people to realise their right of sovereignty."[14] Even the military leaders were (and are) very much aware of the people's avowed belief in and desire for liberal democracy. This is why every military regime, on coming to power, affirms the right of the country to popular rule, expresses its desire to rid the country of indiscipline and corruption and of all other ills that mar our democratic processes, and promisses to return the country, "as soon as possible",[15] to democratic politics. Lastly, the strong belief of the Nigerians in liberal democracy is also very much evident in the various colonial and post-colonial constitutions of the country, the best of which is the 1979 second republican constitution.

But Nigeria is still today under the military government - governed by the Armed Forces Ruling Council (AFRC) with some civilian Ministers. Because of the corrupt, non-accountable, poor administrative and brutal nature of the military government in the country (coupled with the global economic crunch), Nigeria is experiencing severe economic hardships (poverty amidst wealth), a deterioration in social services (where these at all existed before), a breakdown of law and order (no security of person and property, no matter where), and a degradation in image and reputation (at home and abroad). There is a general yearning and agitation for a return to democracy. But a return to which democracy? Surely not to the types of democracy Nigeria had and practised during her first and second republics that always attracted military interventions!

This second part of the work is geared towards the establishment of a stable and lasting democracy in Nigeira: a democracy with a human face - which makes for a disciplined, fair, just and humane Nigeiran society; a good and capable government that will place the good of the society and that of its citizens - thus, the common good - above every other thing else. (This is dealt with in chapter four.) However, we cannot build a lasting democracy in Nigeria without first finding out why our democracies of the first and second republics failed. Thus chapter three is devoted to the problem of democracy in Nigeria. But before then, chapter two delves into the political development of Nigeria.

NOTES

1 Good literatures on the history of Nigeria include: Michael Crowder, **The Story of Nigeria** (London: Faber and Faber, 1962); Sir Alan Burns, **History of Nigeria** (London, 1972); M. C. English, **An Outline of Nigerian History** (London, 1959); E. D. Morel, **Nigeria: Its people and Problems** (London, 1912); C. R. Niven, **A Short History of Nigeria** (London, 1937); Akoi Arikpo, **Who Are the Nigerians?** (Lagos, 1958); Patricia M. Levy, **Nigeria** (New York: Marshall Cavendish, c1993); Allan Carpenter, **Nigeria** (Chicago: Children's Press, c1978); Dorothy B. Sutherland, **Nigeria** (Chicago: Children's Press, c1995); Timothy M. Shaw and Julius O. Ihonvbere, eds., **Nigeria** (Boulder: Western Press, 1992); Kamala Achu, **Nigeria** (New York: Bookwright Press, 1992); Tekena N. Tamuno, **Nigeria: its people and its problems** (Lagos: Panel on Nigeria since Independence History Project, 1989); Helen C. Metz, ed., **Nigeria: A Country Study** (Wahington, D.C., 1992); Peter Holmes, **Nigeria: Giant of Africa** (Lagos: National Oil and Chemical Marketing Co. of Nigeria, 1985); Olav Stokke, **Nigeria: An Introduction to the Politics, Economy and Social Setting of Modern Nigeria** (Sweden: Söderström & Finn, Uppsala, 1970); K. B. C. Onwubiko, **School Certificate History of West Africa, AD 1000-1800,** Books One & Two (Onitsha, Nigeria: Africana-Fep Publishers Limited, c1985); J. F. Ajayi and Ian Espie, eds., **A Thousand Years of West African History** (Ibadan, Nigeria: Ibadan University Press, c1981); James O. Ojiako, **Nigeria: Yesterday, Today, And ...** (Onitsha, Nigeria: African Educational Publishers (Nig.) Ltd., 1981); Eberhard Stahn, **Mai's Weltführer Nr. 3: Nigeria: Reiseführer mit Landeskunde** (Mai's Reiseführer Verlag Buchschlag bei Frankfurt, 1990).

2 The heyday of Nok-Culture (the earliest culture in Nigeria) is reckoned to be from 500 BC to AD 200.

3 This is the result of 1991 census: 88,514,501. However, as at now (end of 1995), the population has come to 95,434,000. (See **Nigeria**, under "Nations of the World," in: **1996 Britannica Book of the Year: Events of 1995**, p. 683.)

4 Due to the dictatorial posture of the present-day government in Nigeria - giving room to the erosion of all democratic principles and institutions, to incessant violations and abuses of world-acclaimed human rights, and to much indiscipline, corruption, insecurity, poverty and squalor - the nation has lost her face, and has fallen from grace to grass, in international politics and amongst international communities (within and without Africa).

5 Nigeria is to Africa what the United States of America is to the world in terms of global peacekeeping.

6 See **Nigeria**, under "Nations of the World," in: **1994 Britannica Book of the Year: Events of 1993**, p. 684.

7 Ibid.

8 Cf. Thurstan Shaw, **Nigeria: Its archaelogy and early history** (London: Thames and Hudson, c 1978).

9 See **Nigeria**, under "Nations of the World," in: **1994 Britannica Book of the Year: Events of 1993**, p. 684.

10 Nnamdi Azikiwe, **Zik: A Selection From the Speeches of** (London: CUP, 1961), pp. 97-99.

11 Ibid.

12 N. Azikiwe, **Democracy with Military Vigilance** (Nsukka: Africa Book Co., 1974), p. 18.

13 Obafemi Awolowo, **The People's Republic** (Ibadan: OUP, 1968), pp. 92-95.

14 Obafemi Awolowo, **The Problem of Africa: The Need for Ideological Reappraisal - Kwame Nkruma Memorial Lectures** (London: Macmillan for University of Cape Coast, 1977), p. 50.

15 Note that "as soon as possible" could be many years - as was the case with the Gowon and the Babangida regimes - because, having tasted the sweet wine of power, the military leaders become intoxicated with power and then would not let go of it.

2. THE POLITICAL DEVELOPMENT OF NIGERIA

Politics, as the art and science of government or as public life and affairs as involving authority and government, has its developmental stages in Nigeria. It ranges from the traditional systems to Western systems (parliamentary and presidential systems) and to military dictatorship. These stages of development will be treated under three periods: before the birth of Nigeria, during the colonial imperialism, and after Nigeria's independence.

2.1. Before the Birth of Nigeria

There was no Nigeria as a nation or state before 1914 (when the two British protectorates of Northern and Southern Nigeria were amalgamated by Frederick J. D. Lugard, later Lord Lugard of Abinger).[1] What existed, prior to this date, was a territory bubbling "with myriads of ethnic groups and dynamic nationalities each with its own well-defined system of Government that compelled compliance with societal laws and norms."[2] There were a number of great kingdoms that had evolved complex systems of government independent of contact with Europe. They include the great Kingdom of Bornu, with a known history of more than a thousand years; the Fulani Empire which for the hundred years before its conquest by Britain had ruled most of the savannah of what is now called Northern Nigeria; the kingdoms of Ife and Benin which had produced art recognised amongst the most accomplished in the world; the Yoruba Empire of Oyo which had once been the most powerful of the states of the Guinea Coast; the city states of the Niger Delta which had grown in response to European demands for slaves and later palm oil; as well as the loosely organised Igbo peoples of Eastern region and the small tribes of the plateau.[3] However, that the fact that these ethnic groups and nationalities were autonomous - each pursuing its destiny and following its chosen direction - does not imply that they had no contact with one another, a point that is often missed by those who overemphasise the ethnic diversity of Nigeria. The fact is that these various peoples who now constitute the modern Nigeria had political and economic connections for centuries, because "sporadic commercial and social contacts had, for centuries long, been in existence, though politically and culturally, each group had remained distinct and separate."[4]

This territory "later became known as the British sphere of influence, following the Berlin Conference of 1884-5 which gave legal force to the British part in the scramble for that area of Africa. The ethnic and cultural groups upon which the British imposed their political domination at that time became the predecessors of the contemporary Nigerian society."[5] And the name, "Nigeria" (proposed by the journalist, Flora Shaw, who later became the wife of Frederick Lugard), was chosen (in 1898/99 by the British House of Commons) out of the many alternatives - such as Guinea Coast, Central Sudan, Niger Sudan, Niger Empire, Nigritia, Goldesia - to designate this vast territory.[6]

The traditional political systems of this period could be classified into two broad categories: one, the centralised political systems, varying from relatively small chiefdoms to very large ones, found in Hausaland ("an effectively blended mix of Hausas and muslim Fulanis in the north"[7]) and in Yorubaland (comprising "a highly structured group in the west"[8]); and two, the non-centralized political systems, found in Igboland ("a highly decentralized confederation of clans held together by common language and a common culture"[9] in the east). Note that Hausaland, Yorubaland and Igboland are the three dominant land areas that constitute the three major "ethnic groups" of modern Nigeria. Our focus therefore will be on these three lands.

2.1.1. The Hausaland[10]

This embraced all the ethnic groups in Northern Nigeria: Hausa, Fulani, Kanuri, Nupe, Tiv, Igala, Idoma, Gwari, Igbirra, Birom, Chamba, Jaba, Sura, and other minor ethnic groups.[11] The advent of Islam in the 11th century, most probably through the Fulani and Arab traders, saw the rapid spread of the moslem religion within the Hausa states; and within the course of the centuries, thanks to the *Jihad* of Usman dan Fodio,[12] Islam quickly developed into a popular religion among the people, and became (from the 15th century onwards) the religion of the ruling classes,[13] giving rise to a political system that was fundamentally "a theocracy organised along essentially feudal lines"[14] - a feudal islamic monarchy - an islamic hegemony.

In Hausaland there was a powerful and efficient emirate system of government. This was a centralised system of administration in which the whole organization revolved around the monarch, the *Emir*.[15] He was very powerful: he had supreme executive and judicial powers and was also the head of a hierarchical system of territorial administration. His power emanated from his being in firm control of coercive forces and instruments and from his authority being based on religion (since the people believed that his authority was divinely sanctioned). Hence, though he ruled in association with a Council of State, he could veto their decisions. Even "a new emir had the power to relieve a number of political officers of their posts and to replace them with his own prote´ge´s as a reward for the latters' loyalty,"[16] because the *Emir* had enormous administrative offices and titles which he dispensed at his pleasure and discretion, and which only those favoured in the social and political ladder within the system were wont to get. And he demanded nothing less than absolute obedience from his subjects, otherwise they lost their social bearings together with the accompanying benefits. Here Okwudiba Nnoli's description of the structure of authority in Hausaland is worth having in detail. He writes:

> The structure of authority was a vertical hierarchy of ranked officials extending from the least powerful to the emir and then to the sultan. Commands flowed from the top downwards while loyalty and obedience flowed in the opposite direction. Deference to authority was such a strongly held value that disobedience, even by the emir, could be punished by removal from office.... It was in the interest of the official to cultivate and retain the favour of the emir through frequent demonstrations of loyalty and obedience. This was the easiest and quickest path to a disproportionate share of the society's surplus. Therefore, the authority relations were despotic in character emphasising relations of power and dependence between subordinates and their superiors.
> The society itself was highly stratified. At the top were the hereditary Fulani nobility who were favoured for office, particularly the ruling dynasties. Slaves occupied the lowest rung of the social ladder. In the middle were the freemen.... Ascription was ... a pervasive aspect of the authority structure. However, a man's fate was entirely determined by blood. Social mobility was possible through becoming the obedient client or loyal follower of the privileged. High office led to personal enrichment. Thus, authority roles were a source, not only of immense prestige, loyalty and respect, but almost the most important means of acquiring wealth and status, overshadowing other alternatives. The emir was at once the wealthiest and most powerful person in the emirate.
> Obviously, this structure of authority put a high premium on deference to authority, loyalty, obedience, and sensitivity to the interests, opinions, views, and demands of one's superiors. It strongly favoured qualities of servility, respect for authority, allegiance to the powerful, and submissiveness. Such a system frowned on self-assertiveness of the individual.... The first and foremost social commitment was loyalty to the emir.... It was a grave sin to fail to discharge duties assigned by one's superior....[17]

On this ground the political system of Hausaland is sometimes called a "religious authocracy."

Apart from its autocracy, the emirate system in Hausaland encouraged the existence of classes, with the lower class always marginalized. There was a sharp division between the ruling class and subject class, and the commoners were largely excluded from participation in the emirate's government and politics.
From the foregoing, it could be concluded that the Hausaland, before the advent of the British, was not a fertile ground for democracy.[18]

2.1.2. The Yorubaland[19]

The Yorubaland comprised the ethnic groups in Western Nigeria: Yoruba, Bini or Edo, Ekoi, Urhovo/Isoko, Ijaw, Itsekiri, and other smaller groups. Very prominent in this land were the Oyo and Benin Empires. Like the Hausaland, the Yorubaland boasted of a vast well-organized kingdom - embracing some centralized kingdoms, each with an *Oba* as the paramount ruler - with a complex monarchical system over which the *Alafin* of Oyo (with his very elaborate court of priests, officials and eunuchs) was the supreme monarch. But unlike the *Emir* of the Hausaland, the Yoruba monarch could not act without the authority of the State Council. In spite of the religious aura which surrounded him - for instance, the *Alafin* was considered as *Ekeji Orisa*, companion of the gods, and the *Oba* was a divine king whose prestige and ritual status far exceeded his political power - one or more Councils of States, consisting of hereditary chiefs and representatives of major territorial groups in the kingdom, were the main decision-making organs. For example, in theory, the *Alafin* was "the fountain of authority and 'companion of the gods'. But in practice, his powers were limited by the *Oyomesi*, an aristocratic Council of State of seven members. Individually, the seven were leaders of the seven wards into which the capital was divided; collectively, they were the king-makers. Headed by *Bashorun* (their 'president' and a sort of prime minister), the *Oyomesi* had the power of getting rid of a tyrannical *Alafin* by asking him to 'go to sleep,' meaning that he should commit suicide,"[20] or by presenting him with an empty calabash or parrots' eggs, meaning that the people had rejected him and then he had to commit suicide. When the office of *Alafin* was vacant, it was the *Oyomesi* that constituted the electoral college that elected a member from the royal family into such an office.

The *Alafin* ruled Yorubaland with the aid of a complex administration. He had a number of important palace officials including titled officers, eunuchs and *Ilari*, whose functions were largely restricted to the palace. Controlling the policy of state were the *Oyomesi*, amongst whom the most important was the *Basorun* who functioned as 'Prime Minister' of the state. Below the *Oyomesi* came the non-hereditary class of *Eso*, or those with military titles. Their leader was the *Kakanfo*, who was the army commander. There was also at a later period the *Ogboni* cult, in the deliberations of which the *Oyomesi* participated. The cult exercised a mediating role between the *Oyomesi* and the *Alafin*.

The political system in Yorubaland, compared to the system in Hausaland, "was hierarchical in form but not authoritarian in content. Command did not flow down from the king to the ranks of obedient officials. On the contrary, power was widely dispersed among partly self-governing units.... Obedience to him (*Oba*) was not total and loyalty was not unquestioning."[21] Again, unlike in the Hausaland, the administrative system in Yorubaland made for "participation by all elements of the society. It was a system in which royalty, freemen and slaves participated."[22] So writes Okwudiba Nnoli on the social structure in Yorubaland:

> Yoruba kingship operated in a social structure containing strong independent units charaterised by lineage, territory, and associational ties based on such criteria as age, religion, and occupation. Most commonly, each of these groups selected its leader as a counterweight to the authority of the Oba. An ascriptive ranking of groups in the society existed. At the top were the royal lineages which could inherit the throne. They were followed by the non-royal lineages capable of taking and inheriting chieftaincy titles, then the commoners whose lineages had no hereditary claims to title. Among the commoners there were hereditary craft occupations of unequal status. Finally, the slaves occupied the bottom rank in the hierarchy.[23]

Thus it could be concluded that the political system in Yorubaland, before the advent of the British, though monarchical, was a fertile ground for democracy: it was not authoritarian and it made room for participation by all.

2.1.3. The Igboland[24]

The Igboland consisted of those ethnic groups in Eastern Nigeria: Igbo (plus the Ika-Igbo), Efik/Ibibio, Ijaw, Ogoja, and other smaller ethnic groups. Unlike the Hausaland and the Yorubaland, the Igboland was charaterised by its extreme decentralization of authority. The Igbos were "people of diffused governmental authority with elders acting mainly as the decision makers."[25] The council of elders had a "chairman" who was one among the equals and his was to co-ordinate rather than to impose. In short, the Igbos were essentially republican - a fact which made them tend "to be largely individualistic and egalitarian."[26] The Igbo saying, *Igbo enwe eze* - literally meaning "the Igbo does not have 'ruler'," a saying which has often been misinterpretated to mean that the Igbo had no 'government' - indicates that rules rather than rulers are the essence of the Igbo system.[27] As A. A. B. Aderibigbe rightly points out,

> The basic social unit among the Ibo was the single village made up of scattered homesteads and linked together by ties of kinship. The largest political unit was no longer than the 'village group'. This last consisted of a number of villages sharing the same cultural identity, a guardian deity and a central meeting place or market. But each constituent village retained the right to manage its own affairs and it was still subject to the moral authority of the head of its lineage, called an *Okpara*, whose symbol was the club-like *ofo*. The village group, however, remained an ideological and political unit in the sense that the constituent villages regarded themselves as members of the larger group, a sense of belonging symbolised by the annual performances of religious rites and by the simultaneous clearing of the various paths leading to the central market. The overall picture for the whole of Ibo country, then, was a very large number of separate political units indicative of what has been called an 'excess of democracy' but certainly not an absence of 'government'.[28]

To this could be added the fact that

> With few exceptions, decision-making in Igbo society was performed not by a single leader but by a council of elders which was highly responsive to the popular will.... There was virtually no rigid stratification of individuals by blood or occupation. The only major ascriptive hierarchical distinction was between freeman and slave. The later [sic] were either secular or religious. Otherwise, age grades, title societies, and other universalistic criteria provided the basis for social status and influence in the society. For example, in many villages the title society such as the Ozo society operated as a political oligarchy controlling decision-making even at public meetings at which all men had a right to speak.

> Deference to authority was very low. Wealth conferred authority and social status.... The societies were open to all freemen. Social mobility, wealth and power were independent of performance in authority roles.... In a general sense, obedience and respect were accorded only to the elders. Authoritative individuals were significant as objects of emulation rather than as recipients of loyalty and obedience.They were to be competed with rather than deferred to. Self-assertiveness and individual initiative were highly valued.
> Thus, Igbo society looked down on people who accepted superiors, depended on them, or relied on them for their progress. Subservience and unquestioning obedience signified weakness and a lack of masculinity. It placed a premium, instead, on occupational skill, enterprise and initiative.... Occupational achievement in pursuit of one's interest was the primary basis for positive social evaluation, the most highly esteemed and rewarded personal quality.[29]

From the above, it could be concluded that, though it lacked a welldefined and a centralized system of administration (like the Hausaland and Yorubaland), Igboland provides the most fertile ground for democracy. Though the *okpara* holds the collective authority of the extended family, he "is by no means a family despot or a dictator, rather he is best thought of as a representative or delegate who must act within the explicit mandate, and represent the views, of the extended family.... The *okpara* is reprimanded respectfully but firmly by the members of his group in the event of his behaving *ultra vires* or failing to measure up to expectation in the village or the town."[30] Therefore, Igboland already had a democracy - the Athenian (Greek) type - which gave ample scope to the individual's ability and initiative, and hence made room for equality, freedom, debate and discussion, representation and participation.

2.2. During the Colonial Imperialism (1861 - 1960)[31]

The abolition of the slave-trade by Britain in 1807 laid the foundations of her legitimate commercial relations with West Africa (to find market for her new industries). Eventually this led her to establish herself politically along the West African coast, the most important stretch of which was that of modern Nigeria. This urge to find market for her new industries brought the British to the shores of Nigeria (or the Niger Districts) in the 1830s - through the British explorers and missionaries.[32] With the partition of Africa (Berlin Conference of 1884-5) and the consequent scramble for Africa, the Niger districts fell under the British control.
As the British greed for wealth and zeal for conquest and expansion grew, she bombarded Lagos in 1851, deposing the slave-trading king of Lagos, Kosoko and replaced him with king Docemo who was sympathetic to British interest. King Docemo then signed the treaty that ceded Lagos to British Crown and Lagos became a British colony (1861).[33] Again it was the bid to consolidate British interests, to expand its trade in the hinterland of the Delta, with its superb river highway, the Niger, that eventually led Britain to proclaim a Protectorate over the

Niger districts (in the *Gazette* of 5th June 1885), and thus lay the foundation of modern Nigeria.[34] From then Britain was deeply involved in the affairs of Nigeria.

How did Britain bring its influence to bear on the myriads of ethnic groups and dynamic nationalities each with its own well-defined system of Government - the Hausaland with its centralized system of government, the feudal islamic monarchy; the Yorubaland with its centralized political system, the traditional-constitutional monarchy; and the Igboland with its non-centralized political system, the segmentary-decentralized republican democracy? In other words, what was the colonial system of administration in Nigeria?

2.2.1. The Colonial Administrative System in Nigeria

At the initial stage, the British influence was felt in Nigeria through the National African Company,[35] the sole British trading company operating in the Niger Delta areas with the aim of securing the area for Britain at the exclusion of other countries like France and Germany. In 1886 this company was granted the Royal Charter, under which "the company obtained political authority over those territories with which the company's agents had signed treaties placing them under British protection. The company was to 'discourage and as far as may be practicable, abolish by degrees any system of domestic servitude existing among the inhabitants'. On the other hand the company was enjoined to interfere as little as possible in the affairs of native chiefs..."[36] The Company later took the name of the Royal Niger Company. This Royal Niger Company operated only in the Southern part of Nigeria, named the Oil Rivers Protectorate, and later in 1893 renamed the Niger Coast Protectorate. The Northern parts of Nigeria were not then involved. What could be said about the North then was that in 1894 a treaty was signed with Bornu placing that territory under the British protection and that, in 1897, the Emirates of Nupe and Ilorin were defeated militarily by the British.

In the course of time, as the unpopularity of the Royal Niger Company grew in the South and as the difficulties of establishing administrative competence over those territories of the North assigned to Britain increased, Britain in 1899 withdrew the company's charter, compensated it for the loss of its privileged position, took over its administrative buildings, and (on Jan. 1, 1900) took control of all the company's territories. Henceforth, the British government exercised direct control over the whole area. The whole of Nigeria was then reorganised into three administrative areas: the Protectorate of Southern Nigeria, with Mr R. Moor as its High Commissioner; the Protectorate of Northern Nigeria, with Sir Frederick Lugard as its High Commissioner; and Lagos, which remained as a separate Colony and Protectorate, under the Colonial Office instead of the Foreign Office. By the year 1906, the Colony and Protectorate of Lagos and the Protectorate of Southern Nigeria were amalgamated into the Colony and Protectorate of Southern Nigeria, after successful military campaigns have been carried against Yoruba and Igbo rulers (between 1886 and 1906) and pacifying missions used to bring Yorubaland and Igboland under British rule. In the North, between 1900 and 1914, centres of resistance to British rule were also attacked and defeated by Royal West African Frontier Force, until the whole area was finally pacified.[37] Hence began the effective British administration in modern Nigeria.[38]

However, the two Protectorates - Northern and Southern Protectorates - had different administrative systems. In the North Sir Frederick Lugard used the system of **Indirect Rule**, whereby he ruled through the existing native institutions. This is how Lord Lugard, in his "Amalgamation Report", published in 1919 just after his retirement as Governor-General, defined Indirect Rule in Northern Nigeria:

> The system of Native Administration in the separate Government of Northern Nigeria had been based on the authority of the Native Chiefs. The policy of the Government was that these Chiefs should govern their people, not as independent but as dependent Rulers. The orders of Government are not conveyed to the people through them, but emanate from them in accordance, where necessary, with instructions received through the Resident. While they themselves are controlled by Government in matters of policy and of importance, their people are controlled in accordance with that policy by themselves.... The courts administer native law, and are presided over by Native Judges.... The taxes are raised in the name of the native ruler and by his agents, but he surrenders the fixed portion to Government.... The attitude of the Resident is that of a watchful adviser not of an interfering ruler, but he is ever jealous of the rights of the peasantry, and of any injustice to them.[39]

By this system, Lugard entirely insulated the North against the revolutionary effects of education by his promise (to the Sultan of Sokoto) that missionaries would not be allowed in the moslem emirates without the Emir's consent. The contrary is the case in the South. Here the missionaries (who were part and parcel of the colonial administration), convinced that their society was superior and also that conversion of the local people would have to be not only from the traditional religion but from the whole way of life which was intertwined with it and supported it, deliberately set out to change the very structure of traditional society with the western lifestyles.

Later, because of economic expediency,[40] among other minor reasons, on Jan. 1, 1914, the Northern and Southern Protectorates were amalgamated by Lord Lugard, and named the Colony and Protectorate of Nigeria.[41] And Nigeria became one Nation, with Lord Lugard as her first Governor-General. However, this unity was very superficial because the administrative distinction between the two Protectorates was maintained. The country was divided into three administrative parts: the Northern and Southern Provinces of Nigeria, which retained their status as a British Protectorate, and each of which was under a Lieutenant-Governor; and Lagos, the capital of the country, which remained a British Colony under an

Administrator - its inhabitants having the rights of British citizens. The Lieutenant-Governors and the Administrator were accountable to the Governor-General of the new country, Lord Lugard. In his general reorganisation of Nigeria, Lugard, on whom great powers devolved, "reduced the already limited powers of the Legislative Council, which in 1906 had been extended to all Southern Nigeria, to a mere cipher by restricting its authority to Lagos Colony alone, and in its place set up an unwieldy Nigerian Council with a majority of officials, and only three nominated Africans from the North and three from the South.... At every turn he avoided acquisition of large administration, so that administration was effectively regionalized under Lieutenant-Governors, a process that only exacerbated the growing differences between the two regions. He amalgamated the Treasury, Railways, Survey, Judiciary, Military, Posts and Telegraphs and Audit. Otherwise everything was left to the Lieutenant-Governors who merely referred to Lugard any matter that seemed to affect Nigeria as whole."[42] As time went on, the country was divided into three Provinces or Regions - Northern, Western and Eastern Provinces or Regions, the last two being the offshoot of the combination of the former Southern Province and Lagos Colony.

It is a pity that Lugard's administration perpetrated tribal consciousness in Nigeria. Lugard always showed preference for the North over the South. Firstly, it was obvious that Lugard centralized the Treasury to enable him "divert revenue that earlier had been properly the South's to balance the Northern deficit.... He even hoped to shift his government headquarters from South to the North which was his spiritual home."[43] Secondly, in the reorganisation of the country, after the amalgamation, he left the administration of the North intact - its islamic administrative statusquo was maintained - but the Southern provinces, which had been acquired piecemeal in widely differing circumstances, he reorganized to bring them in line with the North. In the South, he introduced the "Native Administrative System" - akin to the "Indirect Rule" system operative in the North - which often found the disfavour of the inhabitants because of its foreign nature: there was a big dichotomy between the traditional structure of power in the Western and Eastern Regions and that introduced by the system of indirect rule. "When Lugard toured Yorubaland and Benin it seemed clear to him that the answer to what he considered the administrative chaos of Southern Nigeria was the introduction of the indirect rule of the Northern pattern."[44] It is very unfortunate that Lugard, in deciding to extend his obnoxious and undemocratic "Native Administration" into the South, presumptuously and conspicuously overlooked the political and cultural patterns of the South. For example, in putting the Oba in Emir's shoes Lugard misconceived the position of Oba in Yoruba society: "While the Emir was to a certain extent limited on powers by his counsellors, he was effectively ruler of his emirate. On the other hand, ... the Yoruba Oba was circumscribed in his authority by a large number of checks and balances, effectively only giving voice to a decision that had been arrived at after an intricate process of negotiation and consultation. Certainly he did not possess traditional executive authority that could in any way be construed as measuring up to that possessed by an Emir. No Yoruba Oba had ever collected taxes from his people on a regular basis, whilst the Hausa had accepted his ruler's rights to taxation for several centuries."[45] Another example was in Igboland where Lugard had to force "Warrant Chiefs" on a loosely organized society that had rules rather than rulers. As M. Crowder rightly observes, "If Lugard had difficulties in applying indirect rule to the West, he found it almost impossible to introduce it in the East. Except for the Delta states there were no chiefs of consequence in the Eastern region. A system that depended intimately on a fulcrum of authority, obviously had no application in so loosely organized a society as that of the Ibo and Ibibio."[46] Moreover, in appointing such "Warrant Chiefs" and in the delegation of powers, controversial personalities were sometimes enthroned at the expense of the traditional criteria.[47] This was responsible for the uprisings against the indirect rule system which came up from time to time.[48]

Generally speaking, from what we have seen above, the colonial administration was not geared toward the unity and common-good of the Nigerian Nation. Basing its administration on the classical Roman doctrine of "Divide and Rule", it was really not in the British interest to foster unity among the various ethnic groups in the country. It was motivated by the desire for economic exploitation of the peoples and their resources with a minimum cost to the British. The delineation of the country into administrative units, the appointment of British Officials, and the structures of governance introduced were all guided by this objective. It was to safeguard their rule that the British often created local alien ruling classes and houses with little or no roots in the traditional ruling classes. Thus the "Native Authorities" were mere agents through whom colonial policies were mediated and implemented: collection of taxes, recruitment of forced labour, coercion of the peasantry into the cultivation of cash crops, and the maintenance of law and order. This implies that the rulers, both foreign and native, under colonial administration were completely alienated from the people, the ruled. Moreover, the amalgamation of socially and culturally diverse groups without commensurate uniform administrative policies and strategies, including its constitutions, left the country more divided than united.

All said and done, whatever criticisms may be levied against colonial administration in Nigeria (especially for lumping together groups of mutually incompatible peoples under the same administration and for the use of Indirect Rule system), it had some positive impact on the nation. For instance, in sum, "the British had created a new political unit, and whether they or the people under their administration liked it or not, it was inevitable that a certain number of Africans should begin to identify themselves not with their old tribal allegiances, but with the new political entity known as Nigeria. Thus, whilst Lugard's system of indirect rule tended to preserve tribal consciousness, the needs of the new administration were to produce a new class of Africans - clerks, teachers, traders, parsons, doctors and lawyers who could no longer think in purely tribal terms."[49] This new class of

Nigerians, the elite, was behind the rise of Nigerian Nationalism which led to the struggle for independence.

2.2.2. Towards Independence: New spirit of Nationalism[50]

Of Lugard's successors, the following were credited with the constitutional development of Nigeria[51]: Sir Hugh Clifford, Sir Arthur Richards, Sir John Macpherson, and Sir James Robertson. This thesis will consider Nigeria's political development towards independence under these four men.

2.2.2.1. Under Sir Hugh Clifford

Sir Hugh Clifford, Lugard's successor, in 1922 abolished both the Council and the small Legislative Council for Lagos area and gave the country a constitution (Clifford Constitution of 1922) which established the first ever Nigerian Legislative Council which had a number of elected members, thus giving Nigerians a greater part to play in the government. However, this Council, inaugurated in October, legislated only for the Colony (Lagos) and the Southern Provinces. The Governor alone legislated for the North until 1933 when all the Northern Departments were unified with the Southern Administration. It was during this period, 1922, that Herbert Macaulay, supported by Dr A. Jones, E. Shyngle, T. H. Jackson, K. Kotun, J. T. White and Baulcrick, founded the first ever Nigerian political party, the Nigerian National Democratic Party (NNDP), for the complete enfranchisement of the people of Lagos.

Sir Graham Thompson (Governor, 1926-30) and Sir Donald C. Cameron (Governor, 1930-36) ruled without much consequence. But it was during the latter's tenure (1933) that Lagos Youth Movement (LYM) was formed (with Dr James C. Vaughan, Ernest S. Ikoli, H. O. Davies and Samuel A. Akinsanya at its head) and in 1937 the name was changed to Nigerian Youth Movement, NYM.[52] The Movement had as its aim, inter alia, "the development of a united nation out of the conglomeration of the people who inhabit Nigeria;" "to encourage the fullest play of all such forces as will serve to promote understanding and a sense of common nationality among the different elements in the country" - the aims which it lived out, thus defeating NNDP in the 1938 Legislative Council election by winning all the three seats for Lagos.

2.2.2.2. Under Sir Arhtur Richards

The Governorship of Sir Bernard Bourdillon (1937-44), during which the NYM came into the forefront of the political struggle and a new wave of nationalism fermented, prepared the ground for the Richards Constitution of 1946.[53] Before this constitution, there was the birth, on August 26, 1944, of another political party, the National Council of Nigeria and the Cameroons (NCNC),[54] headed by Herbert Macaulay of the defunct NNDP (as president), with the primary aim of exerting mass pressure in order to accelerate the political development of the country. Then on December 6, 1944, Sir Arthur Richards (later Lord Milverton), Governor (1943-47), prepared a constitutional reform which, he hoped, would promote the unity of Nigeria, provide adequately within that unity for the diverse elements which make up the country, and enable Nigerians secure greater participation in the discussion of their own affairs. With this in mind, Sir Richards, on March 5, 1945, laid on the table of the Legislative Council the scheme of his new constitution: setting up a Legislative Council of forty-five members for the whole of Nigeria, twenty-eight of whom were Nigerians (of whom four were elected and the rest nominated), with a provision for a consultative body, a Regional House of Assembly, to be established in each of the three Regions (to consider and advise on matters referred to them by the Governor). Sir Richards' reason for this provision was "to create a political system which is itself a present advance and contains the living possibility of further orderly advance - a system within which the diverse elements may progress at varying speeds, amicably and smoothly, towards a more closely intergrated economic, social and political unity, without sacrificing the principles and ideals in their divergent ways of life."[55]

Though the Constitution was bitterly attacked, especially by the NCNC which was afraid that Regions once created, would help to crystalize disintegration tendencies, Sir Richards successfully pushed it through the Legislative Council. Then the NCNC protested to the Secretary of State (on March 27, 1945) that the Constitution should not only seek "to secure greater participation by Africans in discussion of their own affairs" but it should also enable them to secure "greater participation in the management of their own affairs." It demanded that the practice of nomination of members should be discontinued and "be replaced by popular representation based on adult suffrage." The Colonial Office defiled the NCNC's protest and gave assent to the Constitution. For this reason the NCNC toured the whole country and collected mandates from Nigerian communities, and sent a mission of the Pan-Nigeria (consisting of six delegates) to London to present their case to the Secretary of State (Rt. Hon. Arthur C. Jones). After receiving and listening to them (on August 13, 1947), the Secretary of State advised them to go home and co-operate in working the Constitution. And so the Constitution eventually came into effect at the beginning of 1947.

In the final analysis, Sir Arthur Richards introduced the first Federal form of Constitution in Nigeria. By this Constitution both the North and South were brought under a single legislative authority for the first time. This implies that for over 33 years of Nigeria's formative stage, the North and South of Nigeria were denied common legislative experience fundamental for the creation of a common outlook on the nation. However, the Constitution's regionalism - it created regional councils for the North, East and West - has been severely criticised as being the foundation of tribalism in Nigerian politics.[56]

2.2.2.3. Under Sir John Macpherson

In April 1948 Sir John Macpherson was appointed Governor of Nigeria, a post he held until 1954 when he became the Governor-General of the Federation of Nigeria (till 1955). Within this period a new political party, the Action Group,[57] was born. This party was a political protrusion of the *Egbe Omo Oduduwa*, a Society of the Descendants of Oduduwa, formed in 1945 by some Yoruba students in London, which held its inaugural Conference at Ile Ife in 1948, with the objectives to "create and actively foster the idea of a single nationalism throughout Yorubaland" and to "co-operate with the existing ethnical and regional associations and such as may exist hereafter, in matters of common interest to all Nigerians, so as to attain to Unity in federation." It is worthy of note that the Action Group, influenced by the rigid regionalism of Chief Bode Thomas,[58] concentrated its activities only the Western part of Nigeria, until 1955 when pressure of public opinion gradually forced it to modify its regional rigidity to become a nation-wide political party with membership in all the legislatures of the country (while still dominating in the West). On coming to office, Sir John Macpherson promptly applied himself to the question of finding a solution to the problems that Richards' Constitution had created. In fashioning his own Constitution,[59] he was going to avoid the mistakes of his predecessors. His Constitution had to be made in consultation with the people. So, the country was indulged in two years of protracted negotiations on the form the new constitution should take. The result was the introduction in 1951 of a Federal Constitution, which greatly increased regional autonomy and established larger and more representative Legislatures with wider powers in the Regions and at the centre. The new Constitution provided for a central legislature of 148 members (half of of them from the North) and an executive council of eighteen members (comprising six officials and twelve ministers (Nigerians), four nominated by each regional assembly). In the regions, the assemblies were enlarged and given legislative and financial powers, and each region had its won executive council with a majority of Africans over official members. Therefore, Macpherson's Constitution was more liberal in its outlook than its predecessors' and much more in keeping with the desires of Nigerians themselves.

The Constitution came into effect in 1952. But before then, in 1951 the country went to a general election, choosing its representatives through the electoral college. And soon after this election, the Government party in the Northern Region was founded - the Northern People's Congress (NPC),[60] a cultural Congress which, like the *Egbe Omo Oduduwa*, was converted into a political organization to meet the requirements of the new Macpherson Constitution. The

Party had the Saduana of Sokoto (Alhaji Ahmadu, the Premier of Northern Nigeria) as its leader. Its motto was "One North, One People, irrespective of region, rank or tribe." Its aims included: "to adopt and cultivate means that would foster better understanding and co-operation between the members of the Association and the Northern community generally;" "to study and strive to preserve the traditions which bound culture to the past, while reforming these traditions to render them capable of meeting modern conditions;" "to educate the Northerners of their civic and political responsibilities, to organize them to accept the leadership of the Northern People's Congress, and to support its candidates for elections;" "to inculcate in the minds of the Northerners a genuine love for the Northern Region and all that is northern, and a special reverence for Religion, Laws and Order and the preservation of good customs and traditions, and the feeling that the sorrow of one northerner shall be the sorrow of all and that the happiness of one is also the happiness of all;" "to make every possible effort in order to hasten the date of Self-Government for Nigeria and the consideration of introducing a 'Permanent Federal Constitution'...." The NPC then, from all indications (in its thoughts and actions), was purely a northern party.

Contrary to all expectations, the 1951 Macpherson Constitution could not work. In 1953 a crisis arose over the issue of self-government, giving rise to the 1954 London and Lagos Conferences[61] which were aimed at finding a temporary solution and removing such provisions of the new constitution as had made it impossible to work. The outcome of the Conferences was the 1954 Federal Constitution with the following provisions: a significant change in the status of the Nigerian civil service - the regionalisation of the public services, giving rise to four separate civil services; so too the Judiciary; the Regional representation on the Council of Ministers, with members now nominated by the party having a majority in the Federal election (instead of by the Regional Legislatures as was before the case); the Council of Ministers should be composed of ten Nigerians and three ex-officio ministers and the ministers should have responsibility for the formulation and execution of policy; the members of the House of Representatives were increased to 184 (with a Speaker, three ex-officio members and six members to be appointed by the Governor-General to represent interests of communities not otherwise adequately represented) and the members were to be elected directly from single member constituencies based on population;[62] the responsibilities of the Federal Legislature were defined, leaving residual powers to the regional Legislatures, and the principle that Federal Law prevailed over Regional Law in case of conflict was established; each Region had the right, subject to certain safeguard to the Federation, to opt for self-government independently of others. On Oct. 1, 1954, the new Federal Constitution of Nigeria came into force. Sir John Macpherson became the first Governor-General of the Federation. The Saduana of Sokoto (Alhaji Ahmadu), leader of the NPC, became the Prime Minister of Northern Region, Dr Nnamdi Azikiwe, leader of the

NCNC, became the Prime Minister of Eastern Region, and Chief Obafemi Awolowo, leader of the Action Group, became the Prime Minister of Western Region.

Then followed the 1954 Federal Government elections, the first to the Federal House of Representatives. This was conducted under different systems: in Eastern Region (Nov. 10), by secret ballot, and all the adults were eligible to vote; in Western Region (Nov. 11) and in Lagos (Dec. 11), by secret ballot, but only those adults who paid taxes in 1953-54 were eligible to vote; and in Northern Region and Southern Cameroons, the electoral college system was used and the various stages of the election were spread over two months. The result of the election showed that, out of the 184 seats, the NPC won 79 seats (all in the North), NCNC, 56 seats (32 in the East, 23 in the West, 1 in Lagos), Action Group-United National Independence Alliance, 27 seats (18 in the West, 7 in the East, 1 in Lagos, 1 in the North), Kamerun National Congress (KNC), 6 seats (all in Southern Cameroons), and others, 16 seats (12 in the North, 3 in the East, 1 in the West). Though the NPC won 79 seats, it failed to secure the absolute majority of seats which would have entitled it to nominate nine ministers in the Federal Government. In a situation like this, the new Constitution empowered the Governor-General to appoint three ministers from each of the Regions after taking the advice of the leader of the party to which the majority of members from the Region belonged. In this way, the NCNC nominated six ministers (having secured the largest number of seats in the East and West) and NPC three; the tenth ministerial post went to Southern Cameroons. Then in 1955 a coalition Government was formed in the centre by the NCNC (which won a majority seats in the East and West) and the NPC (which won an absolute majority in the North only), and the Action Group, teaming up with the other parties in the House, became the official opposition. And the representatives from Cameroons constituted the floating vote.

2.2.2.4. Under Sir James Robertson

Sir James Robertson succeeded Macpherson in 1955 as Governor-General of Nigeria, with Sir Robert Stapledon, Sir John Rankineas, and Sir Gawain Bell, as Governors of Eastern Region, Western Region, and Northern Region respectively, and Mr J. O. Field as Commissioner of the Cameroons. During this period, there were general House of Assembly elections in the Regions.[63] In the West (1956), the Action Group won over the NCNC (48 to 32). In the North (Nov., 1956), the NPC won 100 out of the 131 seats; and the rest was distributed among the United Middle-Belt Congress (12), the Northern Elements Progressive Union, NEPU (5), the Action Group (4), and the Bornu Youth Movement (2). And in the East, the NCNC won over Action Group (64 to 13).

Then followed the Nigeria London Constitutional Conference of 1957,[64] in which the Nigerian delegates asked Britain to grant Nigeria independence in 1959. Nigeria's request for independence in 1959 was rejected and the Conference decided on: a Senate for the Federal Parliament and the enlargement of the House of Representatives; the abolition of the post of Chief Secretary and the creation of the post of the Deputy Governor; Houses of Chiefs for the Eastern Region and the Southern Cameroons; a revised constitution for the Northern Region in view of its stand against regional self-government in 1957; an all-African executive council for Eastern and Western Nigeria; the retention of the police as a Federal subject, so as to insulate it from political influences; the setting up of independent Civil Service Commissions to protect the service; a Premier for the Southern Cameroons; Commissions to inquire into the fears of the minorities and revenue allocation - a delimitation commission (for the division of the country into 320 electoral districts) and electoral commission (for the supervision of elections).

On Aug. 30, 1957, Nigeria had her first all Nigerian Federal Executive Council, with Alhaji Abubakar Tafawa Balewa as the Prime Minister.[65] The various Commissions set about their works.[66] Then followed the transfer of Nigeria's Military Forces from the control of the Army Council to the Defence Council comprising the Prime Minister and three members of the Council of Ministers - the Premiers of Northern, Western, and Eastern Nigeria - plus the Premier-Designate of Southern Cameroons.[67]

Lastly came the "Historic Conference" of Sept. 29 - Oct. 27, 1958,[68] called to consider the reports of the Fiscal and Minorities Commissions and to discuss the request for independence made by Nigeria at the 1957 Conference. The Conference recorded decisions on: fundamental human rights (to be incorporated in the Nigerian Constitution), the Police (only one force under an Inspector-General responsible to the Federal Government), self-government for Northern Nigeria (on March 15, 1959, following the same pattern established in 1957 for Eastern and Western Regions), the position of Lagos (to remain the Federal Capital), the Southern Cameroons (any constitutional changes to be made should take place at the choice of the Southern Cameroons Government which would be formed after the January, 1959, elections), electoral arrangements (uniform electoral qualifications for all future elections to the Regional Houses of Assembly and the Federal House of Representatives), the Minorities problem (the question of creation of more States to wait until after independence), Nigerian Independence (fixed for Oct. 1, 1960), and a number of other matters of purely constitutional routine.

On Dec. 12, 1959, federal elections took place in the 312 single member constituencies throughout the country (of which 174 were in the North, 73 in the East, 62 in the West and 3 in Lagos). About 26 parties, including the prominent ones like the NCNC, Action Group, NPC, Democratic Party of Nigeria and Cameroons (DPNC - which Dr K. O. Mbadiwe formed when he broke away from NCNC), NEPU, KADP, registered for these elections. About 7,185,555 Nigerians voted for the 853 nominees (550 in the North, 183 in the East, and 170 in the West) contesting for the 174 seats. The result of the elections (released on Dec. 21) showed that NPC won the highest votes with 142 seats, followed by NCNC and its ally NEPU with 89 seats, Action Group with 72 seats, and other parties with 9 seats. Since no single party won enough seats to form the National Government, the Governor-General invited Alhaji Abubakar Tafawa Balewa (the leader of the largest party) to form a Government. And on Dec. 20, 1959, a new Federal Government - a coalition government between NPC (with 10 ministers) and NCNC (with 7 ministers) - was formed, with Alhaji Abubakar Tafawa Balewa as Prime Minister.

2.2.2.5. 1960: the year of Independence

The year 1960 was designated for Nigeria's Independence. The Nigerian Constitutional Conference which took place in London (May 10-19, 1960) was a worthy first step in this direction. In this Conference a complete agreement on Nigerian Independence was reached: Nigeria would be a sovereign and an independent Nation on Oct. 1, 1960; she would become a full member of the Commonwealth on Oct. 1; the way in which the decisions of the various Constitutional Conferences would be incorporated in the Constitution for independence was agreed upon - the provisions relating to the appointment of the Governor-General and the Regional Governors, and the powers exercised by the Governor-General and the Governors in discretion, would be exercised on the advice of Ministers after independence; the right of appeal to the Privy Council would be retained after independence, save in the case of election petitions; the Federal Legislature of independent Nigeria would be known as Parliament;[69] there would be mutual advantage to Britain and Nigeria in co-operating in the field of defence; if the Southern Cameroons joined Nigeria it would be with the status of a fully self-governing Region equal in all respects with the other Regions; the Northern Cameroons would form part of Northern Region with the new Divisions and local government arrangements introduced on April 1, 1960; the Nigerian military forces at present in the Southern Cameroons would be withdrawn by Oct. 1, and replaced by United Kingdom forces.

Then came the 'D'day, Oct. 1, 1960. Precisely at 12 midnight a green-white-green banner (Nigeria's flag) replaced the Union Jack on the flagpole and the Nigerian National Anthem was played for the first time. A new era had dawned. Nigeria had become independent. Later that morning, before a large crowd of jubilant people gathered for the Independence celebrations, the Queen's representative, Princess Alexandra of Kent, formally handed the Constitutional Instruments to the Prime Minister, Alhaji Abubakar Tafawa Balewa.

And on Nov. 16, 1960, Dr Nnamdi Azikwe (President of the Nigerian Senate, and formally the Premier of Eastern Nigeria and National President of the NCNC) succeeded Sir James Robertson (the last "colonial" Governor-General in Nigeria) as the first African Governor-General of the Federation of Nigeria; and on this day it was announced (from Buckingham Palace) that the Queen had graciously appointed the new Governor-General to be a member of her Privy Council; henceforth he would be addressed thus: His Excellency the Right Honourable Dr Nnamdi Azikiwe, P.C.

In summary, at her independence, Nigeria inherited from the colonial master, the British, a nation with ugly political and social legacy: a nation that was smack of "weak constitutional and institutional bases for development oriented politics; unbalanced federation; regionalism which engendered mutual jealousy and fear, and erected barriers against free movement of people, goods and ideas, thus encouraging chauvinism; a philosophy of governance in which the masses were perceived as an exploitable group and the leadership unaccountable to the people; regional-based political constituencies; an educational system that alienated the educated from his cultural milieu; a class conscious and capitalistic oriented society in which the state was perceived basically as an instrument for exploiting the people and the resources of the society; and, finally, a society where the rule of law was subject to, and manipulated by, executive pressures."[70] In fact this legacy has remained a major cause of the political, social and economic crises that confront Nigeria since her independence from Great Britain.

2.3. After Nigeria's Independence (1960 - 1995)

This section will concern itself with the political development of Nigeria from October 1960 to December 1995. With her independence, Nigeria had to paddle her own canoe, with its ups and downs. She experienced two republics of democratic administrations and six military dictatorships. And today she is still longing and yearning for a return to civil rule.

2.3.1. The first Republic (1960 - 1966)[71]

The first six years of Nigeria's existence as an independent Nation recorded series of crisis and political instabilities. There was, first of all, the crisis in the Western Region (1962).[72] It developed from within the Action Group which was the party in control of the government of Western Nigeria, caused by the misunderstanding and power struggle between the Premier of the Western Region (Chief Samuel Akintola) and his party (Action Group) boss (Chief Obafemi Awolowo). As the crisis escalated and spread throughout the region, the government of Western Region was closed down and state of emergency was declared in the area by the Prime Minister, Sir Abubakar Tafawa Balewa, (in a meeting of the Federal House on May 29, 1962). The Federal Government took over the administration of Western Nigeria - an Administrator, Senator Dr. Moses A. Majekdunmi, and 16 Commissioners were appointed to oversee the area - until Dec. 31, 1962, when the emergency was lifted.

Then came the 1962 and 1963 census controversies.[73] The May 1962 national population census, the first Nigerian real census, was nullified on Feb. 10, 1963, in a meeting between the Prime Minister and the three Regional Premiers, "in view of a loss of confidence in the figures for the various regions" (because the census figures were manipulated and thus the results were false and inflated). A new national census which took place Nov. 5 - 8, 1963, with strict measures of verification and counting by sight only, passed off well. All the same, the results were contested (even in the courts). In the end, after some adjustments and modifications, on Aug. 29, 1964, the Federal Ministry of Information published the final figures of the census: Nigeria had a population of 55,620,268 (Northern Nigeria 29,758,875, Eastern Nigeria 12,394,462, Western Nigeria 10,265,846, Midwestern Nigeria 2,535,839, and Lagos 665,246). And these figures became the basis for Federal Parliamentary elections.

It is worthy of note that, while the census controversies were going on, a new State, Midwest, was created out of Western Region[74] (after the referendum conducted on July 13, 1963) and interim Government instituted. Then on Jan. 8, 1964, the Federal House of Assembly met to consider the Constitution of the new Region. In the election to the new Region, which took place on Feb. 3, 1964, the National Convention of Nigerian Citizens (NCNC)[75] won overwhelmingly. And on Feb. 8, 1964, Chief Osadebay, the Premier of the Region, formed a Government with a 17-man Cabinet (the Governor, Chief Samuel J. Mariere, and his Ministers) and 11 Parliamentary Secretaries.

Another important event that took place while the census controversies were raging was Nigeria's becoming a Republic on Oct. 1, 1963.[76] This event was the fruit of the suggestion made in November 1961 by Dr Nnamdi Azikiwe and, in December (that same year), favoured by the Prime Minister, Alhaji Sir Abubakar Tafawa Balewa. The Constitution was modified to make it Republican. Some of the modifications in the new Constitution were: the President of the Republic would be elected through an electoral college of members of the Senate and House of Representatives and the tenure of office would be for a period of five years; the Prime Minister would not be removed from office by the President unless as a result of a vote of no confidence in the Government secured on the floor of the House; the power to appoint the country's representatives abroad would be vested in the President acting on the advice of the Prime Minister; non-Nigerians might not become Senators; all Judges would be appointed by the President on the advice of the Prime Minister, and the removal of Judges would be by presentation to the President of an address by a majority of at least two-thirds of all the members of each House of Representatives; the Supreme Court of Nigeria would be the final court of appeal (i.e., no more appeals to the Privy Council from the Supreme Court). After the proposals/modifications have been approved, on Aug. 9, 1963, by the House of Representatives, the new Constitution was embodied in the Republican Constitution Bill, which was passed by the House of Representatives on Sept. 18, 1963, by 254 votes to nil, and, on the following day, by the

Senate by 40 votes to nil. And on Oct. 1, 1963, Dr Nnamdi Azikiwe was sworn in, by the Chief Judge, Sir A. Ademola, as the Republic's first President.

Next, there was the crisis of the federal elections of 1964-65.[77] Before considering this crisis, some noteworthy events that preceded the elections should be underlined. First, there was the formation of a great alliance - the United Progressive Grand Alliance (UPGA)[78] - at Ibadan, on June 3, 1964, by the NCNC, the Action Group (AG) and the Northern Progressive Front (NPF), the Northern Elements Progressive Union (NEPU), the United Middle Belt Congress (UMBC). Second, the Electoral Commission, headed by Mr E. E. Esua, announced some changes, based on the figures of the 1963 population census, in the number of Federal members representing each administrative division: the North was reduced from 174 to 167, the East from 73 to 70, the Midwest from 15 to 14, and the West and Lagos increased from 47 to 57 and from 2 to 3 respectively; it further announced that voters in this election would be searched to ensure free and fair election and that strict security measures would be taken to avoid foul play. Third, on Aug. 20, 1964, another big alliance - the Nigerian National Alliance (NNA) - was formed by Northern People's Congress (NPC), the Nigerian National Democratic Party (NNDP), the Midwest Democratic Front (MDF) and other smaller parties, like Dr Chike Obi's Dynamic Party, the Niger Delta Congress, the Republican Party, and the Lagos State United Front. Fourth, on Oct. 10, 1964, election campaigns started. For the whole period of campaigns, as the President of Nigeria pointed out in his warning-speech on Dec. 10, 1964, there were complaints about

> victimisations, false imprisonment, malicious prosecution, denial of bail for trifle offences, refusal of permits to hold meetings, and beating of political opponents. There have been complaints about denial of the most elementary courtesies to political leaders campaigning in Regions other than their own. It is said that accommodation was refused them in public hotels and rest houses, food and victuals denied them in restaurants and catering establishments, shelter refused them in public buildings during rain storms, and road barriers used to blockade the entrance to towns where they intended to campaign. (There were) intimidatory instances (of) calculated deprivation of Nigerian citizens of their constitutional right to freedom of association, ... (publication of pamphlets by political parties) which incite tribe against tribe and raise disaffection among our multi-national communities, ... (and evidences that the instrument of power were being used) in some respects not only to stifle opposition but also to prevent the forthcoming elections from being free and fair....[79]

Fifth, on Dec. 8, 1964, Nigeria's Federal Parliament was dissolved. Sixth, on Dec. 19, 1964, nominations for the 312 constituencies ended.

Then came the election day, Dec. 30, 1964. Following the boycott of the election by UPGA - the boycott which it announced on Dec. 28 unless "free and fair polling" could be assured - the election was only "partial": "brisk voting" in the North, "moderate" in the West, very limited in Lagos, and non-existent in the

East, with NNA on the lead. Indeed, the election was a disappointment. No wonder the President, in his speech on Jan. 1, 1965, said that "all Nigerian patriots must hang their heads in shame today," because "the first national independence general election has been the signal for assaults on the Constitution and various acts of lawlessness hitherto unknown ... in the history of this country." On Jan. 4, 1965, the President announced that the Constitution left him no alternative but to call on the outgoing Prime Minister, Sir Abubakar T. Balewa, to form a new Government, which would be of "broadly based national" character. So Sir Abubakar announced his new Federal Cabinet on Jan. 7 and its members were sworn-in on Jan. 13 by the President. Then on March 18, 1965, a supplementary election was held in the Eastern Region, thus bringing the Federal general parliamentary elections to an end. And the final result was: NNA 198 seats, UPGA 108, Independents 5, and one seat vacant.

Following the crisis of the federal elections was the crisis of the regional elections in the West in 1965.[80] The Western Nigerian House of Assembly was dissolved on Sept. 18, 1965. The election campaigns were replete with reports of killing (of people), arson and wanton destruction of property. The election took place (on Oct. 11, 1965) in a very tense atmosphere. And by Oct. 12 and 13, two opposing results were being announced simultaneously by NNDP and UPGA. Each claimed to have won the election, and then proceeded to form a government. However, the Chairman of the Federal Electoral Commission, Mr Eyo Esua, announced in November that grave irregularities had occured in the October elections. Without waiting for a solution to the matter, the parties resorted to violence and destruction of life and property. And there was "terror undique" (violence everywhere) in the Region. The Federal Government announced on Jan. 13, 1966, "that the post-election violence in the Western Region had cost the lives of over 160 persons, including 64 civilians killed by the police, 91 killed by other civilians, and seven policemen."[81] This continued unrest in the Western Region, which threatened the peace and unity not only of the Region but of the whole country, could not but attract the military coup d'etat of January 15, 1966.

Summing up our discussion on the first Republic, one cannot but agree with Augustus Adebayo that "the most dominating feature of Nigerian politics (in the first Republic) was the fierce battle among major ethnic groups to control, or at least have a significant share, in the spoils of office in the Federal Government. To achieve this objective, the four Regions - North, East, West and Midwest - often engaged in bitter altercations over matters such as the siting of Federal projects, allocation of Federal grants or the disposition of political appointments."[82] Gavin Kennedy agrees: "it is the conclusion of the study of Nigeria that tribal divisions were the major, if not the sole, explanation for the collapse of the first Federation. In taking account of the realities of tribal divisions, the architects of the Federal State actually ensured that they would be dominant in subsequent years."[83] Indeed the Nigeria's First Republic was surrounded by what Dr A. Ayonrinde called "a dangerous triangle ... of Ethnicity, Religion and Politics," each seeking "power for the ethnic group."[84] The follow-ups of seeking power only for the ethnic group were many and grievous: "political victimisation, murder, politically inspired dismissal from work, arson, acquisition of property without compensation, malicious incrimination of political opponents, insecurity of life and property, violence and recrimination."[85] And the consequence of these follow-ups was a military intervention on Jan. 15, 1966, in the Nigerian politics. This marked the end of the first Republic and the beginning of military rule in Nigeria.

2.3.2. The First Military Administration (Jan. 16 to July 29, 1966)[86]

When Major Kaduna Nzeogwu, the leader of the first coup d'etat in Nigeria, and his colleagues (Major Ifeajuna and co.) struck on Jan. 15, 1966, Nigeria was in a political mess. "There was," as Gen. O. Obasanjo rightly points out, "arson, murder, robbery and general insecurity of life and property. There was in effect a total breakdown of law and order.... (T)here was absolutely no law and order and no security. In other words a state of anarchy had set in."[87] Considering the situation of things then (as seen above), and considering the fact that the Nigerian Army was the one really national institution insulated from the political bickerings of the time, the public saw the military intervention as the only hope of survival for Nigeria: the coup was considered a revolution and its author heroes.[88] This confidence was supported by the programme announced by Major Nzeogwu which included: the restoration of law and order; the destruction of the clumsy and corrupt apparatus through which the politicians perpetrated themselves in power; the elimination of such ills as corruption, bribery and embezzlement; the establishment of a strong, united and prosperous Nigeria with freedom from fear, general inefficiency and freedom to live and strive in every field of human endeavour.[89] Regretably the aims of the coup-plotters were utopian and idealistic. The army was soon infected with the very disease it came to eradicate, thus bringing disunity and disintegration into one of the few truly national institutions of the country. This sad situation eventually plunged the country into a civil war.

In fact, Major Nzeogwu's group were not interested in assuming power but in ridding the country of the corrupt system and those behind the system. Hence they killed some politicians - like Sir Ahmadu Bello (Northern Premier), Brigadier S. A. Ademulegun (Commander of First Brigade), and his wife, Cols. R. A. Shodeinde and Kur Mohammed, Sir Abubakar T. Balewa (the Prime Minister), Chief Okotie-Eboh (the Federal Finance Minister), Brigadier Z. Maimalari, Lt-Cols. J. Y. Pam, A. C. Unegbu and A. Largema, Chief Samuel Akintola (Western Premier), and so on[90] - and detained others (many Ministers, especially from the North, were arrested and detained), while allowing the Government to continue its business. The Federal Cabinet, with many absentees because many Ministers had gone into hiding, met three times on Jan. 15 and once on Jan. 16. In its Lagos meeting of Jan. 16, 1966, the Council of Ministers came "to unanimous decision voluntarily to hand-over administration of the country" as a temporary measure[91] to the army and the police, under the control of Major-General Aguiyi-Ironsi, "with immediate effect." Later that same day, Dr Nwafor Orizu, the Acting President (because the President was in London when the coup took place), in a broadcast to the Nation, invited Major-General Aguiyi-Ironsi to take-over the Government and to make a statement on the policy of the new administration. And so began the military rule in Nigeria, with Major-General Aguiyi-Ironsi as the first Military Head of State of Nigeria.

2.3.2.1. Major-Gen. J. T. U. Aguiyi-Ironsi's regime[92]

Soon after the Acting President's message, Major-Gen. Aguiyi-Ironsi, now the Supreme Commander of the Military Government, announced the decrees suspending the office of the President, the Prime Minister and the Parliament. The same for the offices of the Regional Governors, Premiers and Executive Councils. He then declared a military rule in the centre and in each Region of the Federation. (This is why Major-Gen. Aguiyi-Ironsi "is today only remembered as the ruler who attempted to sail against the Nigerian political current by promulgating a Decree to abolish federalism and convert Nigeria into a unitary state."[93]) Next, he constituted his Supreme Military Council and appointed Military Governors for the four Regions: Lt-Col. Chukwuemeka Odumegwu-Ojukwu (East), Col. R. A. Adebayo (West), Lt-Col. D. A. Ejoor (Mid-West), and Lt-Col. H. U. Katsina (North), and an Administrator for Lagos, Major Mobolaji Johnson.

Major-Gen. Aguiyi-Ironsi lacked the administrative ingenuity required for the handling of the turbulent and boiling atmosphere of the time. It could be said that he did not prepare himself fully for a political leadership role which was thrust on him by the Council of Ministers after the Nzeogwu coup. As Mr Adebayo rightly points out, he "was said to be a 'fine soldier', brought up in the British tradition of putting a clear demarcation between politics and the military. A professional soldier who had risen from the ranks and who had never thought it his business to devote thought and attention to the political and economic problems of his country, was woken up one morning and told to assume the reigns of government as Head of State. Little wonder, therefore, that on assuming office, he had no package of ideas or policies to put before the nation as the goals of national policy or the direction of affairs. Little wonder too, that he depended entirely on advisers ... who placed their own personal ambition above the interest of the nation."[94] And this was to be his tragedy. Not being quick to decision and action, Aguiyi-Ironsi's regime was not to last long: only six months. In a counter-coup of July 29, 1966, planned and executed by the soldiers from the North to avenge their deaths killed in the first coup (which they alleged was organised by the Easterners), he was kidnapped (while on tour in Ibadan where he addressed the traditional rulers on July 28, 1966) and later murdered. And Lt-Col. Yakubu Gowon was appointed in his stead, to begin another military administration.

2.3.3. The Second Military Administration (1966 - 1975)[95]

On July 29, 1966, Major-Gen. Aguiyi-Ironsi (with his host, Col. R. A. Adebayo, the Governor of Western Region) was declared missing from Ibadan where he had addressed the traditional rulers the previous day. For two good days the whereabouts and/or the state of the Head of State was not known. There was interregnum - the Nation was without a leader or government. Confusion gripped the Nigerian populace. Then on Aug. 1, Lt-Col. Yakubu Gowon broke the interregnum when he addressed the Nation, informing her, among other things, that he (Gowon) "had been brought to the position today of having to shoulder the responsibilities of this country and the Armed Forces with the consent of the majority of the members of Supreme Military Council as a result of the unfortunate incident that occurred on the early morning of 29 July, 1966," when "the country was plunged into a national disaster by the grave and unfortunate action taken by a section of the Army against the public, ... done by elimination of political leaders and high-ranking Army officers, a majority of whom came from a particular section of the country,"[96] thus unveiling the mystery about the former Head of State: "the last report was that he and the West Military Governor were both kidnapped by some soldiers. Up till now, there is no confirmation of their whereabouts," and promising "to continue the policy laid down in the statement by the Supreme Commander on 16 January, 1966, published on 26 January, 1966." And so Lt-Col. Gowon assumed office as the new Head of State. However, his position as the Head of State (though recognised by the Governors of Northern, Western and Midwestern Regions and by the Administrator of Lagos) was not recognised by the Governor of Eastern Region, Lt-Col. Odumegwu-Ojukwu, who believed that, following military discipline, Gowon was not the most senior in the Army and so not the right person to succeed the former Supreme Commander. And here began the horn-locking between the two Lt-Colonels, Gowon and Odumegwu-Ojukwu.

2.3.3.1. Lt-Col (and later, General) Yakubu Gowon's regime[97]

He assumed office on Aug. 1, 1966. From the first day of his being in power, Gowon was aware that unitary government pursued by his predecessor was not for Nigeria. This was evident in the title of his maiden broadcast to the Nation: "No trust or confidence in a Unitary System of Government," and in the body of his message: "I have come to strongly believe that we cannot continue in this wise, as the basis of trust and confidence in our unitary system of government has not been able to stand the test of time ... the basis for trust and unity is not there." What to do to end the crisis devastating the nation and to bring about peace and unity in the country became his primary concern. Peace manoeuvres, through Constitutional Conferences attended by representatives of the Regions and Lagos, were called. These Conferences could not harmonise the divergent views and stands of the various Regions. The situation got worse with the sporadic and incessant uprisings and reprisals against the Igbos in the North: a pogrom was unleashed on the Igbos - they (innocent and defenceless men, women and children) were massacred and their property plundered - leading to the repatriation of the Igbos in the North, like refugees (having lost everything - all their means of livelihood - except their heads), to the East.

Since Gowon's Governemnt did nothing to stop this "man's inhumanity to man" meted on the Igbos in the North, the Eastern Region was convinced that the Igbos were unsafe and had no place in the Nigerian polity under Gowon. Thus the Eastern Region hardened and closed its heart and mind to any further peace negotiations being initiated by Gowon and, instead, made bids for secession from the rest of Nigeria. It was when this stalemate was reached that the Ghanaian Head of State, Gen. Ankrah, opted to mediate. And the ground for the peace negotiations shifted to Aburi, Ghana. In the Aburi Communique, signed on Jan. 5, 1967, it was very clear that the Federal Government made many concessions to the Eastern Region. But on reaching home, the Federal side, realising the implications of their concessions at Aburi (which technically meant the disintegration of the Federation), decided to renegade the Aburi agreement. The Eastern Region would not have this; it stood on Aburi decision. (Hence the saying in the East then: "On Aburi we stand!") As none of the sides would bulge, there was tension everywhere and a smell of war in the air. When the Eastern Region seized the revenue due to the Federal Government, one F. 27 plane of the Nigerian Airways and trains, and expelled non-Easterners from its region, it then dawned on the Federal Government that the secession threats from the East were no gimcrack affair. The Federal Government reacted immediately by announcing, on May 27, 1967, a break up of the Federation into twelve States[98] - severing the Eastern Region into three States: East Central State, South-Eastern State and Rivers State, each with a new Governor - with the aim of destablising the unity of the Eastern Region. This strategy from the Federal Government did not deter Lt-Col. Odumegwu-Ojukwu from declaring on May 30, 1967, with the mandate of the Eastern Region Consultative Assembly, the Rebulic of Biafra as an independent and sovereign nation. The Federal Government reacted by deploying troops at Biafra's border. Then it demanded from the Biafran leaders (in its "Count Down" to the latter): among other things, "Public announcement of the withdrawal of the declaration of independence of the so-called Biafra Republic and revocation of the Independence Edict and associated Edicts," and "Public announcement of acceptance and recognition of the Federal Government authority over Eastern Nigeria by the former

Military Governor of East, Lt-Col. Ojukwu or any other Eastern officer," otherwise she faced risk of being crushed.

Biafra leaders rejected the Federal Government demands. Consequently, the Nigerian military Head of State, Lt. Col. Yakubu Gowon, on July 6, 1967, declared what he called "Police Action" on Biafra - which later developed into a total war. This was aimed at crushing what the Nigerian Government described as "the Ojukwu Cessessionist Rebels." But in actual fact, the Nigerian-Biafran war (or the Nigerian civil war) was rather a war between the Igbos and the rest of Nigerians.

The full story of the Nigeria-Biafra war does not belong to this work.[99] But suffice it to say that it was a "war of genocide" against Biafra; that the war, contrary to the expectation of the Federal Army (which thought that it "could crush the East in a few hours"[100]), lasted thirty good months; that Biafrans fought gallantly in defence of their fatherland but, in the end, lost the war to the Federal Government with more manpower and superior weapons (because it was assisted by the British, Russian, USA and Lybian governments). On Jan. 12, 1970, the war was brought to an end with a nation-wide broadcast from the Biafran acting-Head of State, Major General Phillip Effion (by then the Biafran leader, Odumegwu-Ojukwu, had fled the country), declaring Biafran surrender to the Federal Republic of Nigeria and unalloyed acceptance and loyalty to the Head of State and the Government of the Federal Republic of Nigeria. The formal surrender was rendered on Jan. 15, 1970, and accepted by Gen. Gowon, in a colourful ceremony at Dodan Barracks, Lagos. Gowon emerged the heroe of the war, not only in the eyes of Nigerians but also, and much more so, in the eyes of the world: the man who successfully prosecuted the war to sustain the national unity.

The war over, General Gowon called for an atmosphere of "no victor, and no vanquished". He then proceeded to launch his three "Rs": *Reconciliation* (aimed at establishing peace among people who had been warring, and thus at "healing the nation's wound"), *Rehabilitation* (aimed at settling the disabled ones, especially the soldiers, and at demobilising the now excess soldiers and restoring them to civilian living), and *Reconstruction* (aimed at building up the structures destroyed during the war). The people were pleased with Gen. Gowon's three "Rs" and co-operated in carrying them out.

As years passed by, it appeared that Gowon was not thinking of returning the country to a democratic rule. People were being fed up with his unfulfilling promises. Then there was an atmosphere of discontentment and uneasiness among the populace - as human rights and freedoms were abused; corruption at government and official quarters escalated. People were irritated at the ostentatious living, reckless display of arrogance, and wasteful spending of the nation's economy by the military government officials, including the State Governors and Administrator. Nigerians began to complain and to agitate for a return to civil rule. Gen. Gowon then announced in 1972 his nine-point programme for the return of civil rule in 1976: the reorganization of the Armed Forces; implimentation of the Second National Development Plan; eradication of corruption in Nigeria's national life; creation of more States; preparation and adoption of a new Constitution; introduction of a new revenue allocation formula; conduct of a national population census; organisation of genuinely national political parties; and organisation of election and installation of popularly elected government at state and federal levels.

It is very sad that Gen. Gowon abandoned his nine programmes, except the National Population Census of 1973 (which was not even successful, because the census result was rejected as inaccurate), for fun and festivals[101] (at federal and state levels). It is also sad that the General did nothing to stop the corrupt practices of his functionaries. "The State military governors became virtually little gods in their kingdoms, turning the States into their personal estates to do with as they pleased. All sense of public accountability vanished and all forms of excesses and gross abuse pervaded most of the various State administrations.... Most of State Governors became so tyrannical that the people groaned under their administration and pleaded with Gowon to change his Governors. But the Governors were confident that no matter the accusations levelled against them, they could always go to Lagos and explain it offhand to Gowon and everything would end in jokes and laughter."[102] General Gowon would exonerate them or maintain "a criminal silence" over the issue - thus helping to institutionalize corruption and indiscipline. Gen. Gowon could not even discipline his permanent secretaries who had grown wings: "Federal permanent secretaries did not acknowledge the Civil Commissioners as their political masters to whom they should be responsible. Instead they interpreted the role of their Commissioners as that of advisers to the Head of State. The result of this situation was that they felt quite free to pass over the heads of their Commissioners and consult with the Head of State or tender advice directly to him."[103]

Gowon's regime was charaterised by inefficiency and indecision. The public was no longer satisfied with the situation of things. Then came the last straw that broke the camel's back: Gen. Gowon in 1974 postponed indefinitely his promised return to civilian rule in 1976. It then dawned on Nigerians that the Gowon had started to love the seat more than surrendering it to anybody. As time went on, the General was no more in the good books of the military and the civilians. His cup was getting full. And it did, indeed, get full on July 29, 1975, when the General was removed from office in a palace coup conducted by Col. Joe Garba (Gen. Gowon's Body Guard Commander and a relation from maternal side), while the former was attending the OAU meeting (of which he was the current Chairman) in Kampala, Uganda. The Nigerian public received the news of the coup with much joy. By afternoon of the coup day, Brigadier Murtala Muhammed was appointed to succeed the former Head of State, and thus began the third military administration.

2.3.4. The Third Military Administration (1975 - 1979)[104]

The third military administration saw two captains who were birds of the same feather - Brigadier (later General) Murtala Muhammed and Brigadier (later Lt-General and then General) Olusegun Obasanjo (who was the former's deputy and later his successsor when Murtala was assassinated by Dimka). Hence we shall consider the two men - two captains - under one administration.

2.3.4.1. General Murtala Muhammed's captainship[105]

This administration, headed by General Murtala Muhammed, assisted by Lt-General Olusegun Obasanjo, began on July 29, 1975, the day Gen. Gowon was removed from office in a palace coup. It knew the sins of Gowon's administration, how displeasing these were to the Nigerian public. Then it saw as its primary task the removal of "the ghost of General Gowon which could still hunt the new administration" - what Oluleye calls "a process of de-Gowonization"[106] - while the ovation from the public for the coup was still loud. Hence it dismissed all the Military Governors and the Administrator from office and replaced them with new ones who were posted to States other than their own (to shield them from local influences). A panel was set up to probe the ex-Governors and ex-Administrator.[107] Next the administration's axe fell on prominent members of the Supreme Military Council and top civilian officers (like the Inspector-General of Police and his Deputy and the Federal Attorney-General and Commissioner for Justice) whose influence was seen as not conducive to Gowon's effecient performance of State duties.

For better organisation and efficiency and to curtail the excesses of the governors (prevalent in Gowon's time), Gen. Muhammed made two very significant innovations. One, he instituted the Council of States: a body consisting of all the State Military Governors meeting periodically with the Head of State and the Chief of Staff to deliberate on matters affecting the states. With the institution of this council, "the State Governors were no longer members of the Supreme Military Council. Decisions of the Council were handed down to them at the Council of State meetings. In this way, the State Military Governors were brought down to the second rung of the ladder and were placed in a subordinate position to the supreme decision-making organ of the Nation"[108] - a departure from the practice under Ironsi and Gowon. Two, the Head of State told the State Military Governors "to regard their appointment as mere duty posts from which they could be sent to other positions at any time."[109] And he did indeed change them frequently as exigencies of service demanded. As Mr Adebayo rightly observes, "one great blessing of this policy was that State Governors became responsive to public opinion and became conscious of public accountability."[110] And also "conscious of the general impression in the country that Gowon's failure and eventual downfall was partly due to bad official advice, Mohammed speedily cut the Federal permanent secretaries to size. Unless specially summoned, they were no longer to attend meetings of the Supreme Military Council and the Federal Executive Council, on which bodies they previously had right of access and audience under Gowon."[111] However, by relegating top civil servants to the background and keeping them away from policy-making, Gen. Muhammed had ignored and thereby missed the essential ingredients of rational decision-making. One of the failures of his regime!

The next assignment undertaken by the administration was to de-institutionalise indiscipline, corruption and apathy which had eaten deep into the fabrics of the Nigerian society that they had become an integral part of our national political and bureaucratic leadership. To begin this herculean task of cleaning the "Augean stable", the government took a deep look "into the dossiers of the civil servants and officials of parastatals with a view of weeding out the assumed corrupt, indolent and undeserving characters for a better Civil Service."[112] The exercise was very fruitful, for within a short time everyone was shaken out of complacency, everybody became up-and-doing. However the way and manner the purge was done - it was done in a haste and with irrationality - left much to be desired: the baby was thrown away with the dirty water, the wheat and the thorn were weeded together, many honest civil servants fell with a few corrupt and dishonest ones - for example, "drivers, gardeners, gatemen, night watchmen, clerks and messengers fell after their bosses"[113] and even civil servants who were officially sponsored to attend courses were retired for absenteeism while on course - ruining the careers and lives of civil servants. Another major fault of Murtala's regime!

While "de-Gowonization" was going on, the government set in motion its political programme (covering all that needed be done before the return to democracy now firmly fixed for Oct. 1, 1979[114]) which Gen. Muhammed announced on Oct.1, 1975 during his 15th Independence anniversary broadcast to the nation. On Oct. 4, 1975, a 50-man committee, a Constitution Drafting Committee (CDC) - comprising two representatives of the 12 States and prominent articulate men from all over the country, headed by Chief F.R.A. Williams (SAN, a Lagos-based lawyer) - was set up to draft a new constitution for the country in preparation for return to civil rule in 1979. The Committee commenced its work on Oct. 15, 1975. Also a "panel was set up on creation of new states and another one on the siting of the new Federal Capital. States were also active on things like the creation of Local Government Areas and Local Government Elections but under the strict supervision of the Federal Military Government.... On the implementation of the Third National Development Plan, grandiose projects were removed and, or reduced in scope...."[115]

But General Murtala Muhammed was not to live long. His last major function was the creation of 19 States in January, 1976.[116] Then on Feb. 13, 1976, the Head of State was assassinated on his way to the office[117] by Lt-Col. B. S. Dimka and his group, in an unsuccessful[118] coup d'etat meant to re-instate Gowon and his associates.[119] The nation wept and sincerely mourned the death of Murtala, a great man of action. And Lt-General Olusegun Obasanjo took over the leadership mantle - to continue from where General Muhammed had stopped.

2.3.4.2. General Olusegun Obasanjo's captainship

He was appointed to succeed the late Head of State by the Supreme Military Council which met at Dodan Barracks on Feb. 14, 1976, with Lt-Col. Shehu M. Yar'Adua (the former Chief of Staff) as his Deputy. Having learnt some lesson from what happened to his predecessor, General Obasanjo set out immediately to survey and methodically plug all loopholes that could tamper with a successful administration. He moved to Dodan Barracks in order to avoid shuttling up and down between his residence and the office. For intelligence gathering, the "Nigerian Security Organisation" was set up. Soldiers from Gowon's state of origin who constituted the Brigade of Guards were considered a security risk and then flushed out of Lagos, and replaced with new ones. The use of buses to convey many members of Councils for minor functions was introduced in order to prevent identification of key personnel; and all members of the Supreme Military Council were given escorts.[120]

Next, Gen. Obasanjo swung into action to continue and complete what remained of the political programme initiated by his predecessor - viz., creation of local government areas and elections; preparation and adoptation of a new constitution; organization of genuinely national parties; and elections and installation of a civilian government - so as to return the country to democracy as scheduled, on Oct. 1, 1979.

His government embarked on the reform, rationalisation, and institutionalisation of the local government system.[121] Unlike before, when various regions had fashioned different systems for executing government functions at the district levels,[122] the 1976 reforms sought to streamline the local government system and adopt a uniform system throughout the country. The Federal Government put out guidelines for the reforms to be undertaken by states.[123] Each state was expected to build its own local government system suitable to its local circumstances within this framework. Fundamentally these reforms were directed towards greater democratisation and the encouragement of initiative and leadership at local level. Hence the reforms aimed at elevating local government units to the status of being the third tier of government in Nigeria, thereby allocating wide functions to local governments. "Apart from traditional functions of local governments of tax collection, building and running of markets, motor parks, feeder roads and health centres and so on," Mr Sorkaa writes, "the reforms endow local governments with responsibilities for activities which were formerly largely discharged by the other tiers of government. An important example is primary education. There are the additional powers and functions which are exercised concurrently by local and state governments. (See "The Federal Guidelines," par. 5.) Local Governments have power for the establishment of Police Committees in the Local Government Areas. The responsibilities of these Committees include maintaining, under constant review, questions relating to the enforcement of by-laws and other legislations by local governments, and investigating and commenting upon complaints lodged about policemen in Local Government Areas. (See "The Federal Guidelines," par. 61-64.)"[124] The local governments having been created (without violence erupting as a result of the groupings), the local government elections took place peacefully (without rigging or violence). The were no political parties. All candidates stood for elections on their own merit.

There was the inauguration of a new Federal Electoral Commission (FEDECO) on Nov. 15, 1976, by the Head of State. The 24-man Commission, with Chief Michael Ani as its chairman, was to conduct elections into the reformed local Constituent Assembly, delimit constituencies, register political parties and finally conduct elections into state and federal legislatures to return the country to civil rule in 1979.

The Constituent Assembly (CA) with 230 members - 40 appointed by the Federal Government, and the rest elected indirectly by means of a system of electoral colleges based largely on local government units - was inaugurated, with Mr Justice Udo Udoma as its chairman. The CA had two-fold duty: to scrutinise and re-examine the Draft Constitution (amending individual articles where necessary, re-wording and touching up difficult passages), and to legitimise the decisions made by the CDC. The CA began its work of examining the Draft Constitution, clause-by-clause, in Dec. 1976. (Note that the CDC submitted the Draft Constitution to the Head of State on Sept. 14, 1976. It was launched by the Chief of Staff, Brigadier Shehu Yar'Adua, on Oct. 7, 1976, and was thrown open to the public for debate and comments (in any language).[125]) Having finished its work and handed it up to the Head of State, the CA was formally dissolved on Sept. 20, 1978. And after some amendments (17 of them)[126] have been made to the Constitution by the Supreme Military Council, the Head of State signed a decree on Sept. 21, 1978, which promulgated the new Constitution of the Federal Republic of Nigeria into law. The new Constitution would, however, come into effect on Oct. 1, 1979, the day the civilian government would take off. And so, Nigeria now had a presidential Constitution (the American type).

In the same broadcast on Sept. 21, 1978, at which he promulgated the new Constitution into law, the Head of State lifted the ban on politics and political activities. Then political parties began to spring up, and within three months there were 53 of them: the Unity Party of Nigeria (UPN), the Nigerian People's Party (NPP), National Party of Nigeria (NPN), Nigerian Advanced Party (NAP), Nigerian National Congress (NNC), People's Redemption Party (PRP), Great Nigerian People's Party (GNPP), and so on. Among the 53 Parties, only 17 actually met FEDECO's deadline, December 18, 1978, for registration of political parties. And according to FEDECO's announcement on Dec. 23, 1978, only 5 out of the 17 parties (UPN, NPP, GNPP, PRP, and NPN) were qualified to contest the 1979 elections, having fulfilled FEDECO's guidelines that each party that wished to register must send in 10 copies of its constitution and 10 copies of its manifesto.[127] Electioneering campaign began in May 1979. By June 7 all the 5 political parties had submitted to FEDECO the list of their candidates for the year's general elections. Screening of these candidates by FEDECO began on June 11. And by July all was set for the elections: 48 million voters had been registered, polling booths had been constructed, election officials had been trained and security measures provided.

Then came the election period. There were five elections: Senatorial, House of Representatives, State Assembly, Gubernatorial, and Presidential elections. Generally, the elections were conducted on a highly improved franchise than any one in the past history of the country. The greatest feats were the enfranchisement of women in the northern states and the lowering of voting age from 21 to 18. Moreover, that 48 million voters registered for the elections, going by FEDECO's record, shows that for the first time in the history of Nigeria more people participated and helped in determining who should rule them. Now let us have a quick look on the different polls.

The first polls, the senatorial elections, took place on July 7, 1979. People turned out in their millions to exercise their civic right, to elect 95 senators. The result showed that NPN was in the lead with 36 seats (37.9% of total seats), followed by UPN with 28 (29.5%), then NPP 16 (16.9%), GNPP 8 (8.4%), and PRP 7 (7.3%).

The second polls, the election of 449 candidates for the House of Representatives, took place on July 14, 1979. Arrangements for this election were better, and the voters had a better experience, than in the senatorial election. When the result was released, NPN was again leading with 168 seats (37.8% of all the seats), followed by UPN with 111 (24.7%), then NPP 79 (17.4%), PRP 47 (10.9%), and GNPP 43 (9.6%); one seat was reserved for the Federal Capital Territory, Abuja.

The third polls, the state Assembly elections, were held on July 21, 1979. The NPN maintained its lead, despite the unholy alliance between the other four parties (GNPP, NPP, PRP, UPN) announced on July 17 by the GNPP leader, Alhaji Waziri Ibrahim, which was aimed at preventing the NPN from coming to power. (NPP was later, on July 24, to disassociate itself from the alliance.) So the results of the election showed that NPN had a majority in 8 of the State Assemblies (Bauchi, Benue, Cross River, Kaduna, Kwara, Niger, Rivers and Sokoto) and was second in 8 other States (with 36.2% of the total, 1,347, seats in the country), that UPN had a majority in 5 States (Lagos, Ogun, Ondo, Oyo and Bendel) - 24.7%, NPP in 3 States (Anambra, Imo and Plateau) - 16.8%, GNPP only in Borno (11.6%), and PRP only in Kano (10.7%). In all, only NPN won seats in two-thirds of the State Assemblies.

The fourth polls, gubernatorial elections, came on July 28, 1979. And the results were: NPN won 7 States (Bauchi, Benue, Cross River, Kwara, Niger, Rivers and Sokoto); UPN won 5 States (Lagos, Ogun, Ondo, Oyo and Bendel); NPP won 3 States (Anambra, Imo and Plateau); PRP won 2 States (Kaduna and Kano); and GNPP won 2 States (Borno and Gongola).

It now remained the last round of the polls, the presidential elections, scheduled for August 11, 1979. This was the most important of all the elections, because of the place the executive president occupies: he is the Head of State, the Chief Executive of the Federation, and the Commander-in-Chief of the Armed Forces, and he also performs the functions of the Chief Diplomat, the Chief Legislator and the Chief Administrator. This explains the extra-ordinary huge turn out of voters on the election day, more than ever recorded in the previous elections.

Before the elections, FEDECO (on July 19) called on the parties to submit the nomination papers for candidates contesting the presidential election to the Commission on or before August 1. It also made it clear that if a president did not emerge on the election day,[128] there would be a run-off election on August 18. (FEDECO later changed the run-off election date to seven days after the results were known.)

Then came the election day, Aug. 11, 1979. The turnout was very massive and the election was orderly and peaceful. As the results started coming out, it seemed clear to politicians that none of the presidential candidates would emerge a winner in the first ballot. Thus began the problem of what constitutes two-thirds of 19 states.[129] Different answers (from politicians, lawyers, mathematicians and laymen) emerged: for example, NPN gave 12$^{2}/^{3}$ and non-NPN members gave 13. While the debate over 2/3 of 19 states was still going on, FEDECO on Aug. 16, 1979, declared Alhaji Shehu Shagari of NPN the winner of the presidential election and thus the president-elect of the nation. Alhaji Shehu Shagari (NPN) received 5,688,857 votes, followed by Chief Obafemi Awolowo (UPN) with 4,916,651 votes, then Dr Nnamdi Azikiwe (NPP) 2,688,857 votes, Alhaji Aminu Kano (PRP) 1,732,113, and Alhaji Waziri Ibrahim (GNPP) 1,686,489. The non-NPN candidates did not buy FEDECO's re-interpretation of 2/3 of 19 states: "In the circumstance, the candidate who scores at least one-quarter of the votes cast in 12 states and one-quater of two-thirds, that is, at least one-sixth of the votes cast in the 13th state satisfies the requirement of the sub-section (i.e., section 34A subsection 1(c) (ii))."[130] Hence they rejected FEDECO's declaration of Alhaji Shagari as the president-elect of Nigeria. The case was dragged to the Election Tribunal and later to the Supreme Court, each of which upheld the decision of FEDECO. It is good to note here that the decisions of FEDECO, the Election Tribunal and of the Supreme Court were influenced by the Supreme Military Council, whose chairman was the Head of State, Gen. Obasanjo.[131] No wonder "their Justices ... said that the judgement could not be cited in law as a 'precedent'."[132] It must be said that this intervention in the process by the military was uncalled for, very unfortunate and saddening, because it marred the credibility of FEDECO, the Election Tribunal and of the Judiciary - a fact that, as will be shown later, was reflected in the Second Republic when Alhaji Shagari's NPN came to power.

Having been declared the president-elect of Nigeria, Alhaji Shagari on Sept. 27, 1979, offered invitations to the other political parties and their flag-bearers to join him and his party to build "a united, peaceful and stable nation," and to form a "broad-based government"[133] - an invitation which all of them immediately rejected. The NPP later, on Oct. 1, 1979, accepted the invitation (most probably to secure key appointments at the federal level for its members and money for development in the three states which it controlled).

The political programmes of General Obasanjo's regime were completed within the specified time. Gen. Obasanjo creditably honoured his his pledges to the nation, and handed over power to a democratically elected government. This happened on October 1, 1979: in the presence of General Olusegun Obasanjo and his service chiefs and in the presence of the Nigerian public (of all ranks and works of life), the Chief Justice, Mr Justice Atanda Fatai-Williams, swore-in Dr. Alex Ekwueme as Nigeria's first Vice-President, and then Alhaji Shehu Shagari as the first executive President and Commander-in-Chief of the Armed Forces of Nigeria. And in his speech, few hours after he was sworn-in, President Shagari said, among other things, that his "administration is determined that the slogan of the NPN, 'One Nation, One Destiny' shall be translated into reality" and that "there is need for a dedicated leadership and citizenry imbued with faith to cultivate a widespread national feeling for 'One Nigeria'." With this the military rule, which began in 1966, came to an end and the Second Republic took off.

As a credit which it really deserves, in spite of its few weaknesses, the Muhammed/Obasanjo administration remains to date the best government Nigeria has ever had since Independence. In the words of A. Adebayo, "it is no doubt true to state that the four years administration under Murtala/Obasanjo witnessed the best period in the political history of Nigeria from Independence to the Second Republic in 1983, in so far as the administration of the constituent States comprising the Federation was concerned. The four years witnessed a period of restraint and responsiveness to public feelings and a consciousness for public accountability on the part of the State rulers."[134]

2.3.5. The Second Republic (1979 - 1983)[135]

As stated above, the second republic was preceded by 1979 general elections[136] of which Alhaji Shehu Shagari of National Party Nigeria (NPN) was declared the winner. Then on Oct. 1, 1979, Alhaji Shagari and Dr Ekwueme were sworn-in as the first executive President and the first Vice-President of the Federal Republic of Nigeria respectively. And thus began Alhaji Shagari's regime.

2.3.5.1. President Alhaji Shehu Shagari's regime

Alhaji Shagari's administration started on a shaky foundation. Doubts and problems of legitimacy surrounded his appointment as the president of the country. Though the NPP accepted NPN's hands of fellowship in the new government (giving rise to the "NPN-NPP accord"[137]), there were misunderstanding and hatred between NPN and the rest of the parties. The arrogance of the members of NPN was nothing to write home about. This faulty foundation upon which Shagari's administration was built was bound to influence the course of political activities thoughout its tenure, with a possibility of a fall.

1) **Shagari at work**

Shagari's administration took off with the task of organising its house and of sharing functions. On Oct. 9 the National Assembly held its first session: the Clerk of the National Assembly, Alhaji Gidado Idris, swore-in all the 95 Senators and 449 Members of the House of Representatives, and then Dr Joseph Wayas (NPN) was elected president of the Senate and Mr Edwin Umezoke (NPP) was elected the Speaker of the House of Representatives. On Oct. 12 the Senate established two committees: the Rules and Business Committee and House Committee, each with eleven members. On its own part, the House of Representatives set up three committees: the Standing Orders Committee with 8 members, the House Committee with 9 members, and the Public Petition Committee with 17 members. With time the number of committees in each part of the National Assembly grew. The Senate had 20 standing committees, each equally represented by the members of different parties in agreed proportion. The House of Representatives had 26 standing committees, each with 25 members. One big advantage of having these committees is that "both majority and every Nigerian, no matter in what group he belongs, is represented in the country's law making through his representatives. The minority, by the above system, have avoided the tyranny of the majority."[138]

On Oct. 17, President Shagari presented the list of his Cabinet, consisting of 24 Ministers of cabinet rank and 14 of non-cabinet rank, to the Senate for approval.[139] (20 of them - 13 cabinet and 7 non-cabinet - were later approved by the Senate and were sworn-in by the President on Oct. 24.[140]) Next, the President on Oct. 22 re-appointed the 23 federal permanent secretaries who had served with the military administration, and appointed 8 new ones, all of whom (31 in all) were sworn-in on the same day. Then on Nov. 22 he convened the first meeting of the Council of States - "an extra-ordinary body set up by the Constitution and empowered to advise the President on various issues of national importance. Its composition includes the President as chairman, the Vice-President, past Presidents and Heads of State of the country, past Chief Justices of the Federation, one traditional ruler from each State and the State Governors."[141] Other appointments made by President Shagari included: a six-man Revenue Allocation Commission, on Nov. 23, headed by Dr Pius Okigbo;[142] a Contracts Panel, on Dec. 14, made up of 6 ministers, headed by the minister of finance, Prof. S. M. Essang; [143] members of the Electoral Commission, on Dec. 14, with Mr Justice S. O. Ighodaro as chairman, (to be ratified by the Senate);[144] 10 Special Advisers to the executive, on Dec. 20, who were sworn in on Dec. 25;[145] 16 Liaison Officers, on Jan. 29, 1980, as his special assistants for liaison with the state governments;[146] 20 executives for Commercial and Merchant Banks in which the federal government had controlling shares.[147] Lastly, President Shagari, on July 30, 1980, declared his assets before the Code of Conduct Bureau, submitted those of the Vice-President, and said that his ministers and other top government functionaries would soon submit theirs. (This is definitely a good beginning towards accountability. But his lieutenants did not emulate him.)

Apart from organising and structuring his house, Shagari's regime creditably did quite a few other things. "Green Revolution" was launched (Dec. 1979) "to boost food production in a bid to provide 'food and shelter' for every Nigerian." It replaced the "Operation Feed the Nation" of the Obasanjo regime. And a 21-man committee was nominated (May 1980) by the minister of agriculture, Alhaji Ibrahim Gusau, to handle the programme. Many new roads were built and damaged ones repaired. There were "Rural Electrification Programme" and a lot rural self-developments.

2) **Killing the Second Republic**

In terms of political development, the second republic was, generally speaking, a big failure. Shagari's regime saw a resurface of the old "political adam" in the Nigerians - an indication that the politicians had learnt little or nothing from the past. This is probably so because the second republic was "a new wine in an old and unclean skin" - a new system of government (the presidential system) operated by the same old politicians who messed up the first republic. A new wine in such an unclean and polluted skin is bound to get sour and lose its taste very quickly. The second republic saw the resurrection of the old leadership, schooled in the politics of intrigues, insincerity, deceit and the manipulation of ethnic and religious sentiments to sustain themselves in power, who demonstrated no commitment to the letter and spirit of the new and wonderful 1979 presidential constitution. Thus the second republic lacked political leadership capable of galvanising social justice and equality for all Nigerians, irrespective of their state or ethnic origins. And what society (anywhere in the world) could thrive without good leadership? Moreover, Nigeria was "running a presidential system of government alongside with a civil service being run on the British parliamentary system" - another new wine in old skin. "This was the tragedy of the four years of the Second Republic."[148] In fact the politicians of the second republic displayed much ignorance of the presidential system, as we shall now see below.

In the first place, the Second Republic witnessed the politics of hate and spite. Members of one party regarded members of other parties not only as rivals but mainly as enemies. Members of minority parties were victimised in different states. The parties accused one another of political victimisation and intimidation.[149] This hostility existed more between the NPN (that controlled the centre) and the rest of the parties than between the other parties. There was an intense and, in some cases, destructive rivalry between the federal and state governments. On the part of the states, some state governments viewed themselves as "owning" not only the territory but also the people within their states, thereby regarding the federal government as a "stranger". As Mr Adebayo writes: "The Chief Executives of the States which were under different political parties from that of the President in the Federal government, were at pains to demonstrate that the President had no powers to intervene on matters affecting the States and that those who looked to Lagos for salvation were wasting their time.... (And) there was the compelling desire to demonstrate that the government of the political party controlling the State could perform better than the government of the political party controlling the Federal government."[150] There was even the controversy over whether or not to hang Shagari's portrait in public offices. There was also a serious controversy over the appointment of Presidential Liaison Officers (PLO): while Shagari saw it as an innovation to promote co-operation between the states and the centre, the other parties rejected it and warned their officials not to deal with the PLO. Worse still is the fact that most non-NPN governors treated Shagari with contempt[151] - never according him the respect due to a president. Daily, in the different media, President Shagari and his party were ridiculed.

On its own part, the federal government, on many occasions, failed to see that it carried in each state (even if not under its party's control) the same type of responsibility to its people as it did in other states under its party's control. It used its "federal might" on non-NPN governments - by denying or threatening to deny its opponents the "national cake"[152] and by using the federal structures and organisations, like the televisions, radios, newspapers, and even the police, to its own selfish advantage and for the oppression of opponents. This wrong use of the police force by the federal government generated much rancour and conflicts between the federal government (controlled by the NPN) and the state governments (not controlled by NPN) on the one hand, and the police and these state governments, on the other. And in many of such states, the situation created much tension and near breakdown of law and order. This state of affairs generated calls for decentralising the police force or for the establishment of separate state police forces. (Thus, the federal government destroyed the whole rational for a centralised police-force when it completely politicised the force and turned it into one of the most destructive elements in the country - thereby, willy-nilly, rejecting the operational requirements of our federalism.) One good example of the repressive tendencies of the federal government was "the Shugaba Affair": in January 1980, Shagari's administration arrested and deported to Chad the GNPP Majority Leader in the Borno State Assembly, Alhaji Shugaba Abdurrahman, under the pretext that he was not a Nigerian; but thanks to God, when the matter came to the court, "Justice Adefila said that from evidence before him Alhaji Shugaba has been proved to be a Nigerian citizen. He said the applicant is a Nigerian under the 1963 Constitution, and remarked that the minister of Internal Affairs should have carried a thorough investigation about the applicant's nationality before issuing the deportation order,"[153] and the court awarded N10,000 cost to Shugaba.

Secondly, the second republic witnessed abuse of power of the executive. There were "State Governors who felt accountable to no one and demonstrated naked display of power, and utter disregard for public feelings."[154] For instance, "there were some States whose Legislatures were almost entirely dominated by the same political party to which the Governor belonged. In most of these cases, the Governor was also the leader of the party in the State. The checks and balances which ought to exist between the Executive and the Legislature were, therefore, non-existent and this paved the way for the Governor as Chief Executive to manipulate the Legislature as he pleased and have a free day on most governmental and political matters."[155]

Thirdly, the second republic witnessed corruption in its height, especially in high quarters, at both federal and state levels: especially the over-inflation of contracts; payment of huge sums of money to ghost workers; importation of fake products in order to obtain foreign exchange; outright stealing of government property; illegal transfer of public money to private accounts; misuse of overseas tours; misuse of "security funds" by chief executives; and election malpractices. As Mr Adebayo rightly observes: "Throughout the length and breadth of the country, there has been widespread condemnation of the government under Shehu Shagari, as an oppressive, inefficient and most corrupt government. Whatever may be the issues in dispute, there is one that cannot be disputed. There is incontrovertible evidence all around of corruption on an incredible and unparalleled proportion."[156] The federal government and "the Chief Executives of many States indulged in political and financial excesses. Projects of doubtful viability were established against expert advice, political appointments were made merely to satisfy party supporters and without regard to their financial implications on the State...."[157] From high places corruption spread like wild fire and engulfed the whole of the Nigerian society. And the necessary consequences of the existence of this canker worm in the fabrics of the Nigerian nation were the complete collapse of the economy[158] (made manifest in inflation, unemployment, hunger and starvation that had become the lot of every ordinary Nigerian[159]) and, of course, the death of the second republic.

Lastly, the second republic witnessed an election period[160] fraught with horrible conditions, such as:

> the rabid corruption of political office-holders, the failure of some state governors to perform, personality crashes, intra-party feuds, conflicts between some state governments and the federal government and crashes resulting from efforts to superimpose the political party's constitution and structure over the power and authority of elected official, ... the desire to manipulate the power of incumbency in order to remain in power, the challenge to incumbent officials by alienated or opposition elements in the struggle to win access to the state and its resources, the desire to expand the power and sphere of interest of particular parties and the subsequent registration of a sixth political party, ... the nature of the country's economy and society, which by 1983 had shown cracks and conflicts, ... the contradictions of Nigeria's peripheral capitalism, the precipitous decline in oil production and exportation and therefore national revenues and foreign reserve, inflation, unemployment, increasing indebtedness (internally and externally), high crime rate and scarcity of essential commodities, particularly food, ...[161]

3) **The 1983 general elections**

These horrible conditions did indeed affect the 1983 elections. They affected the way the campaigns went: the politicians used these problems as campaign issues - not necessarily to tell the electorate how they would solve these problems and thereby ameliorate the ailing economy of the country and the sufferings of the people, but as a means of pouring venom and aspersion on, and of character-assassinating their political opponents, so as to win some political vantage and thus satisfy their selfish ends and those of their immediate relations and friends. The campaigns turned into war: verbal war, physical confrontations and attacks (with the use of thugs, "vanguards" and weapons), aimed at intimidating and/or eliminating political opponents and/or their supporters, resulting in violence and destruction of life and property. There were, therefore, tension and fear everywhere.

FEDEDCO's level of preparedness for and shabby approach to the elections affected the elections: its registration of a sixth party, the Nigerian Advance Party (NAP), at the last hour, "to take some votes away from the UPN;"[162] its delay in passing the electoral Law which affected its ability to begin the arrangements for the elections on time; its shoddy and suspicious electoral list in which the names of prominent politicians were missing and which contained an incredible number of registered voters; polling booths that had not been constructed in several places and electoral officers that had not been appointed or trained properly when the elections were two months away; non-availability of the corrected voters list for public scrutiny one month to the elections; its decision to alter the pattern of the election - the elections were to begin with the presidential and end with the House of Assembly instead of the other way round as has been the case; its decision to count the votes at the polling stations rather than at the collating centres. There were tension, confusion and suspicion everywhere.

The role of the police also affected the elections. "The period before and after the election saw *the inspector general of police* constantly on television *in full combat uniform warning the public not to invite 'massacres'* by protesting against announced election results. To make this threat credible, leave was cancelled for all officers, top-level meetings were constantly held, *armoured tanks were provided in some states*, notably those opposed to the NPN and about *65,000 policemen were given para-military training and fully equipped for anti-riot duties*. In fact, any visitor to Nigeria shortly before the elections would have concluded that the country was preparing for war. This conclusion would have been strengthened by *the presence of soldiers at all roadblocks all over the country searching all passing vehicles*."[163] This heightened the tension, confusion, suspicion and fear that were already in the air.

The people's attitude also affected the elections. The people were apathetic to FEDECO's call to register for the elections and they were apathetic to their civic duty of going to cast their votes on the election day, because they had lost confidence in FEDECO and in the politicians. And they were afraid of being infected with, and affected by the violence which had, unfortunately, become part of the election processes. "Better to stay at home safe," they people reasoned, "than to go to the polling booths and become injured or killed while voting for people who are insensitve to, and the cause of, my plights and sufferings." Then there were tension, confusion, suspicion, apathy and fear among the people.

The attitude of the Nigerian press also affected the elections. One saw a Nigerian press - newspapers, radios, T.Vs, most of them owned by either the states or by the federal government - which had thrown objective reporting to the winds and which fed the public with varieties of "filth and junk journalism", falsehood and half-truths about the happenings in the country. Each organ and its officers of the mass media kept to the "He who pays the piper dictates the tune" rule, and thus whatever its master did was magnified as good and whatever its master's opponent(s) did was trumpeted as evil and atrocious. "The role of the Nigerian media was severely restricted not only by the corruption and mediocre nature of some journalists but also by the constant threats from the various governments, law-suits and police invasion of media houses all in the effort to ensure conformity with the 'truth'."[164] The press thus became a warfront where one did battle with one's opponents, and where opponents were abused, accused, defamed, castigated, and damned. And so, tension, confusion, suspicion and fear loomed in the air.

To say the least, in the period before the elections "the country was in a state of flux. Uncertainty permeated every nook and corner of society. The public was unsure of whom to believe or trust. Rumours of violence, counter-violence, coups d'etat, even of foreign invasion were rife all over the country and politicians, depending on the extent to which such rumours favoured them, did much to intensify the fears.... The police behaved as (they were) preparing for war against a great power. The politicians behaved as if politics was the only possible avenue of human existence or survival and it was a do-or-die affair. To the politicians, where violence and threats could not compel the electorate to support them, bribery was certain to do it. In the alternative, the people's will could be neglected and the 'required' or desired results announced."[165] With all these, surely nobody expected anything good from the coming elections. However, before the elections, the FEDECO boss, Chief Justice Victor Ovie Whiskey, had re-assured the nation of the preparedness of his commission to conduct the elections; and the police and the army were posted in every nook and corner to maintain peace and order - even though their looks (stern, with red eyes) and equipment (machine-guns, pistols, etc.) portrayed a nation in a state of emergency. But was FEDECO fully prepared for the elections? Did the police and the army do their job as well as they should? The answers to these questions will emerge as we consider the elections themselves.

There were six political parties (NPN, UPN, NPP, GNPP, PRP and NAP) and 65.3 million voters registered for the 1983 elections.

Then came the first of the five elections, the presidential elections, on August 6, following FEDECO's new order. By FEDECO's schedule polling was to start at 7 O'clock and end at 6 p.m. on each day. But it was commonly observed that in practice polling did not commence in most polling stations until 12 noon or even later. The situation reports from almost all the states had it that the electoral officers were late in coming; and when they came, many of them did not have the necessary materials for the election: some had no ballot boxes; those with ballot boxes had no ballot papers or a sufficient quantity of them. What more, though the voters' turn out was very good, many voters could not locate their names in the voters' register, that is, where voters' registers were not missing. Therefore, due to FEDECO's inefficiency and poor performance, many eligible voters were defranchised. What a disappointment and what a fury in the faces of these voters!

The politicians (of all the parties), on their part, had a field day in rigging the elections in all the states. Complaints of victimisation, use of thugs and of fake policemen as polling agents, the manipulation of FEDECO officials and policemen, and alterations of election figures were rife. "The extent of rigging was directly proportional to the amount of resources, access to political power, influence over (FEDECO) officials and the police, available to any political party."[166] The NPN, because of its "federal might", had FEDECO and its officers and the police on its side and thus outplayed the other parties in "the election fraud game" to emerge the *winner* of the 1983 presidential elections: NPN got at least 25% in 16 states, UPN in 7 states, NPP in 4 and PRP in 1; GNPP and NAP did not score up to 25% in any state.

The public was disgusted with FEDECO and with the whole election exercise. It remained for FEDECO to clear its face and re-assure the people, if the other elections were to hold. And the FEDECO boss was fast in doing this: he admitted shoddy performance by FEDECO officials in some places, and he re-assured the nation that his commission would avoid the occurrence of such mistakes in subsequent elections. But FEDECO was far from redeeming its image in the subsequent elections - the same "rigging rule" was observed, with NPN (the biggest rigger) always taking the first place.

In the gubernatorial elections on Aug. 13, 1983, many voters again turned out in good time to elect their governors. Things were not smooth: the same (and even more) electoral irregularities were allegedly committed by FEDECO and some party officials. These irregularities led to social disorder: murder, arson, extreme thuggery and all in the name of politics! The hottest spots were Oyo and Ondo states, followed by Niger and Plateau states, where houses (including polling booths), cars and properties were set ablaze and many people (including some policemen) lost their lives. Consequently, some arrests were reportedly made of some suspects who were alleged to have been involved in electoral malpractices, possession of dangerous weapons and charms, and loitering around polling stations. Also, dusk-to-dusk curfews were imposed in some states and a ban on public meetings and processions was imposed in almost all the states. And further elections in Ondo and Oyo were postponed. However, the results of the gubernatorial elections were later released: NPN controlled 12 states (Anambra, Bauchi, Bendel, Benue, Borno, Cross River, Gongola, Kaduna, Niger, Oyo, Rivers and Sokoto), UPN 4 states (Kwara, Lagos, Ogun and Ondo), NPP 2 states (Imo and Plateau), PRP 1 state (Kano), GNPP and NAP got no state.

The remaining three elections - the Senatorial, the House of Representatives and the State House of Assemblies - witnessed a poor turn out of voters. This could be attributed to the people's disenchantment with, and loss of enthusiasm in the whole process, despite the fact that polling began earlier than in the first two elections. The Senatorial and House of Representatives elections seemed to have been attended by more acts of corruption and electoral malpractices: rigging was rife. This is not to exonerate the State House of Assembly elections which marked the end of a marathon five weeks elections, for it was not without flaws. The senatorial election results showed that, out of the total 96 seats, NPN got 59 seats (won all 5 seats in 10 states: Bauchi, Bendel, Benue, Borno, Cross River, Gongola, Kaduna, Oyo, Rivers and Sokoto, and the one seat in Abuja), UPN got 17 seats (won all 5 seats in 2 states: Lagos and Ogun), NPP got 13 seats (won all 5 seats in Imo State), PRP got 5 seats (all the 5 seats in Kano), GNPP got 1 seat (in Kwara), and NAP got no seat. And in the House of Representatives election results: out of the total 450 seats the NPN won 264 seats, NPP 48, PRP 41, UPN 33, and GNPP and NAP got nil.

In general, the 1983 elections were marked by many conspicuous flaws: non-commencement on schedule; lack of voting materials; incomplete and contradictory particulars of voters on the voters' list and cards; inadequacy of polling booths; voting by under-aged; multiple voting by unscrupulous citizens; notorious and massive rigging; arbitrary dismissals of some trained electoral officers whose sense of objectivity posed some threat to the evil machinations of the favoured parties and on-the-spot appointment of untrained and predetermined ones by FEDECO for reasons best known only to FEDECO itself and the beneficiaries of its goodwill. Even the manner in which the results of the elections were compiled, submitted and released was very pregnant with suspicion: there were cases in which the party agents were not allowed in at the collation centres when they ought to be there; there were reports of electoral officials missing with ballot boxes after the elections; also reports had it that ballot boxes stuffed with thumbed ballot papers were smuggled into the collation centres; some returning officers and/or some deputy returning officers were alleged to have altered the figures of election results with the worst partisan intentions; the election results in some states were suspiciously delayed unnecessarily by FEDECO. The result of these irregularities was the imposition of undesired leadership on the electorate. Any wonder then that there was a general dissatisfaction with the results of the elections? The elections gained a lot of criticisms and condemnation from the general public, especially from the politicians[167] (save, most probably, from the NPN members), the intellectuals,[168] the mass media,[169] the Nigerian Labour Congress (NLC), the Academic Staff Union of Universities (ASUU),[170] and from the army.[171]

The many contestants who lost by FEDECO's verdict refused to accept defeat. They went to court to seek 'redress'.[172] The law courts - High Courts, Appeal Courts and the Supreme Court - were full of electoral cases while the men of the jury sweated it out in their bid to prove the cases of their clients beyond all reasonable doubt. There were series of rulings, appeals and counter-appeals, even up to the Supreme Court where the final verdict was given. The outcome of these court actions was that some who were declared winners by FEDECO now became losers while some who were declared losers by FEDECO now became winners.[173] Sadly enough, many of the courts were partisan in their judgements - an indication that "the judiciary has been terribly corrupted".[174] And there were protests and violence in many places in the country.[175]

4) **The death of the Second Republic**

Despite this general and total dissatisfaction with the 1983 elections and with the NPN (the main brain behind the muddle), members of the NPN were still very proud of themselves and of their "victory". Hence on Oct. 1, 1983, Shagari and Dr Alex Ekwueme, were sworn-in in Lagos by the Chief Justice of the Federation, for a second term in office. On the same day the governors-elect and their deputies were also sworn-in in their various state capitals by their state Chief Judges. But what happened on the swearing-in day in Lagos - "security was tightened, invited dignitaries all wore bullet-proof vests, some arrived late and the speeches were short"[176] - shows that everybody, even members of the NPN, expected "an intervention", "an interruption", be it a coup or violent public reaction.

Though Shagari went on to form his government, everybody knew the time was up for his administration and that a change, for good or for worse, was very imminent. Many newspapers[177] predicted the possibility of a military coup. In short, the public was wont to consider what happened in 1983 not as an election but as a "selection" or "FEDECO awards", and not as a triumph for democracy but as democracy jeopardized. It feared, going by the NPN display of arrogance of power, the possibility of a fascist one-party state being established in Nigeria.[178] It therefore prayed for an intervention, no matter from where, that would effect a change in the present mess.

The people's fear did come true. Barely two months after Shagari had been sworn in, there was another military intervention in the early hours of Dec. 31, 1983. Brigadier Sanni Abacha and his group had ousted the "inept and corrupt" NPN-Shagari administration, to the jubilation of the public. This incidence fulfils the saying of John F. Kennedy: "those who make peaceful change impossible make violent change inevitable." This agrees with Machiavelli's views that when the necessary virtues have decayed, there is no possibility either of restoring them or of carrying on orderly government without them, except by despotic power, and that despotic violence is a powerful political medicine needed in corrupt states. With this coup, the army has buried democracy which the politicians (especially by Shagari and his NPN colleagues and accomplices in the 1983 elections) had already killed.[179] So Shagari's administration became a thing of the past and "will be remembered for the problems encountered in addressing cogent national issues and the disaster of constitutional engineering under a presidential political setting."[180] And thus began another military rule, the fourth one, in Nigeria.

2.3.6. The Fourth Military Administration (1983 - 1985)[181]

In the radio announcement of the fourth coup (first heard over Radio Nigeria about 7 a.m. on 31/12/83), Brigadier Sanni Abacha gave reasons for their coup. He said, among other things:

> You are all living witnesses to the great economic predicament and uncertainty which an inept and corrupt leadership has imposed on our beloved nation for the past four years. I am referring to the harsh intolerable conditions under which we are now living. Our economy has been hopelessly mismanaged; we have become a debtor and beggar nation. There is inadequacy of food at reasonable prices for our people who are now fed up with endless announcements of importation of foodstuff; health services are in shambles as our hospitals are reduced to mere consulting clinics without drugs, water and equipment.
> Our educational system is deteriorating at alarming rate. Unemployment figures including the undergraduates have reached embarrassing and unacceptable proportions.
> In some states, workers are being owed salary arrears of eight to twelve months and in others there are threats of salary cuts. Yet our leaders revel in squandermania, corruption and indiscipline, and continue to proliferate public appointments in complete disregard of our stark economic realities.

> After due consultations over these deplorable conditions, I and my colleagues in the armed forces have in the discharge of our national role as promoters and protectors of our national interest decided to effect a change in the leadership of the government of the Federal Republic of Nigeria and to form a Military Government. This task has just been completed.
> The Federal Military Government hereby decrees the suspension of the provision of the Constitution of the Federal Republic of Nigeria 1979 relating to all elective and appointive offices and representative institutions including the office of the President, state governors, Federal and state elective councils, special advisers, special assistants, the establishment of the National Assembly and the Houses of Assembly including the formation of political parties.[182]

The coup plotters appointed Major-General (later General) Muhammed Buhari the Head of State and Commander-in-Chief of the Armed Forces of the Federal Republic of Nigeria, and Major-General Idiagbon as his assistant.

2.3.6.1. General Buhari's regime

General Buhari assummed office on Jan. 1, 1984. He immediately made his first nation wide broadcast[183] which highlights include:

i) **the reasons for the coup**, ending with: "The change became necessary in order to put an end to the serious economic predicament and crisis of confidence now afflicting our nation;"

ii) **the constitution of the new government**: "the Nigerian Armed Forces have constituted themselves into a Federal Military Government comprising a Supreme Military Council, a National Council of States, a Federal Executive Council at the centre and State Executive Councils to be presided over by a Military Governor to be appointed in due course in each of the states of the federation. Members of these bodies will be announced soon;"

iii) **the nature of politics since 1979**: "The last Federal Military Government drew up a programme with the aim of handing over political power to the civilian in 1979. That programme as you all know was implemented to the letter. The 1979 Constitution was promulgated. However, little did the military realise that the political leadership of the Second Republic would circumvent most of the checks and balances in the Constitution and bring us to the present stage of general insecurity...."

iv) **mismanagement of the economy**: "It is true that there is a world-wide economic recession. However, in the case of Nigeria, it is in fact aggravated by mismanagement.... The situation would have been saved if the legislators were alert to their constitutional responsibilities. Instead, the legislators concerned themselves with salary scales, fringe benefits and unnecessary foreign travels, etc. which took no account of the state of the economy and welfare of the people they represented. As a result of our inability to cultivate financial discipline and prudent management of the economy, we have come to depend largely on internal and external borrowing to execute government projects with attendant domestic price pressures and soaring external debts...."

v) **the 1983 elections**: "The last general elections could be anything but free and fair. The only political parties that could not complain of election rigging are those parties that lacked the resources to rig.... This conclusively proves to us that the parties have not developed confidence in the presidential system of government in which the nation invested so much material resources."

vi) **corruption and indiscipline**: "While corruption and indiscipline have been associated with our state of underdevelopment, these twin evils in our body politic attained unprecedented heights in the past four years. The corrupt, inept and insensitive leaderships in the last four years have been the source of immorality and impropriety in our society. Since what happened in any society is largely a reflection of the leadership of that society we deplore corruption in all its facets.... Corruption has become so pervasive and intractable that a whole ministry has been erected to stem it."

vii) **moment of truth**: ".... We have no doubt that the situation is bad enough. In spite of this, every effort will be made to ensure that the difficult and degrading conditions under which we are living are ameliorated...."

vii) **priority programme**: "The Federal Government will reappraise policies with a view to paying greater attention to the following areas: - The economy will be given a new impetus and better sense of direction; - Corrupt officials and their agents will be brought to book; - In view of the drought that affected most parts of the country the Federal Military Government will, within the available resources, import foodstuff to supplement the shortfalls suffered in the last harvest; - Payment of salary arrears to workers; - Our foreign policy will both be dynamic and realistic. Africa will, of course, continue to be the centrepiece of our foreign policy; - The moral and combat-readiness of the Armed Forces will be given high priority. Officers and men of high personal and professional integrity will have nothing to fear."

Looking critically at the above broadcast, one cannot but observe that "while the reasons given for the coup are quite valid and in fact justified (and this accounts for why the public welcomed the coup with joy), the reasons did not in any way address the crucial structural and fundamental roots of contradictions, crisis and underdevelopment in Nigeria. The coup leaders did not see the problems of corruption, nepotism, waste, unproductiveness of the bourgeoisie, retrenchment and unemployment, social insecurity, etc., as direct or indirect manifestations of the distinctive nature of Nigeria's peripheral capitalism as well as its dependent location and role in the international division of labour."[184] Then it could be said that what happened on Dec. 31, 1983, was "'a change in leadership' ... over the same structures, institutions, class and production relations, external linkages and class contradictions and struggles."[185] This implies that the coup plotters "can only provide at best populist, yet temporary, solutions to the deep-rooted structural contradiction."[186] Moreover, the new regime had not, in their agenda, the restoration of democracy. This further implies that the public would soon, when the temporary jubilation over the removal of the inept and corrupt government was over, be disenchanted with the new military administration, especially with the rate at which the 'goods' are delivered.

The above observations were proved right in the course of Gen. Buhari's regime. Though the regime tried to recover some of the ill-acquired wealth of the actors of the past administration, the public (and more so the middle or junior officers in the army) believed that it did not move decisively against the ousted politicians. Moreover, the regime "put the state apparatus, including its coercive arm, to maximum use and, in that connection, broke the dialogue between the ruler and the led."[187] In other words, in its bid to eradicate corruption and indiscipline and thus enforce discipline - for which it instituted the famous "War Against Indiscipline" - "Nigerians were made to assimilate hastily churned out ethical and moral values, and urged to exhibit them mechanically."[188] The regime became oppressive and despotic: it promulgated decree 4 which threw the freedom of the press to the winds; there were secret military personnel and agents everywhere, nosing around into people's privacy; people's freedom and rights were interfered with and curtailed; and people lived in fear. Much as the people wished and appreciated a military intervention to end the Shagari administration, they did not need Buhari's regime to add to their sufferings and to compound their difficulties. Thus, by the high-handedness of its methods which "caused considerable social dislocations," the Buhari regime had driven a nail into its own coffin. The people, therefore, prayed and waited patiently for another military coup.

The much anticipated coup came on August 27, 1983, to the joy and happiness of all. General Buhari's government was ousted. And General I. B. Babangida took over the mantle of leadership, assisted by Commodore Ebitu Ukiwe, to begin the fifth military administration in Nigeria.

2.3.7. The Fifth Military Administration (1983 - 1994)[189]

The fifth military rule began on August 27, 1983, under the leadership of Gen. Ibrahim Babangida. On assuming office, Babangida first of all abrogated the obnoxious decree 4 (of Buhari) and pledged to uphold the freedom of the press. The public breathed an air of relief. Next, President Babangida announced his political agenda - "Transition Programme" - geared toward returning the country to a civil rule in 1992, and banned the "old politicians" (that is, the Second Republic politicians) from taking part in the politics of the transition programme. The candour with which Babangida's regime announced its transition time-table, and its manner of dramatizing political debates and participatory political involvement in a military setting captivated the minds and imaginations of millions of Nigerians. The public rejoiced. And without wasting time General Babangida set the ball roling towards the Third Republic. Hence Babangida's rulership will be seen under "Towards the Third Republic". However, it could be said here that Babangida's assumption of the title "President" - the first military ruler in Nigeria to do so - raised many questions about the intentions and aims of his administration.

2.3.7.1. Towards the Third Republic (1986 -)[190]

The move towards the Third Republic which began on Jan. 13, 1986, when the Federal Military Government, under Gen. Babangida, inaugurated a Political Bureau to conduct a national debate on the political future of the Nigeria, has seen three different administrations: Babangida's, Shonekan's and Abacha's (the current Head of State). After ten good years, the Third Republic is still an illusion. Nigeria is still under the transition programme. Thus because of the various illusory moves so far towards the Third Republic, our discussion of this phase of Nigeria's political development will not be in detail - only the highlights will be given and according to the three administrations. We shall begin with the architect of the transition programme, General Ibrahim Babangida.

2.3.7.1.1. During General Ibrahim B. Babangida's regime

The General Ibrahim B. Babangida administration could be treated under these three headings: establishment of the "transfer organs", implementation of the "transfer agender", and the 12 June 1993, presidential elections and its aftermath.

1) Establishment of the transfer organs

On 13 January 1986, Babangida inaugurated the first of the transfer organs, the *Political Bureau* (PB),[191] to conduct a national debate on the political future of Nigeria. The Bureau was given the following mandate: to review Nigeria's political history and identify the basic problems which have led to our failure in the past and suggest ways of resolving and coping with them; to identify a basic philosophy of government which will determine goals and serve as a guide to the activities of government; to collect relevant information and data for the government, as well as identify other political problems that may arise from the debate; to gather, collate and evaluate the contributions of Nigerians to the search for a viable political future and to provide guidelines for the attainment of the consensus objectives; and to deliberate on other political problems as may be referred to it from time to time.

Surely this "action of the Federal Military Government marked a significant milestone in the history of Nigeria, as the activities of the Bureau legitimised public debate, encouraged open discussion on issues of historical relevance and re-awakened the democratic spirit."[192]

Of all the transfer organs, the PB was the most successful in discharging its duties. It "submitted a comprehensive report to the government on March 27, 1987. The report was detailed in logic, profound in research, factual in presentation, and impartial in analysis of our historical and political development, together with recommendations on the way forward. The report, no doubt, has become an indispensable encyclopaedia on socio-political development of Nigeria, a scientific diagnosis of the country's political problems, together with recommended antidote to identified ills."[193] This report recommended a four-phased transition to civil rule programme. Events within the first phase, 1987 were the establishment of the Directorate of Social Mobilisation and Political Education; setting up of National Commission on political parties and elections, National Population Commission, the Code of Conduct Bureau and Code of Conduct Tribunal, and National Revenue and Fiscal Commission; setting up of a small-size Constitutional Review Panel to produce the draft of the amended version of the presidential system of government in consonance with the new philosophy of government; creation of new states, if approved; establishment of Area Development Committees and Village with Neighbourhood Committees; and conducting elections into local government councils on non-party basis. The second phase, 1988 was to take care of conducting population census and organising referendum on the Draft Constitution. Events for the third phase, 1989, were: lifting the ban on political activities; registration of two political parties; and elections to local government councils based on the two-party system. And the fourth phase, 1990 was to see to the elections at the state level for governors and legislators (not later than March), the general elections to the National Assembly, and the presidential elections.

The Babangida regime, on receiving the report of the Political Bureau, drew up its own time-table for the political programme: beginning with establishment of more transfer organs in the third quarter of 1987 to the presidential elections and final disengagement by the military in the third and fourth quarters of 1992.[194]

It is noteworthy that the government, in making its own timetable, did not follow strictly the recommendations of the PB. It is also noteworthy that the government, in the process of the transition programme, did not stick to its timetable: there were a lot of alterations and modifications, some of them not very necessary, which "gave rise to allegation and suspicion of a *hidden agenda* - the policy design of the government to abort the logic and goals of re-civilianization in favour of a yet undefined civilianization,"[195] and that some of the items in the agenda were never fulfilled (like SAP-related items).

The second transfer organ was the *National Population Commission* (NPC),[196] established in 1987, as a replacement of the defunct National Census

Board which organized the rejected 1979 census. The NPC had a chairman and an 8-man executive committee appointed by the president (plus other key staffers as resident population commissioners with subordinate staff in all states of the federation). It was empowered to: undertake the enumeration of the population of Nigeria periodically, through censuses, sample surveys or otherwise; establish and maintain a machinery for continuous and universal registration of births and deaths throughout the federation; prepare and maintain a national framework for the delineation exercise for census and sample surveys; collect, collate and publish data on migration statistics - research and monitor the national population policy and set up a national population information bank; arrange for the appointment and training of staff of the Commission; provide information and data on population for purposes of facilitating national planning and economic development; advise the federal government on any population and population related programmes and problems; disseminate information and educate the general public about the functions of the Commission under this decree; and do all such things as may be considered by the Commission to be necessary, desirable, expedient, supplementary or incidental to the performance of the functions or to the exercise of the powers conferred on the Commission under this decree.

The NPC did conduct a national census between Nov. 27 and Nov. 29, 1991, which provisional result, announced by the president on March 19, 1992, in Abuja, showed that Nigeria has 88.5 million people.[197] Both the conduct of the census and the validity of the released figures are still today not accepted by all sections of the country.[198]

The third transfer organ, the *National Electoral Commission* (NEC),[199] was established in 1987, with Prof. Eme Awa (and after two years, Prof. Humphrey Nwosu) as its chairman. NEC had the following specific functions: to organize, conduct and supervise all elections and matters pertaining to elections into all the elective offices provided for in this decree or in the Constitution of the Federal Republic of Nigeria or any other law; to provide clear guidelines, rules and regulations for the emergence, recognition and registration of two political parties; to register two political parties and determine their eligibility to sponsor candidates for any of the elections referred to in paragraph (a) of this subsection; to monitor the organisation and conduct of the political parties; to monitor the financing of the political parties; to monitor the political campaigns and provide rules and regulations which shall govern the political parties; to recommend to the Federal Military Government the amount of public funds required for the organisation and conduct of the affairs of the two political parties; to arrange for the annual examination and auditing of the funds and accounts of the two political parties; to provide rules which shall govern the qualification to vote and be voted for at elections; and to carry out such other functions as may be conferred on it by law. Furthermore, the decree stipulated that the functions of the Commission under paragraph (a) of subsection (i) of this section shall include: the division of the area of the federation or as the case may be, the area of the state, into such number of constituencies as may be prescribed by law for the purpose of elections to be conducted by the Commission; and the registration of voters, the preparation and maintenance of the register of voters for the purpose of any such election.

In the process of executing its duties, one thing became clear to the public about the NEC, viz., it would never be able freely to exercise its functions: "The NEC was created as a practical organ of transition with the objective of implementing the military's transition agenda. The NEC is, therefore, an arm of the ruling military formation in the same way that the old FEDECO helped the Obasanjo regime to establish a re-civilianized republic of its choice between 1979-1983.... Apart from obvious structural and administrative anomalies, NEC's primary handicap is its para-military and undemocratic orientation brought about by the dictatorial clout of its military sponsors.... (Therefore) it is ill-equipped to perform the role of an unbiased umpire and impartial adjudicator. It lacks the clout, the resolve and the independence to conduct a free election...."[200] So NEC, in the end, was a big failure.

The fourth transfer organ was *Mass Mobilisation for Social Justice, Self Reliance and Economic Recovery* (MAMSER).[201] It was established by Decree No. 31 of 1987. Its board of directors included a chairman (to be appointed by the president); one representative each of the following ministries - Information and Culture - Social Development, Youth and Sports - and Employment, Labour and Productivity. Others were a representative of the Directorate of Food, Roads and Rural Infrastructures (DFRRI) and the secretary to the Directorate. Its objectives were: to create a new cultural and productive environment which would promote productive work, self-reliance and self-discipline; to awaken the rights and obligations of a citizen to the nation; to encourage the citizens to actively and freely partake in the discussions and decisions affecting their general welfare; and to promote new sets of attitudes and culture for the attainment of the goals and objectives of the Nigerian state.

To realise these objectives MAMSER was empowered to: establish an appropriate framework for the positive mobilization and education of all Nigerians towards economic recovery and development of a new social and political order, awaken the consciousness of all categories of all Nigerians to their rights and obligations as citizens of Nigeria; inculcate in all Nigerians the value and spirit of civic responsibility, commitment to social justice and economic self-reliance through mobilisation and harnessing of their energies and natural resources into productive use; sensitise, induct and equip all Nigerians to fight against internal and external domination of resources by a few individuals and groups; re-orientate Nigerians to shun waste and vanity and to shed all pretences of affluence in their life styles; promote self-reliance and pride in the consumption of home produced commodities; and prepare the framework for creating the basic institutions and norms of democracy at all levels in society.

To articulate ways for the resolution of other problematic national conditions, the Directorate had also the function: to create consciousness about power and its use and the proper role of government in serving the collective interest of Nigerians; to ensure that materials which appear in the mass media, both electronic and the print, are in consonance with the national objective of self-reliance, social justice, human rights, democratic norms, economic recovery and development; to propagate the need to eschew all vices in public life including corruption, dishonesty, electoral and census malpractices, ethnic and religious bigotry; to propagate the virtues of hard work, honesty, self-reliance, commitment to and promotion of national integration; and to inculcate in all Nigerians the virtues of patriotism and positive participation in national affairs.

The aims and objectives of MAMSER were quite good and generally accepted. In the final analysis the nation gained little or nothing from the MAMSER irrespective of the huge money expended. Set up as a co-relating arm of government ministries, departments and agencies, MAMSER was institutionally restricted. This restriction accounted for its apparent failure. It was impossible for it to even understand what its real mission was, what constituency it was representing, whose interests it was meant to champion, and the most practical ways and strategies of tackling the complex issue of social mobilisation and political education.

The fifth and last transfer organ was the *Centre for Democratic Studies* (CDS),[202] established in 1989 by the president, after he had dissolved the six political associations and established the two government parties (NRC and SDP). The CDS was to organise democratic education and run crash programmes geared toward schooling Nigerians, especially party leaders, aspiring candidates and elected government office holders in the art of governance, democratic norms and practices, and in the basic issues central to the evolution of a new social and political order in Nigeria.

From all indications, the CDS was a failure from its conception. It was a brainchild of the military. It was "the least qualified institution in the country to talk about democracy,"[203] as it had all its programmes and directives from the military that had no appreciation for democracy. Moreover, since democracy is not a classroom affair - it is never learnt in the classroom, the CDS became a waste of national resources.

2) **Implementation of the transfer agenda**

The second move toward the Third Republic by the Babangida administration was the formulation and implementation of the "transfer agenda."[204] This spanned from party formation to the presidential elections and hand-over and final disengagement by the army. While the "transfer organs" were being established, the "transfer agenda" was at the same time in progress.

The Constituent Assembly, once constituted, worked on the constitution. It re-examined and updated the 1979 presidential constitution.

Local government elections on non-party basis took place. It was a big success. Because it was not partisan, there were no unnecessary rivalries and tensions.

Next, there was the formation of political parties.[205] The first quarter of 1989 witnessed the lifting of the ban on partisan political activities. Nigerians who were unaffected by the "blanket ban" (announced by the military after the Dec. 31, 1983 coup), the *new-breed politicians*, quickly came together to form political associations. By April 1989, 80 odd political associations had emerged. However, "the pattern of emergence of the newbreed political associations, their organizational structures and leadership composition showed a remarkable duplication of the political experimentations, at the level of political organization, during the First and Second Republics. The same geo-political and ethno-cultural alliances, axes and configurations were substantially sustained, in the way that the ideological forces cogent during the two Republics were worked into the emergent political associations."[206] Only six out of these many associations passed NEC's scrutiny. NEC then forwarded these six parties to the government for recognition and registeration. This did not happen. Instead, on Oct. 19, 1989, in a broadcast to the nation, "President Ibrahim Babangida, after ridiculing the entire political class and haranguing the newbreed politicians for their ineptitude and incompetence, announced the disqualification and disbandment of the six political associations ... (and) the establishment of two grassroots political parties - the SDP (Social Democratic Party) and NRC (National Republican Congress), (with) 'ideologies of a little to the right and a little to the left'."[207]

The government then went ahead to enact a decree on the formation of the two political parties as legal entities, drew up their constitutions and manifestoes, chose emblems, symbols and flags for them, appointed administrative secretaries to oversee their organisation and running at the federal, state and local government levels. (These secretaries ceased to function when the parties had their congresses and conventions during which party officials were elected.) Furthermore, the government erected secretariats at each Local Government Area for the two parties and was funding them. Funny enough, the two parties were so similar in form and outlook that the MAMSER had to publish a pamphlet on the essential differences in their constitutions and manifestoes. Though the two parties could be found at the ward, local government, state and national levels and though the spectrum of the Nigerian masses was directly involved in their activities, the fact that the government founded the parties and was dictating how they should breathe showed "that the transfer process had entered a stage where it was no longer determined by articulation and synthesization of free social forces, but the mechanical application of a political agenda and modalities enunciated by government."[208] A bad omen, indeed, for the expected democracy.

Then there was local government election on party basis.[209] This took place on Dec. 8, 1990. It was the first election in or of the new dispensation, with its new system of "open ballot"[210] designed and chosen to eliminate rigging and other electoral malpractices that had been the bane of democracy in Nigeria. But, it is very sad to say, the whole exercise was a disappointment. According to A. Nwankwo "the 1990 Local Government election was marked by artificiality. Right from the nomination of the candidates for various elective positions to the actual conduct of the election itself, the process was fraught with falsity and flagrant abuse of electoral procedures. In some cases, candidates emerged without undergoing the party primaries. Sometimes, too, primaries were cancelled by party chieftains who subsequently placed their agents as party contestants. At other times, votes were manufactured mysteriously without regard to the voters' strength in specific wards and local government areas.... During the actual election itself, the inadequacies of the open ballot system were exposed as double accreditation, double voting, manipulation of figures and electoral violence became the rule rather than the exception."[211] Another bad omen for the transition programme!

There followed the creation of new states and local government areas.[212] With the national census conducted in 1991 (which was and still is controversial), the federal government proceeded to create more new states and local government areas.[213] On Aug. 27, 1991, the president, in his broadcast to the nation, announced the creation of nine new states (Enugu, Delta, Osun, Kogi, Taraba, Jigawa, Birnin-Kebbi, Yobe and Abia), bringing the number of states in Nigeria to 30 (plus the Federal Capital Territory, Abuja), and 47 new local government areas. Again, on Sept. 23, 1991, additional 89 local governments were created, bringing the total to 589 in 30 states. And on Dec. 12, 1991, the federal capital was formally moved out of Lagos to Abuja.[214]

Gubernatorial and state Houses of Assemblies primaries and elections then took place.[215] The campaigns left much to be desired. They " were bitter and acrimonious and in some states violent and vicious.... Because of the monetization of the political process, campaigns degenerated into a material contest of the survival of the richest."[216] So too the primaries which "were marked by violence, thuggery, blatant falsification of results and the threats of civil rebellion, unless the whole exercise went according to the calculations and expectations of some dominant political configurations, that the primaries were cancelled in nine States and nine governorship candidates disqualified."[217] However, curiously enough, the governorship and state Houses of Assemblies elections on Dec. 14, 1991, were less violent, but not without election malpractices. The results of the elections were: in the gubernatorial elections the NRC won 16 seats and SDP 14; in the state Houses of Assemblies SDP had control in 17 states while NRC in 13.

The gubernatorial and state Houses of Assemblies elections over, the AFRC, after its Abuja meeting of Dec. 18, 1991, announced the amendment of decree 25 of 1987 and decree 9 of 1989 which amended decree 25, thereby freeing all the politicians banned from transition politics and thereafter (except those, civilians and military, who have been convicted by a court of law or tribunal in any part of the country and, of course, President Babangida whom the AFRC banned from transition politics so as to ensure he does not succeed himself): they were now free to vote and be voted for.[218]

It was then time for senatorial primaries and elections.[219] During the primaries the governors, who controlled the party machineries in their states, determined who became the candidates of the two parties, with the result that "qualification, experience and competence became subordinated to the forces of sychophancy, booth-licking, and insipient clownish loyalty."[220] A big blow to democracy! Even the actual elections on July 14, 1992, were no better: "The election was a charade, a huge national disgrace and an insult to democracy. The results were falsified and figures awarded liberally."[221]

Note that it was only on Dec. 5, 1992, that the National Assembly was inaugurated and its leaders elected.[222]

Lastly came the presidential primaries and elections.[223] The presidential primaries of August 1, 1992, were full of malpractices (like multiple voting, underaged voters, inflated figures) that the results had to be cancelled. Further primaries on Sept. 12, 19 and 26, 1992, did not fare better either. Frauds in these primaries were such that even the presidential candidates themselves and their agents had to protest and call on NEC and the government to cancel the results. Following these protests, the Armed Forces Ruling Council (AFRC), after its meeting of Oct. 6, 1992, decided to suspend the results and asked NEC to inquire into the allegations and to submit a comprehansive report on the matter to it within one week.

The findings of NEC,[224] which it submitted to the government, were tales of frauds, such as: use of money by aspirants to buy votes or achieve undue advantage, falsification of figures, allocation of votes where elections did not take place, favouritism on the part of the parties' executive committees, use of state government machineries by some governors in favour of some aspirants, non-serialization of accreditation slips, late arrival of pre-accreditation materials, non-conduct of primary elections as schedulled, arbitrary cancellation of results by returning officers to favour candidates, mutilation of election results, issuance of fake accreditation slips and voting by non-accredited persons, voting by under-aged and non-party members.[225] Following NEC's report, the AFRC, after its meeting of Oct. 15 and 16, 1992, took some drastic actions. It cancelled the results of the presidential primaries, dissolved the executive committees of the two parties at local, state and federal government levels, and appointed caretaker committees for the two parties which would oversee their affairs pending the conclusion of their local government and state congresses and their national conventions. It instituted a judiciary panel of inquiry to audit and probe the accounts of the two parties, indicted and pardoned the 23 presidential aspirants over electoral fraud, and gave opportunity to fresh aspirants to participate in future presidential primaries. It tasked NEC to provide, within two weeks, guidelines or timetable for the remaining part of the transition programme.[226] The AFRC's decisions were welcomed by the people with joy. Some people (like the 30 state governors) even asked the president to extend the transition to civil rule programme. However, all these demonstrate that our politicians have learnt little or nothing from the past and that the transitional process, based on its faulty foundations, had little hope of success.

In a nation-wide broadcast of Nov. 17, 1992, President Babangida announced, inter alia, the extension of the transition programme from Jan. 2, 1993 to Aug. 27, 1993 and the banning of all the 23 presidential aspirants of both political parties throughout the duration of the transition programme. He re-affirmed his regime's strong commitment to the process of democratisation by adopting the following measures: dissolution of the AFRC by Jan. 2, 1993; dissolution of the Council of Ministers by Jan. 2, 1993; implied abolition of the office of the unelected Vice-President (because most of his functions would be taken over by the chairman of the proposed National Transition Council); establishment of a National Transition Council (NTC) on Jan. 2, 1993; chairman of the NTC to be in-charge of the day-to-day administration of the country throughout the remaining period of the transition programme; the chairman and the members of the NTC shall be ineligible to contest for or hold elective public office for one year after the termination of the transition programme; establishnment of a National Security and Defence Council with the president as its chairman during the remaining part of the transition programme; splitting of the Council in Number 7 into National Security Council and National Defence Council at the end of the transition programme as enshrined in the constitution; swearing-in of members of the National Assembly on Dec, 5, 1992, and the inauguration of the two National Assembly Houses on Jan. 2, 1993; adoption of *Option A4*[227] (one of the eight options recommended by the NEC, as the modality for the nomination of preseidential candidates).

In February 1993 the transition wagon, with regard to the presidential race, took off again. It began with the congresses at ward, local government and state levels - *Option A4* in operation: in the word of Ray Ekpu, "to determine those who have grass roots, those who have roots without grass and those who have neither roots nor grass."[228] Then on March 27, 1993, the national convention - a three-day congress of special delegates of each party- kicked off in Port-Harcourt (for NRC) and Jos (for SPD) to elect, out of the 50 presidential aspirants from the states and Abuja, the party's flag-bearer for the presidential elections.[229] After the conventions, Chief Moshood K. O. Abiola and Bashir Tofa emerged the presidential candidates for SPD and NRC respectively. From now on both men campaigned rigorously for the June 12, 1993, presidential election.

3) **June 12, 1993, presidential elections and the end of the Babangida regime**

On Saturday, June 12, 1993, Nigerians turned out en masse to elect their president. The election witnessed a major innovation in electoral process in Nigerian history - the use of "election umpires"[230] (or election monitoring groups). 3,000 observers - 135 of whom were foreigners (from Britain, USA, France, Denmark, Canada, India, Netherlands, Belgium, China, Italy, Jamaica and Ethiopia) - led by their country's ambassadors or high commissioners in Nigeria monitored the election. International organisations, like the Group of Seven industrialised nations of the world (G7), the United Nations Security Council, were also represented. The whole exercise was quiet, smooth and peaceful. Everybody now waited eagerly for the result.[231]

Meanwhile the so-called Association for Better Nigeria (ABN), led by Arthur Nzeribe, which has been relentlessly campaigning for an extension of Babangida's military rule by four more years, was putting pressure on NEC, through the Abuja high court, not to release the result of the election. This association had, less than 24 hours prior to the election, obtained a high court injunction to restrain NEC from conducting the presidential election pending the determination of the substantive suit before the court. NEC did ignore the court's order and so the election took place. And after the elections a serious legal battle erupted between the Abuja high court (ordering NEC not to release the results) and two other high courts in Lagos and Benin (ordering NEC to release the results).[232]

Amidst this confusion, NEC, on June 16, announced its suspension of the release of the remaining presidential election results, thereby confounding the general public.[233] NEC had earlier released some results from 14 States and, so far, Chief Abiola was on the good lead. Many wondered what would become of the transition programme. On June 26, 1993, Nigerians received the shock of their lives: President Babangida announced the nullification of the June 12 election. He claimed that the two presidential candidates had breached some electoral laws - like widespread use of money. He then unfolded a new plan for another presidential election.[234]

Babangida's new plan was as follows: the two parties were to present candidates for a fresh election by the end of July, 1993; a candidate must not be less than 50 years old, as against the age requirement of 35 in the constitution (most probably to knock off Mr Tofa who was 46); a candidate must "have been a member of either of the two political parties for at least one year to this election" (most probably to disqualify Abiola who joined the SDP only early this January); such a candidate must "possess records of personal, corporate and business interests which do not conflict with the national interests" (most probably to disqualify both Abiola and Tofa who have national and international big business connections); and the 23 presidential aspirants banned last November from participating in the transition process were now free to contest in the next election.

Definitely the government's decisions and plans left much to be desired. If anything, they were a pointer to the derailing of the transition programme[235] - a big set back to the birth of the Third Republic!

Of course, neither Chief Abiola[236] (who saw himself as having won the election), his party, SDP, his tribespeople (the Yorubas), nor the general public, and not even the pro-democracy groups could welcome the annulement of the June 12 presidential election, especially "since the whole world has given a verdict that the election was free and fair and it was the most peaceful in the history of this country."[237] There was also international condemnation[238] (from Britain, the USA, Japan, the European Community, etc.) of Babangida's cancellation of the election.

Then hell seemed to be let loose on earth, on Nigerian earth: there were violent protests and demonstrations, especially in Lagos. People had to flee Lagos to their towns and villages for fear of war.[239] There were court actions (including the one filed by Abiola and his deputy) against the federal government and NEC over the annulled election. The Babangida regime reacted by promulgating three new decrees which restrained the jurisdiction of the courts to entertain any case on the June 12 presidential elections.[240] Moreover, there were protests against Babangida's continued stay in office - protests which nearly paralysed the country. Then the federal government became very hostile to all criticisms and oppositions, even to the media.[241]

On Tuesday, Aug. 17, 1993, the President addressed a joint session of the National Assembly on some important issues concerning the transition programme. The highlights of his address were: the Interim National Government would take over the government on Aug. 25, 1993; the new arrangement would only affect the structure of the federal military government at the federal level, replace, and not extend, the transitional council and it would operate as a constitutional government with specific powers during the interim government and work with the National Assembly exercising its "powers under the law as a necessary complement and balance to the executive powers of the interim government;" the interim government would ensure effective administration of the country, pay special attention to the well-being of its citizens, oversee elections to local governments due in December and encourage the promotion efforts at monitoring and observing elections; it would conduct fresh presidential election and hand over to a democratically elected president at the end of the interim period; a decree would be enacted to give legal basis to the interim government and such law "will be the supreme law of the land, during the interim period and will be binding on all organs of government."[242]

On Thursday, Aug. 26, 1993, Chief Ernest Shonekan, in a brief state ceremony (less than 25 minutes) in Abuja, was sworn-in as the Head of the Interim National Government of Nigeria. The ceremony was performed by Nigeria's

Chief Justice and was presided over by Babangida who then, after the military parade, took his exit from the army and from the seat of power. Thus began the Shonekan's Interim National Government (ING).[243]

To end the discussion on Babangida, the observation of A. Nwankwo becomes relevant when he describes Babangida as a leader who "wishes to leave, not just an enduring legacy, but a multiple succession of sustainable legacies which he hopes will outlive his generation.... Whether in the context of political transition, economic reform programmes, social engineering and re-definition of Nigerian institutional structures, President Babangida wants to appear as an innovator, a visionary realist and a pacesetter."[244] But he so manipulated the transfer organs and agenda that they were stood on their heads - thus making his transition programme, hence the Third Republic, a dream never come true.

2.3.7.2. Chief Ernest Shonekan's Interim National Government (ING) (August 26 - November 17, 1993)

Chief Shonekan came to power on August 26, 1993. He had a herculean task ahead of him. He was to paddle a canoe (the transition programme) that has already hit the rock. Worse still, he was divided between doing the wish of the people and doing the wish of the army - the wish of Babangida - who put him in power. On the one hand, Nigerians were now fed up with the transition programme. All they now wanted was the release of the June 12 presidential results and the installation of Chief Abiola as president. On the other hand, the military government before him had sealed off everything about the June 12 election and had given his Interim Government a mandate to organise a new election and hand over to a democratically elected president.

Aware of these problems - especially of the fact that his ING was not very much welcomed by the people, Shonekan undertook, as his primary task, fence-mending trips and campaigns for support all over the country - to woo Nigerians (especially through the traditional rulers and state governors) to accept his government. He was not successful.

Despite these and other moves, Shonekan faced mounting opposition against his ING,[245] to the point that Wole Soyinka (a Nobel laureate and civil rights campaigner) said "Shonekan is an illegal creation."[246] Even NEC's moves, under its new chairman, Okon Edet Uya, to get the parties agree on a new election timetable also met with stiff oppositions.[247]

Nevertheless both ING and NEC had some sympathisers. There were opponents of the "June 12 saga" who would want the ING and NEC to ignore the June 12 election issue and go on with new arrangement for another presidential election.

The struggle for primacy between the opponents and proponents of the June 12 election was not anything to write home about. It threatened the very peace and unity of the country.[248] It brought division even on the very floor of the Senate - to the point that the senate president (Iyorchia Ayu) and some other principal officers lost their seats.[249] In the final analysis, it led to the downfall of the interim government. On Nov. 9, 1993, a Lagos high court, led by Dolapo Akinsanya, declared Shonekan's ING illegal,[250] to the jubilation of the supporters of Abiola, thereby heightening the tension and insecurity that had since mounted all over the country. This political impasse, coupled with the fuel-price protests and the local governments' sit-tight strikes that were then common place, was a sure signal that a military intervention was imminent.

On Nov. 17, 1993, Shonekan's government crashed as Abacha bulldozed his way into power, signalling Nigeria's return, once agian, to military rule.[251] This was a coup with a difference: "No gun was fired, armoured tanks did not roll out into the streets, neither was there a dawn broadcast." Shonekan was simply made to resign (after only 80 days in office).[252] The ING which Shonekan called "a child of circumstance" and Gen. Sani Abacha "a child of necessity" was thus killed and Babangida's transition programme that cost the nation time (10 good years) and billions of Naira struck off. All democratic institutions and processes at local government, state and federal levels were abolished. Nigeria came back to square one. What a waste of time? What a waste of money? What a waste of skill and manpower? The people were disappointed - not because they loved Shonekan and hated Abacha, but simply because they "are sick and tired of 'military messiahs'."[253] However, the people's longing and yearning for a return to civil rule still remains unflagging. Will Abacha satisfy their longing and yearning?

2.3.8. The Sixth Military Administration (1993 -)[254]

The sixth military administration began on Nov. 17, 1993, the day Shonekan's ING was forced to resign. By the time of writing this work (up to December 1995) General Sani Abacha's regime was on, with plans for returning the country to a democratic rule in 1998. Therefore treatment on this administration is limited to the transition programme during General Abacha's regime, up to December 1995 (inclusive).

2.3.8.1. General Sani Abacha's regime[255]

In his maiden broadcast[256] to the Nation on Nov. 18, 1993, Gen. Sani Abacha, Head of State and Commander-in-Chief of the Nigerian Armed Forces, stated, among other things: "the Interim National Government is hereby dissolved;" - "the National and State Assemblies are also dissolved;" - "the State Executive Councils are dissolved. Brigade Commanders are to take over from the governors in their states until administrators are appointed. Where there are no

Brigade Commanders, the Commissioners of Police in the state are to take over;" - "all local governments are dissolved. The Directors of Personnel are to take over the administration of the local governments until administrators are appointed;" - "the National Electoral Commission is hereby dissolved;" - "all former secretaries of federal ministries are to hand over to their Directors-General until ministers are appointed;" - "the two political parties are hereby dissolved;" - "all processions, political meetings and associations of any type in any part of the country are hereby banned;" - "any consultative committee by whatever name called is hereby proscribed;" - "Decree 61 of 1993 is hereby abrogated."

On the formation of his government, he said: "A Provisional Ruling Council, PRC, is hereby established. It will comprise: the Head of State, Commander-in-Chief of the Armed Forces of the Federal Republic of Nigeria as Chairman; the Chief General of Staff as Vice-Chairman; the Honourable Minister of Defence; the Chief of Defence Staff; the Service Chiefs; the Inspector-General of Police; the Attorney General and Minister of Justice; the National Security Adviser." Further on administration, he said: "Legislative powers will reside in the Council; States will be governed by civilian administrators to be appointed later; also a Federal Executive Council will be put in place."

On security: "Our security system will be enhanced to ensure that lives of citizens, property of individuals are protected and preserved. Drugs trafficking and other economic crimes such as 419 must be tackled and eliminated.

On the media: "On the closed media houses, government is hereby lifting the order of proscription with immediate effect...."

On the political and economic situation of the country: "We require well thought-out and permanent solutions to these problems if we are to emerge stronger from them. Consequently, a Constitutional Conference with full constituent powers will be established soon to determine the future constitutional structure of Nigeria. The Constitutional Conference will also recommend the method of forming parties which will lead to ultimate recognition of political parties formed by the people. While the Conference is on, the reorganisation and reform of the following major institutions will be carried out - the Military, the Police, the Customs, the Judiciary, NITEL, NNPC, NEPA, the Banking Industry and Higher Educational Institutions."

Finally Gen. Abacha promised that his regime "will be firm, humane and decisive. We will not condone nor tolerate any act of indiscipline...."

From Gen. Abacha's address, it was clear that his regime was not a continuation of Babangida's, even though he was part of the latter's admninstration. He put aside everything about Babangida's transition programme by demolishing all democratic institutions and processes. Abacha's was purely a military dictatorship, his unchaining the closed media houses notwithstanding. Also clear from his address was the fact that he was not in hurry to return the country to a civil rule: no timetable was given. Any plan in this regard depended on the outcome of the Constitutional Conference that would be established (as if Nigeria's socio-political problems lie within the leaves of the constitution). And his regime seemed to be poised to revive the ailing public institutions - a herculean task indeed.[257]

The first thing Abacha did was to institute his 32-man Federal Executive Council in which every state of the federation was represented. But the Council as constituted has one major problem: it is an assembly of prominent men and women of opposing views, what Muyiwa Akintunde called "a rainbow team".[258] And one wonders if such a Council would ever easily reach a consensus on any matter.[259]

Next, the Abacha regime set up panels to probe the ailing public institutions. The probe began with the Judiciary[260] (seeing Mohammed Bello, Chief Justice of the federation and some others out of office) and NIPOST,[261] then followed the Customs,[262] the Nigerian Ports Plc,[263] the banking industry,[264] the NNPC,[265] and so on. The results of the probes revealed that each of these institutions was filthy and stinking. For instance, there was gross indiscipline on the part of the institutions' executives, such as mismanagement of the finances and the affairs of the institutions.

Another move was the inauguration on Jan. 19, 1994, of a 19-member Constitutional Conference Commission (CCC).[266] This was followed by the inauguration of the national campaign for constitutional conference in Abeokuta, Ogun state[267] - for public debates on Nigeria's future. Nigerians were divided on the proposed constitutional conference - many were not really sure what they wanted - making the conference appear like a battle ground where scores had to be settled on territorial integrity, revenue allocation, citizenship and so on.[268] Amidst the struggles and confusions evident in the constitutional conference, the participants at Azikiwe/Gowon national symposium came to a man about the unity of the country: "Nigeria must remain one."[269]

After Abacha's hundred days in office, Nigerians felt that his regime was heading nowhere with regard to the country's socio-economic and political problems.[270] There arose many doubts over the regime's agenda, especially over its tenure. Pressed to the wall by these doubts, the government released the first phase of its political programme which took off with the inauguration of a 15-man Constitutional Conference Election Committee (CCEC). This committee was charged with the election of members of the Constitutional Conference by May 28, 1994. "Five delegates are to be elected from each ward. The delegates would meet at the local government level to elect three candidates for the actual Constitutional Conference. The three conference delegates to be so elected would represent each senatorial district.... The conference will have barely four months to carry out its assignment. The final report is expected to be submitted to the Provisional Ruling Council by November 28. Government will then consider the report and produce a new constitution. By December 30, the new constitution is expected to be released, creating room for the emergence of the second phase of the political programme on January 6 and lifting of the ban on political activities on January 17, 1995."[271]

After a shaky start - due to the alleged unpreparedness of CCEC,[272] the boycott of the ward election by notable politicians who demanded the release of the June 12, 1993, presidential election results and the swearing-in of the winner,[273] the National Democratic Coalition's (NADECO's) uncompromising attitude towards the Government,[274] and the arrest of Chief Abiola (after he had declared himself the president of Nigeria)[275] - the Constitutional Conference was eventually inaugurated by General Abacha with a 30 point agenda.[276]

The delegates then settled down to business.[277] Some of their early decisions included: rotation of the presidency between the north and the south;[278] military rule in Nigeria to end on Jan. 1, 1996;[279] creation of states and local government areas to be handled by Provisional Ruling Council.[280] It is noteworthy here that the decisions of the NCC were subject to the federal government's approval.

To address the problem of hard drugs in Nigeria, the federal government reorganised the National Drug Law Enforcement Agency (NDLEA), to make it more efficient for the drug war.[281] Gen. Abacha also launched "War Against Indiscipline and Corruption" (WAIC) - a programme many believed the regime was morally unfit to execute, due to the questionable wealth of its officers, and due to the increasing involvement of serving and retired military personnel in armed robberies.[282]

As time passed by, it appeared that Abacha had not the solution to the nation's socioeconomic and political problems. The inflation rate had gone up, so high (over 300%) that the Nigerian currency lost its value and the prices of everything skyrocketed (to the point that many people could no longer afford the basic minimum of the essentials of life). Workers, especially teachers, were being owed salaries and allowances. There were no good roads, no good water-supply, and no constant electricity. The phones were not functioning. The country's educational institutions were very appalling - in infrastructure, structure and standard.[283] The hospitals were existing only in name: they were consulting clinics where no drugs are dispensed. What more, corruption and indiscipline became the order of the day; crime rate soared; and there was much insecurity of life and property. In short, the people were facing biting and unbearable hardships.[284]

Nigerians began to react against the government's apparent indifference to their plights. There were strikes for one claim or another every now and then.[285] Protests and demonstrations against the government became more prominent. Consequently the government began to take stringent and, very often, ruthless measures against criticisms and oppositions.[286] The government's clamp down on oppositions - with its concomitant abuse of people's rights and freedom - brought Abacha's regime in a bad light (within and without the country). The only thing the people now wanted was: Abacha must go! And it was no surprise that there was an attempted coup early March 1995 on Abacha's regime?[287]

1) Abacha's transition to civil rule programme

Because of these recent happenings, General Abacha in March 1995 reconstituted the Federal Executive Council, with 36 members as against 33 in the former, including 7 serving military officers and 3 women. Only 8 members of the former cabinet were retained.[288] The government also proposed a consultative body to supervise a transition programme that was yet to be drawn up[289] - an action that people saw definitely as a play for time (following the open-ended tenure given to it by the Constitutional Conference[290]). Then on June 17, 1995 (exactly one year after its inauguration by Abacha), the National Constitutional Conference presented to Abacha its finished work (the new draft constitution). Gen. Abacha received it with much joy, saying that the PRC was going to consider the draft for approval. He then announced the lifting of ban on politics.[291] This was generally received with joy throughout the federation. Next, the federal government began the restructuring of National Electoral Commission (NEC) in order to put it on course.[292] And on Oct. 1, 1995, in his independence anniversary broadcast, the Head of State, Gen. Abacha announced a transition to civil rule programme which would last three years (that is, up to Oct. 1, 1998).[293] Here is the detail of his transition timetable:

i) 1995 last quarter, October - December: approval of draft constitution; lifting of all restrictions on political activities; establishment of the National Electoral Commission of Nigeria (NECON); creation of Transitional Implementation Committee, National Reconciliation Committee, and Federal Character Commission; appointment of panel for creation of states, local governments, and boundary adjustment.

ii) 1996 first quarter, January - March: election and inauguration of local government councils on non-party basis.

iii) 1996 second quarter, April - June: creation of states and local governments; commence process of political party registration.

iv) 1996 third quarter, July - September: registeration of political parties; delineation of constituencies; production of authentic voters' register.

v) 1996 fourth quarter, October - December: election of local government councils at party level.

vi) 1997 first quarter, January - March: inauguration of party-elected local government councils; consolidation of new political party structures; tribunal sitting and conduct of any local government bye-elections.

vii) 1997 second quarter, April - June: party-state primaries to select candidates for state Assembly and governorship elections; screening and approval of candidates by the NECON.

viii) 1997 third quarter, July - September: state Assembly elections.

ix) 1997 fourth quarter, October - December: election of state governors; sitting of state election tribunal and conduct of bye-elections.

x) 1998 first quarter, January - March: inauguration of state Assembly and state governors; party primaries to select candidates for national Assembly elections; national Assembly election campaigns.

xi) 1998 second quarter, April - June: national Assembly elections; primaries to select candidates for presidential elections; commencement of nation-wide campaigns for the presidential elections.

xii) 1998 third quarter, July - September: presidential elections.

xiii) 1st October, 1998: swearing-in of new president and final disengagement.

The timetable when released met with a lot of criticisms from home and abroad. Prominent among the criticisms was that the length of the transition period was unnecessarily too long. The public feared a repeat of Babangida's long (ten years) and fruitless transition programme. Yet the military government, being what it is, overlooked all criticisms and remained stiff with its programme.

The option now left to Nigerians is to accept the timetable as it has been drawn. The onus is left now to the politicians to abide by the rules of the game to make the programme succeed. It is my conviction that the realisation of the dream of Nigerians - the return of the nation to democracy - depends very much, on the one hand, on the conduct of the politicians - their avoiding all ethnic and/or religious bias, and all electoral malpractices that ruined the first and second republics, and, on the other hand, on the military government remaining faithful to its promise - monitoring the programme closely, yet with less interference, and keeping to the timetable.

Returning Nigeria to a civil rule is one thing, having a sustainable democracy in Nigeria is another. From the above treatment of the political development of Nigeria (from colonial administration to the present day), there are many problems which militate against a sustainable democracy in Nigeria. These problems need to be highlighted, in order to get rid of them. And it is the object of the next chapter to trace and highlight these problems.

NOTES

1 Cf. A. H. M. Kirk-Green, **Crisis and Conflict in Nigeria: A Documentary Sourcebook 1966-1969**, Vol. 1 (London. New York. Ibadan: OUP, 1971), p. 142; Obafemi Awolowo, **Path to Nigerian Freedom** (London: Faber & Faber, 1947), pp. 47-48; Alhaji Ahmadu Bello, "House of Representatives (Lagos): Debates, 1953," in: **My Life** (London: Cambridge University Press, 1962), p. 133; Prof. Onigu Otite, "On the Concept of A Nigerian Society" in: A. O. Sanda (ed.), **Ethnic Relations in Nigeria: Problems and Prospects** (Nigeria: Dept. of Sociology, University of Ibadan), pp. 3-16, esp. pp.3-6.

2 Alhaji Shehu Musa, C.F.R., "Ethnicity, Social Cohesion and National Integration," in: **Round-Table Meeting on Ethnicity in Nigeria, Implications for National Development** (Kuru, Nigeria: National Institute for Policy and Strategic Studies, 1983), p. 42.

3 See M. Crowder, "The Birth of Nigeria," in his book: **The Story of Nigeria** (London: Faber and Faber, 1962), pp. 19-30; cf. Emeka Odumegwu-Ojukwu's "Prometheus unbound," in his book: **Because I Am Involved** (Ibadan. Owerri. Kaduna: Spectrum Books Limited, 1989), pp. 15-16.

4 Emeka Odumegwu-Ojukwu, **Because I Am Involved** (Ibadan. Owerri. Kaduna: Spectrum Books Limited, 1989), p. 15; cf. Prof. Onigu Otite's "On the Concept of Ethnicity in Nigeria" in: **Round-Table Meeting on Ethnicity in Nigeria: Implications for National Development** (Kuru, Nigeria: National Institute for Policy and Strategic Studies, 1983), p. 6.)

5 Dr A. O. Sanda (ed.), **Ethnic Relations In Nigeria: Problems and Prospects** (Nigeria: Dept. of Sociology, University of Ibadan, 1976), p. 117.

6 See A. H. M. Kirk-Green, "Who cioned the name 'Nigeria'?" in: **West Africa**, Dec. 22, 1953. Cf. Dorothy Wellesley, **Sir George Goldie - Founder of Nigeria** (London, 1934), pp. 98-99. There are other views as to the origin of the name "Nigeria": Prof. Onigu Otite writes that "'Nigeria', a name derived from the River Niger and given to this arbitrary set of social relationships, was coined by the London Times issue of 8 January 1897, although it had no British Government Official recognition until 1899 when the British House of Commons debated the Royal Niger Company Bill (Kirk-Green 1956). Edokpayi (1957) argues, however, that the word 'Nigeria' had in fact been used in 1859-60 by William Cole in his Journal of an African Timber Trader or Life in the Niger and that it was Saunders Otley and Co. of London who first gave press publication in 1862 to the word 'Nigeria'." (See Onigu Otite's "On the Concept of A Nigerian Society" in: A. O. Sanda (ed.), op. cit., p. 6.) On his part, E. Odumegwu-Ojukwu holds that "the very name Nigeria is meaningless, yet, for what it set out to do, it was most appropriate. As a noun, it was at best a half-truth; as an adjective, it was suitably elastic to accommodate future exposition of the imperial design. The name, we are told, was born of the amorous dementia of a certain Flora Shaw. It was coined some four thousand miles away to encompass peoples on whom the romantic eyes of the lady had not set...." (His "From Avernus we rise," op. cit., p. 55.)

7 E. Odumegwu-Ojukwu, op. cit., p. 15.

8 Ibid.

9 Ibid.

10 **A Thousand Years of West African History**, edited by J. F. Ade Ajayi and Ian Espie (Ibadan, Nigeria: Ibadan University Press and Nelson, 1981), provides a good treatment of the history of "The Hausa States" on pp. 90-112. See also Michael Crowder's "Sudanese States" in his book: **The Story of Nigeria** (London: Faber and Faber, 1962), pp. 31-45; C. S. Whitaker, Jr., **The Politics of Tradition: Continuity and Change in Northern Nigeria, 1946-1966** (Princeton, New Jersey: Princeton University Press, 1970); and M. G. Smith, "The Hausa of Northern Nigeria," in: J. L. Gibbs, ed., **Peoples of Africa** (New York: holt, Rinehart and Winston, 1965).

11 For the details of early Hausa social and political organization, see C. C. Ifemesia, "States of the Central Sudan," in: J. F. Ade Ajayi and Ian Espie, eds., op. cit., pp. 107-108.

12 Through the holy war, the "Jihad", of Usman dan Fodio (a Fulani) which began in 1804, the islamic religion spread to the whole region of Northern Nigeria and became

the foundation upon which the life of the people would have to be directed. Cf. M. Crowder, "The Holy War of Usman dan Fodio" in: sic, op. cit., pp. 78-95.

13 The leaders of the communities were always the first targets of zealous Islamic proselytes. Their conversion automatically and rapidly led to the transformation of their communities into an Islamic area. Cf. E. A. Ayandele, **The Missionary Impact on Modern Nigeria 1842-1914: A Political and Social Analysis** (London: Longman, 1966), p. 4.

14 Okwudiba Nnoli, **Ethnic Politics in Nigeria** (Enugu, Nigeria: Fourth Dimension Publishers, 1978), p. 130.

15 The Emir owed his appointment to the Sultan of Sokoto, the spiritual and temporal head of Sokoto Empire, because the emirate was supposed to be a vassal state in this Empire.

16 Okwudiba Nnoli, op. cit., p. 30.

17 Ibid., pp.130-131.

18 See, for example, A. D. Yahaya's detailed analysis of the undemocratic nature of local government in the emirate areas of Northern Nigeria up to 1974, in his "Representation in Local Government - The Emirate Case," in: **Nigerian Journal of Public Affairs** (Vol. 11, No. 1, May 1976).

19 For detailed study of the Kingdoms of the Yorubaland, see M. Crowder, "Kingdoms of the Forest," in: sic, op. cit., pp. 46-56; A. A. B. Aderibigbe, "Peoples of Southern Nigeria," in: J. F. Ade Ajayi and Ian Espie, eds., op. cit., pp. 191-201.

20 A. A. B. Aderibigbe, "Peoples of Southern Nigeria," in: J. F. Ade Ajayi and Ian Espie, eds., op. cit., p. 195.

21 Okwudiba Nnoli, op. cit., p. 133.

22 Ibid.

23 Ibid.

24 For more readings on the politics in Igboland, see: J. F. Ade Ajayi and Ian Espie, eds., op. cit., pp. 201-205; M. M. Green, **Ibo Village Affairs** (London: Sidgwick & Jackson, 1947); Daryll Ford and G. I. Jones, **The Ibo and Ibibio-speaking Peoples of South Eastern Nigeria** (London: International African Institute, 1950); Simon Ottenberg, "Ibo Perspectivity to Change," in: W. R. Bascom and M. J. Herskovits, eds., **Continuity and Change in African Cultures** (Chicago: University of Chicago Press, 1958); G. T. Basden, **Niger Ibos** (London, 1968); I. Nzimiro, **Studies in Igbo Political System: Chieftaincy and Politics in 4 Niger States** (London, 1972); B. O. Odinamadu, **Politics and Igbo Elites** (Ibadan, 1979); E. N. Njaka, **Igbo Political Culture** (Evanston: Northwestern University Press, 1974); L. U. Ejiofor, **Dynamics of Igbo Democracy: A Behavioural Analysis of Igbo Politics in Aguinyi Clan** (Ibadan: University Press Limited, 1981); E. Isichei, **A History of the Igbo People** (London and Basingstoke: MacMillan Press Ltd., 1976).

25 Akase Paul Sorkaa, "Democratic Values and Limitations of Local Government Reforms," in: Sam E. Oyovbaire, ed., **Democratic Experiment in Nigeria - Interpretative Essays** (Benin City, Nigeria: Omega Publishers, c1987), p. 113.

26 Ibid.

27 Cf. M. M. Green, **Ibo Village Affairs** (London: Sidgwick & Jackson, 1947), p. 8.

28 A. A. B. Aderibigbe, "Peoples of Southern Nigeria," in: J. F. Ade Ajayi and Ian Espie, eds., op. cit., p. 202.

29 Okwudiba Nnoli, op. cit., pp. 131-132.

30 Lambert U. Ejiofor, **Dynamics of Igbo Democracy: A Behavioural Analysis of Igbo Politics in Aguinyi Clan** (Ibadan, Nigeria: University Press Ltd., 1981), p. 40.

31 For details on this subject, see M. Crowder, op. cit., pp. 108-257; K. O. Dike, **100 Years of British Rule in Nigeria, 1851-1951** (Lagos, 1957); K. O. Dike, **Trade and Politics in the Niger Delta, 1830-1885** (Oxford, 1962); E. A. Afigbo, **The Warrant Chiefs: Indirect Rule in Southern Nigeria, 1891-1929** (London: Longmans, 1972); A. H. M. Kirk-Green, **Lugard and the Amalgamation of Nigeria: Documentary Record** (London, 1968); James O. Ojiako, **Nigeria: Yesterday, Today, And...** (Onitsha, Nigeria: African Educational Publishers (Nig.) Ltd., 1981), pp. 7-84.

32 Cf. M. Crowder, "Explorers and Missionaries," in: sic, op. cit., pp. 118-133.

33 Cf. M. Crowder, "the Growth of Legitimate Trade," in: sic, op. cit., pp. 134-154.

34 Cf. M. Crowder, "The Consolidation of British Interests," in: sic, op. cit., pp. 155-168.

35 Cf. M. Crowder, "Company and Consuls," in: sic, op. cit., pp. 169-190.

36 Ibid., p. 169.

37 Northern Nigeria had been profoundly influenced by the Holy War of Usman dan Fodio, and because of the coherent organization of the Fulani Empire, it presented a formidable resistance to British encroachment into its territories. Sir F. Lugard had to surmount this resistance with his force equipped with superior weapons - as seen in the words of Hilaire Belloc: "Whatever happens we have got the maxim gun and they have not." For more details, see M. Crowder, "Emirs and Maxims," in: op. cit., pp. 191-203.

38 Cf. M. Crowder, op. cit., pp. 205-207.

39 Ibid., pp. 217-218. Cf. **"Annual Report for Northern Nigeria," 1902, Nr. 409**, p. 105. For more on Indirect Rule, see Frederick D. Lugard, **Report on the Amalgamation of Northern and Southern Nigeria and Administration** (London, 1920); Donald Cameron, **Principles of Native Administration and their Application** (Lagos, Nigeria, 1934); Lord Hailey, **Native Administration in British African Territories, 5 vols.** (London, 1951); Margery Perham, **Native Administration in Nigeria** (London, 1937); Akase P. Sorkaa, "Democratic Values and Limitations of Local Government Reforms," in: Sam E. Oyovbaire, ed., op. cit., pp. 113-116.

40 "The Northern Protectorate," writes M. Crowder, "was running at a severe deficit, which was being met by a subsidy from the Southern Protectorate, and an Imperial Grant-in-Aid fro Britain.... This conflicted with the old-age colonial policy that each territory should be self-subsisting.... (I)t was felt that the prosperous Southern Protectorate could subsidize its northern neighbour until such a time as it became self-supporting...." (Ibid., p. 213.)

41 Cf. Frederick D. Lugard, **Report on the Amalgamation of Northern and Southern Nigeria and Administration** (London, 1920).

42 M. Crowder, op. cit., pp. 215-216.

43 Ibid., p. 216.

44 Ibid., p. 219.

45 Ibid.

46 Ibid., p. 221.

47 Cf. E. A. Afigbo, **The Warrant Chiefs: Indirect Rule in Southern Nigeria, 1891-1922** (London: Longmans, 1972), pp. 37ff. See also M. Crowder, op. cit., p. 231.

48 Worthy of mention are the "Aba Women's Riot" and the riots in Calabar and Opobo in 1929. See M. Crowder, op. cit., pp. 231-233. Cf. **Memorandum as to the Origin and Causes of the Recent Disturbances in Owerri and Calabar Provinces, Appendix 111**; P. K. Uchendu, **The Role of Nigerian Women in Politics, Past and Present** (Enugu, Nigeria: Fourth Dimension Publishing Co. Ltd., 1993), pp. 37-45; Harry A. Gailey, **The Road to Aba: A Study of British Administrative Policy in Eastern Nigeria** (New York: New York University Press, 1970); Sylvia Ross, **African Woman: A Study of Igbo of Nigeria** (New York: Frederick Praeger Publishers, 1965); J. C. Onwuteaka, "The Aba Riot of 1929 and Its Relation to the System of Indirect Rule," in: **The Nigerian Journal of Economics and Social Studies**, Nov. 1975.

49 M. Crowder, op. cit., p. 225.

50 For details, see M. Crowder, on "The Rise of Nigerian Nationalism," "Three Constitutions," and "Independence Achieved," in: sic, op. cit., pp. 225-273; Nnamdi Azikiwe, **Political Blueprint of Nigeria** (Lagos, Nigeria, 1943); see also his **Development of Political Parties in Nigeria** (London, 1957); Obafemi Awolowo, **Path to Nigerian Freedom** (London: Faber & Faber, 1947); J. F. Ade and Bashir Ikara, eds., **Evolution of Political Culture in Nigeria** (Ibadan: UPL and KSCAC, 1985); James O. Ojiako, op. cit., pp. 11-84; Prof. J. F. Ade Ajayi, "Decolonisation," in his **The Problems of National Integration in Nigeria: A Historic Perspective** (Ibadan: Nigerian Institute of Social and Economic Research, 1984), pp. 5-7.

51 For details of the constitutional development of Nigeria, see M. Crowder, op. cit., pp. 242-257; Kalu Ezera, **Constitutional Developments in Nigeria** (London, 1960).

52 Dr Nnamdi Azikiwe, **The Development of Political Parties in Nigeria** (London, 1957), pp. 6-8.

53 Cf. M. Crowder, op. cit., pp. 242-245.

54 Cf. Dr Nnamdi Azikiwe, **The Development of Political Parties in Nigeria**, p. 10.

55 From the **Despatch from the Governor of Nigeria to the Secretary of State for the Colonies, December 6, 1944**. Quoted in: James O. Ojiako, op. cit., p. 13.

56 Dr Kenneth Dike, in his **100 Years of British Rule in Nigeria**, comments: "Undoubtedly the Richards Constitution is a dividing line in Nigerian Constitutional development. Before it the keynote in Nigerian politics was unification towards a centralized state and the realization of a common nationality.... But with Richards' Constitution this tendency towards unification was on the whole arrested...." (Quoted in: M.Crowder, op. cit., p. 242.)

57 Cf. Dr Nnamdi Azikiwe, **The Development of Parties in Nigeria**, p. 18, and M. Crowder, op. cit., pp. 247-248.

58 Chief Bode Thomas, a Lagos prominent Lawyer, started (in 1948) to expound, in a Lagos newspaper, a political philosophy that sought to divide Nigeria into three regions. For details of his theory, see Dr Nnamdi Azikiwe, **The Development of Parties in Nigeria**, pp. 15-17.

59 Cf. M. Crowder, op. cit., pp. 245-251.

60 Cf. Dr Nnamdi Azikiwe, **The Development of Political Parties in Nigeria**, pp. 18-19.

61 Apart from the problems of the Constitution, the 1954 Conferences also treated the problems relating to "minority groups" which were agitating for their own States, like "a Midwest State" (from Western Region) and "a Calabar-Ogoja-Rivers State" (from Eastern Region). Cf. James O. Ojiako, **Nigeria: Yesterday, Today, And ...,** pp. 18-20.

62 The constituencies, when drawn, were 92 in the North, 42 each in the East and in the West, 2 in the Federal Territory, and 6 in the Southern Cameroons.

63 See **Nigerian Year Book 1958**.

64 Cf. J. O. Ojiako, op. cit., pp. 28-38.

65 Cf. ibid., pp. 38-39.

66 Cf. ibid., pp. 40-50.

67 Cf. ibid., pp. 50-51.

68 For details, see ibid., pp. 53-66.

69 This is understandable because "The British ... believed and thought that for any dependent community to aspire to the status of national independence and nationhood, it must adopt the British parliamentary form of government and demonstrate its ability to practise it." See A. Adebayo, op. cit., p. 63.

70 Quoted from **Report of the Political Bureau, March 1987** (Abuja, Nigeria: The Directorate for Social Mobilisation, "MAMSER," 1987, p. 31.

71 For details, see James O. Ojiako, op. cit., pp. 96-227.

72 Cf. Ibid., pp. 96-147.

73 Cf. ibid., pp. 150-157, 173-174, 177-183.

74 Cf. ibid., pp. 163-172.

75 This is the new name for the former "National Council for Nigeria and the Cameroons"(NCNC) since after Nigeria's independence, when Southern Cameroons ceased to be part of Nigeria.

76 Cf. ibid., pp. 158-162.

77 Cf. ibid., pp. 185-213.

78 One spectacular thing about this Alliance is that it caused the "marriage of two strange bed-fellows", the NCNC (dominant among the Igbos) and the AG (dominant among the Yorubas), the two most dominant parties in the Alliance. The two parties, before the Alliance, never saw "eye to eye" and they were more antipathetic to each other than either was to the NPC (dominant among the Hausas). Their coming together was meant to stop the NPC from dominating the oncoming Federal election.

79 Quoted in: J. O. Ojiako, op. cit., pp. 199-200. (My Brackets)

80 Cf. ibid., pp. 214-222.

81 Ibid., p. 221.

82 A. Adebayo, op. cit., p. 43.

83 Gravin Kennedy, **The Military in the Third World** (London: Gerald Duckworth & Co. Ltd., 1974) - quoted in: A. Adebayo, op. cit., p. 52.

84 Dr A. Ayonrinde, "Ethnicity in Nigeria: Implications for National Development," in: **Round-Table Meeting on Ethnicity in Nigeria: Implications for National Development** (Kuru, Nigeria: National Institute for Policy and Strategic Studies, 1983), p. 17.

85 General Olusegun Obasanjo, "The Demise of the Rule of Law in Nigeria under the Military: Another Point of View," in: Folarin Shyllon and General Olusegun Obasanjo, **The Demise of the Rule of Law in Nigeria under the Military: Two Points of View** (Ibadan, Nigeria: Institute of African Studies, University of Ibadan, c1980), p. 31.

86 For details, see Adewale Ademoyega, **Why We Struck** (Nigeria: Evan Brothers (Nigerian Publishers) Ltd., 1981); Robin Luckham, **The Nigerian Military: A Sociological Analysis of Authority and Revolt, 1960-67** (London: Cambridge University Press, 1971); Alexander A. Madiebo, **The Nigerian Revolution and the Biafran War** (Enugu, Nigeria: Fourth Dimension Publishers Co. Ltd., 1980); A. H. M. Kirk-Green, **Crisis and Conflict in Nigeria, Vol. I** (London: Oxford University Press, 1971); Major-General James J. Oluleye, **Military Leadership in Nigeria, 1966-1979** (Ibadan, Nigeria: University Press Limited, 1985); R. E. Mgbeahurike, **The Ethical Challenges of Constant Military Intervention in Nigerian Politics to Nigerian Politics - Studies in the Political Ethics of Nigeria from 1960-1989** (Roma: N. Domenici-Pe´cheux, 1989); Oyeleye Oyediran, ed., **Nigerian Government and Politics under Military Rule, 1966-79** (London: Macmillan Publishers, 1984); Okey Achike, **Groundwork of Military Law and Military Rule in Nigeria** (Yugoslavia: Fourth Dimension Publishers, 1980); B. O. Nwabueze, **Military Rule and Constitutionalism in Nigeria** (Ibadan. Owerri. Kaduna. Lagos: Spectrum Law Publishing, 1992); Folarin Shyllon and Gen. Olusegun Obasanjo, **The Demise of the Rule of Law in Nigeria under the Military: Two Points of View** (Ibadan, Nigeria: Institute of African Studies, University of Ibadan, c1980).

87 Gen. Olusegun Obasanjo, "The Demise of the Rule of Law under the Military: Another Point of View," in: F. Shyllon and Gen. O. Obasanjo, op. cit., p. 23.

88 Cf. Emeka Odimegwu-Ojukwu, **Because I Am Involved** (Ibadan. Owerri. Kaduna, Nigeria: Spectrum Books Limited, 1989), p. 31. See also Major-General Joseph N. Garba, "Military Administration and the Nigerian Society," in: **Nigeria in Transition: A Critical Examination of thr main Political, Economic and Social Aspects of the Nigerian Society** - Seminar on Nigeria in Transition, 1979, Kaduna, Nigeria, (Lagos: Federal Ministry of Information, 1980), p. 29.

89 See **Report of the Political Bureau, March 1987** (Abuja, Nigeria: Directorate for Social Mobilisation, MAMSER, 1987), p. 32; cf. **New Nigerian Newspaper**, Jan. 17, 1966.

90 The details of the pattern of the killings which accompanied the coup - the politicians killed were mainly from the North, few from the West, and hardly any from the East - and the fact that coup plotters struck in Lagos, Ibadan and Kaduna and not in Enugu, made room for the coup to be considered (especially by the people from the North) as an Igbo affair. This resurfaced and heightened the tribal sentiments (this time even among the army) that was aflame during the first Republic. This resulted in the killing of the Easterners (the Igbos in particular) by the Northerners, in a counter-coup of 1966, and lastly in a civil war. Cf. Major-General J. J. Oluleye, **Military Leadership in Nigeria, 1966-1979** (Ibadan, Nigeria: University Press Limited, Ibadan, 1985), p. 27.

91 The actual words used in the terms of invitation were: "until such a time as law and order has been restored." This implies that the military was summoned as "a police action" to save the country from final collapse, to restore law and order so as to permit, soon again, politics according to the established rules. But this was not to be. A temporary measure became a normalcy. The army entrenched itself in power and sent the civilians on an indefinite leave. As E. Odumegwu-Ojukwu put it: "The armed

forces, thus freed from the burden of its antecedents, realised not only that it could join in the contest, but also that it was itself the true arbiter of the contest which it found that it will win." (Sic, op. cit., pp. 30-31 and 33.)

92 Cf. Major-General James J. Oluleye, op. cit., pp. 29-37.

93 A. Adebayo, op. cit., p. 49.

94 A. Adebayo, op. cit., pp. 50-51; cf. Major-Gen. J. J. Oluleye, op. cit., p. 32.

95 For details, see this chapter, footnote no. 86; cf. N. U. Akpan, **The Struggle for Secession** (London: Frank Cass, 1972); Brigadier D. M. Jemibewon, **A Combatant in Government** (Nigeria: Heinemann Education Books (Nig.) Ltd., 1979); Lindsay Barret, **Danjuma: The Making of a General** (Enugu, Nigeria: Fourth Dimension Publishers Co. Ltd., 1979); Gen. Olusegun Obasanjo, **My Command** (Nigeria: Heinemann Educational Books (Nig.) Ltd., 1980).

96 He was referring to the counter-coup of July 29, 1966, organised by Northern soldiers, against the Igbos and their allies, to avenge the deaths of the Northerners killed during the first coup d'etat of Jan. 13, 1966, which they believed was master-minded by the Igbos against the Northerners. It was in this couter-coup that the Head of State, Major-Gen. Aguiyi-Ironsi, with his host, was kidnapped and murdered.

97 See Major-General James J. Oluleye, op. cit., pp. 38-167.

98 The twelve States were: North Western, North Central, Kano, North Eastern, Benue-Plateau, Kwara, Western, Lagos, Midwestern, East Central, Rivers, and South Eastern.

99 For details about Nigeria-Biafra war, see Major-Gen. J. J. Oluleye, op.cit., pp. 38-144; cf. N. U. Akpan, **The Struggle for Secession, 1966-1970** (London: Frank Cass, 1971); Zdenek Cervenka, **A History of the Nigerian War, 1967-1970** (Ibadan, Nigeria: Onibonoje Press, 1972); John de St. Jorre, **The Nigerian Civil War** (Hodder and Stoughton, 1972); A. H. M. Kirk-Greene, **Crisis and Conflict in Nigeria, Vol. II** (London: Oxford University Press, 1971); Sir Rex Niven, **The War of Nigerian Unity** (Nigeria: Evans Brothers (Nigeria Publishers) Ltd., 1970); Gen. Olusegun Obasanjo, **My Command** (Nigeria: Heinemann Educational Books (Nig.) Ltd., 1980); Alexander A. Madiebo, **The Nigerian Revolution and the Biafran War** (Enugu, Nigeria: Fourth Dimension Publishers, 1980); A. Nwankwo, **Nigeria: The Challenge of Biafra** (London: Rex Collins, 1972).

100 The **New Nigeria** of March 8, 1967, quoted the Military Governor of Northern Region, Lt-Col. H. U. Katsina, as saying, "the Army could crush the East in a few hours if the Supreme Commander gave the go-ahead."

101 Here one cannot but remember "FESTAC" (Festival of Arts and Culture) organized by Gowon's administration in 1974 for the whole of Africa. This festival engulfed millions of Naira: "Festac Town" had to be built and volvo and mercedez cars imported in their hundreds before the festival (for carrying visitors) - all at exorbitant and inflated prices. Do not ask me what became of these luxurious cars after the festival! Your guess is as good as mine.

102 A. Adebayo, op. cit., p. 53.

103 Ibid., p. 52. This was a sharp contradiction to the practice in the prime ministerial form of government in which the Minister or Commissioner is the political master of his department who decided policy, while the permanent secretary is his chief adviser and the instrument of executing policy.

104 For details, see this Chapter, Footnote No. 92.

105 In early January, 1976, Brigadier Muhammed made some promotions in the Armed Forces. He "catapulted himself from the rank of Brigadier to General and backdated it to the august date, 29 July, 1975. The backdating confused people as to the motive behind the new General.... Below him, Brigadiers Obasanjo and T. Y. Danjuma were shot up to the rank of Lieutenant-General." See J. J. Oluleye, op. cit., pp. 176-177.)

106 Major-General James J. Oluleye, op. cit., p. 169.

107 "The Governors and the Administrator of Gowon's regime ," writes Major-Gen. Oluleye, "were given a fair hearing. A panel was set up to ascertain how rich they were and how the riches were acquired. The findings were an eye sore, as many of them were on the ladder to becoming millionaires. Except Brigadiers Mobolaji Johnson and Oluwole Rotimi, others were booted out via dishonourable discharge after they were divested of their ill-gotten gains." (Ibid., p. 176.)

108 A. Adebayo, op. cit., p. 56.

109 Ibid.

110 Ibid.

111 Ibid., pp. 55f.

112 Major-General J. J. Oluleye, op. cit., p. 170; cf. A. Adebayo, op. cit., p. 54.

113 Major-General J. J. Oluleye, op. cit., pp. 170-173; cf. A. Adebayo, op. cit., p. 55: "But much as there is virtue in speed of execution and a 'no-nonsense' approach to decision-making, there is a limit to which a decision-maker can haste and hurry without doing violence to the process of decision-making. Here Murtala Mohammed's style of governance suffered from lack of careful and deliberate consideration of major policy issues."

114 What must be done before the return to civil rule included: creation of more states; creation of local government areas; conduct of local government elections; implementation of the national development plan; preparation and adoption of a new constitution; organisation of genuinely national parties; elections and installation of a civilian government; siting of a new federal capital; purging of the civil service and parastatals; and implementation of universal primary education.

115 Major-Gen. J. J. Oluleye, op. cit., pp. 173-174.

116 The new 19 States were: Anambra, Bauchi, Bendel, Benue, Borno, Cross River, Gongola, Imo, Kaduna, Kano, Kwara, Lagos, Niger, Ogun, Ondo, Oyo, Plateau, Rivers and Sokoto.

117 General Muhammed maintained a low profile in order to correct Gowon's flambouyant excesses. So he usually drove himself to places (as he did on this day of days that he met his doom) and even for functions, armed escorts were of no necessity. Hence it was very easy for the "coup boys" to plan and execute their coup without being detected by the Army or Services Intelligence Organisations.

118 The coup began at 8.30 a.m. and collapsed at 1 p.m.

119 See the unannounced strategy of the coup plotters and the Federal Government's statement on the death of Gen. Muhammed in: Maj-Gen. J. J. Oluleye, op. cit., pp. 180-184.

120 Ibid., pp. 191-193.

121 See Akase Paul Sorkaa, "Democratic Values and Limitations of Local Government Reforms," in: Sam E. Oyovbaire, **Democratic Experiment in Nigeria, Interpretative Essays** (Benin City, Nigeria: Omega Publishers, 1989), pp. 118-130.

122 Cf. ibid., pp. 112-117.

123 See **The Federal Government Guidelines on Local Government Reforms** (Kaduna: Government Printer, 1975); cf. Brigadier, Shehu M. Yar'Adua, **'Forward' to the Federal Government Guidelines on the Local Government Reforms of 1976**.

124 See A. P. Sorkaa, op. cit., p. 120. (My brackets.)

125 For the summary and criticisms of the Draft's content, see James O. Ojiako, op. cit., pp. 232-248.

126 For the 17 amendments announced by the Head of State, see James O. Ojiako, op. cit., pp. 251-254.

127 For the account of the origins and manifestoes of these parties, see R. Joseph, "Political Parties and Ideology in Nigeria," in: **Review of African Political Economy**, No. 13, May-August, 1978.

128 To win the Presidency on the first ballot, the decree says that a candidate must have not less than one-quarter of the votes cast at the election in each of at least two-thirds of the 19 States of the Federation apart from leading other contestants in the total number of votes cast at the election. But the question is: "What is two-thirds of 19 States?" - a question that puzzled the whole Nation after the presidential elections and to which there was no unanimous answer.

129 Cf. J. O. Ojiako, op. cit., pp. 300-316.

130 **Daily Times**, August 18, 1979.

131 Major-Gen. J. J. Oluleye reports on the meeting of the Supreme Military Council on August 14, 1979 at Dodan Barracks to consider section 34(2) (1)(b) of the Electoral Decree No. 73 of August 1977, and he concludes: "From the above, it will be seen that Chief Michael Ani (FEDECO Chairman) acted on the authority of General Olusegun Obasanjo (the Head of State) select group of the Supreme Military Council. He never acted on his alone as his statement will very much like the whole world to believe. Mr. Nnamani, the Attorney General of the Federation had briefed the Dodan Barracks meeting thus (as contained in the minutes): ...." (Sic, op. cit., pp. 203-204.)

132 Major-Gen. J. J. Oluleye, op. cit., p. 206.

133 **Daily Times**, August 17, 1979, p. 1.

134 A. Adebayo, op. cit., p. 57.

135 For details, see Toyin Falola and Julius Ihonvbere, **The Rise and Fall of Nigeria's Second Republic, 1979-84** (London: Zed Books Ltd., 1985); James O. Ojiako, **Nigeria: Yesterday, Today, And...** (Onitsha, Nigeria: African Educational Publishers (Nig.) Ltd., 1981), pp. 261-405; **Report of the Seminar on Nigeria In Transition: A Critical Examination of the main Political, Economic and Social Aspects of the Nigerian Society, Kaduna, Sept. 11-13, 1979** (Lagos, Nigeria: Federal Ministry of Information, 1980); Abubakar Y. Aliyu, ed., **Return to Civilian Rule** (Zaria, Nigeria: The Institute of Administration, Ahmadu Bello University, Zaria, 1982); Niyi Oniororo, **Nigeria's Future: Revolution Not Reformation** (Lagos, Nigeria: Nigerian Council of National Awareness, 1980); Abubakar S. Mohammed and Tony Edoh, ed., **Nigeria: A Republic In Ruins** (Zaria, Nigeria: Dept. of Political Science: Distributed by Ahmadu Bello University Bookshop, 1986); James O Ojiako, **First Four Years of Nigeria Executive Presidency: Success or Failure?** (1983).

136 See Abubakar Y. Aliyu, ed., "Formation of Political Parties and the 1979 Elections: Consequences and Implications," in: sic, op. cit., pp. 182-254; Oyeleye Oyediran, ed., **The Nigerian 1979 Elections** (Illupeju, Lagos, Nigeria: Macmillan Nigeria, 1981);

Ebenezar Babatope, **Nigeria, "Elections 1979": The Betrayal of a Nation** (Ibadan, Nigeria: Deto Deni Productions, 1979); Amadu Kurfi, **The Nigerian General Elections 1959 and 1979 and the aftermath** (Lagos, Nigeria: MacMillan Nigeria, 1983).

137 See the details of the agreement between the two parties on Oct. 1, 1979, in: J. O. Ojiako, op. cit., pp. 340-342. Note that this accord later, in 1981, broke up and NPP then joined the Progressive Alliance whose primary goal was fighting the NPN and dislodging it from power in 1983 - cf. T. Falola & J. Ihonvbere, op. cit., pp. 77-78.

138 J. O. Ojiako, op. cit., p. 338.

139 Cf. Ibid., pp. 346- 350.

140 Cf. ibid., pp. 352-354.

141 Ibid., pp. 357-358.

142 Cf. ibid., pp. 358-360.

143 Cf. ibid., p. 363.

144 Cf. ibid., pp. 363-364.

145 Cf. ibid., pp. 364-365.

146 Cf. ibid., p. 368.

147 Cf. ibid., pp. 368-369.

148 A. Adebayo, op. cit., p. 99; but read pp. 92-100 for details.

149 Cf. **Times International**, Jan. 14, 1980, and **New Nigerian**, Jan. 22, 1980.

150 A. Adebayo, op. cit., pp. 57-58.

151 There was this special case in 1980 when President Shagari made a state visit to Bendel State: Shagari had a personal confrontation with the State Governor, Ambrose Alli. The Governor neither came to welcome him on arrival nor did he accord Mr President the honour and respect due to him.

152 "Early in the life of the Second Republic," according to T. Falola and J. Ihonvbere, "Shagari's lieutenants always threatened the states with funds, reminding them that they would go cap in hand to Lagos for money. State governors and functionaries replied that the money belonged to all and Shagari had no right to deny any state its share." (See T. Falola and J. Ihonvbere, op. cit., p. 79.)

153 J. O. Ojiako, op. cit., pp. 390- 392.

154 A. Adebayo, op. cit., p. 57

155 Ibid.

156 Ibid., pp. 59-60, also pp. 20-23.

157 Ibid., p. 58.

158 According to T. Falola and J. Ihonvbere, "By 1981, the treasury had become virtually empty, and the Shagari government had to beg all over the world for loans.... All the nineteen state governments incurred heavy external debts, totalling about $8 billion by March 1983. The federal government itself negotiated for a N2.5 billion from the IMF, signed a N1.5 billion loan agreement with a consortium of 25 European, American and Middle East banks in July 1983, and it was also reported in November that the United States granted it credit loans totalling $180 million. These debts mortgaged the country's ability to take several autonomous decisions or policies at home or externally.... During the December 1983 Sixth Annual Congress of the UPN in Abeokuta,

Chief Awolowo ... announced that 'Nigeria has become a bankrupt nation which cannot pay its foreign indebtedness which now stands at between $16 billion and $20 billion'." (Sic, op. cit., pp. 113-114.)

159 Cf. **The Guardian**, Dec. 24 & 29, 1983; **Sunday Sketch**, Dec. 25, 1983; **Concord**, Dec. 21 and 25, 1983.

160 See **Round-Table Meeting on the 1983 General Elections** (Kuru, Nigeria: National Institute for Policy and Strategic Studies, 1983); Julius O. Ihonvbere, **The 1983 Elections and the Buhari Coup in Nigeria: Contradictions in a (Semi-) Peripheral Political Economy** (Halifax, N.S., Canada: Centre for African Studies, Dalhousie University, 1985); Toyin Falola and Julius Ihonvbere, "The 1983 Elections and the Coup," in: sic, op. cit., pp. 206-234.

161 T. Falola and J. Ihonvbere, op. cit., p. 206.

162 Ibid., p. 207.

163 Ibid., p. 211. (My italics.)

164 Ibid., p. 212.

165 Ibid. (My brackets.)

166 Ibid., p. 216. (My brackets.)

167 See, for example, Chief Obafemi Awolowo's comments in: "Awolowo Interviewed," **West Africa**, Nov. 21, 1983, p. 2674.

168 See, for example, Wole Soyinka's condemnation of NPN as the biggest defaulter in the election malpractices: in: Wole Soyinka, "The 1983 Elections and the Foreign Press," **The Guardian**, September 10, 1983.

169 See, for examples, the editorials of all non-government owned papers between August and December 1983: they exposed the nature of the Police-FEDECO-NPN alliance.

170 See the Academic Staff Union of Universities (ASUU), National Executive Council Communique, "The 1983 Election Crisis, Dangers Ahead and the Way Out", n.d., p. 2.

171 See, for an example, Major-General M. Buhari, **Text of an Address to a World Press Conference**, Lagos, Jan. 5, 1984.

172 For some of these cases and how non-neutral the courts were, see T. Falola and J. Ihonvbere, op. cit., p. 224-225.

173 A good case in point was in Ondo where FEDECO declared Chief Akin Omoboriowo (NPN) the winner and Chief Michael Ajasin (UPN) the loser of the gubernatorial election. The Supreme Court later ruled that Chief Ajasin, and not Chief Omoboriowo, was the winner.

174 "Awolowo Interviewed", **West Africa**, Nov. 21, 1983, p. 2674; cf. "Awolowo's Last Throw", **Africa Now**, May 1983, pp. 14-16.

175 Cf. ibid., pp. 225-226.

176 T. Falola and J. Ihonvbere, op. cit., p. 227.

177 **The Punch**, in its Oct. 1, 1983 issue, noted that there was really nothing to celebrate on the occasion of the country's 23rd. Independence anniversary and second inauguration ceremony, giving the fact that the waste, recklessness and abuse of power of the past four years (Oct. 1979 - Oct. 1983), and lamented the fact that the country had learnt little or nothing from its turbulent past - a fact evident from the "just concluded elections." And **Sunday Triumph**, Aug. 21, 1983, warned that the conduct of the pre-

sidential election was such that "violent change was inevitable and that Shagari and the NPN must be reminded in the event they forgot of the consequences of the rigged elections in 1965."

178 See "Averting a One-Party State," **National Concord** (Editorial), Aug. 20. 1983; and Edak B. Ene-Ita, "A One-Party System of Government in Nigeria?," **The Guardian**, Oct. 18, 1983.

179 See Gen T. Y. Danjuma (Rtd.) who, in an interview, said: "Democracy has been in jeopardy for the past four years (1979-1983). It died with the 1983 elections. The army only buried it. They didn't kill it. The politicians killed democracy...." (Sic, "12²/³ Dented our Image". Text of interview with A. Ogan, **Guardian**, Jan. 22, 1984, p. 3.)

180 Arthur A. Nwankwo, **Nigeria: The Political Transition and the Future of Democracy** (Enugu, Nigeria: Fourth Dimension Publishing Co. Ltd., 1993), p. iii.

181 Cf. S. G. Ikoku, **Nigeria's Fourth Coup d'etat: Options for Modern Statehood** (Enugu, Nigeria: fourth Dimension Publishing Co. Ltd., 1985), and T. Falola and J. Ihonvbere, op. cit., pp. 228-232.

182 S. G. Ikoku, op. cit., pp. 166-167.

183 Cf. Major-General Buhari, **New Year Day Broadcast to the Nation**, Jan. 1, 1984, in: S. G. Ikoku, op. cit., pp. 170-171.

184 T. Falola and J. Ihonvbere, op. cit., pp. 228-229. (My brackets.)

185 Ibid., p. 230.

186 Ibid., p. 229.

187 Arthur A. Nwankwo, op. cit., p. iii.

188 Ibid., p. 18.

189 For details, see Arthur A. Nwankwo, **Nigeria: The Political Transition and the Future of Democracy** (Enugu, Nigeria: Fourth Dimension Pub. Co., 1993); **Nigeria, Rebuilding Democracy** in: **TIME**, No. 48, Nov. 28, 1994; **Executive Lawlessness in the Babangida Regime:** A Report of the Civil Liberties Organisation (Lagos, Nigeria, March, 1991).

190 For details, see Arthur A. Nwankwo, **Nigeria: The Political Transition and the Future of Democracy** (Enugu, Nigeria: Fourth Dimension Pub. Co., 1993); **Nigeria, Rebuilding Democracy** in: **TIME**, No. 48, Nov. 28, 1994; Arthur Nwankwo, **Nigeria. Political Danger Signals** (Enugu, Nigeria: Fourth Dimension Publishing Co. Ltd., 1991), Arthur Nwankwo, **Retreat of Power: The Military in Nigeria's Third Republic** (Enugu, Nigeria: Fourth Dimension Publishing Co. Ltd., 1990); **Report of the Political Bureau, March 1987** (Abuja, Nigeria: The Directorate for Social Mobilisation, MAMSER, 1987); **Transition to Civil Rule Programme**, Vol. 1 (Lagos, Nigeria: Federal Government Printer, 1987); "Nigeria: Rebuilding Democracy," in: **TIME**, No. 48, Nov. 28, 1994.

191 For details about the Political Bureau, see Arthur A. Nwankwo, op. cit., pp. 36-44.

192 **Report of the Political Bureau**, March 1987, p. 3.

193 Ibid.

194 Gen. Babangida had a sixteen-phased programme: i) 3rd Quarter, 1987: establishment of the Directorate for Social Mobilization, establishment of a National Electoral Commission, and establishment of a Constitution Drafting Committee; ii) 4th Quarter, 1987: elections into the local governments on non-party basis; iii) 1st Quarter, 1988:

establishment of National Population Commission, Code of Conduct Bureau, Constituent Assembly, Code of Conduct Tribunal, and inauguration of National Revenue Mobilisation Commission; iv) 2nd Quarter, 1988: termination of Structural Adjustment Programme (SAP); v) 3rd Quarter, 1988: consolidation of the gains of Structural Adjustment Programme; vi) 1st Quarter, 1989: promulgation of a new constitution, and release of new fiscal arrangements; vii) 2nd Quarter, 1988: announcement of two recognised and registered political parties; viii) 4th Quarter, 1989: elections into local governments on political party basis; ix) 1st and 2nd Quarters, 1990: elections into legislature and state executives; x) 3rd Quarter, 1990: convening of state legislatures; xi) 4th Quarter, 1990: swearing-in of state executives; xii) 1st Quarter, 1991: census; xiii) 3rd Quarter, 1991: census; xiv) 4th Quarter, 1991: Local Government elections; xv) 1st and 2nd Quarters, 1992: elections into Federal Legislatures, and Convening of National Assembly; xvi) 3rd and 4th Quarters, 1992: Presidential elections, swearing-in of the new President and final disengagement by the Armed Forces.

195 Ibid., pp. 104-107.

196 A. A. Nwankwo, op. cit., pp. 44-54.

197 Cf. **Guardian**, March 20, 1992; **New Nigeria**, March 20, 1992; **Daily Star**, March 21, 1992; **Frankfurter Allgemeine**, 14. April 1992, p. 7.

198 Cf. A. A. Nwankwo, op. cit., pp. 46-54.

199 Cf. ibid., pp. 54-62.

200 Ibid., pp. 60-62.

201 Cf. ibid., pp. 63-76.

202 Cf. ibid., pp. 76-80.

203 Ibid., pp. 78f.

204 For details of the transfer agenda, see A. Nwankwo, op. cit., pp. 99-284

205 Cf. ibid., pp. 109-126.

206 Ibid., p. 110.

207 Ibid., p. 117. (My brackets.)

208 Ibid.

209 For the general conduct and result of this election, see **Newswatch**, April 8, 1991, pp. 18-19; cf. A. Nwankwo, op. cit., p. 126.

210 On the "open ballot" system, see **Newswatch**: April 8, 1991, pp. 18-19; - Nov. 23, 1992, p. 10.

211 A. Nwankwo, op. cit., p. 126.

212 Cf. ibid., pp. 130-136; also **Newswatch**, Oct. 7, 1991, pp. 12-18.

213 Cf. ibid., pp. 130-136.

214 Cf. **Newswatch**, Dec. 23, 1991, pp. 27-33.

215 Cf. ibid., pp. 136-145; also **Newswatch**, Oct. 21, 1991, pp. 21-23; - Oct. 28, 1991, pp. 9-13; - Nov. 4, 1991, pp. 9-16; - Dec. 23, 1991, pp. 34-35; - Dec. 30, 1991, pp. 13-18.

216 A. Nwankwo, op. cit., p. 137; also **Newswatch**, Nov. 11, 1991, pp. 11-12.

217 Cf. **Newswatch**, Dec. 9, 1991, pp. 9-16.

218 Cf. **Newswatch**, Dec. 30, 1991, pp. 25-27.

219 Cf. A. Nwankwo, op. cit., pp. 148-151; also **Newswatch**, June 8, 1992, pp. 33-35; - July 13, 1992, pp. 9-16; - July 20, 1992, pp. 13-20; - Aug. 3, 1992, pp. 9-15.

220 A. Nwankwo, op. cit., p. 148.

221 Ibid., p. 149.

222 Cf. **Newswatch**, Dec. 21, 1992, pp. 21-22.

223 A. Nwankwo, op. cit., pp. 151-152, 241-284; also **Newswatch**, Aug. 17, 1992, pp. 11-18; - Sept.14, 1992, pp. 28-30; - Sept. 28, 1992, pp. 24-26; - Oct. 5, 1992, pp. 46-49; - Oct. 19, 1992, pp. 14-19; **TELL**, Oct. 12, 1992, pp. 16-18.

224 Cf. **Newswatch**, Nov. 16, 1992, p. 14; - Dec. 7, 1992, pp. 14-20.

225 Cf. Text of President Ibrahim Babangida's press briefing in Abuja, Oct. 9, 1992, in: **Sunday Sketch**, Oct. 11, 1992, p. 21.

226 Cf. **Newswatch**, Oct. 26, 1992, pp. 10-17.

227 "Option A4" involves the selection of state-flag bearers of the two political parties by the Ward, Local Government and State Congresses of the parties. For more information on option A4, see **Newswatch**: Nov. 23, 1992; - Feb. 1, 1993, pp. 9, 16-17; - March 8, 1993, p. 8; - March 29, 1993, p. 6; - April 12, 1993, p. 9; April 26, 1993, pp. 15 & 17; **African Concord**, May 10, 1993, p. 31.

228 Ray Ekpu, "Gowon's Waterloo," in: Preface to Cover, **Newswatch**, March 8, 1993, p. 8; cf. the same issue of **Newswatch**, pp. 9-15, the article, "Crash of an Ambition," which describes how Yakubu Gowon, Nigeria's ex-Head of State, was defeated during the primaries in his Local Government Area.

229 Cf. **Newswatch**, March 29, 1993, pp. 9-17.

230 Cf. **Newswatch**, June 21, 1993, p. 13.

231 Cf. ibid., pp. 10-18.

232 Cf. **Newswatch**, June 28, 1993, pp. 18-21.

233 Cf. ibid., pp. 8-21.

234 **Newswatch**, July 5, 1993, pp. 16-18.

235 Cf. **TELL**, July 26, 1993, pp. 14-20.

236 Cf. **Newswatch**, July 5, 1993, pp. 9-10.

237 Cf. **African Concord**, July 19, 1993, pp. 14-19, esp. p. 15.

238 Cf. **Newswatch**, July 5, 1993, pp. 14-15; - August 16, 1993, pp. 13-14; - August 30, 1993, pp. 28-29.

239 Cf. **African Concord**, July 19, 1993, pp. 20-25; also **Newswatch**: Aug. 9, 1993, pp. 18-20; - Aug. 23, 1993, pp. 11-15; - Aug. 30, 1993, pp. 26-27.

240 Cf. **Newswatch**, August 2, 1993, pp. 9-13.

241 Cf. "Crack-down: War against the press," in: **Newswatch**, Aug. 9, 1993, pp. 10-14; also "The Big Noose" in: **Newswatch**, Aug. 30, 1993, pp. 30-32.

242 Cf. **Newswatch**, Aug. 30, 1993, pp. 8-14.

243 Cf. "Shonekan Takes Over," in: **Newswatch**, Sept. 6, 1993, pp. 10-16. (The list of the members of Interim Federal Executive Council is found on p. 12.) See also "Babangida's Last Minutes" in: **Newswatch**, Sept. 20, 1993, pp. 10-15.

244 A. Nwankwo, op. cit., p. iii.

245 Cf. Sam Olukoya, "Walking a Tight-Rope", in: **Newswatch**, Sept. 20, 1993, pp. 20-21.

246 Cf. Wole Soyinka, in an interview with Newswatch, in: **Newswatch**, Sept. 27, 1993, pp. 32-37.

247 Cf. **Newswatch**, Sept. 20, 1993, pp. 21-22.

248 Cf. **Newswatch**, Oct. 18, 1993, pp. 12-15.

249 Cf. **Newswatch**, Nov. 15, 1993, pp. 12-17.

250 Cf. **Newswatch**, Nov. 22, 1993, pp. 12-16. Even Tai Solarin, educationist and social critic, argued (in **Newswatch**, Nov. 22, 1993, pp. 15-23) that "if the election of June 12 is not upheld, Nigeria should be allowed to break up."

251 Cf. Godwin Agbroko, "Change of Guard", in: **Newswatch**, Nov. 29, 1993. pp. 9-14; see also the excerpts of the maiden broadcast by Gen. Abacha on Nov. 18, 1993, in: ibid., p. 18, and Nats Agbo's "Good Bye, Aso Rock," in: ibid., pp. 19-20.

252 See the full text of Shonekan's speech to members of the ING, Nov. 17, 1993, in: **Newswatch**, Nov. 29, 1993, p. 21.

253 Ray Ekpu, "Not for love of Soldiers," in: **Newswatch**, Dec. 6, 1993, p. 6.

254 Cf. "Nigeria: Rebuilding Democracy", **TIME**, No. 48, Nov. 28, 1994.

255 Cf. Muyiwa Akintunde who, in order to show Abacha's lust for power, described him as "Cat with Nine Lives" - in: **Newswatch**, Nov. 29, 1993, pp. 15-17.

256 Cf. ibid., p. 18.

257 Cf. Utibe Ukim, "Cancerous Babies: Government vows to fix Nigeria's ailing public institutions. But can it put them on the straight and narrow path?" in: **Newswatch**, Dec. 6, 1993, pp. 17-18.

258 Cf. Muyiwa Akintunde, "Firming Up: Abacha moves gingerly and assembles a rainbow team. Can they solve the problems?" in: **Newswatch**, Dec. 6, 1993, pp. 11-16.

259 One good example is the conflicting statements from the members of the Federal Executive Council on the constitutional conference. See Godwin Agbroko, "Flips and Flops," in: **Newswatch**, Jan. 17, 1994, pp. 10-14.

260 Cf. ibid., p. 10

261 Cf. **Newswatch**, Jan. 31, 1994, pp. 14-15.

262 Cf. **Newswatch**, Nov. 7, 1994, pp. 8-11.

263 Cf. **Newswatch**, Nov. 21, 1994, pp. 30-33.

264 CF. **Newswatch**, Aug. 7, 1995, pp. 18-29.

265 Cf. **Newswatch**, Aug. 21, 1995, pp. 23-24.

266 Cf. **Newswatch**, Jan. 31, 1994, p. 23. Note that human rights activists, led by Gani Fawehinmi and seven other lawyers, challenged the composition of the Commission. They went to a Lagos high court on Jan. 18 asking the court to restrain the inauguration of the Commission on the ground that 18 out of the 19 members were morally unfit, because they were among those indicted by Sani Abacha, as a Brigadier-General, when he announced the coup of 1993 that terminated the Second Republic.

267 Cf. ibid., pp. 24-25.

268 Cf. Nats Agbo, "What Do We Want?," in: **Newswatch**, Feb. 28, 1994, pp. 10-15.

269 Cf. **Newswatch**, April 11, 1994, pp. 27-28.

270 Cf. **Newswatch**, April 4, 1994, pp. 10-13, 18 & 19.

271 Cf. Nats Agbo, "Phase One," in: **Newswatch**, May 9, 1994, pp. 10-14.

272 Cf. **Newswatch**, May 23, 1994, p. 23.

273 Cf. **Newswatch**, May 30, 1994, pp. 10-16.

274 Cf. **Newswatch**, June 13, 1994, pp. 10-15.

275 Cf. Abiola's arrest, **Newswatch**, July 4, 1994, pp. 9-15; Abiola's declaration of himself as president on June 11, **Newswatch**, June 27, 1994, pp. 8-12; Abiola's preparation for June 12, 1994, **Newswatch**, June 6, 1994, pp. 9-16 and June 20, 1994, pp. 11-15; Abiola on trial for treason, **Newswatch**, July 18, 1994, pp. 9-14 and Aug. 8, 1994, pp. 8-10; Trade Unions fight for Abiola, **Newswatch**, July 25, 1994, pp. 10-15.

276 Cf. **Newswatch**, July 11, 1994, pp. 11-16; - July 18, 1994, pp. 15-16.

277 Cf. **Newswatch**, Oct. 10, 1994, pp. 7-8; - Nov. 21, 1994, p. 36.

278 Cf. **Newswatch**, Oct. 17, 1994, pp. 17-18.

279 Cf. **Newswatch**, Dec. 19, 1994, pp. 12-16. Note that the Constitutional Confrerence in May 1995 reversed this decision and gave Gen. Abacha a blank cheque to determine when to go. Cf. **Newswatch**, May 8, 1995, pp. 10-13.

280 Cf. ibid., pp. 17-19.

281 Cf. **Newswatch**, May 9, 1994, pp. 15-16.

282 Cf. **Newswatch**, May 16, 1994, pp. 11-18 (fabled wealth of the military); - Dec. 12, 1994, pp. 21-22 (military involvement in armed robberies).

283 Cf. **Newswatch**, Dec. 12, 1994, pp. 14-20.

284 Cf. **Newswatch**, Nov. 28, 1994, pp. 13-18.

285 Think of the incessant strikes by teachers and staff of our institutions of learning; think of the workers' strike organised by the Nigerian Labour Congress (NLC) and of Oil-Workers' strike that nearly paralysed the country. Cf. **Newswatch**, Aug. 1, 1994, pp. 24-28; - Aug. 8, 1994, pp. 15-17; - Aug. 15, 1994, pp. 10-16.

286 See Government's hard-line position on agitations by trade unions and others, in: **Newswatch**, Aug. 29, 1994, pp. 10-14; the Government(?) offensive against pro-democracy groups, in: **Newswatch**, Sept. 12, 1994, pp. 8-13; the proscription of *Guardian*, *Concord* and *Punch* groups of newspapers by Government, in: **Newswatch**, Sept. 19, 1994, pp. 26-31.

287 Cf. **Newswatch**, March 13, 1995, pp. 12-18; - March 27, 1995, pp. 10-14; - June 12, 1995, pp. 17-18; - July 31, 1995, pp. 8-14 and Aug. 7, 1995, pp. 9-14 (on local and international plea not to kill the alleged coup plotters).

288 Cf. **Newswatch**, March 27, 1995, p. 18.

289 Cf. **Newswatch**, May 15, 1995, pp. 28-29.

290 The Constitutional Conference reversed its last Dec. 6 decision that fixed Jan. 1, 1996, as the terminal date for the Abacha regime. It now gave Gen. Abacha a blank cheque to determine when to go. Cf. **Newswatch**, May 8, 1995, pp. 10-13.

291 Cf. **Newswatch**, July 10, 1995, pp. 8-13.

292 Cf. **Newswatch**, Aug. 7, 1995, pp. 15-16.

293 Cf. **Newswatch**, Oct. 9, 1995, pp. 13-18.

3. THE PROBLEM OF DEMOCRACY IN NIGERIA

From the last chapter, it is obvious that democracy is not new in Nigeria and/or to Nigerians. "Before the collapse of the First Republic, it was fashionable to describe Nigeria as an African model of democracy. This sentiment was expressed in different ways by Nigerians, both academics and politicians, as well as by foreign observers."[1] At independence, on 1 October 1960, Nigeria opted for or, rather, inherited from her colonial master (the Great Britain) the parliamentary system of democracy. This system of democracy lasted only six years. For, in 1966, the army, not satisfied with the state of affairs in Nigeria, sent the corrupt, ethnocentric, and confused politicians packing, and with them all democratic institutions and policies. Then in 1979, when the army was ready and willing to withdraw to its barracks, another democratic era began in Nigeria. This time around, Nigeria, not satisfied with the British parliamentary system, opted for the American presidential system of democracy. This again was short-lived - only four years. In 1983 the army struck again to re-impose military dictatorship. Since then all the efforts, time and money expended towards re-introducing democracy in Nigeria have not borne much fruit, even though there is today, more than ever before, much yearning and longing for democracy.

Why has democracy failed to take root in Nigeria? Is the fault with the systems of democracy Nigeria had adopted or with the Nigerian managers of the systems? Why can democracy not thrive in a country (Nigeria) so blessed with huge natural resources and personnel?[2] Confronted with such questions, everybody appears to be helpless. As Augustus Adebayo rightly observes: "An intriguing aspect of the problem is that everyone appears to be aware that public affairs are not being run the way they ought to be. Everyone grumbles under his breath at the sorry state of public affairs."[3] Are Nigerians then incapable of good government, of democracy? I would not want to buy William Bossman's view that "the Negroes are all without exception crafty, villainous and fraudulent and very seldom to be trusted and a man of integrity is as rare among them as a white falcon."[4] Nor would I accept Sir Richard Burton's view that "the Negro is always a child, that never develops, and that the race is an inferior one which neither education nor anything else can raise to the level of the White."[5] Both of these are definitely biased and rooted in racism.

The black person, and here the Nigerian, is definitely very capable of democracy. The fact is that Nigeria, as a nation, is still very young, and so it falters and makes mistakes - stumbles and falls - in its search for lasting democracy. But Nigeria must get up, be on its feet again and keep moving ahead. Nigeria must learn from its past mistakes, to reach its destination and goal: to become a disciplined, fair, just and humane society - a democratically developed state.

It is the onus of this chapter to delve into and probe the problem of democracy in Nigeria: to seek out those things that hinder the growth of enduring democracy in Nigeria, in order to enable the country learn from its mistakes and then forge ahead to build a stable and lasting democratic society. Thus much attention shall be paid to the negative - rather than to the positive - aspects of the Nigerian polity. And the focus will be on the following headings: national unity factor, leadership factor, socio-economic factor, justice and security, indiscipline and corruption, and mass media factor.

3.1. National unity factor[6]

"Every kingdom divided against itself is heading for ruin; and no town, no household divided against itself can stand." (Matt. 12:25) These words of wisdom from Christ brings to light how difficult it is for Nigeria to stand as a nation when its component parts are divided against each other and hence how difficult it is for democracy to thrive in such an atmosphere of disunity.

Some 32 years ago, the then President of Nigeria, Dr Nnamdi Azikiwe, in his independence anniversary broadcast on Oct. 1, 1964, was very much concerned about the fragile unity of the country. He asked: "Is Nigeria four years after independence and a year after becoming a republic, still a group of tribes or is it a nation?" And referring to election struggles he asked why it was that in the first year of Nigeria's existence as a Republic, our leaders took delight "in beating the tom-tom of tribal hatred and fouling the air of God with vituperations against ourselves, all in the name of politics?"[7] How would Nigerians answer the above two questions today (32 years later)? The answer is that Nigeria is still today "a group of tribes," still struggling to become "a nation," and that our leaders are still very much "beating the tom-tom of tribal hatred" and of religious discriminations, "and fouling the air of God with vituperations against ourselves, all in the name of politics." In other words, Nigeria is still very much a house divided against itself. Unity is still a big problem in Nigeria and has to be addressed by Nigerians. As E. Odumegwu-Ojukwu rightly observes: "The source of our problem is rooted in our fear of unity - ... our lack of will to transform our primordial instincts and create a modern polity. It is ... a matter for great regret that this country of ours has suffered greatly as a result of the all pervasive disunity that has characterised all government action since our accession to independence in 1960. This disunity has distorted, complicated and to a large extent stultified every developmental effort undertaken by government. The effect of the shibboleth called dichotomy is so well-known that it has become a cancer in our body politic. Because we have no cure, and because we do not even seek a cure, it continues to spread thereby enhancing its virulence. Today, when we look at Nigeria - no matter from what direction, no matter the focus of perspective, everything which we see bears the frightful aspect of a dichotomy: the north/south dichotomy, the east/west dichotomy, majority/minority dichotomy, muslim/christian dichotomy, military/politician dichotomy, socialist/capitalist dichotomy, urban/rural dichotomy, the traditional/modern dichotomy.... The list is long and seemingly interminable."[8]

The problem of unity in Nigeria could be attributed to the faulty foundation of the Nigerian state, ethnicism and religious-divide.

3.1.1. Faulty foundation of the Nigerian state

Britain has been and is still being accused of having sowed the seed of disunity in Nigeria.[9] As shown in the previous chapter, before the arrival of the Europeans, the area now known as Nigeria bubbled with myriads of ethnic groups and dynamic nationalities each with its own well-defined system of government that compelled compliance with societal laws and norms. After subjugating them (by military force), Britain (in 1914) amalgamated these socially and culturally diverse groups without consulting them and without a consensus from them. According to Dr Olu Akinkoye, "the British used force to persuade the citizens. There was very little effort by the British to resocialize the citizens into the membership of a larger society known as Nigeria. Their terms of reference in the colonies did not include the development of national consciousness in the colonies."[10] Evidently, no nation could be built with force, but with the mutual consent of the different groups willingly agreeing to form one nation - a type of social contract. This agrees with Shepherd's view that for any nation, national unity and internal stability and national development for that matter, are determined to a large extent by the presence of national consensus and public order.[11] Moreover, the amalgamation was without commensurate uniform administrative policies and strategies, including its constitutions, thereby leaving the country more divided than united. For example, Lugard's administration perpetrated tribal consciousness in Nigeria. Lugard always showed preference for the North over the South. For instance, it was obvious that Lugard centralized the treasury to enable him "divert revenue that earlier had been properly the South's to balance the Northern deficit.... He even hoped to shift his government headquarters from South to the North which was his spiritual home."[12] Another example is Richards' Constitution (1946) which principle of regionalism has been severely criticised as being the foundation of tribalism in Nigerian politics. In short, the colonial masters, for their selfish economic interests, preferred a divided Nigeria to a unified one, and so no attempt was made at the integration of the different groups. Hence Nigeria lacked and still lacks a common character.[13] Let me cite some authors to buttress my points. According to Henry I. Ejembi:

> The colonial establishment was able to learn the essential lesson of the close unity forged by the different elements in the early nationalist struggle.... This essential lesson was that such unity was dangerous to continued imperialist control of Nigeria after 'independence' if the system was rid of ethnic tensions. This lesson they incorporated into the Richards Constitution of 1946 and the Mcpherson Constitu-

> tion of 1951 by urging the entrenchment in the Constitution of 'ethnic diversity' and what they glibly referred to as 'unity in diversity in Nigeria's national life'.[14]

In the same vein Prof. Sanya Onabamiro writes:

> The British ruled over Nigeria for sixty odd years. Basing their administration on the classical Roman doctrine of 'Divide and Rule', it was naturally not in their interest to foster unity among the various ethnic groups in the country, let alone employ education as an instrument for shaping the society. This doctrine of 'Divide and Rule' was institutionalised in the Arthur Richards' Constitution which carved the country into ethnic Regions, each to seek its own interest and develop along its own lines, at its own pace, the long-term consequences of which are still very much with us today.[15]

On his part, Prof. J. F. Ade Ajayi observes that:

> For the different peoples, incorporation into Nigeria was the result of force, conquest and loss of sovereignty, not of any consultation or desire to develop existing linkages. Common subjection to British colonial rule did provide new integrative factors such as British statutory laws, the railways and network of roads, new administrative, mining, and port urban centres where workers from different parts of the country mixed. But British colonial rule also discouraged some existing linkages. As each part of the country was encouraged to produce for the British market and to import essential goods also from abroad, the network of trade routes for internal trade and exchange were weakened. Prosperity began to be sought more from dependence on the foreign market than on mutual interdependence within an internal trading system.
>
> The Indirect Rule system, developed in the North between 1900 and 1914, and extended to southern Nigeria after 1914, was based on the principle of semi-autonomous Native Authorities. This fostered a type of 'divide and rule' policy....
>
> ...(There) was great unevenness in the spread of development associated with colonial rule. In particular, whereas missionaries were left relatively free and were even subsidised to establish schools and training colleges in Southern Nigeria, the colonial office held a tighter rein on education in Northern Nigeria. This was done partly to discourage Christian missionary influence on western education in the North, and partly also to keep education as much as possible as a factor to strengthen the abilities of the emirs and the old aristocratic classes to rule, and discourage the premature rise of what was called an 'educated proletariat'. This uneven development has become a major factor in sewing the seeds of distrust and fear of domination among the different peoples, thus strengthening the forces of internal group solidarity.
>
> ... The Clifford Constitution of 1922 ... provided for some elective representation of Lagos and Calabar and nominated representation of other Southern provinces but allowed no representatives of the Northern provinces to sit on the Legislative Council. The Governor in his discretion legislated for the North.... This also meant that until the Richards Constitution came into effect in 1946, representatives of northern and southern peoples had no opportunity to sit together to debate.[16]

The end result of all these is that, at independence in 1960, the colonial masters bequeathed the Nigerians, instead of one nation or one Nigeria, "three

Nigerias". In other words, "political independence was attained against a background of 'three Nigerias', controlled by three often hostile political parties. The system was thus marked by a weak centre, a lot of acrimony and instability. The striving to overcome this built-in instability was to become one of the major factors constraining the development of democratic practice in Nigeria."[17]

3.1.2. Ethnicism

In his book "How to be a Nigerian", in the chapter on "Unity in Diversity", Peter Enahoro writes:

> Europeans talk about weather; *Nigerians talk about tribe*.
> The Nigerian society is strictly organised into a variety of tribes. So consuming is the devotion to tribe that if St. Peter were a Nigerian, four-fifths of us would be wasting our time in church and Heaven would soon spill out The Gatekeeper's tribal group of Nigerians.
> Tribes transcend individuality.
> You would hear one Nigerian describing another Nigerian to a third Nigerian. If the third Nigerian is at sea and does not know to whom his informant is referring, the first Nigerian would then bring him ashore with: 'I am talking about that Yoruba man.'
> ....
> But the reference to his tribe already points to the kind of man he is *certain* to be. The gentleman in question may never be known by name throughout the conversation, but the fact that he is Yoruba, or Ibo, or Efik is sufficient to identify him.
> Not only is his social, political and economic outlook determined immediately, even his possible reaction to a given situation, his secret thoughts, are reasonably suspected on the understanding that members of the same tribe are all alike!
> ....
> All members of a tribe are brothers.
> This feeling of close affinity in the tribe is more than fraternal sentiment. It fills the place of employment agency....[18]

From Peter's "Unity in Diversity" one can decipher three realities: firstly, there exists ethnic pluralism or diversity in Nigeria - "The Nigerian society is strictly organised into variety of tribes;" secondly, ethnic pluralism is good in itself - "All members of a tribe are brothers;" and thirdly, ethnic pluralism can be bad when it degenerates into ethnicism - "This feeling of close affinity in the tribe is more than fraternal sentiment. It fills the place of employment agency." These three realities will guide our discussion on ethnicism as a hindrance to the rooting of democracy in Nigeria.

We have already seen that Nigeria is a complex and pluralistic society: with as many as between 250 and 400 nationalities or ethnic groups, each with its own language and customs. So there is nothing like "Nigerian culture" or "Nigerian language". "What we often erroneously refer to as Nigerian culture is a mechanically juxtaposed and uncommunicating cultural traditions."[19] Ethnic or cultural diversity is not bad in itself nor does inter-ethnic competition need to breed disunity. Surely, a country with a variety of cultures is today the envy of the world. But the situation changes and becomes bad when the different cultural patterns are in opposition to one another - that is, when the people become ethnocentric.[20] Hence we must distinguish "ethnic pluralism" from "ethnicity", using the words of Prof. O. Otite:

> ... ethnicity does not consist in mere ethnic or cultural heterogeneity, the mere identification of ethnic or cultural group entities.... Mere socio-cultural diversity poses no real problem. What is crucial comprises the interactions and the interrelationships as the various identifiable socio-cultural groups struggle and manouvre themselves over the control of access to the nation's scarce resources. In the process, there is always the tendency for people not only to place their ethnic values and interests over those of other ethnic groups but also over those of its nation. Hence ethnicity becomes not only a cultural phenomenon but also a structural category, an instrument of social organization in fields of competition. Any rewards in this parochial endeavour strengthens desire for, and the success in, consolidating ethnic boundaries.[21]

We have also seen that colonial rule, rather than enhance the richness of cultural diversity in Nigeria, instituted and encouraged ethnicism by dividing the country into three regions, each dominated by one tribe. Thus, "the history of Nigeria's independence since British rule to date has witnessed a progressive growth of tribalism into the structural centre of our national development. During the colonial rule, no attempt was made at the integration of the tribes. They ruled autocratically through alliance with traditional rulers, professionals, businessmen and bureaucrats."[22] And "after independence, the elites who took over from the colonialists were themselves not sufficiently socialised into any Nigerian tradition. They were by and large members of their own ethnic groups."[23] And so ethnicism became a canker worm in the fabrics of the Nigerian polity.

Therefore, the problem of ethnicism - or tribalism,[24] as some would prefer to call it - is very much with us. It clouds and colours all our thoughts, words and deeds. "Ethnic mistrust and tension," laments C. Gahia, "run high. Tribal loyalties remain stronger than national loyalty. All the tribes complain of one form of domination or the other. The Hausa-Fulani are accused by the other tribes of monopolising political power. The Hausa-Fulani accuse the Yoruba of dominating the economy and the public service. The Igbo blame their woes on Hausa-Fulani political domination and Yoruba domination of the economy and the federal bureaucracy. Minorities accuse the major tribes of political, religious and cultural oppression.... Tribal sentiments permeate national life in Nigeria. Everything in the country has its own tribal tag. Allegations of ethnic discrimination in appointments, jobs, admission into schools, business transactions and the sharing of amenities cut across and can be heard in every state of the federation.... Every leader the country has produced has been seen primarily in tribal or sectional terms. And there is hardly any official policy that has not been seen to derive from the sole aim of promoting one ethnic interest or the other."[25]

Among other factors that aggravate ethnicism in Nigeria - such as place of birth and abode: 70% of children in Nigeria are born and live most of their lives in rural villages and so "the child becomes thoroughly initiated into 'his ethnic system' before learning any other 'system'," unlike in the more developed countries where a greater proportion of children are born in cities, and grow up in heterogeneous urban places;[26] the problem of acute scarcity of resources;[27] the colonial urban setting;[28] the myth of cultural diversity[29] - pernicious manipulations from the elite takes the first place. The Nigerian elite manipulate ethnic sentiments to their own selfish interest and benefit. According to Prof. O. Otite, "the elite that mobilize members of their ethnic groups on the basis of their shared cultural symbols and sentiments camouflage their personal and emerging class interest. In other words, those who gain from ethnicity are the elite and their various agents, clients, or sub-elite. Hence ethnicity becomes a cover, an instrument of exploitation of their generality of the underprivileged members of an ethnic group, and a strategy of controlling and distributing, not contributing to, national resources."[30] And Alhaji Shehu Usman agrees: "the educated elite, more than anybody else, must bear the blame for the present confusion. For, the flames of most of the rancour and bitterness that have poisoned our political system have been fanned by this educated elite, who should know better, but who have allowed themselves to be blinded by selfish ambition."[31]

In the end, one sees that ethnicism is an evil wind that blows Nigeria no good: it militates against national integration and the rooting of democracy in the country. In the words of I. M. Akor: "In Nigeria over the years, ... it is because of this ethnic form of social and political organisation that the democratic process has failed to function normally."[32]

3.1.3. Religious-divide

There are three main religions in Nigeria: Christianity, Islam and Traditional religions. About 49.0% of Nigerians are Christians, about 45.0% Muslims, and about 6.0% traditional religionists. This discussion on "religious-divide" will be concerned with Christianity and Islam which are less accommodative of each other and tend "to be more combative, particularly Islam since the idea of reformist Islam is to exclude all other religions and to seek to create an Islamic theocracy."[33] Traditional religions will be left out because they are generally accommodating to both Christianity and Islam and thus pose no threat to national unity.

Christianity and Islam "drew its followers into a common culture, but also urged them to remain combative and exclusive. As each believer was integrated, he was also alienated from his neighbour who did not follow his religion."[34] O. Nnoli agrees:

> Religion was another divisive factor in the social relations among Nigerians arising from precolonial differences. In this respect, the relevant distinction is between Muslims and non-Muslims. Islam was introduced into Northern Nigeria about five hundred years ago. However, its effects on the population was greatly intensified and its area of dominance expanded after 1804 when Fulani religious leaders in the town of Sokoto waged a holy war that brought most of Hausaland under the orthodox Islamic leadership of the Sultan of Sokoto. In the South, on the other hand, only a portion of Yorubaland came under islamic influence. The rest remained animist. During the colonial period many of them embraced Christianity, in some cases with enthusiasm, even fanaticism.
>
> Religious differences have a high potential for separating people from one another. Throughout history these differences have been the basis of tension, animosity, hostility, and even war. Many times a certain fanaticism is associated with religious beliefs which excludes social relations with people of different religion, or hampers mutual trust and confidence when such relations happen to exist.... For example, the orthodox Islamic doctrine in the North which confines married women to the purdah makes moslem men unconfortable when they interact with non-Moslems accompanied by their wives, who do not even wear veils.
>
> Religious beliefs and feelings have historically been among the strongest and most enduring factors compelling human beings to cluster together in exclusive communities sharing bonds of association....
>
> Such exclusiveness increases the social distance between members of different religious groups. In Nigeria, this fact is reinforced by the distinction which Islam makes between the believer and the unbeliever. This distinction explicitly discourages serious mutually rewarding interaction between members of the two groups. It conceives of their relationship as essentially a struggle in which one will inevitably prevail over the other and in the conduct of this struggle, the jihad or holy war is a self-fulfilling instrument.... One of the consequences of this distinction is the tendency for a long time of the Moslem North to be oriented to Mecca and the Arab world in general.... The inevitable consequence of this external orientation is the increase in the social distance between the North and South of Nigeria.[35]

What more, Christianity and Islam were relatively ethnic bound: the North was essentially muslim, the East essentially christian, and the West a mixture of both. This situation was made worse by the colonial masters who, knowingly or unknowingly, instituted the religious-divide, like they did ethnicism, in Nigeria. "As a deliberate policy, and in deference to the reservations of varying interest groups, Christian missionaries ... were kept out of the Northern region. This had the effect, first of all, of accentuating differences in the country as between the 'Muslim North' and the 'Christian South', thus making religion an important ingredient in regional politics in colonial Nigeria."[36] And Nigerians being naturally a religious people, they are prepared to lay down their lives in defence of their faith. This explains why any issue touching on religion is always very sensitive and, at times, explosive. No wonder Sir Alhaji Abubakar Tafawa Balewa warned that "it would be the end of happiness in this country when religion is brought into politics."[37] This also explains why there are sometimes religious disturbances (between Muslims and Christians) in the country.[38] To cite some examples, there were religious riots in Kano - Yan Awaki Ward (1980), in Maiduguri - Bulunkuti

(1982), in Kaduna - Rigasa (1983), in Yola - Jimeta (1984), in Gombe - Maitatsine (1985), again in Kaduna - Kafanchan (1987). This further explains why Nigeria is a secular state: its constitution maintains the separation of state and religion while upholding the "right to freedom of thought, conscience and religion."[39]

Despite the secular nature of Nigeria, and in spite of the watchful eyes of the society and the "innate" desire of the government not to carry out any act which could be seen as favouring a particular religion, cases of policies motivated by religious influence abound. The politicians are still full of ethnic and religious sentiments. And there are evidences of manipulation of religion. As with ethnicism, there are cases of political offices being distributed on religious affiliation lines. Sometimes, political decisions are made to please particular groups because of religious pressures from members: like the formulation of the foreign policy attitude toward the Middle-East problems,[40] or the attempt by the Babangida administration in 1987 to force Nigeria into the Organisation of Islamic Congress (OIC).[41]

Again, as in the case of ethnicity, the Nigerian elites are only too ready to exploit or manipulate religion whenever they think it suits their immediate political advantage to do so, without regard to the longer term implications.[42] Let me cite some examples. Politicians go under the shadow of religion during their campaigns - presenting an election as a battle between Muslims and Christians or between Catholics and Protestants - in order to whip up religious sentiments, to enkindle the fire of hatred (or revolt), in their followers against "the imagined enemy." The first military coup d'etat (1966) was seen as the calculated act of the christian-east against the muslim-north, just as the consequent massacre of the easterners by the northerners was regarded as the calculated act of the muslims against the christians. The civil war that followed these confusions was termed a war between Christians and Muslims. There was also the so-called "sharia debate" in the Constituent Assembly. "In the course of its deliberations," Adigun A. B. Agbaje writes, "discussions on provisions for a parallel Sharia (Muslim) legal system up to the highest appellate levels in the country led to the emergence of two hostile religious camps, viz: Muslim, which endorsed the proposals, and Christian, which opposed it. The opposition carried the day but the battle was carried by embittered assemblymen into the public and the press. Again, press coverage followed predictable lines, with the *New Nigeria* (a Northern newspaper) leading the battle for the adoption of the proposals. The administration had to intervene at the highest level to defuse the tension which, in fact, was beginning to create camps within the military itself."[43] There are many other examples of the manipulation of religion in Nigeria.[44]

Because of the problems of mutual distrust and of conflicts and unrests associated with religious divisiveness (based on ethnic divisions) in Nigeria, it is extremely difficult to foster unity in the country and, therefore, difficult for democracy to find a firm footing.

3.1.4. Consequences of the divisive factors

Two outstanding consequences of the divisive factors demand our attention here The first is that Nigerians are made strangers in their fatherland. There is lack of mutual acceptance of one another's full citizenship of Nigeria. One is only an acceptable citizen within one's region. Once outside one's region, one's citizenship diminishes (if not ends). For example, thirty-six years after independence, "Nigerians are only granted contract appointment in certain areas of their fatherland (and) foreigners are given preference over Nigerians for employment in parts of Nigeria. Nigerians cannot buy land in parts of Nigeria. Nigerians cannot fully exercise their political rights in certain parts of Nigeria."[45] In public transactions much emphasis is laid on "state of origin" than on "place of birth" and qualification - thus making nonsense of some of government's policies, like tax-payment in one's place of abode (and not in one's state of origin). It makes nonsense of the objectives of the "National Youth Service Corps" designed to expose Nigerian youths to various areas and cultures of their country, thus to foster national unity. At this juncture the questions posited by E. Odumegwu.Ojukwu demand our attention: "What is the sense of asking the question 'state of origin' in a country in search of unity? Why must students from different areas of our country suffer discrimination even though their parents have lived and paid taxes in the state within which they seek education? Why do we establish federal schools to integrate our youth, send them to National Youth Service Corps to be better integrated only to separate them promptly in employment when they become adults? Why do we persist in stigmatising a Nigerian citizen with the disabilities of an area he probably has never visited let alone lived in? Why can't a free born Nigerian citizen have the right to change his state - the right to free movement within his country?"[46]

The second major consequence of the divisive factors is lack of patriotism evident in the lives of Nigerians. Tribal loyalties remain stronger than national loyalty. "The demonstration of a Nigerian community and commitment to that community has been relatively minimal or at least uneasy.... The history of political institutions in this country attests to the fact that the interests of individuals and groups have tended to take precedence over the interests of the country as a whole."[47] There is no sense of the common-good. And this hinders the cultivation of a sustainable democracy in Nigeria.

3.2. Leadership factor[48]

If the saying, a nation is like its leaders, is anything to go by, then the Nigerian leadership should be blamed for the failure of democracy in the country. "The trouble with Nigeria," Chinua Achebe writes, "is simply and squarely a failure of leadership. There is nothing basically wrong with the Nigerian character. There is nothing wrong with the Nigerian land or climate or water or air or anything else. The Nigerian problem is the unwillingness or inability of its leaders to rise to the responsibility, to the challenge of personal example which are the hallmarks of true leadership."[49] Obviously there are many things wrong with Nigeria, apart from the leadership issue. Chinua Achebe only tries to bring out leadership as a major factor that underlies other factors.

Since independence, Nigeria has been bogged by the leadership problem. Apart from the fact that the country has not been blessed with a nationally accepted leadership,[50] there is also the fact that Nigerian leaders have failed to perform well. The first fact is associated with the problem of unity and will be solved when the unity problem is solved, and so it will not bother us here. The second fact - the poor performance of Nigerian leaders - is the object of this discussion. The reasons for poor leadership in Nigeria include: poor mentality of being in power; lack of vision and misplacement of values; lack of accountability; apotheosis of mediocrity accruing from the "federal character" or "quota system" principle; militarism.

3.2.1. Wrong mentality of being in power

There is a general mentality about being in power - a mentality of personal aggrandisement, of being in a higher class, of showmanship and flamboyance, of lordship, and not of service - very much evident in the Nigerians (both leaders and the led) which is very unhealthy for a democratic polity. This general mentality emanates from the way most Nigerians conceive 'government'. This is well brought out by S. G. Ikoku:

> To the average Nigerian, *government is business*. The ordinary people see government as *a benefactor*. Things have to be done for the people. If not free everything, then at least little or no taxes. The successful representative is he who promises free this and free that while holding out the prospect of diminishing taxation. The professional class see government as *the godfather*. Once a diploma is obtained and a friend or relation is in public office, the way to position and affluence is paved. The business community see government as *the goose that lays the golden egg*. It provides the juicy contracts, ranging from petty supplies to giant projects. All that is needed in order to make a fortune is connection. And connection is founded upon and reinforced by blood and marriage links, old school ties, club membership, ethnic origin, and above all pecuniary inducement.
> The public servant regards public office as the *opportunity to make good*. The professionals, academics as well as businessmen consider some presence in the corridors of power as the *secret to success*. Competence does not really matter. The politician sees being in public office as *the chance of a lifetime to get his share of the national cake*. This thinking lies at the root of the Nigerian malaise....[51]

As stated above, the Nigerian politicians, who constitute the leading class, see being in office as "a chance of a lifetime to get (their) share of the national cake." They are not interested in serving the people and the nation, but in enriching themselves. Of course, this *sharing of the national cake mentality* leads to the looting of the public treasury, without any commensurate interest shown in creating, accumulating and augmenting that loot. And since "loot by its very nature is a diminishing asset, it is therefore not surprising that (thirty-six years) after independence we have come to see and scrape the bottom of the barrel."[52] Obviously democracy can hardly survive on the looting of the national treasury.

The *colonial mentality* exhibited by Nigerian leaders poses its own problem. On assuming the leadership mantle from the colonial masters, the Nigerian new leaders "immediately embarked on the use of the political machinery to pursue their class interests of amassing wealth and privileges against the interest of the majority of the country, the workers and peasants. Oblivious of the conditions of their people and the inherent injustice of the situation they quickly moved into the white salary scales and GRA residential areas to break racist monopoly of these privileges. Thus, the Nigerian leaders were more desirous of imbibing the life style and privileges of colonialism than in abolishing its injustice and oppression of the Nigerian masses...."[53] Hence, "the sum total of Nigerian independence became and has remained the symbolic replacement by black faces of white faces - the content and direction of government has not changed."[54] This colonial mentality makes Nigerian leaders feel that they belong to a different class from the masses - creating a distance between leaders and the rest of the people. In their ivory tower they hardly feel the sufferings and hardships of the ordinary people, and rarely address themselves to the people's problems.

To maintain their 'other classness', the Nigerian leaders 'live big', live the life of *showmanship and flamboyancy*. They show off their wealth (even if ill-amassed), and their status (even if it is dubious how he arrived there). Fanfare colours most of their activities. They want to be recognised and be heard in every occasion. They like much noise. There is too much noise around them: on the road, there is the convoy of vehicles led by a police vehicle with siren "blasting out deafening noise to scatter and disperse all members of the public going about their lawful duties by foot or vehicle;"[55] in a place of visit, there are the "diversional amusements" meant to entertain them ("groups of schoolchildren [sic] dance and sing, half-naked maidens to dance, sing and titillate, and able-bodied men to perform acrobatic displays"[56]), and the vote of thanks, full of flatteries, given to the them.[57] There is too much noise about them: due to the overwhelming, and very often undue, publicity from the mass media. And there is much noise from them: their speeches "open with a long and sonorous recital in recognition of the various dignitaries present"[58] and very often lack substance - a type of 'oratocracy'.[59] Consequently, the important business of government is left undone or half-done. This agrees with A. Adebayo's view that "if one discounts the various forms of *sound* and *fury* which take up the daily working life of the African ruler, there is practically nothing left. It is ... little wonder that there is hardly any development anywhere around.... The stark reality is that once the sound and fury of the African ruler is taken away, the rest of his government is 'signifying nothing'."[60]

Another consequence of the showmanship and flamboyance of the Nigerian leaders is that much wastes are involved. Let us take the outing of the Nigerian leader for example.[61] Each outing of the leader involves elaborate arrangements. The ground of the assembly have to be ready with canopies (if in the open air), chairs, tables, loudspeakers. The police have to be alerted "to send a contingent of men to control the traffic, maintain law and order and ensure security." The press has to be invited to cover the ceremony and is "expected to fill the air and the front pages of their newspapers with the activities of the central figures of the show." All these constitute a big waste of energy, time, money and other resources. A. Adebayo gives a rough estimate (calculated on annual basis) of financial wastes on such personality visits[62]: transport has N600,000.00, manpower gulps N900,000.00, equipment and materials take N350,000.00, and refreshments (food and drink) get N250,000.00. And he concludes: "The items that have been costed above amount to an estimated sum of about N2 million annually. A sum of about N2 million is thus frittered away annually by a government whose majority of population live in squalor and penury."[63] All these, without mentioning the non-quantifiable costs,[64] which Adebayo calls "invisible costs, invisible yet dangerously potent." These wastes are in fact dangerously infecting both the ethical and political values of the society, as they equally undermine efforts to achieving a sustainable democracy in the country.

The Nigerian leaders strongly believe that *might is right*. They dominate more than they serve. They would want everybody to know that they are in-charge here, therefore no tolerance of opposition. Anybody with opposing view is branded an enemy (who must be eliminated).[65] A peep into the political history of Nigeria shows that "since Colonial days, successive executives have demonstrated the relative importance of the executive and its potentials for operating as a super-ordinate branch of government with tentacles for stultifying the other branches. The avenues for turning chief executives even into petty tyrants in governmental process were exposed, especially during the First and Second Republics."[66] Obviously no democracy can thrive on such dictatorship!

Allied to the problem of *might is right* is the *personality cult* problem. The Nigerian leaders, by the mere fact of being in power, consider themselves the centre of all activities and the custodian of wisdom and knowledge (irrespective of how educated or illiterate they are), who must be referred to on every matter. This relegates the important role of experts on issues to the background. And to complement their aura of self-importance, the Nigerian leaders gather many sycophants around them, who adore and flatter them, and for whom the leaders' friends and enemies automatically become their friends and enemies as well. Thus the society is divided along personality lines, with one group fighting against another. Moreover, "personality cult in a fissiparous, pluralistic, competitive society such as ours can only exacerbate jealousy and as such be counter productive."[67] Hence it is unhealthy for a democratic polity.

3.2.2. Lack of vision and misplacement of values

Lack of vision and misplacement of values have been the bane of the Nigerian leadership. Many Nigerian leaders are only politicians and hardly statesmen. (While a politician is concerned with the next election, a statesman is concerned with the next generation.) Nigerian leaders are so immersed in today that they never remember yesterday nor imagine tomorrow. In taking critical decisions they hardly ask themselves: "Will it be good for the nation, not just today but after I am gone?" Because they lack vision, Nigerian leaders become so narrow-minded and myopic in their plans and actions. They do not rise beyond self and self-interests. A. Adebayo underscores the point in his observation:

> An over-riding consideration in the minds of a great many rulers when taking decisions on public issue, is the need to cater for their future political welfare. For example, many rulers want to be financially secure and to insure their future against financial insecurity.... Because of (this), many rulers award contracts for projects whose social and economic utility is dubious. The rulers are mainly concerned with receiving their own kick-backs on signing the agreements....[68]

In the same vein, Nisi Osundare writes:

> For fear of being misunderstood, let me quickly submit that this country has its share of skilful, accomplished, even upright politicians. But unfortunately, this breed of men and women is in a lamentable minority. The field is literally taken over by a group of opportunistic, myopic men and women who cannot differentiate personal interests from national interests, who operate from an absolute lack of principle. It is this category of politicians who prepare the ground for military intervention in the first place; it is their easy compromise which endows military rule with oppressive longevity.[69]

It is not that Nigeria lacks the civil service machinery which should help the leaders in their decision-making. As A. Adebayo states: "our successive political rulers had the civil service machinery at their disposal, to collect data and information and analyse the various alternatives needed for policy-making. But to what extent have the politicians allowed themselves to be guided by the expertise of the civil service?"[70] Because they neglect expert advice, public decision-making by Nigerian rulers is in many instances the very antithesis of rationality, as some examples below illustrate.

Many Nigerian leaders ignore expert advice in the siting developmental projects. A. Adebayo writes: "most Nigerian politicians are mainly preoccupied with the defeat or destruction of their political opponents and any weapons which come to hand are considered useful and appropriate in achieving this end. Therefore, decisions about siting of industries and various forms of infrastructure and amenities are based, not on the reports of feasibility studies or on the degree of importance to the social and economic development of a community, but on the need to buttress the ruler's political base and punish political opponents with a view to pressurising them to declare support for him."[71] And he goes on, "while other areas in the community, in terms of need, geographical and infrastructural suitability are more deserving of certain social and economic projects or amenities, the ruler shuts his mind to the considerations and sites the projects in his own area; the same is true of the provision of infrastuctures like electricity and water supply schemes and the siting of industries."[72]

Close to the above is the fact the Nigerian leaders find it difficult to continue the policy and/or project initiated by their politically-opposed predecessors, irrespective of how good and important these are to the welfare of the people. As A. Adebayo rightly observes: "when the baton changes hand and a Governor from a rival political party succeeds the erstwhile Governor, as it happened in a number of States during the last general elections in Nigeria in August, 1983," the new governor often embarks "on a policy of vendetta, demolishing almost everything that the former Governor had done and wreaking vengeance on those known to be friendly or loyal to him."[73] This explains the presence of many abandoned policies and projects all over the country.

Just as the Nigerian leaders abhor opposition, they cherish loyalty. Their decisions are therefore bent in favour of their loyalists, just as the latter influence their decisions. A. Adebayo agrees: "Political leaders and rulers particularly cherish such friends on whose personal loyalty they can always rely. Human weakness, however, sets in when major public decisions are based on the views and wishes of favourites and personal friends, without due and proper examination and assessment of other possible choices or alternative courses for action.... It is a travesty of the principles of public decision-making to base decision-making solely on the views of those who profess to be protecting the ruler's political interests. A ruler's personal friends and favourites will often tell him what they know would delight him. It is here that flattery and adulation abound. A ruler who continually receives advice from such source, cuts himself off from reality and is heading fast towards the brink of political disaster."[74]

Because of their lack of vision, the Nigerian leaders present jumbo budgets - unrealistic projections - not in tune with their treasuries. In the end they winds up with deficit budgets. They then seek for ways of raising money, such as asking for external loans, to finance their projects, thereby plunging the state or the nation into unwarranted debts.[75]

Like in the making of budgets, the Nigerian leaders indulge in making unnecessary expenditures without taking into account the strength of the treasury. In the end, they discover that their state is running on deficit. This was what happened to Nigeria during the second republic: "In 1979, the nation had a foreign exchange reserve of about N3 billion. As a consequence of the Iranian revolution and the boost in Nigeria's oil sales, there was a rapid increase in the external reserves which stood at N5.6 billion in December 1980. However, the squander-mania of the Shagari administration ensured that the foreign exchange reserve was soon wasted. Between 1980 and 1981, the value of imports rose astronomically from N9.095 billion to N13.159 billion. This was 45% increase in only 12 months. Thus, by 1982, the nation was running a balance of payment deficit of N1.5 billion, while outstanding payment arrears are estimated at over N2 billion in May 1983."[76]

3.2.3. Lack of accountability

Another major bane of democracy in Nigeria is "arrogance of power based on complete lack of accountability from its leaders. All else - corruption, traffic jams, police brutality, etc. etc. are simply expressions and details of these."[77] Kyari Tijani gives an impressive definition of accountability: "Political accountability, the act of rendering to the political community the true account of the discharge of its duties by the leadership of that community, for the purpose of adjudging by the community itself whether or not it wishes to continue to accept this particular leadership group, is the very basis on which democracy is based. Periodic election is but a mere process of, and functions for achieving and enforcing accountability. Accountability is therefore the value component of democracy which decrees elections. There is thus no democracy if there is no accountability and there is no accountability if there is no election."[78] From this definition, accountability is more than mere rendering of monetary account, it involves the whole of one's stewardship. It implies running an open government, whereby citizens are duly informed of the true position of the nation's economic, financial and political situation. It also implies public officers being sincere and responsible to their duties and to the public. Accountability springs from the fact that the leader is a servant, and as such he must render account of his stewardship to the electorate. It is a civic right of the electorate to receive such a true account of the stewardship of the leaders.

Unfortunately to expect such honest account of stewardship from any Nigerian leader is rather to expect an impossibility. It is an indisputable fact that such ugly situation is in itself a wreck of democracy. It is a situation in which Nigeria today still finds itself. Tunji Olagunju rightly expresses the situation thus:

> Our past experience in working with democratic institutions has shown that government was neither hardly responsive nor accountable to the desires of majority of the people.... First, the citizens themselves feel less powerful and effective: they show little or no personal concern about their own society. Even when they do, the mechanisms then available were not effective in responding to their interests. Consequently, they have almost literally and paradoxically demonstrated a strong desire for any form of government that could cater for their interests. Secondly, the content of politics has been concerned more with acquisitive power

> of office than a socially desired discharge of duties and responsibilities. Consequently, there has been very little concern on the part of rulers for the welfare and advancement of the individual and social justice. Thirdly, ... the demonstration of a Nigerian community and commitment to that community has been relatively minimal or at least uneasy. The experience before the war showed clearly that the large majority of the socially mobilised people was more willing to sacrifice the interests of the national community for those of the person and immediate groups. The history of political institutions in this country attests to the fact that the interests of individuals and groups have tended to take precedence over the interests of the country as a whole....[79]

The worst situation of non-accountability in the history of Nigeria was during the second republic. The following citations attest to this. According to A. Adebayo: "In the four years of the presidential system of government, from Oct. 1979 to Dec. 1983 under Alhaji Shehu Shagari, the country witnessed the rise of State Governors who felt accountable to no one and demonstrated naked display of power, and utter disregard for public feelings."[80] And Kyari Tijani agrees: "This lack of accountability came out fully in many actions of the Shagari administration, both throughout its first tenure, and since the inception of the current one. The infamous Bakolori massacres; the Black Maria incident; and the purported deportation of Shugaba Abdurrahman (Majority Leader in the then Borno State House of Assembly) all occured in the early part of 1980, and others such as the bungled revenue allocation formular, the Presidential Liaison Officers (PLO) 'palaver' etc. came later."[81]

3.2.4. Federal character and Quota system: Apotheosis of mediocrity

Federal character - which metamorphosed into *quota system* - derives its legal basis from sections 14 (3) and (4) of the 1979 Constitution of the Federal Republic of Nigeria. According to section 14 (3),

> The composition of the government of the Federation, or any of its agencies, and the conduct of its affairs shall be carried out in such a manner as to reflect the Federal character of Nigeria and the need to promote national unity, thereby ensuring that there shall be no predominance of persons from a few states or from a few ethnic or other sectional groups in that government or in any of its agencies.

And according to section 14 (4),

> The composition of the Government of a State, a Local Government Council or any of the agencies of such government or council, and the conduct of the affairs of the government, or council or such agencies, shall be carried out in such a manner as to recognise the diversity of the peoples within its areas of authority and the need to promote a sense of belonging and loyalty among all the peoples of the Federation.

In effect the *federal character* demands representation of all the ethnic groups in all federal institutions and establishments. It does not matter even if the required qualification for the office is not met by anyone from certain state. Recruitments, appointments and promotions are more often not based on qualification and merit but on "state's merit." All this is to reflect *federal character*, and a ploy to favour the so-called "educationally disadvantaged areas." Eventually these are the people who dominate in all the top offices at the federal sector - the army, the police, the navy, the airforce, the judiciary. The political supreme offices also are controlled by them. Opportunity for others to climb up are not readily given.

In all its ramifications the so-called *federal character* poses a lot of problems. Apart from promoting national disunity (the very thing it intends to prevent) - through "the reinforcement of ethnic membership as a basis for other participation in social, economic and political life of the nation (which) occurs in its crudest representations at the level of political patronage and the distribution of strategic positions at different levels of government,"[82] and through "the renewed identification with ethno-cultural and linguistic groups and associations, as well as the cultivation of micro loyalties"[83] - it sacrifices merit and institutes mediocrity. Tribe, and not merit, now serves as the main consideration of recruitment or appointment, recognition of natural talents and admissions to institutions of higher learning (where *quota system* is used to reflect the *federal character*). And from the point of view of leadership, a person who is not qualified or well-qualified for a leadership post is made a leader (because he comes from the so-called "disadvantaged area" - "one-eyed man in a blind country" - at the expense of a well-qualified and experienced personality (who comes from the so-called "advantaged area"). In the end, the state suffers from the non-performance of the inexperienced leader - the nemesis of mediocrity.[84] And obviously no democracy can thrive in such a state of mediocrity.

3.2.5. Militarism

The military is part of leadership factor of the nation. Hence it is part of the problem of democracy in Nigeria. The military has been in power for twenty-six out of the thirty-six years of Nigeria's independence. Thus to say that it has contributed most to Nigeria's faltering is just to state the obvious.

Two reasons could be adduced for military interventions in Nigeria. The first reason - which refers mainly to military coup d'etat against civil regimes - is non-performance by the civil leadership, manifested in the corporate threat or deprivation, intra-class rivalry and bitter competition among politicians, which lead to a decay of the necessary public virtues and the failure of civil leadership to promote economic development and maintain law and order. Machiavelli once said that when the necessary virtues have decayed, there is no possibility either of restoring them or of carrying on orderly government without them, except by despotic power, and that despotic violence is a powerful political medicine needed in corrupt states. This explains the enthusiasm with which many Nigerians welcome the arrival of the military on the scene - as a saving grace. (Note that this enthusiasm does not imply that the people wish an indefinite military rule.) The second reason - which refers mainly to military coup d'etat against military regimes - is the bureaucratic struggle of modern civil-military elite: the lust for power by the military. Jibril Ibrahim writes: "It was former President Shehu Shagari who argued that there were only two political parties in Nigeria, the military and the National Party of Nigeria. Nobody doubts that the Nigerian Army is virtually a political party composed of men who have no antipathies to political power and its perquisites."[85] This explains the fact of their reluctance to quit once on the throne.

Although the military is unencumbered by bureaucratic processes and is, therefore, better able to take decisions on sensitive matters without too much pussyfooting - much quicker than the politicians, although the military has contributed its quota towards the development of the country and has radicalised the political system, as Sam Oyovbaire took pains to point out,[86] and although the military has produced the best government Nigeria has ever had from independence to date (that is, the Murtala/Obasanjo regime), "military intervention in politics is not only an aberration, it is to some extent a negative way of solving political problems, because the military is not trained for partisan politics."[87] A military regime, as far as democratic processes are concerned, is a square peg in a round hole. Its modus operandi is every inch anti-democratic. As Mr Adebayo rightly points out: "A military regime cannot properly be described as operating within a political system. All military governments come to power by illegal and unconstitutional means, that is through *coup d'etat*, involving the use of force."[88] No matter how enlightened its programmes or liberal its aspirations, the military establishes physical force rather than verbal persuasiveness as the mechanism underlying decision-making and guaranteeing the success of public policies. Under the military, the rule of law is thrown to the wind: the military make retrospective or retroactive legislations, compulsorily acquire property without prompt payment of compensation, make arbitrary arrests and detention without trial, and oust the jurisdiction of the ordinary courts of the land to interprete or pronounce on the validity of legislation. This places the military government above the law.[89] Folarin Shyllon writes: "They passed Decree after Decree which violated the rule of law. They set up special tribunal after special tribunal the composition of which offends against the rule of law and fundamental human rights of the Constitution of the Federation. In order that the legality of such tribunals might not be challenged, they ousted the jurisdiction of the ordinary courts of the land and prohibited appeals. Every special tribunal they set up is not a tribunal but a negation of one.... It is incapable of administering justice according to law because of its composition and arbitrary powers. The exercise of arbitrary power is neither law nor justice."[90]

Having intervened from time to time, the military in each case has not been able to resolve the crisis of legitimacy and development under which the civilian regimes have crumbled. Some of the problems have become compounded by the military rule: indiscipline and corruption have skyrocketted, the economy has nose-dived into the deeps, the people's plights and sufferings have become innumerable and unbearable, all social institutions and services have deteriorated, and the country seems to be in a stand-still. Then it is clear that military rule is "one step forward and two steps backward." Thanks to God, the Nigerians know this; hence their continuous and persistent calls for military disengagement from politics.[91] Though Chairman Mao had said that power flows from the barrel of a gun, the truth remains that power, real power flows from the voice of the people, and that a country that gives its leadership to the military is finished and ruined. And Nigeria is no exception. Until the military ceases to intervene in the country's political process, Nigeria would not have a sustainable democracy.

3.3. Socio-economic factor[92]

It is a fact that democracy cannot be established in a country where the basic social and economic structures and services are lacking and where the majority of its people are living in penury and squalor. This is yet another problem of democracy in Nigeria. Despite Nigeria's abundant human and natural resources (see pages 111-112), poverty and misery still stare its citizens in the face as the economic and social structures and services are in bad shape (that is, where they exist at all). Some reasons can be given for these: poor economic planning and structures, lack of social structures and services, education problem, and so on.

3.3.1. Poor economic planning and structures

Before and since independence (Oct. 1960), efforts at harnessing Nigeria's economic resources were focused on agricultural production for export. At independence, the country was self-sufficient in food with agriculture contributing 70% to gross domestic product (GDP) and over 80% to exports. But with the sudden oil boom in the 1970s there was a shift of emphasis from agriculture to oil which had become a reliable source of government revenue and of easy money for urban dwellers. The result of this neglect of the agricultural sector was a progressive fall in the output of food and cash crops, so that Nigeria which was number one exporter of palm oil became an importer of nearly all commodities. Consequently, by 1983, food importation alone amounted to nearly 16% of total imports (with rice gulping 26% of the total food imports).

With the oil boom ($4 a barrel in 1973 to $42 a barrel in 1980), Nigeria's revenue rose astronomically - from N.509 billion in 1970 to N1.893 billion in 1973, N5.365 billion in 1974, N7.00 billion in 1977 and N13.323 billion in 1980.

Rather than use this oil revenue "for more effective and meaningful economic planning and development, we went on shopping spree. In one year alone, our import bill from Britain rose to two billion naira. We preferred to purchase rather than produce."[93] In the industrial sector, as Joseph Ode rightly points out, "most 'manufacturing' activities consisted, in the main, of assembling, blending, bottling or repackaging of components of goods hitherto imported with the ultimate objective of producing the components locally.... Foreign contractors and suppliers of equipment besieged the country for their own share of the revenue.... They supplied capital goods and equipment for, sometimes, ill-designed projects which got stalled in the process of construction but the money already spent on equipment was not returned.... It was thus during the same period ... that Nigeria was lured not only into the courts of the credit agencies of Europe but also into the net of the international capital market.... The arrival of petroleum did not only lure Nigeria into the debt trap, it also diverted the country's attention from developing other sources of revenue - agriculture and industry - and created an insatiable taste for foreign consumer and industrial goods. With the booming of oil revenue, Nigeria imported anything under the sun, including, allegedly sand and sawdust. Imports of machinery and equipment for industries accounted for 50% of total imports.... But while the level of imports was rising, exports of non-oil goods were declining. Thus the country which recorded a favourable trade balance of N55.4 million in 1966, N4,439.3 million in 1974 began to record deficits from 1978. The deficits persisted for 12 years, broken only temporarily in 1979 and 1980."[94] Then came the sudden oil doom in the 1980s - due to the global oil glut.

With the collapse of the world oil market, with its concomitant dramatic fall in Nigeria's oil earnings and untold and unexpected hardships on Nigerians, came in 1986 the introduction of the *structural adjustment programme* (SAP), aimed at market reforms (which bore the imprint of the IMF: devaluation of the naira and so on, though the government would not admit it because the nation, in a national debate in 1985, has rejected the Fund).[95] SAP did not help the ugly situation. If anything, SAP worsened and complicated the country's economic crisis[96]: giving rise to retrenchment of workers (leading to increased unemployment), an inflationary spiral (64-80% in 1995[97]), borrowing spree (leading to huge external debts - US $32,245,000,000 by Dec. 31, 1991[98]), rise in internal public debts, decline in social services, and so on. Consequently, there is a drastic fall in the standard of living. Thus one concludes with O. Nnoli that "Nigeria's growth in the national wealth has been growth without development. Hence, it has been accompanied by growth in scarcity and inequality...."[99]

The Vanguard newspaper (Dec. 19, 1995, p. 18) gives us an over view of the Nigerian economy today: "Available indicators in the first six months of 1995 ... show that the Nigerian economy is still in deep recession, displaying a number of unhealthy characteristics. Among the main features are:- lack of economic growth; - persisting low level on industrial capacity utilization which in fact declined to 26.97% from 29.04% recorded a year ago; - an annual inflation rate of

80% in the twelve months to June 1995; - rising unemployment as new jobs were not created while labour shedding in industries was a natural response to declining factory operations; - the combination of inflation and slow-down in economic activity meant a pervading stagnation; - a heavy build-up of unplanned inventory of finished goods arising from flagging domestic aggregate demand. This compounded the problem of low capacity utilization; - lack of new investments which constitute the principal source of economic growth."

As stated above, this economic crunch has very adversely affected the living standard of the people. With the high inflation rate and the depreciation of the Nigerian currency, "most Nigerians," in the words of Utibe Ukim, "can no longer afford a decent meal or a comfortable accommodation.... The rising cost of health-care services has driven many back to traditional healers. Education too is fast joining the preserve of the rich with the recent spate of increases in school fees.... The high cost of food is particularly taxing for the lowly-paid workers.... For most middle-income earners, sustaining an average-sized family is a real problem.... Postal charges are up too. In January, they went up by 650%.... Electricity charges are about to go up from the present average rate of 32 kobo per one kilowatt.... School fees have also gone up.... Two other areas that have witnessed remarkable increases in prices are accommodation and transportation.... The sharp rise in the prices of building materials has forced many people to abandon their buildings halfway.... Transport fares just keep rising too. Passengers are no longer sure what they will pay at any time.... On the average, transportation cost has increased by more than 120% in Lagos in the last few months...."[100] All these, with a per capita income of about N8,153.16 (that is, about N679.43 per month - about $30.88, going by government official exchange rate of N22.00 to $1[101]).

As if this is not enough, there are widespread reports of non-payment or delay in payment of workers' salaries, or even cut in salaries. Moreover, many workers in the private sectors are underpaid,[102] that is, if they are not retrenched.

In the face of these harsh realities, the urge to survive at whatever cost (by "cook or crook") becomes paramount. Prof. O. K. Ogan puts it this way: "Surely if a water-tanker driver or a gateman was allowed in this country to go without his salary for the first three months following his employment in the Civil Service ... it is idle to blame him if he does a lucrative business sidetracking the official address to which he has been dutifully assigned, and selling the water a few yards further down the road at N50 to N100 a tank. It is equally idle to show surprise when the night-watchman collaborates with thieves to burgle you at night so that he can find food for his family from the proceeds of selling your radio, television or electronic set."[103] This explains the high rate of indiscipline, corruption and crimes prevalent in Nigeria today.

3.3.2. Lack of social structures and services

The poor economic situation of the country inevitably affects the social structures and services. Where these social services and amenities existed before, they are fast "crumbling like cookies".[104] Baffled by the dilapidating social structures, A. Adebayo writes: "And what have the Nigerian governments got to show for the impressive annual budgets, the array of top ranking functionaries with high sounding titles, the endless overseas trips and the hustle and bustle of apparent devotion to work? Its telephones which stay dead for several months and years, electricity which is erratic and uncertain, postal services which are irregular and undependable, water taps that refuse to drip no matter how much you turn it. To cap all these, there is squalor and poverty, with a few over-wealthy individuals who have profited amidst the encircling gloom and who display their wealth with callous indifference."[105] This summarises the problem at hand, but we shall go further for more details. We shall begin with education.

3.3.2.1. The education problem

Every government, including the Nigerian, knows the importance of education as the greatest investment that any nation can make for the quick development of its economic, political, social and human resources. According to Gen. Abacha, Nigeria's Head of State, "Education and general enlightenment are crucial for national development and understanding. Our educational system must be one that insures the availability of an indigenous skilled workforce for economic growth of our industries. Education, health and shelter are among the inalienable rights which a democratic government should guarantee its people."[106] The importance attached to education in Nigeria has seen a rapid development of educational institutions and infrastructures and massive enrolments at all levels. Nigeria can today boast of more than 34,904 primary schools (with more than 12,712,087 pupils and over 344,221 teachers; showing pupil-teacher ratio of over 36.9:1),[107] more than 5,595 secondary schools (with more than 2,723,791 students and over 136,677 teachers; showing student-teacher ratio of over 19.9:1),[108] about 376[109] vocational or teacher training institutions (with about 391,583 students and about 15,738 teachers; showing student-teacher ratio of 24.9:1)[110] and over 140 higher institutions - comprising 41 universities, 39 polytechnics and 60 colleges of education.[111] And Nigeria's literacy rate, by 1990, is about 50.7% (age 15 and over of the total population) - males 62.3% and females 39.5%.[112]

Good as the above report may seem, Nigerian education is crumbling. There is lack of equal opportunity for primary and secondary education for all. Education has become too expensive - school fees are very high, so too the cost of books, uniform and other academic requirements - that only the rich can afford it.[113] Consequently, the enrolment in education at all levels has been on the decline and withdrawals have been on the increase - as a result of parents' reaction to the removal of subsidies on educational services and the imposition of levies and increases in fees.[114] In theory, primary education is today free throughout the country (except in privately owned schools), but the many levies imposed on the pupils very often make nonsense of the "free education." Some parents, especially those who are poor, those with many children and/or those who have no stable income, cannot afford the money. This implies that children from poor families are denied the opportunity even of primary education. The situation is worse in secondary and tertiary institutions where fees and levies are paid. In secondary schools, fees differ from state to state. Even within the states levies vary according to schools. And these fees are higher in privately owned schools. Utibe Ukim comments that "the cost of government-moderated examinations like the senior secondary school examination certificate and the general certificate of education examination has gone up."[115] Therefore, not all those who passed out of the primary schools have the opportunity to attend secondary schools. And in tertiary institutions, "State-owned tertiary institutions are leading the way in higher school fees, while at federal universities the increases are so far in areas like post-graduate studies, certificate and remedial courses."[116] Hence the poor has no hope at all for tertiary education.

There is also the problem of lack of adequate facilities and qualified teachers. Many of the nation's educational institutions at all levels lack both accommodation and instructional facilities. Indeed our institutions of learning display a profound deterioration of physical facilities. "Books, for instance, have been priced out of reach of students who need them. School libraries do not contain useful books anymore. Students are forced to spend a lot of money to photocopy relevant portion of textbooks, and buy handouts prepared by lecturers"[117] at high costs. The situation is made worse by lack of qualified teachers. With the introduction in 1976 of the "universal primary education," UPE, the number of pupils intake was so high that there was serious lack of teachers in primary schools. The government introduced "crash programmes" (in the name of teachers training colleges, TTC) to raise primary school teachers. Hence every dick and harry (even market women) went to TTC and "crashed" out as "teachers". The effect of this was the recruitment of unqualified teachers into primary schools. The story is the same in secondary schools. The phenomenal jump in enrolment in primary schools was to have massive growth rates implications on secondary schools. Again through "crash programmes" and "sandwich courses" unqualified teachers found their way into secondary schools. What more, "the desultory programmes of education was to become more confusing with the introduction in the fourth national development plan of the 6-3-3-4 system of education. By this secondary education was divided into two phases of junior secondary school, JSS, and senior secondary school, SSS. But the programme immediately ran into hitches because of lack of qualified teachers and equipment especially in technical education."[118]

The lack of qualified teachers in Nigerian schools is made worse by the exit of well qualified teachers from the school system. Because of poor salaries, and even the non-payment of the salaries, the well qualified teachers leave the school to take to private business or even travel outside the country to look for better paid jobs.

There is next the problem of the disjointed educational programmes. Every now and then the educational institutions are closed down because of one strike or another (from teachers and/or students) - demanding for payment of arrears of salaries and allowances, for new salary scales, better conditions of service and increased welfare for students, and so on. Not much then is covered for the semester or for the session. In the end, only "half-baked literate persons" are produced. What future has a nation with such "half-baked literate" future leaders? It is a well known fact (and Plato indicated this in his *The Statesman and the Laws*) that "ignorance is the ruin of states."

Lastly, there is the problem of orientation. Nigeria has elitist educational system which is white-collar job oriented. It is not geared towards productivity and inventiveness. Nigeria inherited it from the British. It is not the best for Nigeria, because it is geared towards the enhancement of the few and the exploitation of the many. Horst Eliseit (a German journalist) observed the social and economic consequences of pronounced elitist education and said in an article written in April 1971 entitled "African Balance": "In the social field the dominant feature is the contrast between a small educated, governing class of highly paid state officials, enjoying the support of a few wealthy cliques, and the broad masses living in poverty and backwardness."[119] Harry G. Johnson (Professor of Economics at the University of Chicago) agrees. Describing what he called the legacy of the British colonialism in his article, "A Word to the Third World," written in October 1971, he said: "the purpose of a nation is not to promote economic development in any meaningful sense, but to enable its educated elite to survive and prosper on good salaries and with confidence in their own superiority over people who merely work for living."[120] Gen. Olusegun Obasanjo was quite aware of this problem when he, as the then Head of State, in Dec. 1977, at a convocation in Ahmadu Bello University, said: "The responsibility of the University to our youth, and therefore to our future, is truly great. This responsibility would not have been discharged if all the we produce is a long list of graduates, who are elitist, self-opinionated and materialistic, and who thus set themselves apart from the very people who brought them up when they were helpless."[121] Unfortunately Nigerian educational institutions produce many graduates who are elitist, self-opinionated, and materialistic, and who set themselves apart from the common people (whom they exploit and manipulate). Definitely a situation of this sort does not augur well for a sustainable democracy.

3.3.2.2. Other social services

Other social services here include health care, electricity, water, communication services (transportation, postal and telephone services). These are the social services which people in developed world take for granted, but which in developing world, like in Nigeria, are luxury.

Health care. The health care statistics of Nigeria indicate that health care in Nigeria is not very healthy after all. 1986 report shows the following: physicians 16,003 (1 per 6,573 persons); hospital beds 90,668 (1 per 1,160 persons); infant mortality rate (1990-95) 96.0.[122] However, according to the world development report of the World Bank (1993), "Nigeria had one doctor to 6,666. America on comparative level had 420 persons per doctor. Also about 1.4 hospital beds are available to 1,000 persons in the country."[123] Though the 1990-95 projections put life expectancy in Nigeria at 50.8 years for males and 54.3 years for females [with birth rate per 1,000 population at 46.5 (world average 26.4) and death rate per 1,000 population at 14.0 (world average 9.2)[124]], a recent World Health Organisation, WHO, report shows that "only 49 per cent of Nigeria's population have access to adequate health care delivery with a 52-year-life expectancy."[125] There are not enough hospitals to take care of the many sick. Even the few existing ones lack both basic and major equipment and the available facilities are deteriorating. To use the words of Sani Abacha, the hospitals have become "mere consulting clinics without drugs, water and equipment."[126] Nigerians are used to "OṢ" (meaning "out of stock") often written on their cards by the pharmacist against doctor's prescriptions. The patients must then buy their drugs from drug stores in town, even when they are on admission in hospital. (Many of these drug stores in town are owned by the doctors and pharmacists working in the hospitals where these patients are admitted. Their drugs are very costly and some of them are fake.) Because of non-availability of health care to the common man, and because of the high cost of the meagre available one, many Nigerians have resorted to quack doctors, traditional native healers, and spiritual healing homes.

Electricity supply. This is not available to all: either it is not available in an area or some people cannot afford the cost. Even in those places where you have electricity, it is erratic and uncertain because there is always constant power failures (of course, without warning and without assurance of its return soon). No wonder the National Electric Power Authority, NEPA, has been nicknamed "Never Expect Power Always"! Consequently, the food stuff, meat and drinks in the refrigerator and deep freezer go bad; industrialists find it difficult to function well; and life generally becomes miserable. To beat NEPA, some people buy and install generators in their homes and/or in their working places, not minding the nuisance and hazards which the noise and polution from these generators constitute to people's health and to the environment.

Water supply. Many communities in Nigeria - especially in rural areas - do not have potable water. They rely on rivers, streams, ponds and rainfall for their water supply. "In 1986, the Directorate of Foods, Roads and Rural Infrastructure, DFRRI, was set up to develop rural areas. In the first phase of rural development, the directorate claimed to have supplied 250 communities in each state with potable water. By 1992, DFRRI claimed that it had provided potable water to 5,000 communities. But fact-finding teams by government itself showed that many of DFRRI's bore-hole projects were not functioning."[127] Moreover, the communities that have potable water do not have constant water supply. More often than not, the taps are dry - they would not drip no matter how much you turn them; and sometimes when they run you are fed with coloured water (dirty, muddy, rusty). Consequently, to make ends meet, people have to buy water (sometimes from sources that are suspect). Obviously lack of good water supply constitutes health-hazard to many Nigerians.

Transportation. Nigeria has no good network of roads. The available roads have all gone bad and they are no better than death-traps. In urban areas, there is always heavy traffic and thus traffic jams and hold-ups. To worsen the situation, transport fares keep rising, such that passengers are no longer sure what they will pay at any time. This problem is made more complex by the fact that "we have no alternatives to almost anything. Life is comparatively easier in other countries facing the same situation as we do because there are alternatives. If taxi goes up in London or New York, for instance, the subway or the bus is a veritable alternative. If the air fares rise, the rail or the couch becomes a comparatively cheaper alternative. Here, the rail has since been abandoned. The government-owned buses are unable to compete with the rickety private buses in our towns and cities. Inevitably, we fall back on the private buses and pay the higher fares for lack of viable alternatives."[128]

Postal and telecommunication services. These are not better off. "Postal charges are up too. In January (1993), they went up by 650 percent. Postages for local mails went up from 50 kobo to N1.50. To post one kilogram local parcel, you need between N40 and N60. Overseas letters attract between N20 and N40, depending on their destination."[129] Letters now take very long time to reach their destinations within and from Nigeria. For example, before it took a letter posted in Nigeria roughly two weeks to arrive Germany, today it takes months.

Telephone is not found everywhere in Nigeria. It is seen a luxury. But, for those who have it, its prices have also gone up, and the services are irregular and undependable. The telephones hardly work. They can stay dead for several months and years. "In fact," writes P. Enahoro, "a telephone is a gadget for recording silence.... It is all part of the welfare services provided by a very considerate State which no doubt believes that a regular exchange of insults among its diverse citizens is a good thing for drawing people close. Unfortunately, not many people appreciate the value of this scheme; in spite of the fact that Government spends large sums annually to ensure that telephones are not in working order and if they are, that telephone operators know the appropriate swear words in vogue. The aim of every telephone operator is to contradict you. To call you when you do not wish to be called; not to answer when you are calling. To refuse to admit that you have the wrong number; never to put you through to the right number."[130]

The postal and telecommunication services have so decayed that the workers violate their customers' rights of privacy: they steal people's mails and tap people's telephone messages.

From the catalogue of woes seen in this discussion on socio-economic conditions of Nigeria, one conclusion is inevitable, viz.: Nigeria is poor and Nigerians are living in poverty. The country is ranked by World Bank among the world's poorest[131]: in 1991 the 13th and recently the 11th poorest nation in the world. It is a fact that democracy cannot thrive where the economy is poor and where the people are living in poverty. This is so because poverty diminishes the power of freedom: a poor person is not free. In his *Law of freedom*, regarding the commonwealth, Gerrard Winstanley holds that the root of all bondage is poverty - "A man had better to have had no body than to have no food for it" - and that true freedom means that all equally have access to the use of the earth and its fruits.[132] Moreover, Nigeria's poverty is even more pronounced because of lack of alternatives; and democracy (or, better capitalism) survives on the basis of alternatives.[133]

This awful situation of things is often utilised by some politicians to manipulate and exploit the common people. Writing on universal suffrage and economic conditions, Hamilton rightly says: "A power over a man's subsistence amounts to a power over his will."[134] This agrees with Kant's view that suffrage "presupposes the independence or self-sufficiency of the individual citizen."[135] This explains why Nigerian politicians are able to buy over the voters in an election.[136] Because the people are poor - they are not free and self-subsistent - they see an election as an opportunity to get money out of the politicians. Their motto becomes "If you give me money, I vote for you." And in the end, it is the highest bidder, and not the best qualified, that wins in an election. This is one of the major reasons why Nigeria has never had a fair and free election. And it constitutes a big hindrance to the building of a sustainable democracy in Nigeria.

3.4. Justice and security[137]

When one thinks of justice and security, one's mind goes straight to the judiciary (as the custodian of the rule of law and the administrator of justice) and to the police (as law-enforcement agents). The failures and successes of these two bodies in their honourable duties invariably impact the political albeit the democratic state of any nation, Nigeria inclusive.

Nigeria's constitution upholds the concept of the rule of law: that the law is supreme over any person or group of persons in the society; that nobody is above the law and nobody has the right to tamper with the process of its application.

Nigeria's constitution maintains the separation of powers between the three organs of government - the executive, the legislative and the judiciary - with the judiciary as the impartial arbiter in interpreting and administering the law. Furthermore, our constitution guarantees, among other things, the fundamental rights of man[138]: right to life; right to dignity of human person; right to personal liberty; right to fair hearing; right to private life; right to freedom of thought, conscience and religion; right to freedom of expression and the press; right to peaceful assembly and association; right to freedom of movement; right to freedom from discrimination. Now, a question arises: if our Constitution has committed the country to the principles of democracy and social justice, and has made the security and welfare of the people the primary purpose of government (with economic, social and educational objectives), why do we have a lot of injustices and lack of security in Nigeria? Where lies the problem?

Cassius' words, "The fault, dear Brutus, is not in our stars, but in us who are the underlings,"[139] paves the way for our answer. In other words, the fault is not with our constitution, but fundamentally in the managers of our constitution - the government, the judiciary and the law enforcement agents. Thus we have executive lawlessness, lawlessness in the judicature and police lawlessness. There is the problem of ignorance of the law by the common man and of the high cost of justice.

Before delving into how the administrators and protectors of our law have become its violators, let us consider the problem of the **ignorance of the law** by the common man and of the high cost of justice. Many Nigerians are very ignorant of the laws of the land. "The concept of the rule of law is an alien concept to the Nigerian society. It is hardly understood by the ordinary person. Except for the professionally trained legal minds and a few other privileged persons in the society, the language in which laws are written is usually very difficult to be understood, hence the general ignorance of the law.... The situation has made the law to remain essentially an elitist property, understood only by the gentlemen in the legal profession who have succeeded in turning the interpretation of the law into a very lucrative business in the society."[140] The common man hardly knows his fundamental rights. This ignorance of the law by the common man is often exploited by those in the legal profession and by other agents concerned with the administration of justice. The police, for instance, likes dealing with people who are ignorant of the law more than with those who know their rights, because it can easily frighten and then extort more money from the former more than it can from the latter. Even those in the legal profession do exaggerate the cases of their clients, once they realise that the latter are ignorant of the law - to frighten them and to impress on them how serious and grievous their cases are, in order to get more money out of them - rather than educate them on their rights. Therefore, the common man is done injustice under the law by men of the law. (How fitting here are the words of the psalmist: "Can judges who do evil be your friends? They do injustice under the cover of law; they attack the life of the just and condemn innocent blood" - Psalm 94: 20-21.) And the government is doing little or nothing to educate the people on the laws of the land and to provide means of helping the people to keep the law.

To the above could be added the **high cost of justice**. The fees charged by the lawyers are generally very high that the common man cannot afford them. Therefore, only the wealthy can afford to hire a good lawyer, and, so, the rich often stand the better of justice administration.

Now to the **executive lawlessness**. Though Nigeria's constitution provides for separation of powers, thus making the judiciary independent of the executive and the legislative, in practice the judiciary is not independent - it is politicised and has inclination towards the executive. This could be a carry-over from the colonial system. During the colonial time, there "was the tendency of colonial judges to want to safeguard the interest of the executive against those of the other branch of government, the legislature.... 'What came out of Nigeria's colonial experience in the realm of law was not a robust legacy of the rule of law, but a notion of it which Nigerians might appreciate and nurture.'... Thus the problem of the Nigerian political system has remained the issue of the total independence and impartiality of the judiciary which is unfettered by executive pressures."[141] This is more prevalent during the military rule. Under the military, the rule of law is thrown to the winds: the military make retrospective or retroactive legislations, compulsorily acquire property without prompt payment of compensation, make arbitrary arrests and detention without trial, and oust the jurisdiction of the ordinary courts of the land to interprete or pronounce on the validity of legislation. This places the military government above the law.[142]

Considering all that is happening in Nigeria, one will agree with T. A. Imobighe that "there is a growing loss of confidence in the country's laws since they have failed to give the ordinary citizen protection against the excesses of the power elite. The loss of confidence has more or less assumed a fatalistic proportion because the country's judicial system and other law enforcement agents virtually exist to serve and defend the interest of these exploiters."[143] Going by the rule of law, everybody is equal before the law and the law is no respecter of persons. Not so in Nigeria. Here, everybody is unequal before the law, and the law is a respecter of persons and money. Justice is very often tilted in favour of the powers that be and of the rich. This is the place where "governments, both military and civilian, have too often shown complete disrespect for the rule of law. These practices undermine the public's confidence in the government, the law, and the administration of justice. Thus the entire nation suffers. Often acts of executive lawlessness go unchallenged or, even worse, unreported. Furthermore, these violations of the rule of law are perpetuated at all levels of government and even by some semi-governmental organisations such as universities. Clearly, once the top ranks of the government demonstrate their lack of respect for the judiciary, others follow suit and begin to ignore the legal limits of their authority."[144] This was particularly the case during the second republic when many governors took the law into their hands. Consequently there were cases of politically motivated dismissal of employees, arbitrary restructuring of government bodies and skewed distribution of resources contrary to existing laws.[145]

There is next the **lawlessness in the judicature**. Many of the men and women of the legal profession (who are expected in law to be neutral in their view of law and facts in order to make the game fair) are known to spurn their oath of office and then become partisan in certain cases before them, thereby violating the very law which they ought to protect. Cases abound of Nigerian judges who are biased and in favour of the government against defendants.[146] Moreover, it is difficult for the common man to obtain justice. For example, the average Nigerian worker who is struggling "for justice from landlords, shareholders and managerial agents and rentiers, among others," is just struggling in vain, as those who are in control of the legal system are the "judges most of whom derive more of their income from their position as landlords, shareholders, and all types of rentiers, than their salaries, allowances, pensions and gratuity."[147]

Lastly, there is the **police lawlessness**. The police are law enforcement agents. They are supposed to protect the people against any violation of their rights. But, what we see is a police force that not only takes the law into its hands but also violates the rights of the people it is supposed to protect. "Illicit behaviour by police ranges from excessive use of force, wide spread harassment, defiance of constitutional court orders or decisions, systematic police perjury to criminal negligence of duty. Physical assault on suspects and other innocent citizens by police officers is daily occurrence in Nigeria even though such act is in contravention of section 31 (a) and 33 of the constitution."[148] Hence, with the police, the security of the people is never guaranteed. And like the judiciary, the police are partisan: "The police force in Nigeria has never been known to defend the course of the poor or to be really neutral in politics. It is also known to be ridden with corruption and ineffectiveness. However, its behaviour between 1979 and 1983 convinced the average citizen that the majority of the police officers were card-carrying members of the ruling NPN. Other than the frequent massacres of peasants (as was the case in Bakolori, Sokoto state), students and workers, most of the state police commissioners operated as military governors and had the belief that they had the power to determine the future of any politician."[149]

It therefore becomes clear (from the above discussions) that those who are mandated with responsibility of managing the affairs of the country have turned out to constitute themselves greatest danger to the security of the country. Surely a government that does not abide by its own rules cannot seriously expect others to respect either that government or its laws! And since government's attitude to the question of the rule of law provides a very good thermometer for measuring the state of the health of legality and of law and order in a given society, one can conclude that there is not much justice in our judicial system and that there is no security of life and property in Nigeria. Lawlessness seems to be the order of the day. And where there is no law, there cannot be justice. According to Thomas

Hobbes: "In that state of nature (where) war of everyman against everyman prevails, nothing can be just. The notions of right and wrong, justice and injustice have there no place. Where there is no common power, there is no law: where no law, no justice. Force and fraud, are in war the two cardinal virtues."[150] Nigeria may not be in a state of war, but the horrible situation of things in the country demands "a state of emergency" as force and fraud have become the society's cardinal virtues. As E. Odumegwu-Ojukwu puts it: "Everywhere, the citizen of this country is assaulted with violence: in his home where he is obliged to erect and inhabit his own prison, in his place of work which he has to turn into a fortress and in the streets where his fears border on schizophrenia. The helpless Nigerian has watched helplessly the degradation of his society: robbery with violence has become so much an everyday affair that the robbers and the criminals have become folk heroes of our new society. With mouth agape, 'the Nigerian' has watched a national metamorphosis where 'Keeping the Peace' has become 'Killing the Peace'. Wherever he looks there is violence: in sports, in politics, in religion."[151] In the same vein, Prof. O. K. Ogan writes:

> In the past decade Nigerians have shown an uncanny and obsessional expertise in defeating the purpose of every law enacted, and flouting it fragrantly. We must be the world's best forgers and embezzlers of public funds, and it is seldom that any of our multifarious high-powered inquiries has produced effective results or even verdicts. We can decode every cypher, however complicated, neutralise every safety device, however fool-proof, the other nations of mankind may have guaranteed them to be - that is, other races with the most sophisticated technological expertise; but Nigerians can always 'fix' that.
>
> In all departments of government as well as in the private or public sector any file marked 'top secret' is sure to have had its content committed to memory by the messenger. Every secret or classified information is public knowledge. Investigations into acts of fraud occupy more space in our national press than any other news item. The code of conduct and disciplinary procedure of any institution, private or statal and parastatal alike will clearly list out what the principals of that organistion define as taboo; but it is idle to assume that anyone takes notice of such trivia. Every certificate of roadworthiness, every driving licence and soon I bet every certificate of tax clearance also bears a price tag. Every bank or business house attacked by armed robbers must know that the forces behind the robbery exist right under its nose, master minded by a powerful crime ring within its walls.
>
> Any Nigerian hawking a West African Examinations Council certificate with ten A's anywhere in Britain is quietly snubbed in favour of a Grade III from any other West African territory. Our expertise in crime is thus genuinely and widely acknowledged. One could go on citing examples ad nauseam. It is a catalogue that draws from every sphere of local human endeavour, private or public.[152]

It cannot therefore be over-stressed that situation as this mars growth and development of democracy.

3.5. Indiscipline and Corruption[153]

Indiscipline and Corruption are "twin-brothers" that have become household words in Nigeria. They are bedevilling phenomena which have plagued the nation unabated since its independence. Indeed, indiscipline and corruption have become the cankerworm in the fabrics of the Nigerian society which has defied all attempts to eradicate it.[154] Though indiscipline and corruption are related and often go together, they are not identical: while every corruption involves indiscipline, not every indiscipline is corruption. Hence they have to be treated separately.

3.5.1. Indiscipline

It is difficult to define indiscipline. The dictionaries define it simply as "lack of discipline." To ascertain the meaning of indiscipline therefore, we must know the meaning of discipline. *The Concise Oxford Dictionary* gives five sets of definitions of discipline. We shall concern ourselves with the first set of definitions: "control or order exercised over people or animals;" "the system of rules used to maintain this control;" "the behaviour of groups subjected to such rules." Indiscipline then is lack of any or all of the above definitions. As Chinua Achebe has it, "indiscipline is *a failure or refusal to submit one's desires and actions to the restraints of orderly social conduct in recognition of the rights and desires of others*. The goal of indiscipline is self-interest; its action, the abandonment of self-restraint in pursuit of the goal."[155] Because indiscipline borders on the self and on the violation of the common-good, it is very difficult, if not impossible, for democracy to take root in a soil where the virus of indiscipline dominate. This is the plight of Nigeria.

Considering the present state of affairs in Nigeria, E. Odumegwu-Ojukwu laments: "We see a society where there is total lack of discipline.... In short, ours is a society where we are not our brothers keepers, which is very un-African."[156] Truly "indiscipline pervades our life so completely today that one may be justified in calling it the condition *par excellence* of contemporary Nigerian society. We see and hear and read about indiscipline in the home, in the school, in the public service, in the private sector, in government and in legislative assemblies, on the roads, in the air."[157]

Some examples of acts of indiscipline in the Nigerian society are quite illustrative. Firstly, in public places: Nigerians hardly follow the rule of "first come, first served" - shamelessly jumping the queue is the order of the day. X may be waiting for attention in a public office when Y (also in need of attention) arrives, and Y will be attended to before X. This happens either because Y knows somebody, or somebody who knows somebody, who works in that public place, or because Y is somebody of affluence and/or of influence. Secondly, on our roads:

it is the survival of the fittest, with the drivers flouting traffic rules with impunity. The bigger your vehicle is, the mightier you are on the road. The truck driver would like to keep the bus driver out of the way; the bus driver the car driver; the car driver the motorcyclist; the motorcyclist the cyclist; and the cyclist would frighten the pedestrian off the way. In the end, it is the weakest, the pedestrian, who suffers the most. Thirdly, in the civil service: many civil servants use their official time for private business and thus leave their work undone. Other examples abound. But these three enough to drive home my point: indiscipline is a blatant violation of natural justice and of the common-good, and it poses a great danger to the rooting of democracy in Nigeria.

3.5.2. Corruption

Corruption is not new in the Nigerian politics. It is as old as Nigeria itself and, as stated earlier, has defied all attempts to wipe it out. Even as far back as 26 February 1952, the Emir of Gwandu moved the following motion in the Northern House of Chiefs:

> That this House, agreeing that bribery and corruption are widely prevalent in all walks of life, recommends that Native Authorities should make every effort to trace and punish offenders with strict impartiality and to educate public opinion against bribery and corruption.[158]

During the first republic, the President of Nigeria, Dr Nnamdi Azikiwe, was worried about the level of corruption in the country that he warned that with the vice permeating the country "the prestige of our nation dwindles to the vanishing point, defacing our national image and bringing shame to those who wear the 'agbada' of Nigerian citizenship." At the same period, in 1963 to be precise, Ronald Wraith and Edgar Simpkins observed that "in Africa, corruption flourishes as luxuriantly as the bush and the weeds which it so much resembles, taking the goodness from the soil and suffocating the growth of the plants which have been carefully and expensively bred and tended. The forces ranged against it are negligible."[159] This agrees with Utibe Ukim's observation that "in Nigeria, corrupt practices are truly a way of life and nobody seems to have a clue to taming the monster."[160] Moreover, "corruption in Nigeria is not about a few individuals who pilfer from public purse, it is the system. The problem is neither economic nor even political, it is moral.... Corruption is now so deeply rooted that it is doubtful if it can be dug out."[161] Indeed, corruption has become so rampant and commonplace that for many Nigerians bribery is no longer evil but a mode of thank you, a "dash" - a way of "expressing gratitude in anticipation of services about to be rendered."[162]

Corruption is very much evident in the *misappropriations of public time, funds and property*. There is what I may term "white-collar crimes"[163]: taking work supplies for personal use - like using official stationery for private purposes; using government drugs, dressings and hospital equipment for private purposes; using the company phone for personal long distance calls; using government labour for private work; time theft and unauthorised absenteeism - like using government time for private work; misuse of government motor vehicles for private purposes; demanding sex from a female applicant for jobs; demanding money from applicant for jobs or contracts; tampering with applications, contract documents and payment vouchers; misuse of overseas tours - to gallivant round and enjoy a life of ease and pleasure for some time and also to amass and build up income in foreign exchange from the "estacode allowances".

There are election malpractices[164]: bribing the voters to vote for oneself or for somebody else; contriving to get one person to vote more than once in one particular election; encouraging and allowing unregistered persons, under-aged persons and aliens to vote; stuffing the ballot boxes with ballot papers before the day of election; scaring away opponent voters; disenfranchisement of individuals and entire communities either by under supplying of voting materials, by refusing to build booths in requisite numbers or at well-known designated places; by not allowing the full time of voting, or by simply not sending any electoral staff; bribing election officials to stay away from their appointed posts; getting Returning Officers to falsify the results of voting; and the worst of all, the collusion of the Electoral Commission (the supposedly "unbiased organiser and umpire" of elections) and of the police (the supposedly "neutral law-enforcement and peacekeeping force") with the powers that be to effect election frauds. (Note that Nigeria has never had a hitch-free or free and fair election.)

There is the big money corruption[165]: like obtaining import licences under false pretences - huge sums of money are sent abroad into private accounts for importation of goods which are never shipped, and, in some cases, to cover up their crimes the dupes ship sand or sawdust; the inflation of contracts in order to receive kickbacks which go into the coffers of political parties and into private pockets - the end result of this is that infrastructural works are poorly constructed and do not last, because a contractor finds that by the time he has handed money round to all those whose favour must be won in government, the balance of the contract money is nowhere near enough to execute the project to standard; payments are approved and paid for contracts which are never executed all to enable the functionary concerned to make quick money; payment of salaries to fictitious workers; fictitious travelling claims and allowances; financial excesses and misuse of security funds by chief executives.[166] It is a well-known fact that quite a number of government functionaries amass millions of naira, and a few are known to have hit the billion mark. Some of them own private jets, fleets of ships, chains of business enterprises, even palatial mansions in the western world's capitals.

What encourages the spread of corruption is the general attitude of Nigerians to wealth and riches. Nigerians worship material success. Wealthy people who are known to be corrupt are regularly courted and honoured by communities, religious bodies, social clubs and other private organisations, thereby encouraging the "get-rich-quick attitude." A. Adebayo testifies to this: "the generality of Nigerians worship material success, no matter by what means the success is achieved. This goes to the roots of our sense of values.... A junior official who lives far beyond his means and rides cars, builds houses annually, is regarded with envy and admiration by the generality of Nigerian public. When they speak about him they say that he is making it. They regard him as particularly fortunate. In civilized communities, a person who is living beyond his station in life or who has come into some sudden mysterious wealth will be regarded as suspect by society and will be avoided by decent people. A few years ago, a story was published about a Nigerian who gave a present of about N4 million to his English girlfriend in Britain. It was reported that the lady promptly rejected the gift, pointing out that sudden accession to wealth would make her a subject of suspect and scorn in society and her friends and neighbours would keep away from her."[167] And Dr T. A. Imobighe agrees: "there is the unabated obsession for material wealth. In Nigeria today, the belief in money has been substituted for a belief in the nation. It is the rich that gets recognition in the society not those who render honest service to the nation."[168] Public probity is therefore thrown to the winds. Nobody - especially those who benefit from the largess of the corrupt people - asks questions, like how somebody who was nobody yesterday comes into much money today. Even a public servant who is honest in his work and thus does not get rich overnight is considered a failure by his people. This sad situation is well brought out by Prof. O. K. Ogan thus:

> What is the reaction to public probity? Does the honest Permanent Secretary in Nigeria have any credibility?.... Any high executive in Nigerian society is thought to be in big business. He is the king pin in the award of contracts; therefore our society assumes that he will channel everything into his own pockets. His family and friends and hangers-on invariably expect this, so if they don't see this happen, they imagine that he must be less competent than his colleagues, or just a liar.
>
> ....
>
> A person amasses a lot of wealth through ill-gotten gains, and so, as is customary in this country of crooks, he will live a very lavish and ostentatious life to show off his wealth. It is generally known for a fact that he is a thief but he will try to bolster up his image with revolting extravagance such as throwing lavish parties to which he invites the world and his wife. Do you need to accept his invitations? How many Nigerians would feel compromised by being seen enjoying the largesse of such a monster? On the contrary many people in our community will go to any lengths to advertise their commitment and alliance, even sparing no pains to enhance their friendship with such a character.[169]

This lack of probity has degenerated into decadence and lawlessness. There is the unfortunate and unhealthy pre-occupation or an obsession with "What can I get away with?" rather than "What can I put in?" For many people this has become a full-time occupation and the only purpose in life. And there is much disrespect for the law: "In the past decade Nigerians have shown an uncanny and obsessional expertise in defeating the purpose of every law enacted.... Our expertise in crime is thus genuinely and widely acknowledged."[170] This definitely hinders the development of democracy.

Corruption has many far-reaching effects. According to Peter Eigen,

> Corruption has far graver consequences than the mere funneling of scarce resources into the pockets of unethical civil servants. As former U.S. congressman John Brademas has pointed out, corruption is 'a major obstacle to the advance of democracy and economic groth.... By undermining trust in political institutions and public officials and by distorting government policy against the best interests of the majority, corruption impairs the process of democracy. The effects of corruption are especially pernicious in emerging democracies, for the abuse of public office subverts popular confidence in the very idea of self-government.' Corruption gives rise to oligarchy. It allows leaders to cling to power while resisting governmental reform, curbing personal freedom, and abusing basic human rights. Corruption hinders the creation of free markets. The magnitude of bribes, rather than the quality of products or services, determines what sells. Hence corruption is conducive to fundamental mistakes in project selection and project design - often with catastrophic consequences for both society and the environment.
>
> This process hinders the growth of competitiveness, frustrates efforts to alleviate poverty, and makes real economic progress impossible. A self-perpetuating cycle can develop, with a broad expectation of corruption causing an increase in its incidence. Such a system rewards the unscrupulous and demoralizes the honest. A 'brain drain' often follows, as people who reject the system emigrate to countries in which they will be rewarded for their skills and productivity.
>
> ....
>
> ... All too often, a corrupt environment channels resources to nonproductive areas such as the police, the armed forces, and other organs of social control and repression as the elites move to protect their positions and wealth. In a vicious circle, corruption and autocratic rule feed upon each other and become mutually dependent.[171]

To these could be added the erosion of national consciousness and patriotism among Nigerians. This is, indeed, very serious and pathetic, as Dr T. A. Imobighe indicates: "This lack of national consciousness is manifested in the prevailing attitude of most Nigerians that the country exists to be exploited to aggrandize self and close associates rather than an entity to be developed. A nation whose citizens lack a national consciousness and patriotism is a nation that has lost its soul. Such a nation falls easy prey to internal disruptions and external violations. The situation in the country is particularly serious in that the lack of national consciousness and patriotism has permeated all sectors of public life, be they the security enforcement sector or the strategic resource management sector."[172] And democracy has no chance of survival in a country where decadence and lawlessness thrive and where national consciousness and patriotism are lacking.

3.6. Mass media factor[173]

Another major problem of democracy in Nigeria is the mass media (radio, television and newspapers and magazines). Although there is freedom of the press in our constitution, the Nigerian press is everywhere in chains - in chains from its proprietors and in chains from the government. So, rather than inform, the press is often prone to misinform the public. This impedes the democratic process.

A foreigner looking at the rate with which many newspapers and magazines spring up in Nigeria, especially during the civil rule, would immediately conclude that Nigeria is a reading country, where public information is very much valued. But if he were to stay long in Nigeria or if he were to do some investigation into "why these newspapers and magazines?," he would soon discover, to his chagrin, that the whole thing is political: each newspaper or magazine represents a politician or a political party or a political view or the views and particular interest of the proprietor. Indeed "Nigerian politics media politics. Whatever you may say about Nigerian politicians, you must admit that they know the value of the news media in political struggles. In the first republic most of our journalists were politicians in the scruffy garb of journalists. After all, we won independence, thanks largely to the gallons of ink they poured out in the struggle for independence. In the second republic, we opened the dam of ink on ourselves. No one knows how many newspapers there were. They made politics exciting for those who had the stomach for scurrilous and yellow journalism. Most of the newspapers died even before the military chaps cocked their guns at the Shehu Shagari administration."[174] That emphasises why the politicians and/or political parties invest much in the print and electronic media: in order to acquire an effective publicity machine to reach the electorate, reinforce themselves and promote their political interests, since the press has become "a veritable weapon in the struggle for the minds of men and, as the struggle (becomes) more contentious and often bloody, for the breaking of the heart (and often times the head) of opponent and spectator alike."[175] Some examples will help to buttress the point. During the second republic, Alex Ekwueme (of the National Party of Nigeria, NPN) set up the *Trumpet* in Anambra state to promote the party's interest in the state and to help fan the embers of division within Nigerian People's Party, NPP (the ruling party in the State);[176] Dr Nwakamma Okoro (NPN member) set up *The Nation* in Imo state to provide competition for NPP state-owned *Statesman*;[177] in Bendel State, Chief Anthony Enahoro (NPN) established the *Sun* to "scorch" the Unity Party of Nigeria, UPN, administration of Ambrose Alli;[178] and so on.

This brings us to the heavy censure of the press by the proprietors of the mass media. Nigeria has "a legacy of practice that seeks to subordinate the media, through ownership, through control, either financial or moral, to the leadership of society."[179] The saying, "He who pays the piper dictates the tune" is very true in the relationship between the mass media and their owners. As E. A.

Jaja rightly points out, there is "a direct corollary ... between financial control, on the one hand and content, on the other.... Party activists find their way on to the payroll as editors and writers, and the paper becomes primarily a vehicle for building legend out of the party and the men in power."[180] What this means is that the proprietors of the press determine the editorial policy, and thus editorial freedom precludes the publishing of any material detrimental to the political interests of the proprietors.[181] To ensure this, the pattern of top editorial recruitments into the various press emphasizes loyalty and reliability, and a whiff of suspicion is enough to lead to dismissal of the concerned editor.[182] This then makes the mass media partisan.

A major consequence of the press censure is the sacrificing of professional ethics and standards, informed by visions of the liberal order.[183] News reporting loses its objectivity. Everything is seen from the point of view of the proprietor - only what the master wills, says and does is important. The press ceases to be open to and accommodative of opposing views. Political opponents of the master automatically becomes also opponents and enemies of the master's press, with the result that nothing good could ever be reported about and from these opponents. The opponents are meant for "slaughter" - hence the mud-smearing or mudslinging, the character-assassination, in a word: the yellow journalism that is the lot of the Nigerian press. Thus, one of the pillars on which democracy stands - the journalistic pluralism, the willingness of the press to publish all shades of opinion (even opinion opposed to its own) - is thrown to the winds. Then the public is misinformed, fed with truncated news, lies, and, at best, with half-truths. News is slanted to suit particular interests. As T. Obadina, a clumnist with the *Punch*, puts it: "the reader gets the truth he pays for: If he buys *Concord* he gets *Concord*'s brand of truth, and if he buys *Sketch* he gets *Sketch*'s brand of truth."[184] Therefore, news reporting in Nigeria, going by normal standard, leaves much to be desired. A. Adebayo puts the matter thus:

> Pick up any newspaper in an African country, and every page will be filled with the picture of the ruler and what he says and does. The only other feature which will fill the newspaper will be bric-bat mud-slinging between rival political parties. Curses, name-calling, mutual accusations of the most vile nature - all these run from page to page alongside the oratorical activities of the ruler....
>
> Let us compare this with the situation in the civilized world. In those countries, once the elections are over, the newspapers put away party political duels and dwell on social and economic issues. The politics you read of are the political decisions of government as they affect the social and economic life of the nation, and also the interplay of world politics. Besides these, you will not read of President Ronald Reagen or Mrs. Margaret Thatcher on pages of newspapers. They go about their work quietly and unobtrusively. They do not rush round at weekends collecting chieftaincy titles, the expences of which are borne by government treasury and the news and pictures of which fill the newspapers throughout the following week.[185]

There is next the censure of the press by the government. This is normal with the military government. Military rule, not being democratic but dictatorial, welcomes neither opposition nor criticism. Therefore, unless the press dances to the tune of the military government it is bound to be suppressed. Mr Agbaje summarises the situation this way: "the military administration ... (shows) a preference for 'administrative' handling of journalists and media houses, including detention of 'recalcitrant' journalists without trial, raids and laying of siege in the premises of erring newspaper houses, dissolution of boards of government-owned newspapers whenever necessary, and outright proscription. To complement all this (is) a controlled system of news management on the part of government."[186] It is really an uphill task fighting for press freedom under military government. And one can rightly say that press freedom under military rule is like water in the desert.

Nevertheless, many seasoned journalists still continue to brave the hostilities to their profession from many angles. Consequently some have spent and some are spending months in detentions, some lose their jobs, some even paid for it with their lives. In the same vein, there are some media houses and institutions that defy all threats from the powers that be, in order to remain true to their profession. Such newspapers and magazines - like *Newswatch* (Nigeria's weekly newsmagazine) and *Tell* (also a weekly magazine) - are owned by nonpoliticians and are not subordinated, through ownership or through control, either financial or moral, to the leadership of the society or to the whims and caprices of their proprietors. They are non-partisan and so they endeavour to present the public with objective news: unbiased facts and true pictures of events. In these media every shed of opinion can be read. They are critical as well as educating. And with them Nigerian press has a future.

Conclusion

Although there are other minor factors militating against the spirit of democracy in Nigeria (which have been overlooked in this work for lack of time and space), these six factors (considered above) constitute the major hindrance to building a sustainable democracy in the Nigeria. The task facing this nation and its well meaning citizens is how to get rid of these cancerous problems from our body politics. In other words, how do we establish a just, free and fair society in which there shall be no discrimination (of tribe, religion or sex); in which the government shall be effective, responsible and accountable; in which the welfare of the citizens shall be primary; discipline and honesty shall be part and parcel of the people's life; and whereby the rule of law remains supreme, and the mass media is free to do its work of objectively informing, educating and entertaining the public? In short, how do we build a stable and lasting democracy in Nigeria? This all important question is the concern of the next chapter.

NOTES

1 Tunji Olagunju, "Transition to second experiment - Some political issues" in: Sam E. Oyovbaire, ed., **Democratic Experiment in Nigeria: Interpretative Essays** (Benin City, Nigeria: Omega Publishers, c1987), p. 33.

2 A. Adebayo, **Power in Politics** (Ibadan, Nigeria: Spectrum Books Limited, 1986), pp. 2-3.

3 Ibid., p. 3.

4 W. Bossman, **A New Accurate Description of the Coast of Guinea** (Translated from Dutch and printed in London, 1705), p. 146 - quoted in: A. Adebayo, op. cit., p. 4.

5 Sir R. Burton, **A Mission to Gelele, King of Dahome**, 1864 - quoted in: A. Adebayo, op. cit., p. 4

6 For details on this subject, see J. F. Ade Ajayi, **The Problems of National Integration in Nigeria: A historical perspective** (Ibadan: Nigerian Institute of Social and Economic Research, 1984); **Report of the Seminar on Nigeria in Transition** (Lagos: Federal Ministry of Information, 1980); **Round-Table Meeting on Ethnicity in Nigeria: Implications for National Development** (Kuru, Nigeria: National Institute for Policy and Strategic Studies, 1983); Okwudiba Nnoli, **Ethnic Politics in Nigeria** (Enugu, Nigeria: Fourth Dimension Publishers, 1978); Onigu Otite, **Ethnic Pluralism and Ethnicity in Nigeria: With Comparative Materials** (Ibadan, Nigeria: Shaneson, 1990); Larry J. Diamond, **Class, Ethnicity, and Democracy in Nigeria: The Failure of the First Republic** (Syracuse, N.Y.: Syracuse University Press, 1988); Dr. A. O. Sanda, ed., **Ethnic Relations in Nigeria: Problems and Prospects** (Nigeria: Dept. of Sociology, University of Ibadan, 1976); B. I. Ngwoke, **Islam, the O.I.C. and Nigerian Unity** (Enugu, Nigeria: I. Ngwoke, 1986); Hypolite Adigwe, **Nigeria Joins the Organisation of Islamic Conference, O.I.C.: the Implications for Nigeria** (Onitsha, Nigeria: Archdiocesan Secretariate, Cath. Archdiocese of Onitsha, 1986); Abubakar S. Mohammed & Tony Edoh, eds., **Nigeria: A Republic in Ruins** (Zaria, Nigeria: Dept. of Political Science, 1986); Yusuf B. Usman, **For the Liberation of Nigeria** (London: New Beacon Books Ltd., 1980); Peter Enahoro, **How to be a Nigerian** (Ibadan, Nigeria: The Caxton Press (West Africa) Ltd., 1981); Sam E. Oyovbaire, ed., **Democratic Experiment in Nigeria: Interpretative Essays** (Benin City, Nigeria: Omega Publishers, 1987); K. A. Busia, **Africa in search of Democracy** (London: Routledge & Kegan Paul, 1967); **Report of the Political Bureau, March 1987** (Abuja: Directorate for Social Mobilisation, MAMSER, 1987), pp. 24-30, 186-201.

7 Quoted in: James O. Ojiako, **Nigeria: Yesterday, Today, And...** (Onitsha, Nigeria: African Educational Publishers (Nig.) Ltd., 1981), p. 190.

8 E. Odumegwu-Ojukwu, op. cit., pp. 1-2 & 186.

9 Cf. A. O. Sanda (Dr), ed., **Ethnic Relations in Nigeria: Problems and Prospects** (Nigeria: Dept. of Sociology, University of Ibadan, 1987), pp. 118-119, and Okwudiba Nnoli, **Ethnic Politics in Nigeria** (Enugu, Nigeria: Fourth Dimension Publishers, 1978), pp. 154, 112-123.

10 Olu Akinkoye (Dr.), "Ethnicity and Social Cohesion," in: **Round-Table Meeting on Ethnicity in Nigeria: Implication for National Development** (1983), p. 85.

11 Cf. C. O Nwanunobi, "Ethnicity and National Integration: New Directions," in: **Round-Table Meeting on Ethnicity in Nigeria: Implications for National Develop-**

ment (Kuru, Nigeria: National Institute for Polica and Strategic Studies, 1983), pp. 111ff.

12 Michael Crowder, op. cit., p. 216.

13 Cf. E. Odumegwu-Ojukwu, op. cit., pp. 3-4.

14 Henry I. Ejembi, "Ethnicity and Political Development in Nigeria: An Outline of a Discussion," in: **Round-Table Meeting on Ethnicity in Nigeria: Implications for National Development** (Kuru, Nigeria, 1983), p. 38, also pp.58-60, 63-64.

15 Sanya Onabamiro (Prof.), "The place and role of education in the evolution of an egalitarian society," in: **Report of the Seminar on Nigeria in Transition** (Lagos: Federal Ministry of Information, 1980), p.89.

16 J. F. Ade Ajayi, **The Problems of National Integration in Nigeria: A Historical Perspective** (Ibadan: Nigerian Institute of Social and Economic Research, 1984), pp. 4-6.

17 A. R. Mustapha, "Repression and the Nigerian Political Economy," in: A. S. Mohammed & T. Edoh, eds., **Nigeria: A Republic in Ruins** (Zaria: Dept. of Political Science, 1986), pp. 25-26.

18 Peter Enahoro, **How to be a Nigerian** (Ibadan, Nigeria: The Caxton Press (West Africa) Ltd., 1981), pp. 3-6; cf. A. O. Sanda, ed., "On the Concept of a Nigerian Society," in: sic, op. cit., pp. 3-16.

19 Ekpo Eyo (Dr.), "Nigeria's Traditional Ideals: Culture as an instrument of National Unity," in: **Report of the Seminar on Nigeria in Transition** (Lagos: Federal Ministry of Information, 1980), p. 24

20 A. A. Akiwowo emphasises and expounds the fact that "ethnic rivalries and jealousies give rise to tribalism." See his article, "The Sociology of Nigerian Tribalism," in: A. O. Sanda, ed., op. cit., pp. 21-24.

21 Onigu Otite (Prof.), op. cit., pp. 9-10; cf. Dr M. Zakayi Kano, "Ethnicity and Social Cohesion," in: **Round-Table Meeting on Ethnicity in Nigeria: Implications for National Development** (1983), pp. 93-94.

22 Kasim A. Sambo, "Ethnicity in Nigeria: Implications for National Development," in: **Round-Table Meeting on Ethnicity in Nigeria: Implications for National Development** (1983), p. 77.

23 Olu Akinkoye (Dr), op. cit., p. 86; cf. E. Odumegwu-Ojukwu, op. cit., p. 137.

24 Note that many people use "tribe/tribalism" and "ethnicity/ethnicism" interchangeably. But we can distinguish "tribe/tribalism" from "ethnicity", although both may operate on the same principle. An ethnic group could be said to consist of one or more smaller entities called "tribe". Ethnicity "is more macro-divisive and more salient with more far-reaching consequences than tribalism. Ethnicity is the more appropriate concept in analysing symbol-based discriminations at the national level." (See Prof. Onigu Otite, "On the Concept of Ethnicity in Nigeria," in: **Round-Table Meeting on Ethnicity in Nigeria: Implications for National Development** (Kuru, Nigeria: National Institute for Policy and Strategic Studies, 1983), p. 9; cf. Alhaji Shehu Musa: "This is where I must differ with those who regard ethnicism as being synonymous with tribalism...." - his "Ethnicity, Social Cohesion and National Integration," in: **Round-Table Meeting on Ethnicity in Nigeria** (1983), p. 43; and also A. A. Akiwowo, op. cit., p. 17.

25 C. Gahia, "The Tribal Bugbear," in: **Newswatch**, October 10, 1994, pp. 35-36; cf. Olu Akinkoye, op. cit., p. 87; A. Bamishaiye, "Ethnic Politics as an Instrument of Unequal

Socio-economic Development in Nigeria's First Republic," in: A. O. Sanda, ed., op. cit., pp. 71-90; and E. Odumegwu-Ojukwu, op. cit., pp. 18-20.

26 Cf. Olu Akinkoye, op. cit., pp. 82-83.

27 Cf. ibid., p. 87; see also Okwudiba Nnoli, op. cit., pp. 69-106.

28 Cf. Okwudiba Nnoli, op. cit., pp. 35-36.

29 Cf. ibid., pp. 107-112.

30 Onigu Otite (Prof.), op. cit., p. 11; cf. A. O. Sanda, op. cit., pp. 120-121; A. B. Akinyemi, "Ethnic Politics: A Non-conformist View," in: A. O. Sanda, op. cit., pp. 135-145; O. Nnoli, op. cit., pp. 140-248; Y. R. Barongo, "Ethnic Pluralism and Democratic Stability: The Basis of Conflict and Consensus," in: Sam E. Oyovbaire, ed., **Democratic Experiment in Nigeria: Interpretative Essays** (Benin City, Nigeria: Omega Publishers, 1987), pp. 70-76.

31 Alhaji Shehu Usman, "Ethnicity, Social Cohesion and National Integration," in: **Round-Table Meeting on Ethnicity in Nigeria: Implications for National Development** (Kuru, 1983), p. 48.

32 Idoko M. Akor, "National Integration and the Material Basis of the Ethnic Ideology in Nigeria," in: **Round-Table Meeting on Ethnicity in Nigeria** (Kuru, 1983), p. 52; cf. K. A. Busia, **Africa in search of Democracy** (London: Routledge & Kegan Paul, 1967), p. 111.

33 J. F. Ade Ajayi, op. cit., p. 9.

34 Ibid., p. 3.

35 Okwudiba Nnoli, op. cit., pp. 128-130

36 **Report of the Political Bureau, March 1987**, p. 29.

37 "Is that NPC Policy," in: **West African Pilot**, Editorial, June 17, 1960.

38 See, for example, Jibril Ibrahim's analysis of the immediate and long term causes of the outbreak of religious violence between Muslims and Christians in Kaduna State in 1987: in his article, "The Politics of Religion in Nigeria: The Parameters of the 1987 Crisis in Kaduna State," published in: **Review of African Political Economy**, no. 45/46, 1989, pp. 65-82.

39 Cf. **The Constitution of the Fed. Republic of Nigeria: 1979, sec. 10; 1989, sec. 37.**

40 While the Muslims were sympathetic towards the Arab nations, the Christians had their sympathy for Israel, and the Federal Government adopted a so-called "neutral stand" toward the Middle-East countries. However, this "neutral stand" of the Federal Government is very ironical: although the Government refused the establishment of an Israeli Embassy in Nigeria, it had good relationship with the Arab world. Cf. A. B. Akinyemi, **Foreign Policy and Federalism** (Ibadan, Nigeria, 1974), p. 103.

41 This affiliation "is said" to have been cancelled, following the many protests and demonstrations from the Christians. However, we should not forget the attempts made by Ahmadu Bello in 1961 to drag Nigeria into a "Confederation of Muslim States" - cf. "No Sir Ahmadu!" in: **Daily Times**, Editorial, June 28 and 29, 1961.

42 Cf. Emeka Odumegwu-Ojukwu, op. cit., pp. 186-187.

43 Adigun A. B. Agbaje, **The Nigerian Press, Hegemony, and the Social Construction of Legitimacy, 1960-1983** (Lewiston: E. Mellen Press, 1992), pp. 242-243; cf. **New Nigeria:** June 2, 1977, p. 1; - Sept. 13, 1977, pp. 2 & 34; **Nigerian Tribune**, Sept. 17, 1977, p. 4; **West Africa**, May 8, 1978, p. 901; **African Contemporary Record**, 1978-

79, p. B739; J. J. Oluleye, op. cit., p. 201; Olusegun Obasanjo, **Not My Will** (Nigeria), pp. 61-62.

44 Cf. Yusufu's "The Manipulation of Religion in Nigeria Today: Its Social and Political Basis," in his book, **For the Liberation of Nigeria** (London: New Beacon Books Ltd., 1980), pp. 78-91.

45 Emeka Odumegwu-Ojukwu, op. cit., pp. 20 & 55.

46 Ibid., p. 22.

47 Tunji Olagunju, "Transition to the Second Experiment - Some Political Issues," in: Sam E. Oyovbaire, op. cit., pp. 35f.

48 For details see Chinua Achebe, **The Trouble with Nigeria** (Enugu, Nigeria: Fourth Dimension Publishing Co. Ltd., 1983); A. Adebayo, **Power in Politics** (Ibadan: Spectrum Books Ltd., 1986); Emeka Odumegwu-Ojukwu, **Because I am involved** (Ibadan. Owerri. Kaduna: Spectrum Books Ltd., 1989); **Report of the Seminar on Nigeria in Transition** (Lagos: Federal Ministry of Information, 1980); **Round-Table Meeting on Ethnicity in Nigeria: Implications for National Development** (Kuru, Nigeria: National Institute for Policy and Strategic Studies, 1983); Okwudiba Nnoli, **Ethnic Politics in Nigeria** (Enugu, Nigeria: Fourth Dimension Publishers, 1978); Abubakar S. Mohammed & Tony Edoh, eds., **Nigeria: A Republic in Ruins** (Zaria, Nigeria: Dept. of Political Science, 1986); Yusuf B. Usman, **For the Liberation of Nigeria** (London: New Beacon Books Ltd., 1980); Y. B. Usman, ed., **Political Repression in Nigeria** (Zaria, Nigeria: Gaskiya Corporation Ltd., 1982); Peter Enahoro, **How to be a Nigerian** (Ibadan, Nigeria: The Caxton Press (West Africa) Ltd., 1981); Sam E. Oyovbaire, ed., **Democratic Experiment in Nigeria: Interpretative Essays** (Benin City, Nigeria: Omega Publishers, 1987); **Report of the Political Bureau, March 1987** (Abuja: Directorate for Social Mobilisation, MAMSER, 1987); Ralph Adams Cram, **The Nemesis of Mediocrity** (Boston: Marshal Jones Company, 1919); S. G. Ikoku, **Nigeria's Fourth Coup d'etat: Options for Modern Statehood** (Enugu, Nigeria: Fourth Dimension Pub. Co. Ltd., 1985); F. Shyllon and O. Obasanjo, **The Demise of the Rule of Law in Nigeria under the Military: Two Points of View** (Ibadan: Insitute of African Studies, University of Ibadan, 1980); O. Obasanjo, **A March of Progress: Collected Speeches of His Excellency Lt. Gen. Olusegun Obasanjo** (Lagos: Federal Ministry of Information, n.d.).

49 Chinua Achebe, **The Trouble with Nigeria** (Enugu, Nigeria: Fourth Dimension Publishing Co. Ltd., 1983), p. 1.

50 Cf. Mike Akpan, "Politics of Leadership," in: **Newswatch**, Oct. 10, 1994, pp. 25-27.

51 S. G. Ikoku, **Nigeria's Fourth Coup d'etat: Options for Modern Statehood** (Enugu, Nigeria: Fourth Dimension Publishing Co. Ltd., 1985), p. 107.

52 E. Odumegwu-Ojukwu, op. cit., pp. 105 & 176; cf. K. A. Sambo, op. cit., p. 79. (My brackets.)

53 Okwudiba Nnoli, op. cit., pp. 145-148.

54 Emeka Odumegwu-Ojukwu, op. cit., pp. 28-30, 45-46, 49; also pp. 4-7.

55 Ibid., p. 8.

56 Ibid., p. 10.

57 Emeka Odimegwu-Ojokwu observes that in Nigeria "followership has become such that our leaders are seduced and tyrants made out of them. We are sycophants. We

even applaud executive imbecility. We genuflect to mediocrity and defend the indefensible executive indiscretions." (Cf. sic, op. cit., p. 178.)

58 A. Adebayo, op. cit., p. 9.

59 According to Adebayo, "Oratocracy is ... government by speechmaking." - ibid., p. 6.

60 A. Adebayo, op. cit., pp. 1-2.

61 Cf. ibid., p. 6.

62 Cf. ibid., pp. 12-13.

63 Ibid., p. 13.

64 Cf. ibid., pp. 14-16.

65 Cf. Emeka Odumegwu-Ojukwu, op. cit., p. 90.

66 **Report of the Political Bureau, March 1987**, pp. 96-97.

67 Emeka Odumegwu-Ojukwu, op. cit., p. 143.

68 A. Adebayo, op. cit., p. 36; cf. Emeka Odumegwu-Ojukwu, op. cit., pp. 20 & 89.

69 Nisi Osundare, "The Limits of Opportunism," in: **Newswatch**, Aug. 16, 1993, p. 37.

70 A. Adebayo, op. cit., p. 30.

71 Ibid., pp. 35-36.

72 Ibid.

73 Ibid., pp. 58f.

74 Ibid., pp. 36-38.

75 Cf. **Newswatch**, Jan. 11, 1993, pp. 39-40.

76 A. R. Mustapha, "Repression and the Nigerian Political Economy," in: A. S. Mohammed & T. Edoh, eds., op. cit., p. 35.

77 Kyari Tijani, "Democracy, Accountability and the State of the Nation," in: A. S. Mohammed & T. Edoh, eds., op. cit., pp. 2-3.

78 Ibid., pp. 4-5, & 17.

79 Tunji Olagunju, "Transition to the Second Experiment - Some Political Issues," in: Sam E. Oyovbaire, ed., op. cit., pp. 35-36.

80 A. Adebayo, op. cit., p. 57.

81 Kyari Tijani, op. cit., pp. 2-3; cf. Y. B. Usman, ed., **Political Repression in Nigeria** (Zaria, Nigeria: Gaskiya Corporation Ltd., 1982).

82 A. O. Sanda, "Ethnicity and National Integration: New Directions," in: **Round-Table Meeting on Ethnicity in Nigeria: Implications for National Development** (Kuru, 1983), p. 102.

83 Ibid., pp. 102-104.

84 Ralph Adams Cram's book on the sad implications of mediocrity is worth reading: **The Nemesis of Mediocrity** (Boston: Marshal Jones Company, 1919).

85 Jibril Ibrahim, "The Transition to Civil Rule," in: Adebayo O. Olukoshi, ed., **The Politics of Structural Adjustment in Nigeria** (London: J. Currey; Ibadan: Portsmouth; N.H.: Heinemann, 1993), p. 136.

86 Sam E. Oyovbaire, op. cit., pp. 175-187.

87 Major-General J. N. Garba, "Military Administration and the Nigerian Society," in: Sminar on Nigeria in transition (1980), op. cit., p. 29.

88 A. Adebayo, op. cit., p. 48.

89 To cite two examples: the Constitution (Suspension and Modification) Decree No. 1, 1966, sec. 3 (1) states: "The Federal Military Government shall have power to make laws for peace, order and good government of Nigeria or any part thereof with respect to any matter whatsoever;" sec. 6 declares that: "No question as to the validity of this or any other Decree or any Edict shall be entertained by any court of law in Nigeria;" and the Federal Military Government (Supremacy and Enforcement of Powers) Decree No. 28, 1970, sec. 1 (2) (b) states, inter alia: "any decision, whether made before or after the commencement of this Decree, by any court of law in the exercise or purported exercise of any powers under the Constitution or any enactment or law of the Federation or of any State which has purported to declare or shall hereafter purport to declare the invalidity of any Decree or of any Edict (in so far as the provisions of the Edict are not inconsistent with provision of a Decree) or the incompetence of any of the governments in the Federation to make the same is or shall be null and void and of no effect whatsoever as from the date of making thereof" and the judiciary "owes its present existence to the military regime which has always had the power to abolish, if it has so wished, the whole constitution and rule this country by Decree." (Cf. **Law Notes and Reviews** (1970), No. 6, pp. 30-31; also Folarin Shyllon, "The Demise of the rule of law in Nigeria under the military," in: F. Shyllon and O. Obasanjo, op. cit., pp. 3-5.)

90 Folarin Shyllon, op. cit., p. 16.

91 Cf. **Newswatch**: - Nov. 23, 1992, pp. 36-37; - Nov. 16, 1992, pp. 9-16; - Feb. 8, 1993, p. 3; and - May 17, 1993, p. 25.

92 Cf. Adebayo O. Olukochi, ed., **Politics of Structural Adjustment in Nigeria** (London: J. Currey; Ibadan; Portsmouth, N.H.: Heinemann, 1993); T. A. Oyejide, et al., **Nigeria and the IMF** (Ibadan: Heinemann Educational Books (Nigeria), 1985); **Report of the Seminar on Nigeria in Transition** (Lagos: Fed. Mins. of Information, 1980); Peter Enahoro, **How to be a Nigerian** (Ibadan, 1981); Emeka Odumegwu-Ojukwu, **Because I am Involved** (Ibadan, 1989).

93 Emeka Odumegwu-Ojukwu, op. cit., p. 93, also pp. 58-59.

94 Joseph Ode, "Rich But Poor," in: **Newswatch**, Oct. 10, 1994, pp. 28-30.

95 Cf. Adebayo O. Olukochi, ed., **Politics of Structural Adjustment in Nigeria** (London: J. Currey; Ibadan; Portsmouth, N.H.: Heinemann, 1993), pp. 1-9, 38, 129-130.

96 Cf. ibid., pp. 3-4, 43-51, 82.

97 Cf. **Vanguard Newspaper**, Dec. 11, 1995, p. 11, and Dec. 19, 1995, p. 18.

98 See **Nigeria**, under "Nations of the World," in: **1994 Britannica Book of the Year: Events of 1993**, p. 684.

99 Okwudiba Nnoli, op. cit., p. 252

100 Utibe Ukim, "Out of Reach," in: **Newswatch**, April 19, 1993, pp. 16-21. For market survey - showing how the prices of foodstuffs have hit the roof, see **Vanguard**: - Dec. 11, 1995, p. 11; - Dec. 14, 1995, pp. 12-13; - Dec. 18, 1995, p. 13.

101 Note that the government-pegged official exchange rate (of N22.00 to $1) is far from the normal and more realistic market exchange rates of N80.00 to $1 which would bring the average monthly income of the Nigerian (N679.43) to $8.49.

102 There is much exploitation of wage labour in Nigeria. In a government sponsored study of labour and productivity in the mid-1970s, "The result obtained did show that labour was under-compensated relative to its productivity in seven out of ten selected industries.... The evidence was that in most industries, wage rates did not advance as fast as productivity and cost of living increases. In fact in some industries the average wage rate was below the subsistence wage." (See **Economic and Financial Review**, Vol. 13, No. 1, C.B.N., June, 1975, p. 13; cf. A. R. Mustapha, "Repression and the Nigerian Political Economy," in: A. S. Mohammed & T. Edoh, eds., op. cit., pp. 33-34.)

103 O. K. Ogan (Prof.), op. cit., p. 43.

104 This is the phrase Wale Akin-Aina used to describe the social services in Nigeria. See **Newswatch**, Oct. 10, 1994, pp. 33-34.

105 A. Adebayo, op. cit., p. 3.

106 Gen. S. Abacha, "Insuring Democracy's Steady Growth" - speech during the inauguration of the Constitutional Conference - in: Country: Nigeria Rebuilding Democracy, in: **TIME**, No. 48, Nov. 28, 1994.

107 This is 1989-90 estimate - cf. **Nigeria**, under "Nations of the World," in: **1994 Britannica Book of the Year: Events of 1993**, p. 684.

108 Ibid.

109 This is 1987-88 estimate - cf. ibid.

110 This is 1988-89 estimate - cf. ibid.

111 From JAMB: "Universities and Courses available during the 1994/95 Academic Year".

112 See **Nigeria**, under "Nations of the World," in: **1994 Britannica Book of the Year: Events of 1993**, p. 684.

113 Cf. **Newswatch**, April 19, 1993, p. 19.

114 Cf. **TIME**, No. 48, Nov. 28, 1994.

115 **Newswatch**, April 19, 1993, pp. 18f.

116 Ibid., p. 19.

117 Ibid.; cf. **Newswatch**, Jan. 11, 1993, pp. 16-17.

118 **Newswatch**, Oct. 10, 1994, p. 33.

119 Quoted in: Sanya Onabamiro (Prof.), "The Place of and Role of Education in the Evolution of an Egalitarian Society," in: **Report of the Seminar on Nigeria in Transition** (Kaduna, 1979), op. cit., p. 92.

120 Ibid.

121 Ibid.

122 See **Nigeria**, under "Nations of the World," in: **1994 Britannica Book of the Year: Events of 1993**, p. 684.

123 **Newswatch**, Oct. 10, 1994, p. 34.

124 See **Nigeria**, under "Nations of the World," in: **1994 Britannica Book of the Year: Events of 1993**, p. 684.

125 **Newswatch**, Oct. 10, 1994, p. 34.

126 In his radio announcement of the fourth coup d'etat on Dec. 31, 1983 - cf. S. G. Ikoku, op. cit., pp. 166-167.

127 **Newswatch**, Oct. 10. 1994, p. 34.

128 Dan Agbese, "The Price War," in: **Newswatch**, April 12, 1993, p. 7.

129 **Newswatch**, April 19, 1993, p. 18.

130 Peter Enahoro, op. cit., pp. 43-45.

131 See "Global Report Card" in: **African Concord**, Sept. 30, 1991, p. 38.

132 Cf. G. H. Sabine & T. L. Thorson, **A History of Political Theory**, fourth edition (Chicago et al.: Holt, Rinehart and Winston, Inc., 1973), p. 455.

133 Cf. Dan Agbese, "The Price War," in: **Newswatch**, April 12, 1993, p. 7.

134 Mortimer J. Adler, ed., **Great Books of the Western World, Vol. 1: The Syntopicon I** (Chicago et al.: Encyclopaedia Britannica, Inc., 1990), p. 241.

135 Ibid..

136 See, for examples, NEC's report on the September 1992 presidential primaries (where money played a key role) in: **Newswatch**, Dec. 7, 1992, pp. 14-20; and the report on the Ward Congress on Feb. 6, 1993 in: **Newswatch**, Feb. 22, 1993, p. 21.

137 Cf. Sam E. Oyovbaire, ed., op. cit.; **A Report of the Seminar on Nigeria in Transition** (Lagos, 1980); A. S. Mohammed & T. Edoh, eds., op. cit.; F. Shyllon & O. Obasanjo, op. cit.; **Executive Lawlessness in the Babangida Regime: A Report of the Civil Liberties Organistion** (Lagos, Nigeria: Civil Liberties Organistion, 1991); E. Odumegwu-Ojukwu, op. cit.; Yusufu B. Usman, "Social Justice and Patriotism: The Real Alternatives Facing Senior Nigerian Executives Today," Text of a paper presented at the concluding seminar of the 5th Senior Executive Course at NIPSS, Kuru, Sept. 26, 1983.

138 See **The Constitution of the Federal Republic of Nigeria (Promulgation) Decree 1989, No. 12**, part II, chapter IV, sections 32-41.

139 William Shakespeare, **Julius Caesar**, Act I, Scene II - Cassius to Brutus.

140 Report of the Political Bureau, March 1987, p. 100.

141 Ibid., p. 29.

142 For some examples, cf. Executive Lawlessness In the Babangida Regime: A Report of the Civil Liberties Orgnisation (Lagos, 1991), pp. 1-13; see also F. Shyllon & O. Obasanjo, op. cit., pp. 1-17, 39.

143 T. A. Imobighe, "Chasing the Shadow: The Illusory Battle for Law, Order and Security in Nigeria," in: A. S. Mohammed & T. Edoh, op. cit., pp. 53-54.

144 **Executive Lawlessness in the Babangida Regime**: A Report of the Civil Liberties Organisation (Lagos, Nigeria: Civil Liberties Organisation, 1991), p. 1.

145 Cf. Ejembi A. Unobe, "Government Lawlessness during the first four years of Nigeria's Second Republic: Implications for politics of law and order," in: A. S. Mohammed and T. Edoh, eds., op. cit., pp. 70-73; and F. Shyllon & O. Obasanjo, op. cit., pp. 12-15.

146 Examples are found in: A. S. Mohammed and T. Edoh, op. cit., pp. 74-76.

147 Yusufu B. Usman, "Social Justice and Patriotism: The Real Alternatives Facing Senior Nigerian Executives Today," Text of a paper presented at the concluding seminar of the 5th Senior Executive Course at NIPSS, Kuru, Sept. 26, 1983.

148 Ibid., p. 65. And for examples of police lawlessness, pp. 65-70; cf. F. Shyllon and O. Obasanjo, op. cit., p. 14.

149 T. Falola & J. Ihonvbere, op. cit., p. 211.

150 T. Hobbes, **Leviathan**, Intro. by A. D. Lindsay (N. Y.: Dulton & Co., 1950), p. 105.

151 Emeka Odumegwu-Ojukwu, op. cit., p. 26.

152 O. K. Ogan (Prof.), op. cit., p. 42.

153 Cf. Chinua Achebe, op. cit., pp. 27-43; A. Adebayo, op. cit., pp. 19-29; Kyari Tijani, "Democracy, Accountability and the State of the Nation," in: A. S. Mohammed and T. Edoh, eds., op. cit., pp. 1-20; Peter Enahoro, op. cit., pp. 35-37; Emeka Odumegwu-Ojukwu, op. cit., pp. 56-57.

154 "Every Nigerian leader," writes Mercy Ette, "has attempted to dislodge the worm but none has ever succeeded." For how each leader did this, see Mercy Ette, "The Worm Lives," in: **Newswatch**, Oct. 10, 1994, pp. 37-38.

155 Chinua Achebe, op. cit., p. 27.

156 Emeka Odumegwu-Ojukwu, op. cit., pp. 56-57.

157 Chinua Achebe, op. cit., p. 27.

158 A. Adebayo, op. cit., p. 19.

159 R. Wraith and E. Simpkings, **Corruption in Developing Countries** (London: George Allen and Unwin Ltd., 1963).

160 Utibe Ukim, "Anatomy of Corruption," in: **Newswatch**, March 13, 1995, pp. 10-17.

161 **The Economist**, June 8th, 1996, p. 50.

162 Peter Enahoro, "The 'Dash'," in: sic, op. cit., pp. 35-37.

163 Cf. A. Adebayo, op. cit., pp. 20-22.

164 Cf. ibid., p. 22; Kyari Tijani, op. cit., pp. 5-15; **Newswatch**: - Nov. 30, 1992, p. 8; - Dec. 7, 1992, pp. 14-20; - March 8, 1993, pp. 10 & 13; - March 29, 1993, pp. 6 & 13; - April 12, 1993, pp. 9 & 19.

165 Cf. Ibid., pp. 15-16 and 22-23; Chinua Achebe, op. cit., p. 39-43; **Newswatch:** - Dec. 28, 1992, p. 42; - March 1, 1993, pp. 16-18; - March 13, 1995, pp. 10-17.

166 According to Adebayo: "The provision of security funds has been a regular feature of annual budgetary system since the colonial times. During the military regime from 1966 to 1979, the average annual expenditure of each State Government on Security was about N25,000. In the Federal Military Government it was about half a million naira. With the inception of the Second Republic, Security Votes escalated beyond belief. State governments voted anything between N2 million to N6 million annually for security. And in the final analysis, what form of security did a State government have to spend N6 million annually upon? The money was not meant to pay for Police or the Armed Forces personnel or equipment, matters which are the exclusive responsibility of the Federal Government. But the interesting point is that this is a vote which traditionally is not subject to audit. The Chief Executive is at liberty to dip his hands into it at any time and withdraw as much as he likes." (Ibid., p. 23.)

167 A. Adebayo, op. cit., pp. 24-25.

168 T. A. Imobighe, "Chasing the Shadow: The Illusory Battle for Law, Order and Security," in: A. S. Mohammed & T. Edoh, eds., op. cit., p. 54, also pp. 42f.; cf. E. Odumegwu-Ojukwu, op. cit., pp. 175 & 183.

169 O. K. Ogan (Prof.), "Public Servant and Public Probity," in: **Report of the Seminar on Nigeria in Transition** (Lagos, 1980), pp. 43-44.

170 Ibid., pp. 40-42, esp. p. 42.

171 Peter Eigen, "Combatting Corruption Around the World," in: **Journal of democracy**, vol. 7, no. 1, Jan. 1996 (Baltimore, MD: John Hopkins University Press), pp. 160-161.

172 T. A. Imobighe, op. cit., p. 55.

173 Cf. Adigun A: B. Agbaje, **The Nigerian Press, Hegemony, and the Social Construction of Legitimacy, 1960-1983** (Lewiston: Edwin Mellen Press, 1992); **Report of the Seminar on Nigeria in Transition** (Lagos: Fed. Mins. of Information, 1980).

174 **Newswatch**, May 17, 1993, p. 7.

175 Adigun A. B. Agbaje, op. cit., p. 161.

176 Cf. ibid., p. 189.

177 Cf. ibid., p. 190.

178 Cf. ibid.

179 Alfred E. Opubor, "Public Communication Policies And The Mass Media In The New Nigeria," in: **Report of the Seminar on Nigeria in Transition** (Lagos, 1980), p.81.

180 E. A. Jaja, "Problems of an African editor," in: **African Report**, 11, 1 (Jan. 1966), pp. 40-42.

181 For examples, see Adigun A. B. Agbaje, op. cit., pp. 177-196.

182 For examples, see ibid., pp. 197-199.

183 Cf. ibid., pp. 146 & 154.

184 T. Obadina, **The Punch** (Lagos), Sept. 21, 1981, p. 5.

185 A. Adebayo, op. cit., pp. 17-18.

186 Adigun A. B. Agbaje, op. cit., p. 230. For more details on the military and the mass media, see ibid., pp. 216-268.

4. BUILDING A STABLE AND LASTING DEMOCRACY IN NIGERIA

The last chapter dealt with the various problems that impede the growth of enduring democracy in Nigeria: lack of unity, poor leadership, militarism, poor socio-economic institutions and services, lack of social justice and security, indiscipline and corruption, and constrained mass media. It is the task of this chapter to seek solutions to these problems, and thus to suggest possible ways of building a stable and lasting democracy in Nigeria.

By this title, "building a stable and lasting democracy in Nigeria," emphasis is laid on the word "building" as against "importing". For democracy to work and last in any given society, it must germinate and grow from the soil of that society, though its seed be foreign. As a way of life, and not just merely a system of government, democracy should not be wholesale imported or imposed.[1] It must spring from the people, from their culture.

The problem of many developing countries (Nigeria included) has been the attempt to import democracy as practised in Europe (Britain) and in the USA and to plant it on their soil hook, line and sinker. At best, these countries eventually succeed in establishing "a little democracy" which, according to Charles W. Ferguson, "is a dangerous thing."[2] Although the institutions and principles of democracy are everywhere the same and they must be found in any democracy for that democracy to be worth its name, the "soil textures" for their germination and growth are not the same. This explains why there are different democracies, like "American democracy" and "British democracy."[3] Thus, there must be in Nigeria "Nigerian democracy," no more and no less. The late Prime Minister of Nigeria, Sir Alhaji Abubakar Fafawa Balewa, in a rather jocular reply to a fellow parliamentarian, made a similar point: "I find it difficult to know what is really meant by 'democracy'. In America people practise 'democracy', in the United Kingdom there is 'democracy'. France is 'democratic', sir, but they are all different kinds. So may be our 'democracy' in Nigeria may be yet another kind of 'democracy'."[4] Yes, Nigerian democracy must "be yet another 'democracy'." Nigerian culture is different from other people's culture, and democracy must be part and parcel of a people's culture for it to be stable and last. This agrees with Adebayo Adedeji's projections for Africa: "Democratization in Africa will be sustainable and credible only if it comes as an integral part of the transformation of the continent's political and socioeconomic structures. Quick fixes and shortcuts, or any attempted mimicry of inappropriate foreign models, would be exercises in futility. The new African democratic, transformational ethic ... cannot be developed by others on behalf of African people, but only by Africans themselves, acting in light of their own values, perceptions, concerns, and aspirations. Only the people can drive the process forward."[5] And Nwafor Orizu agrees: "In short, to African democracy must be something African to have permanence; it must be something lively to have attraction; it must be something creative to have appeal; it must be something spreading outward to have a following; it must be something now - here to have promise; it must be something practical to have realism; it must be something true to draw faith; it must be something altruistic to have a future, and it must be something godly to have reverence."[6]

This is not to say that Nigeria cannot learn or borrow anything good in democracies as practised in other countries.[7] Surely there are a lot to learn from countries like the USA. Just as no culture is static but develops and grows, so also democracy. The process of developing and growing implies picking up certain (helpful) values from other cultures or democracies and discarding certain (unnecessary) others. However, this healthy interdependence of cultures or democracies is not the same as "importation of culture or democracy."

Another problem that needs immediate attention is the myopic view of the concept and scope of democracy evident in Nigeria. Nigerians very often see democracy only as a political system (a system of government) and hardly as an economic system and/or as a moral-cultural system (a way of life). Hence, "building a stable and lasting democracy in Nigeria" demands the need to widen the concept and scope of democracy in Nigeria.[8] Democracy is more than a system of government. As John Dewey observes: "Democracy is much broader than a special political form, a method of conducting government, of making laws and carrying on governmental administration by means of popular suffrage and elected officers. It is that, of course. But it is something broader and deeper than that. The political and governmental phase of democracy is a means, the best means so far found, for realizing ends that lie in the wide domain of human relationships and the development of human personality. It is ... a way of life."[9] Therefore, to have democracy as only a system of government will not do. For leaders, to be in-charge, work out programmes and dish them out from above is not enough; and for the citizens, "to vote is not enough."[10] Man is not only a political being but also an economic as well as a moral-cultural being (a seeker after the good and the true). Hence every individual lives simultaneously within each of the three systems. According Michael Novak,

> Political freedom without economic freedom is shallow; economic freedom without political freedom is fickle. The two need each other and reinforce each other. Both need the guidance, self-restraint, and institutional checks set upon them by institutions of morals and culture: by a free press, by free universities, by free churches, and by free associations of many sorts.
>
> All three systems work together as one whole: the political system (democratic), the economic system (social market, free, capitalist), and the moral and cultural system (pluralist). For a stable and economically dynamic democracy, all three systems are required, each with its own proper health and in equilibrium with the other two.[11]

Democracy then involves the development of the human person (politically, economically and morally). This development will be impossible unless the principles and institutions of democracy (cf. part 1, chapters 3 & 4 respectively) are in place. And even when these principles and institutions are in place, the development of the human person would not have been accomplished unless man is habituated to them. This is why the moral-cultural aspect of democracy - the cultivation of *democratic virtues* - is very important. Michael Novak rightly argues that "one of the great strengths of democratic thinking is that it is *practical*. Democracy is a *praxis*, not a theory. As a practice, it has two locations: one in the *habits* and the dispositions of a people, and one in a set of living *institutions* and functioning procedures.... Any people who wish to create a stable democracy must learn to practise certain specific democratic *virtues*."[12] This implies that neither institutions alone nor habits alone can a stable democracy make. In other words, "democracy lives not only in specific habits but in specific *institutions*. Habits are not enough: institutions are required. Even a virtuous people will suffer under poor political institutions.... Human rights can only be defended by certain working institutions."[13] Nigeria needs therefore "to concentrate on building democratic *habits* and democratic *institutions*," and not just democratic institutions alone.

Therefore, to build a stable and lasting democracy, Nigerians (beginning from the home to the public places) must cultivate the democratic habits and match them with the democratic institutions. Both the governors and the governed must live out the principles of democracy and both must co-operate to establish and maintain a fair and just society, a society in which personal rights, human welfare and collective preference (the three tests for democracy) are tops.[14]

This chapter wishes to draw the attention of Nigerians to the human aspects of democracy which they have been neglecting. Hitherto, Nigeria has focused all its attention on structures without relating them to the human person for whose good these structures are supposed, in the first place, to be established. Now is the time to take serious the anthropological and social dimensions of democracy which boil down to one thing: human welfare and development - putting the good of the human person and the common good at the centre of all systems and structures. In other words, this thesis wishes to put a human face on "Nigerian democracy." To do this, this chapter is divided into three sections. The first section deals with the development of the human person - mental, political, socio-economic and cultural-moral dimensions. The second section brings out the various roles of the family, the community, the school, the religious bodies, the state and the mass media, in the development of democracy as a way of life in Nigeria. And the third section, the conclusion, is a call to patriotism.

4.1. The Development of the Human Person

Democracy has a human face which is very often neglected. This human face of democracy points to the fact that the human person is at the very centre of everything - a primary position it occupies from nature.[15] This implies, as Pope

John Paul II emphasises, that the human person *transcends* the social structures in which his life unfolds; that the structures are made *for man* and not vice versa; and that the structures are made *by man* and hence the principle of their dynamic development is the human person.[16] What all these boil down to is that "the human person may never be sacrificed for political interests, national or international, whichever they may be.... The principle to follow is not that of allowing economic, social and political factors to prevail over man, but, for the dignity of the human person to be put above everything else...."[17]

This concept of the human face of democracy must be born in mind in all aspects of human development. Then democracy is geared toward the development of man - "of every man and of the whole man."[18] But what constitutes true and authentic human development? Authentic human development "is not a straightforward process, as it were automatic and in itself limitless, as though, given certain conditions, the human race were able to progress rapidly toward an undefined perfection of some kind."[19] Again, "just as one's life does not consist in the abundance of the things he possesses,"[20] so too true development is not measured by the number of physical structures (like big and tall buildings) a country has; neither is it measured by the availability of socio-economic structures nor by the number of its millionaires. It is rather measured by how much freedom and social justice the people enjoy. "True development," in the words of Pope John Paul II, "implies ... a lively *awareness* of the *value* of the rights of all and of each person. It likewise implies a lively awareness of the need to respect the right of every individual to the full use of the benefits offered by science and technology. ... In order to be genuine, development must be achieved within the framework of *solidarity* and *freedom*, without ever sacrificing either of them under whatever pretext.... In other words, true development must be based on the *love of God and neighbour*, and must help to promote the relationships between individual and society."[21] Human development could be divided into four, viz.: mental, political, socio-economic and cultural-moral developments.

4.1.1. Development of the mind

The development of the mind is the basis of all other developments. Unless a people is developed in mind, every of its efforts at political and socio-economic development is bound to fail. Thus mental development of the people must take the first place in Nigeria's bid to build a stable and lasting democracy.

Development of the mind demands the provision of functional education, be it formal (as in the school) or informal (as in the family or in the adult education or through the media). As such good and sound formal education of the citizenry lays sound foundation for flourishing democracy. Since "education is learning to express oneself best" (a definition which stems from the meaning of the word education - *to draw out*), then, argues Arthur Armstrong, "if each human being can learn how to 'draw himself out', or learn to express himself best, then we can have a genuine democracy - and only then."[22] Put in another way, "one of the requisites of democracy is an educated people. If all want to share in the good of life to the fullest degree possible, they realize that knowledge and trained minds are required. Also, in a complicated society such as ours, we can't any longer learn from just experience (trial and error); we have to get some formal education if for no other reason than to save time, expense and energy."[23] And it is generally accepted that "it is the function of education, at every level of maturity from the kindergarten to adult classes, and in every area of living, to promote democracy and consciousness of democracy among our people."[24] This is so because, following the thoughts of Plato in *The Republic*, "education is the positive means by which the ruler can shape human nature in the right direction to produce a harmonious state.... If the citizens are well educated they will readily see through the difficulties that beset them and meet emergencies as they arise.... With a good system of education almost any improvement is possible; if education is neglected, it matters little what else the state does."[25]

It is true that Nigeria, since independence, has experienced rapid development of educational institutions and infrastructures and massive enrolments at all levels, yet its standard and quality of education leaves much to be desired. (See part 2, 3.3.2.1. above.) Hence something must be done to enhance Nigeria's educational development - wipe out illiteracy, and improve the academic standard of its educational institutions.

The first step towards the mental development of Nigerians is to recognise the fact that education is a natural right. "The natural law ... gives man the right to share in the benefits of culture, and therefore the right to a basic education and to technical and professional training in keeping with the stage of educational development in the country to which he belongs."[26] Moreover, democracy demands *equal opportunity* for all, including equal opportunity in education for all. Therefore, all Nigerians should have equal opportunity of acquiring at least the basic education - and here, primary and secondary education. And this *equal opportunity* can be attained in Nigeria if, and only if, primary and secondary education are made free and compulsory for all. (Plato and Aristotle agree that the most important force in moulding citizens is a compulsory system of education.[27])

Nigeria already operates the system of "universal and compulsory primary education". But this system is not yet working well, because nothing is being done to make sure that every child goes to school - that is, to make sure that all parents send all their children to school - or to make sure that all obstacles (like the many levies in our primary schools) which hinder children from poor families from attending school are removed. My position is that not only primary but also secondary (at least junior secondary) education should be free and compulsory. This would afford every Nigerian the basic education, after which one pursues whatever carrier in life one chooses. The government should make sure this basic education is truly free - by providing all the necessary equipment needed in primary and secondary schools and making it illegal for any school to impose taxes or levies on the pupils and students. The government should also enforce the law of compulsory education by seeing to it that any parent or guardian that fails to send his or her child to school is brought to book. By rigidly implementing and enforcing the policy of free and compulsory primary and secondary education illiteracy will definitely be wiped out of Nigeria.

The second step towards mental development of Nigerians is to raise the standard and quality of education in the country. Mr A. Adebayo writes in this regard thus: "The issue of standard and quality of education is very important. We strive after universal and compulsory primary education. But there is a point below which education is scarcely worth having because a large number of semi-literate people will benefit neither the country nor themselves. A thousand people with advanced professional or technical skill would make a greater impact on national development than a hundred thousand people who could barely read and write. The goal of education for the purpose of national development and ethical orientation should therefore be a compulsory universal education well above primary six level, which must take cognisance of character formation and integrity. Otherwise, education is not worth having."[28]

To achieve solid and qualitative education of the people, and complete eradication of illiteracy the following obstacles are to be removed: the issues of lack of adequate facilities (like classrooms or lecture halls, libraries and laboratories); insufficiency of qualified teachers in the schools; disjointed educational programmes (due to frequent strike actions by teachers or lecturers and/or by students and subsequent frequent closure of schools by the authorities); poor educational orientation (more theory and less practice - not geared towards productivity). These must be squarely addressed and lasting solutions found to them. Without going into details with regard to these issues, it must be stressed that more attention be paid and more fund devoted to education in Nigeria than is hitherto the case. Instead of proliferating universities, colleges of education and polytechnics in the country (with the result that a state may have over four higher institutions, all sick), available resources should be channelled toward enlarging, improving and developing the existing ones. It is not necessary, for instance, that every state must have a federal university. Rather, one such university, well developed and equipped, could be for 3 to 5 neighbouring states, each state with a campus of the university. It is also not necessary that every university must have all departments and offer almost every course; instead, universities should be identified with a particular field, with allied subjects, and equipped and developed as such - so that a university of medicine, for example, would have departments for chemistry, biology, physics, mathematics, etc. and none for history, geography, economics, and so on.

It is noteworthy that the suggestions made in 1979 by Professor Sanya Onabamiro,[29] with regard to achieving an egalitarian educational system in the country, are already in operation, viz: 1) that the state control on secondary education should be relaxed "to enable voluntary agencies and local communities to give more active co-operation to the Government in achieving progress in secondary education and to get parents more committed in the process of their children's education;" 2) that the federal government monopoly on university education should be relaxed "to enable rich philanthropists and industrial magnates to establish private universities subject to guidelines and regulations imposed by the Government;" and 3) that arrangements should be made "for the establishment of an Open University in addition to making some of the existing Universities grant external degrees." If these suggestions are taken more seriously, they would definitely help to enhance the standard of education in Nigeria.

Next, the living and studying conditions in Nigerian schools should be made very conducive for students, and teachers or lecturers should be well paid and they should receive their salaries and allowances as when due. These would stop incessant strike actions by students and teachers or lecturers and subsequent closure of schools and disruption of academic programmes.

Another thing that should be done to improve the standard of education in Nigeria is to make sure that the prices of education materials, reading and writing materials like books, are such that the students can afford them. The government should subsidise education equipment or materials.

Lastly, we can talk about the content of education itself. The content should be such as would make the students self-sufficient and productive at the end of their courses. The "6-3-3-4 system" of education we have in Nigeria (since 1984) is very good and, if implemented to the letter, would produce "productive" rather "white-collar" graduates. About this system of education, Prof. Onabamiro writes, inter alia,

> The essence of this educational system, as modelled on the U.S.A. pattern, is that it should have a pyramidal structure. ... The base of that pyramid is the Primary Education which must be available to all children for six years from the age of six years. But when primary school comes to an end the children, being only twelve years old, will still be too young to obtain gainful employment. Therefore places must be found for them in the *Junior Secondary Schools* where they will have the opportunity of being exposed to a variety of pre-vocational activities along side their normal academic studies.
>
> In the course of the three years the continuous assessment compiled on every child, plus the results of the periodic tests, will identify his or her natural bent and general abilities. As a result of these exercises those who will leave school at the age of 15 will have an idea of what sort of vocation they want to pursue, while those who have the potential for further study will go into the *Senior Secondary Schools* for another period of three years.
>
> The top of the pyramid is the segment on High Education, provided in universities and polytechnics for those students from the Senior Secondary Schools who show an aptitude and desire for pursuing their education for a few more years.[30]

To summarise, the Nigerian government should invest a lot in education. Its annual budgets should give priority to education. And it should enforce free and compulsory primary and secondary education for all and do all in its power to improve the falling standard of education in the country. Once these are done, illiteracy will be wiped out in Nigeria and all other development plans of the country will begin to yield fruits, fruits that will endure. This does not mean that the government should abandon or neglect all other developments until all Nigerians have become literate. No, all that pertain to human development go hand-in-hand. With this, our attention shifts to political development.

4.1.2. Political development

Man, as a socio-political animal, lives in a civic society or community. This civic community comprises individuals, families and various groups who, in the words of Vatican Council II,

> are aware of their own insufficiency in the matter of establishing a fully human condition of life. They see the need for that wider community in which each would daily contribute his energies toward the ever better attainment of the common good. It is for this reason that they set up the political community in its manifold expressions.
>
> Hence the political community exists for that common good in which the community finds its full justification and meaning, and from which it derives its pristine and proper right. Now, the common good embraces the sum of those conditions of social life by which individuals, families, and groups can achieve their own fulfilment in a relatively thorough and ready way.
>
> Many different people go to make up the political community, and these can lawfully incline toward diverse ways of doing things. Now, if the political community is not to be torn to pieces as each man follows his own viewpoint, authority is needed. This authority must dispose the energies of the whole citizenry toward the common good, not mechanically or despotically, but primarilly as a moral force which depends on freedom and the consciencious discharge of the burdens of any office which has been undertaken.[31]

It follows then (from this quotation and from St. Paul, Rom. 13:1-5) "that the political community and public authority are based on human nature and hence belong to an order of things divinely foreordained; (and) that political authority, whether in the community as such or in institutions representing the state, must always be exercised within the limits of morality and on behalf of the dynamically conceived common good, according to a juridical order enjoying legal status."[32]

Democracy, as a political system, has got certain universal principles and necessary institutions which are for the common good. (See part I, chapters 2 and 3, above.) These principles and institutions of democracy are not new to the Nigerians. They were very much in place during the first and second republics. But because Nigerians lacked and still lack the cultural-moral aspect of democracy - the democratic virtues or habits - democracy could not take root in the country. The problem then is matching theory with practice. In theory Nigeria has "equality of all before the law", but in practice there is no "equal opportunity for all" in virtually everything; "survival of the fittest" is the order of the day; and, of course, the rich or affluent ones and those at the corridors of power are "more equal" than the rest of the people. In theory Nigeria has the bill of rights, but in practice the people do not even know their rights, talk less of enjoying them. In theory Nigeria has the rule of law, but in practice what exists is "the rule of men" (with its concomitant insecurity). Again, in theory the judiciary is independent, but in practice it is in shackles, under the executive control. To overcome these political impasses and to make democracy a reality in Nigeria, the following actions must be taken: too much emphasis laid on, and the too much importance attached to, politics must be reduced; the masses must be politically educated and made aware of their rights and duties; there is need for effective and responsible government; there is need for good citizenship; ways must be found to end the "coup culture" in Nigeria; and the country must be ruled according law and order rather than by the whims and caprices of men.

4.1.2.1. Politics is not everything

Nigerians, as already stated, hold democracy as a system of government and hardly as an economic system and as a way of life. This explains why democratic virtues are hardly reflected in our economic dealings and in our daily activities. What more, for many Nigerians politics everything: the air they breathe, their speech, their means of livelihood, and so on. Indeed, politics has become the easiest way to power and affluence. Hence people use any available means - they lie, cheat, maim, kill - to attain political power. And today virtually everything, every organisation and institution has been politicised, including even neutral bodies like the police, the army, the judiciary, the civil service, the schools, the churches, and so on. Consequently the society as a whole is in a mess, being infected with politics which, in Nigeria, is regarded as "a dirty game."

But politics is not everything.[33] Life is more than politics. To politicise everything is to imperil democracy itself. As M. Novak rightly points out:

> Political passions must not be allowed to become too hot, for democracy like metal melts when temperatures are too high.... For when politics embraces everything it corrupts such independent goods as truth, the university, journalism, the clergy, the family, and even friendship. The totalization of politics is not virtue, but a primary disease, the incubator of totalitarian practices. Politics, like the state, must be limited.[34]

Therefore, to build a stable and lasting democracy in Nigeria, politics must be limited to its own sphere. Economic and moral aspects of democracy must also have their own way. Politics must be sanitised with and by moral values, so that it would cease from being "a dirty game" to being a means of enhancing human development. And those organisations and institutions - the police, the army, the judiciary, the civil service, the electoral commission, the schools, the churches, etc. - which are supposed to be neutral for the sake of the common good, must remain so: they must be neutral, be left neutral and be seen to be neutral.

4.1.2.2. Political education and awareness

James M. Spinning once said: "We aren't educated until we come truly to find democracy not just in the machinery of government but in the hearts of men." The people are supposed to take active part in the way their society is run. This is *political participation*. "It is in full accord with human nature that juridical-political structures should, with ever better success and without any discrimination, afford all their citizens the chance to participate freely and actively in establishing the constitutional basis of a political community, governing the state, determining the scope and purpose of various institutions, and choosing leaders."[35] Hence the people must be politically educated and aware: they must know their rights and duties (especially to vote freely in the interest of advancing the common good); they must know the happenings around them (for instance, what their government is doing, the way it is doing it and why it is doing it); and so on.

No doubt, "civic and political education is today supremely necessary for the people, especially young people. Such education should be painstakingly provided, so that all citizens can make their contribution to the political community. Let those who are suited for it, or can become so, prepare themselves for the difficult and most honourable art of politics."[36] Therefore, in our effort to build a stable and lasting democracy, sincere effort must be made to enhance civic and political education and awareness - formally (through school education) and informally (through the family, adult education, and the mass media). (For details see part 2, 4.2., below).

4.1.2.3. Effective and responsible government

Nigeria needs effective and responsible government: a government that would uphold and defend the rights of all citizens, maintain public order and tranquillity, and promote the common welfare; a government that would promote socio-economic welfare and public health; a government that would care for cultural and moral values. To have such a government, good leadership is a sine qua non.

Nigeria has always lacked good leadership. (See part 2, 3.2., above.) Consequently good government has always eluded it. Solution must therefore be found to the problem of leadership in Nigeria, if the country is to enjoy true democracy and authentic development. Such solution must be based on certain good political habits: leadership is service; a leader is there for the common good; a leader is a person of integrity; a leader is accountable to the people; a leader is oriented toward the future; a leader has a spirit of sportsmanship.

1) **Leadership is service**[37]

Nigerians must change their mentality about government and about being in public office. Instead of regarding government as business, a benefactor, a godfather, the goose that lays the golden egg, and instead of seeing public office as an opportunity to good and quick money, the secret to success, the chance of a life-time to get one's share of the national cake, Nigerians should consider leadership a *service*. Anybody in public office is, and should be seen as, a *public servant*: one who serves the public, and not one who lords it over the public. This follows very much from Christ's teachings on leadership:

> You know that among the pagans the rulers lord it over them, and their great men make their authority felt. This is not to happen among you. No; *anyone who wants to be great among you must be your servant*, and *anyone who wants to be first among you must be your slave*, just as the Son of Man came not to be served but to serve, and to give his life as a ransom for many.[38]
>
> If anyone wants to be first, he must make himself last of all and servant of all.[39]
>
> Do you understand what I have done to you? You call me Master and Lord, and rightly; so I am. If I, then, the Lord and Master, have washed your feet, you should wash each other's feet. I have given you an example so that you may copy what I have done to you.[40]

Christ climaxed his teaching on leadership by laying down "his life as a ransom for many" - his death on the cross - thereby indicating how selfless a service leadership should be.

The leader is thus a servant and not a master. He or she receives the mandate - the power - to rule from the people. It follows then that those are masters who give the mandate while he or she is a servant to whom the mandate is given. It is said in politics that sovereignty rests with the electorate and not with the elected.

Therefore, Nigerian leaders and/or those who aspire to lead must bear in mind the fact that they are servants and as such can never be greater than the people, the masters.[41] "No servant is greater than his master, no messenger is greater than the one who sent him" (Jn. 13: 16). Rather the servant must be "faithful and wise enough ... to give (his master) his allowance of food at the proper time" (Luke 12: 42-46), because "what is expected of stewards is that each one should be found worthy of his trust" (1 Cor. 4: 2). With this in mind, the "might is right attitude" - the arrogance - of many a Nigerian leader would be a thing of the past and our leaders would dedicate themselves to the service of the people to which they are sworn-in.

2) **A leader is there for the common good**

The public servant or leader is there, not for himself or herself nor for his/her relations and friends (to enrich himself or herself or his/her relations and friends) but, for the common good - for the good and well-being of individuals, families and groups in the society. A ward officer is there, not for his/her family and extended families but, for all the members of the ward. A local government officer is there, not for his/her family and relations, nor for his/her ward but, to serve everybody in the local government area. A state officer is there, neither for his/her family and relations, ward nor for his/her local government area but, for all the components of state. A national officer is there, not for his/her family and relations, ward, local government area, senatorial zone and state but, for the whole nation - his/her constituency is the whole country. What these boil down to is that a leader - no matter at whichever level of the ladder he/she might be, though he/she ought to protect and fight for the interest of those who voted him/her into power - should never allow any private interest to override the common interest. In other words, a leader must not be selfish or sectional where common good is concerned. This would make for peace and unity in the community, be it at ward, local government, state or national level. (More on common good and national unity in 4.1.4.1., below.)

3) **A leader is a person of integrity**

A leader is honourable, honest, and truth conscious. He/she conducts his/her life and affairs in an honourable manner that he/she becomes a light in the darkness for his followers to see with, the salt that gives taste to the society, and a tower built on a hill that others look up to. Being a person of honour, he/she does not go back on his/her words. He/she keeps his/her promise to the people. He/she is time conscious and does not keep the people waiting too long for him/her when he/she has an appointment with them. He/she does not need or take kickbacks or bribes in order to do his/her work nor does he/she allow lobbyists to influence his/her decisions through unwholesome means. He/she gives each person his/her due because everything is on merit. He/she does not help himself or herself with the common purse but, instead, makes do with his/her wage. Being a respectful person, he/she respects those around him/her and under him/her and does not carry himself or herself too high as to impose himself or herself and/or his/her views on his/her followers, knowing that "a successful democracy cannot be a nation of followers, but it also cannot be a nation of bullies - people who force others to obey them."[42] And being an honest and truth-conscious person, he/she is always prepared to give an account of himself or herself and of his/her office to the electorate.

This integrity aspect of leadership is very important in Nigeria where public officers have discarded honesty and have embraced the life of bribery and corruption, with the result that they serve the public only when their palms have been greased and/or their pockets stuffed with some "gifts". Public officers are known to demand money and even sex from people before giving them what is their due. Thus appointments to public offices are made and employments and other offers (like contracts) are given not by merit but by being able to satisfy the greed and sensual urges of the public officers. It is therefore when, and only when, public officers in Nigeria have learnt to live above board in honesty and integrity that equity and justice will reign in our midst and then, it would be easier to build a stable and lasting democracy in the country.

4) **A leader is accountable to the people**

Since a leader is a servant who should be honest, he/she must be accountable to his/her master (the electorate), otherwise he/she stands the chance of being fired from his/her post. This is an important lesson that Nigerian leaders must have to learn. And the Nigerian electorate must also learn to be, and play the role of, a master. It must insist always that its servants render accurate accounts to it, during and after their tenure of office. The point here, therefore, is: not only that the leaders should be accountable to the people, but that they should be made accountable.

Nigerian leaders are known to be corrupt and non-accountable to the people. (See part 2, 3.2.3., above.) Though the press very often does call everybody's attention to corrupt practices of public officers, though at times panels are set up to probe such allegations, nothing happens in the end: such public officers are hardly brought to book for their deeds and/or misdeeds. As the draft charter on corruption prepared during the Murtala regime by the Centre for Advanced Social Science, CASS, Port Harcourt,[43] indicates: "it is not enough to detect and expose corruption," it must be adequately punished. It is a sorry story that, according to CASS, "in Nigeria, the prospects of being punished for corruption have always being small, the chances that the punishment will be anything but token," especially if the office of the culprit is high.

Being in office or having been in office should offer no one an immunity from being accountable to the people or from being brought to book to face charges against one's illegalities while in office. Nigeria should borrow a leaf from what is happening in some other countries around the world. Some examples will do. In Brazil, President Fernando Collor de Mello was (in 1992) driven out of office because his brother accused him of corruption. In Mexico, a former police boss was (in 1993) arrested and prosecuted for accepting bribe from a drug-trafficker. In the USA, ex-president Richard Nixon was not spared the agony of "watergate" scandal (while in office). President Bill Clinton was accused of knowing of and permitting a fraud by some of his officers while he was the governor of Arkansas (20 years ago) - the famous "whitewater affair". Even his wife, Hilary Clinton, had to appear (Jan. 26, 1996) before the Grand Jury to answer questions about the "affair" and later, on April 27, 1996, President Clinton himself gave four hours testimony (in tape) on the issue. And on May 28, 1996, the governor of Arkansas and two others were convicted of fraud by the "whitewater affair" Grand Jury - partially vindicating the Clintons - and the governor resigned from office. In South Korea, the two former presidents (Chur, who came to power through a military coup in 1978, and Roh, who was in power for five years, up to 1993) were charged to court for, and convicted of, bribery and corruption while in office. In Italy, Silvio Berlusconi, the ex-Italian prime-minister was brought to book for alleged corruption - taking bribe and illegal financing of political parties - and link with the "mafia" when he was in office. In Venezuela, the two time famous president and one of the eldest statesmen of Latin America, Mr Peres (who left office three years ago), was found guilty (May 30, 1996) of misusing 17 million dollars of public funds and sentenced to more than two years house detention. And in Columbia, for over eight months the president was probed and pressurised to resign, because his election campaigns two years ago were alleged to have been financed with money from the drug cartel, until June 13, 1996, when the lower house cleared him of the offence (to the disappointment of many people within and without Columbia). There are many other instances, but these few are enough to wake Nigerians up from their deep slumber and encourage them to demand an adequate account of and from their officers or leaders.

Nigeria must fight against corruption and encourage accountability on all levels. The tendency of Nigerians to rationalise corruption has helped to consolidate it in country, as the CASS charter indicates: "wealthy people who are known to be corrupt are regularly courted and honoured by communities, religious bodies, social clubs and other private organisations" and those who benefit from the largess of these corrupt people rarely ask questions. Nigerians must change and begin to challenge all corruption and corrupt officials. They must minimise or put a stop to their worship of material success. Anybody who is living beyond his/her station in life or who has come into some sudden mysterious wealth should never be regarded with envy and admiration by the generality of Nigerian public, nor should he/she be given a place of honour in public gatherings. Rather, as is done in civilised communities, such a person must be regarded as suspect by society and should be avoided by decent people. Such a person should be reported to the appropriate authorities for questioning and for other necessary actions (including legal prosecution). If, after prosecution, such a person is found guilty of corruption, his/her ill-gotten wealth should be confiscated, he/she must make all the necessary refunds and he/she must be sent to jail (his/her sentence depending on the gravity of his/her offence).

All top government officials must declare their assets on assuming office and on leaving it. Any officer with incredulous increment of assets - because his/her assets are now more than what his/her salary (plus allowances) could procure - must be brought to book. After the legal prosecutions, he/she must forfeit all the illegally acquired assets and then be sent to prison. A public officer found guilty of bribery and corruption or gross abuse of office should be summarily dismissed from office, made to make refunds (where necessary), and then sent to gaol. And an ex-public officer who is found guilty of abuse of office or of corrupt practices while in office must be brought to book, made to refund any ill-amassed wealth and be given a jail sentence. These measures would put some sense of discipline into public officers and help curb corruption and lack of accountability in our society.

Moreover, *ethics committee* should be introduced in the Nigerian local government, state and national assemblies to probe and discipline members who are dancing out of line, as is the case in the USA Obviously, this would help the people's representatives to live an honourable life expected of them, "honourable members" that they are called.

5) **A leader must have a vision**

A leader is a statesman, not just a politician. While a politician is concerned with the next election, a statesman is concerned with the next generation. As a statesman, a leader is not so immersed in today that he or she never remembers yesterday nor imagines tomorrow, and he or she is not so narrow-minded and myopic in his plans and decisions that he or she does not rise beyond self and self-interest. Rather he or she is a person of vision who, in making a critical decision, asks himself or herself: "Will it be good for the nation, not just today but after I am gone - after I have left office?"[44]

Nigerian leaders must therefore stop presenting "jumbo budgets" - unrealistic projections - that are not in tune with their treasury. This would save them from running into deficit and then going for external loans which plunge the state or nation into unwarranted debts. In the same vein, Nigerian leaders must indulging in unnecessary expenditures that leave the state/nation so much in debt, thereby constituting a big burden for future generations. This would help to liberate Nigeria from over-indebtedness to the developed countries, and then help to give her the air of freedom to pursue her development programmes.

Moreover, a leader should always have constructive and realistic plans. Such plans should take into account the effects, short and long term, his/her policy would have on the people and on the country at large. It is very sad to have a leader wake up one morning and announce a policy that must be executed within a short time, without minding how unprepared the people are for the new policy and without minding what the people would suffer in the course of executing the new policy. Think, for example, of what the people go through, what they suffer, whenever Nigeria changes its or one of its currency. This change is never by gradual withdrawal of old currency by the central bank while the new is put into circulation (as is done in developed countries). Rather a date is fixed - always a short duration - within which the people must get rid of their "old" currency, and after which the "old" currency ceases to be a legal tender. Imagine the rush - many a time, last minute rush - of the people to the banks and the time they have to waste at the banks, waiting to be attended to, due to the large crowd that daily besiege the banks with their money to be changed. Again, think of how certain policies that affect the people's life are changed in Nigeria without due notice or enough notice to the people. For example, the change in the postal charges was so "sudden" and without enough information to the people that people who came to post their letters with the old amount (say, N1.50 for normal overseas letter) received a shock of their lives when they were told that they needed now between N30.00 and N40.00 (depending on what part of overseas) to post the same letter. This is simply "planlessness". Therefore, Nigerian leaders must have vision, draw their plans according to this vision, and execute such plans according to the needs and welfare of the people.

6) **The spirit of sportsmanship**

A leader must have the spirit of sportsmanship. Rather than consider his/her political opponents as enemies, the Nigerian leader should see and take them as rivals in the political game. There is always a winner and a loser in every competition, political competition inclusive. So if he or she loses (for example in an election), he or she should accept defeat and congratulate his or her victorious opponents rather than cry "woe!" and foul play, and let hell loose on them.[45] And if he or she wins, he or she should extend a hand of friendship to his or her opponents rather than exclude them from the plan of things in the state and deny them governmental amenities and support - to punish them and to pressurise them to declare support for him or her.

The public officer should learn to change his or her policy or decision when this is not to the liking of the masses, even though he or she had earlier thought that his or her policy or decision was the best for the people. The mentality that the leader is always right must be changed. Being in power does not confer wisdom, so that the leader becomes the custodian of knowledge and wisdom, nor does it make one above mistake, so that the leader becomes impeccable. Therefore, the Nigerian leader should be flexible and not fight shy of being corrected, for no man is all-knowing and all-perfect.

Nigerian politicians should learn what it is to be a good opposition. Instead of always trying to undermine the policies of the party in power (in order to discredit it), the party in opposition should support the programmes of the ruling party meant for the common good and for the interest of the nation. Nigerians should borrow a leaf in this regard from the developed countries. For example, on Wednesday, November 17, 1993, the US House of Representatives (dominated by the Republicans, who are always at battle neck with President Clinton's ruling party, the Democratic party) passed NAFTA (North America Free Trade Agreement) by 234 to 200 votes, and President Clinton pointed out that the Republicans voted more than the Democrats in favour of the bill.

The Nigerian public officer should learn to resign from office when he/she has fallen out of favour with the masses - like when he/she finds himself or herself in a certain mess or scandal that is unworthy of his/her office, or like when the government adopts a policy that is contrary to faith and morals. This is the practice in the developed world[46] and it is very worthy of emulation by Nigerians.

With good leadership in place, Nigeria would be sure to have a good government, and thus a stable democracy. But this is not enough. Nigeria also needs good citizens - citizens who are aware of their rights and obligations and who would go about their daily businesses with the interest of the common good and of the nation at heart.

4.1.2.4. Good citizenship

Just as Nigeria needs efficient and responsible government, so also it needs good citizens for a democratic polity.[47] Citizens have their many rights and their corresponding duties. Here the political rights and duties of Nigerian citizens are stressed, with the aim of making them aware of their roles towards installing efficient and responsible government in the country.

A citizen should love his/her country. This duty rests in the law of nature, because the fatherland is the community of people to which the citizens are bound by common mores and culture; and because they are indebted to their country for protection and promotion of the common weal. All those Nigerians who live like mercenaries in their own country - those public servants who are lackadaisical and nonchalant about their official duties, calling them "no man's business" and still collect their salaries at the end of each month - those who are interested more in what they would gain from the country than in what they would put in - those who sabotage the efforts and plans of the nation, and so on - should have a change of mind and then do their duty to their country. (More on this later, in part 2, 4.3.)

A citizen should in conscience obey and respect civil authority, to the extent that the objective common good demands, even when this authority oversteps its competence and oppresses the people.[48] This is no blind obedience: "Still it is lawful for them to defend their own rights and those of their fellow citizens against any abuse of this authority, provided that in so doing they observe the limits imposed by natural law and the Gospel."[49]

It is the obligation of citizens to pay taxes - a duty deriving from the citizens' obligation to contribute their share to the necessities of the state, whose help they need, by which they profit, and which also assumes certain obligations in the citizens' place and stead. It is very sad that many Nigerians - government and non-government functionaries - indulge in tax evasion. This must stop, in order for the country to grow and to meet up with its many obligations. (More on this later, in part 2, 4.3.)

A citizen has both the right and duty to participate in the political processes: to vote and be voted for during an election. He/she is bound to do this in the interest of advancing the common good. As the Catholic Bishops' Conference of Nigeria would have it, "it is as a member of the electorate and government that the christian citizen should show how he can contribute equitably to the common good and manifest simultaneously both civic and religious virtues."[50]

Regrettably some Nigerians do not fulfil their civic responsibilities, because they regard politics as "a dirty game". This attitude is not the best. "To let politics become a cesspool," according to Howard Crosby, "and then avoid it because it is a cesspool is a double crime." This is because those who tag politics "a dirty game" and then eschew it are doing harm to themselves and to the nation: they are giving mandate to the "unworthy candidates" to ascend the platform of government. In the words of Donald G. Bloesch: "It would be a mistake ... to detach ourselves from the political turmoils of our time on the grounds that we need to keep ourselves pure from ideological contamination.... But such an attitude simply indicates that secularism has triumphed in a new way, because the world of politics and economics is then abandoned to the principalities and powers arrayed against the kingdom of Christ."[51] Some other Nigerians fail in their civic duty because they allow their vote to be bought with money. By so doing they sell their right, their freedom and their conscience to the highest bidder, and thereby allowing men and women of dubious character to ascend the throne of leadership. This too must stop.

Nigerians must therefore use their democratic rights in such a way as to ensure that the right persons are chosen to lead. Before the elections, they should watch for the qualities of leadership in those campaigning for their votes. These two sayings should be their guide: "They lead the best who dare to lead where others fear to tread; they do not cover up their faults but right their wrongs instead," and "a good leader knows the way, shows the way, and goes the way." They should look for men and women of honour and integrity, described by Mokwugo Okoye as: "Strong minds, great hearts, true faith and ready hands; men (and women) whom the lust of office does not kill; men (and women) whom spoils of office cannot buy; men (and women) who possess opinions and a will; men (and women) who have honour; men (and women) who will not lie; men (and women) who can stand before a demagogue and damn his treacheries without winking; tall men (and women), sun-crowned, who live above the fog in public duty and in private thinking."[52] With such close watch on the aspirants to leadership, "we must not confuse champions for leaders, nor prominence for pre-eminence. We must not confuse eloquence for honesty, neither must we confuse silence for wisdom. We must not confuse good looks for efficiency nor bravado for courage."[53]

To help Nigerians decide whom to vote for when the elections come up, debates should be organised among the political aspirants, especially among those aspiring to the executive posts of governorship and presidency, to ascertain their knowledge of the problems of the country and how they intend to solve such problems. The candidate who shows better knowledge of the problems and who has better proposals for solving them should be expected to win the election when the time comes, rather than the candidate with more money who makes many promises but lacks what it takes to tackle the nation's problems. Such debates are a type of opinion pole. This system is used, for example, in the USA and it is very effective. Nigeria should adopt it.

And during the elections, Nigerians should vote for men and women of integrity - men and women who will provide Nigeria with efficient and responsible government. Dr Nwafor Orizu (the president of the Nigeria Senate in 1964), in his *The Leadership We Want*,[54] lists eleven sterling qualities which anybody aspiring to leadership in Nigeria should have. These qualities are worthy of mention here; and they include:

A catalogue of achievements which must be based on patriotic motivations and national designs. A leader must be somebody Nigerians can trust and who must have grown from the roots of unshakeable faith in the country - a faith "supported by a long-standing hardwork, self-sacrifice, devotion to the principle of freedom and loyalty to the things Nigerian." This implies that inexperienced people should not be voted into office.

Selflessness. "Leaders should be such persons as do not seek their own alone. They must be people who respect other people and are sympathetic with the problems of others in a world where every person is sacred to himself." This implies that any candidate who is very much after himself and his own (friends and relations) - at the negligence of others - should not receive the people's vote.

A pure heart. "While they (the leaders) may make mistakes, their mistakes must not issue from bad motive or wicked designs. They should not connive over wrongs, nor think evil of those that disagree with them. When a leader is generally broad-minded, then he is qualified to lead Nigeria."

Ability to get the best out of the worst. Nigeria needs leaders "who have the ability to meet all emergencies without despair, whose intellect or emotion may not be swamped by discouragement or cynicism or by ingratitude or hatred, who are spiritually shock-proof in order to be able to resist the whirl wind of international diplomacy in the midst of cross-currents of internal oppositions."

The fear of God. "A nation without morals is bound to go the way of Sodom and Gomorrah.... Morally superior people have the chances of survival in spite of all the transient successes of wicked people. Leadership must behave in such a way as to show religious tolerance; and show the growing youth that it pays to be truthful, honest, industrious and faithful." (Benjamin Franklin, a one time president of the USA, stands out as an example here. In 1787 a convention was called in his country to revise the Articles of the Confederation. For weeks delegates reviewed ancient history and analysed modern governments, searching for insights. But nothing suited the infant nation. Finally, Benjamin Franklin, a distinguished gentleman, rose and said: 'In this situation of this assembly, groping as it were in the dark to find political truth and scarce able to distinguish it when it is presented to us, how has it happened that we have not hitherto once thought of humbly applying to the Father of Lights to illuminate our understanding.' So, Mr Franklin believed there was a sovereign God who could provide guidance to those who sought it and that leaders should rely on God for enlightenment. Thus a Nigerian leader must be a Franklin.)

Loyalty. "No nation can really exist until those who lead have grown so loyal as to forget themselves and forfeit a good deal of pseudo liberties in the service of the nation. They must suspend all other loyalties; throw away all other interests when they conflict with the nation's interest; suspend every discordant views which tend to disintegrate; and absorb all the shocks of centripetal influences on our culture and tradition." And a leader "must be loyal to his party - it makes no different what party. He must be loyal to his religion - no matter what religion. He must be loyal to his teachers - from his infant to the college. He must be loyal to his friends - both on Palm Sundays and on Good Fridays of life. He must be loyal to the royal in him, and translate all these loyalties to the highest form of loyalty - loyalty to the nation and loyalty to God."

Ability to represent the collective yearning of the entire nation. The leaders "must represent all the grievances, suppressed ambitions, vague longings, unexpressed rights, imposed handicaps; they must symbolise the spirit of the age by identifying themselves with the joys and sorrows of every citizen when taken collectively...."

Citizenship of the world. The leaders "must not narrow their gaze at Nigeria. Their diplomacy must be such as to internationalise Nigeria while solidifying it; to remain the brothers of all nations with prejudice towards none; to isolate our new nation from aggressive entanglements, while clinging to friendly co-operation of those whose principles of life suit our national purposes."

Ability to deliver. "Anybody who opts to ask for the people's votes for the presidency must let the voters know ahead of time that he knows the problems of the country in all its details, covering the interests of all peoples in all works of life. Showing the knowledge of these things is one thing; stating unequivocally the solutions the leader intends to apply to each and every one of them is the more important thing."

Nigerians should keep these qualities in mind while choosing their leaders. Moreover, they must bear in mind that the kind of leaders they choose will determine the kind of government they will have: good leadership equals good government, and bad leadership equals bad government. So, they must always ask themselves this question: What kind of leaders do we need? Emeka Odumegwu-Ojukwu's projections are worthy of note here. He writes:

> What kind of leaders do we need? We need leaders who are servants of the people, not their masters. We need leaders who will serve first the common man. We require leaders who will ensure fairness and equity to the various groups. We need leaders who must be the embodiment, and at all times, exemplify the ideas, of our nation. We need leaders who will keep alive the flames of our national aspirations. We want leaders who will be trusted friends of the people and protectors of the disadvantaged and oppressed. We require leaders who will have the right judgement both of people and of situations. We need leaders who will attract the right kind of lieutenants and who can best further the interest of the people. We want leaders who must be accountable to the people and are subjected to the will of the people. We need leaders who must be fanatical for the people's welfare and must at all times stand for justice and symbolise good government. We want leaders who will possess the ability to inspire the people out of despondency. We need leaders who can submerge excessive personal prestige and who are not vainglorious.
>
> ....
>
> We should no longer tolerate leaders who think that leadership is merely a game of frivolities. We have no need of leaders who spend more time in disco and midnight parties than in attending to the affairs of the state. We have no need for leaders who have proved that they can be juvenile in every inch of their conduct and are better suited to be band managers.
>
> Leadership is a business for serious minds. We do not want leaders who are erratic, whimsical and vindictive because they lack the maturity required for leadership. We do not want leaders who push their ignorance of the basic tenets of democracy to the extreme point of referring to our people as subjects. In a democracy, such as ours, the people are the masters and the leaders only their servants.[55]

If Nigerians could bear all these in mind while choosing their leaders, Nigeria would have good leaders, and thus good government, and the country would be a better place for all. Therefore, the citizens cannot afford to joke with their civic responsibilities.

Apart from the important task of choosing their leaders, Nigerians have also the onerous task of keeping a close watch on their leaders to make sure that they keep to the rules of the game. "Vigilance," writes Dr N. Orizu, "is one of the attributes of effective democracy. There must, therefore, be a prompt checking of the enemies of democracy: African democracy must fight against those who deny human rights, who condone inequality before the law, bureaucratic tyranny, repression of the labor class, unequal pay for equal ability and equal work, secret connivance over discriminations based on color, religion, or nationality, imperialism, secret diplomacy, unequal treaties, and calculation of power in terms of destructive elements."[56] Therefore, any leader who does not live up to expectation should be denied the mandate come the next election.

4.1.2.5. The Rule of Law and the Guarantee of Basic Rights and Freedoms

There is nothing wrong with the Nigerian constitution but with its managers. The lawlessness of the executive, of the police and of the judicature, coupled with the people's ignorance of the law, makes nonsense of the rule of law in the country. (See part 2, 3.4., above.) Therefore, to make the rule of law a reality in Nigeria, the following must be done: all must have respect for the rule of law; the people should be educated on their rights, and these rights must be protected; and the country's judiciary must be truly free and independent.

1) **Respect for the Rule of Law**[57]

There must be respect for the rule of law from both the rulers and the ruled. The rule of law implies that the law is supreme in the land. This means that before the law all are equal - nobody is and should be above the law - and the law is no respecter of person. Hence, being a leader or on top does not give one immunity from the law, nor does it make one master of the law (as a good many Nigerian leaders would assume). As Frederick the Great (18th century) rightly put it: "In court the laws must speak and the ruler must keep quiet" - indicating that the leader is under the law. Therefore, our government must be that of laws and not of men. Everything has to follow the "due process of the law" and there should be no arbitrary rule. Here the primary question, before any decision is taken, is: "What does the law say?" And having known what the law says, then all are bound to do what the law says, otherwise the defaulter - it does not matter who he/she is, whether the president of the country or the street-cleaner - pays the penalty for breaking the law.

To have respect for the rule of law, the people should be law-conscious. Majority of Nigerians are not very much law-conscious. This is not necessarily because they care less about the law (though some Nigerians would always want to circumvent the law in order to get what they want), but because they are not aware of the existence of many laws that govern them. Many a time those in authority make laws without consulting the people for whom the laws are made, and without informing them about, or educating them on, such laws when they are made. Consequently, many Nigerians do not know what the law says about many things. One might not even know about a law until one "unknowingly" falters and is arrested by the police who would tell one, when one claims ignorance of the law, that "ignorance of the law is no excuse". This should not be. The rule of law derives from the people. According to L. Stapleton, "a rule is law only for people who participate in the making of the laws or consent to them, and who are protected by basic rights, evinced in precedural safeguards, making their consent voluntary. For all others, even if they submit to the compulsion, the norms are not law but plain force."[58] Not only that law derives from the people, "but the process as a whole must be satisfactory to the citizens, or they have the power to change it."[59]

Let us look at what obtains in the developed countries. Take the USA for example. The people's opinions are taken into consideration before laws are made. When such laws are made, the people are constantly kept aware and mindful of them through different media and in the appropriate places. Thus in all public places - be it in the airports or seaports, or in the buses, trains, boats, ships, aeroplanes, or in business premises (like eating and/or drinking places), or in recreational places, or in academic premises, etc. - one is reminded of, one hears and/or reads, what the law says about the way of behaving or doing things in those places. The result is that the Americans are very conscious about their laws, be they federal or state laws. Nigeria should borrow a leaf from the US in this regard.

To have respect for the rule of law, the law itself should be reasonable and workable - capable of being kept and enforced. What is a law if it is not reasonable and workable, if the people are not afforded the means of obeying and keeping it, and if the government cannot enforce it? Mr Boek rightly points out that "a law does not meet the intentions of those who passed it unless it is enforced and those disobeying it, penalized."[60] Think of a law in Nigeria which prohibits Nigerians from burying their dead anywhere except in the cemeteries. This, in a culture where it is normal or traditional to bury one's dead at home and as such there are no burial grounds or cemeteries. It would have been wiser to provide the people with cemeteries before enacting the law. Or think of another law in Nigeria which makes it mandatory for Nigerians to register their "births" and "deaths" - without providing the people with the necessary "clinics". Or think yet of another law in Nigeria which out-laws "tribal marks" - in a society where these "facial marks" are traditionally "something" of beauty and/or honour. Surely, such laws as these are not reasonable, and they can neither be kept nor enforced. They are only a sham, a child's play.

In contrast, think of the situations in developed countries, where laws are made and means provided to help the people keep the laws. Here laws are enforceable. Take Germany for example. Here the law forbids burning of anything (even papers) in the open. The people are provided with public "dustbins" or "garbage cans" where they should dispose of their "wastes". Dustcarts or garbage trucks come every week to take the wastes to refuse collection centres. Furthermore, the law mandates the people to separate their wastes for easier processing at refuse collection centres. To make this possible, dustbins of different colours are provided to classify the wastes. Again the law forbids people to ease themselves or to defecate in the open. Consequently, toilets are provided in all public places and houses, at strategic places, and in long-distance-public-vehicles.

Normally laws are made for the welfare of the people - to help them live an orderly and peaceful life in the society, and not to punish them. This implies that laws should not be made just for the sake of making laws, but to help the people live a secured life. "A decision as to whether or not a regulation is necessary has to be based on the effect of having or not having it on the quality of life of all the people who would be affected by the regulation."[61] It then follows that the government regulations must be essential to be able to greatly improve the quality of life of the people. "Essential regulations," in the words of Boek, "are those that have been shown to be needed through objective analyses of the risks to all forms of life on which they are focused, along with the actual effect of the regulations on reducing those risks."[62] Therefore, the Nigerian government must make sure that its laws are essential, reasonable and workable: that they are capable of improving the life of the people, of being obeyed by the people and of being enforced by its agents.

It must therefore be emphasised that everybody - the government and its law enforcement agents, and the citizens - must be law abiding. This stems from the fact that all are equal under the law and that the law is no respecter of person. On the part of the governed, the citizens must be law conscious and must cherish and inbreed a strong respect for law. However, his/her obligation to obey the law is based on his/her consent to the method of its making or agreement with the direction it gives, or both. Thus it could be said with Stapleton that "in a democracy, the citizen has a moral obligation to obey the law, whether or not he considers it wise, because he has consented to the method of its making. If, however, the law directs him to perform an action that would cause serious injustice, he cannot be considered obligated to obey it. To take any other view robs conscience of all integrity. But this principle holds only in cases where obedience to the law would cause real injury to a vital principle."[63] On the part of the government, it must abide by the rule of law (the constitution). It must never introduce any law arbitrarily or act arbitrarily. To this belong the prohibition of retrospective laws (especially when these would be injurious to the citizens) and the 'law of protection of trust'. Thus the state business must be open, measurable, foreseeable and calculable. The government must guarantee the legal process which guarantees the autonomy and independence of the judiciary, not only in view of the protection of the individual but also in view of the commitment of the state power to the constitution and the law. And the government agents and agencies too must respect and obey the spirit and letters of the law. Thus, when both the government and the governed observe "constitutional morality," justice and peace become the order of the day, and the stability and growth of the democratic polity is assured. A quotation from J. F. Kennedy will buttress as well as summarise our points:

> Our nation is founded on the principle that observance of the law is the eternal safeguard of liberty and defiance of the law is the surest road to tyranny.
> The laws which we obey includes the final rulings of the courts as well as the enactments of our legislative bodies. Even among law-abiding men few laws are universally loved.
> But they are uniformly respected and not resisted.

> Americans are free, in short, to disagree with the law, but not to disobey it. For in a government of laws and not of men, no man, however prominent or powerful, and no mob, however unruly or boisterous, is entitled to defy a court of law.
> If this country should reach the point where any man or group of men, by force or threat of force, could long deny the demands of our court and our Constitution, then no law would stand, no judge would be sure of his writ and no citizen would be safe from his neighbors....[64]

2) **Guarantee of basic rights and freedoms**

With regard to fundamental human rights, Nigerian constitution provides the list of individual rights or liberties - the bill of rights - that are protected against the exercise of state power. The bill of rights contains certain "unalienable rights" - the civil rights or civil liberties which protect the citadel of man's individualism. These rights include the freedom of speech, of assemblage and of the press; religious freedom; freedom of unauthorised search and seizure, the right of trial by jury. And they are never to be encroached upon without mortal danger to democracy. "The safeguards of the Bill of Rights," Bingham observes, "rest on the assumption that no man is to be merely a means to some other man's end, even if the other man be a government official. The criminal himself is a citizen with inviolable rights, till the formalities of trial, sentence and execution are complied with. The writ of *habeas corpus*, by which even the enemy of society is assured his day in court, was the first foundation stone of modern democracy."[65] This highlights the equality of all before the law and the fact that an accused person cannot be deemed guilty without being given a chance to defend himself.

As stated in part 2, 2.4. (above), the common man in Nigeria is ignorant of his/her fundamental rights, and this lack is often exploited by those in the legal profession and by the law enforcement agents to extort money from him/her. Therefore, the common man is done injustice under the law by men and women of the law. To tackle this problem, Nigeria's primary task should be to educate the citizen on their fundamental human rights and obligations - through formal education (in the schools), through informal education (adult education and seminars), and through the mass media (newspapers, radios and televisions). Secondly, the state must check and stop the abuse of people's rights by its agents, especially by the police who have become people's foes instead of their friends.[66] The state is a means, not an end - it exists for the sake of the individuals of which it is composed, not vice versa. Hence it is bound to defend the civil liberties. Such a defence is the essence of democracy, for it is an assertion of the dignity and worth of the individual.

3) **Independent and respectable judiciary**[67]

Nigerian constitution provides for separation of powers - the distribution of power among such functionally differentiated agencies of government (the legislature, the executive, and the judiciary). The reason is to prevent any one branch of government from becoming supreme: to prevent the misuse of power and thus to secure the freedom of the individual. According to Madison, "the accumulation of all powers, legislative, executive, and judiciary, in the hands, whether of one, a few, or many, and whether hereditary, self-appointed, or elected, may justly be pronounced the very definition of tyranny."[68]

With this provision of separation of powers in our constitution, one would imagine that the Nigerian judiciary is free and independent. But it has been shown (in part 2, 3.4. above) that the judiciary in Nigeria is not very free and independent. If Nigeria is to have a stable and lasting democracy, the independence of the judiciary must be reaffirmed and religiously respected.

It is very essential that the judiciary be independent to be able to perform its enormous and all-important function. According to S. K. Padover, the courts of justice serve a triple function: "On the level of individual relationships they adjudicate differences with objectivity and impartiality.... A second function of an independent judiciary is that of clarification of the rules by which the communities live - it provides for a government of laws and not of capricious men. Third, such a judiciary imposes legal restraints on the arbitrary power. By defining the laws and defending the rule of law, independent courts can put a damper on willful personal power and overweening political ambition."[69] Although there is no complete separation between the judiciary and the executive or the legislature, democracy fares better when the judiciary enjoys greater autonomy from the other branches of government, to maintain its very essential impartiality and to avoid being exposed to political influences and pressures.

In this regard, Nigeria must uphold certain devices used in democratic states to ensure the independence of the judiciary. One is the permanency of the judge's position. A judge is usually appointed to hold office 'during good behaviour' and so he may not be removed from office by any vent of the wind. For instance, in the USA the federal judges may be removed only by impeachment before Congress; and in Britain they may be removed only by an address of both Houses. Two, the judges should be provided with social prestige and adequate salaries. These enable a judge to maintain a certain standard of living that is above par and which reduces the chances of greed and wanton pursuit of wealth. Third, a judge is rendered immune from action in relation to the decisions he may take within his jurisdiction. The fourth is non-political appointment of judges.[70] This is meant to prevent any judge from being partisan, which would definitely mar his/her juridical impartiality. Lastly, the quality and calibre of persons to be appointed as judges must be taken into consideration. It is very necessary to have the right kind of men and women behind the law. In the words of T. Roosevelt, "while good laws are necessary, while it is necessary to have the right kind of governmental machinery, yet the all-important matter is to have the right kind of man behind the law. A State cannot rise without proper laws, but the best laws that the wit of man can devise will amount to nothing if the State does not contain the right kind of man, the right kind of woman."[71] As J. R. Lewis rightly points out, "the judge, after all, is not a being of Olympian detachment; he is a man, with all man's prejudices, failings, experiences and partiality. He will try to be impartial, and perhaps will succeed as far as is humanly possible. But the qualification of 'humanly possible' must be noted. The judge is not a computer. There is always a human element in his decision, an element influenced by his education, his home background, his social surroundings, his personal experiences, his philosophies of life.... In order to be able to overcome the worst of his prejudices and ensure that justice is done, the judge must be an exceptional man. He must be honest, a man of integrity and wisdom; he must above all be impartial, allowing no emotional feelings personal to himself to sway his judgement. He must be well versed in the law, since he is called upon to apply it, and he should thus have a sound background of legal training and practical experience."[72] Therefore, only those who have a knowledge of law and the constitution along with the respect of other lawyers and citizens, who are supposed to be unbiased without any opinions about issues that come up in the court until the evidence is presented, and who have a strong belief in democracy and sufficient experience with the court system to have maturity of judgement should be appointed judges in Nigeria.

On its own part, the judiciary must always assert and uphold, in words and deed, its independence. It must endeavour to preserve the liberties of the individual, to protect the constitution, to uphold legal rights against the encroachments of the state and the individual and the pressure group. It must ensure that the law is applied without fear or favour, whether a man is Igbo, Hausa or Yoruba, christian or muslim, president or ordinary labourer, lawyer, litigant or thief. Justice must go to whom it is due, not to the mighty (as to those in power), not to the highest bidder (as to the rich). The men and women of the legal profession must make sure that the poor of the land obtain justice. They should stop exploiting the common man's ignorance of the law (in order to get much money out of him/her). And they should bring their services within the reach of the common man by lowering their present high charges which only the rich can afford.

To help keep the judiciary on the right course, a legal review board for lawyers should be established. "This board would review decided cases to determine if appropriate conclusions have been reached, based on the facts. Corrupt lawyers could then be disciplined."[73] Not only that, well-trained lawyers in the nation should help to prevent members of the judicial system from perverting the constitution with their decisions. "One way lawyers do this is by writing about decisions in relation to the Constitution in law journals and by presenting talks at meetings of lawyers."[74] Also public access to all court papers should be provided, and this would force the "judges to be extra careful because their decisions would become historical documents."[75] Moreover, all Nigerians, "whether or not they are lawyers, must pay attention to decisions of judges to make sure they do not violate the Constitution or laws of (Nigeria). Because citizens are free to speak and write about decisions they believe are incorrect, judges who make them can be influenced to carefully consider the constitutionality of the issues before they give their decisions."[76]

4.1.2.6. Civilian control of the military

There can never be a lasting democracy in a country where the military have the will to take the law into their hands, to oust duly elected leaders, and to assume political roles - roles very much alien to their calling. The military's role is to defend the country against external aggression. As pointed out in part 2, 3.2.5. (above), incessant military interventions in the political life of Nigeria is one of the major reasons why democracy has not taken root in the country. The military often justify their interventions in the name of democracy: to save the country from collapsing (due to the irresponsible, selfish and corrupt practices of the politicians which are ill-winds that blow democracy no good). But it is clear could not perform better than the civilians they overthrow: when they disengage, they always leave the country more battered than they found it when they came to power. This goes a long way to indicate that military interventions are not the solution to Nigeria's political maladies. So writes E. Odumegwu-Ojukwu,

> To be frank, the entry of the military into Nigerian politics has not fulfilled its promise.... (I)t installed indiscipline and has succeeded in legitimising it as a normal system for changing governments. It has not solved the social problems, neither has it solved the economic problems. It has destroyed the delicate balance of our political structure without putting in its place a better structure. It has destroyed public morality both spiritual and carnal.[77]

Therefore, a stop has to be put to military coups in Nigeria if the country is to make any headway toward having a stable and lasting democracy. As the Nigerian Head of State, General Sani Abacha, in 1994 put it: "It has become imperative that through a permanent, irrevocable and binding arrangement, we permanently end the coup culture in Nigerian politics."[78] The question now is: How do we stop the military from intervening in the political affairs of Nigeria?

One may immediately opine that as soon as the politicians begin to play the game of politics according to the rules - not trying to win at all cost, not regarding politics as a do-or-die battle, not being too selfish and corrupt, etc. - military coup in Nigeria would be a thing of the past. This position appears very logical but it has a big flaw. Politicians are not angels and they will never be. If we were to wait until the politicians became angels or saints in politicking before the military cease from intervening in the Nigerian politics, then we would have to wait *ad infinitum*. Without encouraging the recklessness and corrupt practices of our politicians, it must be stressed that the military should allow the politicians to make mistakes and then to learn from their mistakes. The sayings "practice makes perfection" and "experience is the best teacher" are important here.

Some people, like Nnamdi Azikiwe (the first President of Nigeria), Chuba Okadigbo (a lecturer turned politician), Arthur Nwankwo (a political analyst), Sam Ikoku (an old time politician), Olusegun Obasanjo (a former military Head of State), General S. Abacha (the current military Head of State), have argued that since the military have been deeply immersed in the Nigerian political life - out of the 36 years of Nigeria's independence, 26 years have been spent under military rule - it would be difficult to disentangle it from politics. In the words of S. Abacha: "The armed forces should never be removed from the concerns and anxieties of the society they serve."[79] Therefore, for these people, there should be a joint military-civilian rule - *diarchy*[80] - in Nigeria. Dr Nnamdi Azikiwe had in 1972 proposed that, in addition to the legislature, the executive and the judiciary forming the three arms of the state, the armed and security forces should constitute the fourth arm. His reason is that "without the active cooperation of the armed and security forces, neither of the three arms of the state would function effectively in the government of human beings."[81] In his bid to provide Azikiwe's proposal "with some teeth in a functional sense," Dr Okadigbo came up with the theory of "balancing the ballot and the bullet forces in our body politic," saying:

> there will be need for the representation of the armed forces in the senate of the republic. There will be four members of the armed forces elected within the armed forces and functional within the senate.... These persons shall represent the various levels within the armed forces, namely, from the rank of private to lieutenant, from captain to lieutenant-colonel and from the rank of colonel to the rank of general. There will be one extra member who may be the head of the forces in an ex-officio capacity.... The armed forces will, at least, be involved in the process of political development of the country. This will give them a place for dialogue within the system. We can hear their points of view and we can articulate them. We can explain to them our own points of view and thus evolve a system of dialogue between the force of the bullet and the force of ballot. The two forces can, at least, be in concert.[82]

Advocating "positive integration of civilians and the military," Arhtur Nwankwo posits his "theory of cimilicy"[83] which involves "mobilising all democratic forces within the armed forces and civil society with a view of taking state power from the hands of the elite classes" - the "politicisation of the armed forces and the militarisation of civilians." He writes: "Cimilicy is the most primary condition and, in fact, the first step which must be taken in future democratisation of Nigerian affairs.... It would be misleading to expect to operate a stable political formation in Nigeria without (first) settling the question of cleavages in civilian military relations." The strategy of "cimilicy", according to Nwankwo, derives from "a realisation that, given the increasing recourse to violence by the neocolonial establishment and the intensive militarisation of existing political institutions, the present stalemate can be broken only with the same coercive mechanisms with which it is imposed" - in other words, "the only option for opposing (the) military blackmail is paradoxically the military option."

I am highly opposed to diarchy in all its forms - be it as Zik's "fourth arm theory of government" or as Okadigbo's "balance of bullet and ballot forces" or as Nwankwo's "cimilcy" - for the one reason that it is undemocratic, and so it will never lead to the establishment of a stable and lasting democracy in Nigeria. In the first place, diarchy is "a mixture of opposites," civilians with the army - democracy with authoritarianism, which will never work. This agrees with Niyi Osundare's view that diarchy is

> an odd mixture of coercion and persuasion, a frustrating yoking together of brutal rigidity and civil latitude, a suit made of a curious combination of khaki trousers and *babanriga*. Diarchy is an arrangement doomed to failure. It is a tricky conspiracy of the military and civilian elite to gain power and maintain their hold on it. It is a dangerous sabotage of the people's freedom and libertarian ideal. It is also a farce with a mask with hidden fangs, for while the civilian segment gives diarchy a democratic veneer, the military wing plays the real enforcers with their monopoly of violence and brutality. The military crush the people under their boots, the civilian covers up the blood with folds of *agbada*. A philosopher once said: 'Unhappy is the land ruled by soldiers;' to which we add: unfree is the country ruled by diarchists.[84]

In the second place, to allow diarchy is to encourage and perpetuate military coups in Nigeria (the very evil we intend to eliminate), for then we shall be acknowledging that the military have a right to be in government.[85] And thirdly, such involvement of the military in politics would surely divert and distract the military from their professional role of national defence, thereby weakening Nigeria's military preparedness in case of external aggression. Therefore, it is obvious that diarchy will neither solve the problem of military coups in Nigeria - it will not stop the military from intervening in Nigerian politics, nor will it enhance the building of a stable and lasting democracy in the country. However, if the military personnel wish to play the game of politics, as citizens of Nigeria they have every right to do so, "but to do so they must obey the rules. They should resign and not return to the forces after. They should stump the campaign trail, soliciting votes, instead of stalking the presidential palace, and taking it by storm."[86]

One major way of stopping military interventions in Nigerian politics is to maintain the subservient role of the military,[87] what Samuel P. Huntington calls "objective civilian control" of the military.[88] This involves: 1) a high level of military professionalism and recognition by military officers of the limits of their professional competence; 2) the effective subordination of the military to the civilian political leaders who make the basic decisions on foreign and military policy; 3) the recognition and acceptance by that leadership of an area of professional competence and autonomy for the military; and 4) as a result, the minimisation of military intervention in politics and of political intervention in the military - efforts should be made to restructure and redirect the military toward military missions and to get them out of a wide range of less-than-military activities.

Such civilian control of the military must be one of the strong values held by all citizens in a democracy. W. E. Boek writes: "The civilian authority over the military cannot be by just one branch of the government, such as the executive. Instead, civilian control has to be a basic tenet of the Constitution and policy of the people with authority vested in more than one branch, and it must include the elected legislature."[89]

Good enough, part I, section 1(2) of the 1989 the Nigerian constitution stipulates that "the Federal Government of Nigeria shall not be governed, nor shall any person or group of persons take control of the Government of Nigeria or any part thereof, except in accordance with the provisions of this Constitution." But sad enough, this provision is not taken very serious. This negligence must stop and the letters of the constitution upheld. Therefore, any person or group of persons (the military inclusive) who topples or attempts to topple a duly constituted government should be brought to book and tried for treason, if not immediately, after he/she (or they) has (or have) relinquished the usurped office. This would definitely help to eradicate the "coup culture" in Nigeria.

At this juncture, it is clear that political development alone will not offer Nigeria a stable and lasting democracy. There is also need for socio-economic development: free market economy and social welfare and services.

4.1.3. Socio-economic Development

The society is meant for man and not man for the society. What this implies is that "in the socioeconomic realm, ... the dignity and total vocation of the human person must be honoured and advanced along with the welfare of society as a whole. For man is the source, the centre, and the purpose of all socioeconomic life."[90] Therefore, all socio-economic policies and structures must be for the good, development and fulfilment of man - as individuals, families and groups - and for the better attainment of the common good. And every plan, policy, action and structure which does not protect, project and propagate the dignity and welfare of the human person must be rejected as unjust. It is in this light that the socio-economic developments in Nigeria ought to be seen, if Nigeria is to establish a genuine, stable and lasting democracy.

4.1.3.1. Economic development

Economic development or growth is very essential for the democratic process. In fact, there is a mutual relationship between economic growth and democracy[91]: democracies generate economic growth (more than dictatorships), and the level of economic growth has a very strong effect on the duration of the survival of a democracy. Przeworski et al. maintain that "poor democracies, particularly those with annual per-capita income of less than $1,000, are extremely fragile: based on our study, the probability that one will die during a particular year is 0.12. This rate falls to 0.06 in the $1,000 to $2,000 range, to 0.03 between $2,000 and $4,000, and to 0.01 between $4,000 and $6,000. These numbers mean that a democracy can be expected to last an average of about 8.5 years in a country with per-capita income under $1,000 per annum, 16 years in one with between $1,000 and $2,000, 33 years between $2,000 and $4,000, and 100 years between $4,000 and $6,000."[92] (Note that the current per capita income in Nigeria is below $200.) They agree with Larry Diamond and Juan Linz that "economic crisis represents one of the most common threats to democratic stability,"[93] and rightly hold that "inflation also threatens democratic stability. A democratic regime has a 0.023 chance of dying and an expected life of 44 years when the annual inflation is between 6 and 30 percent; and a 0.064 chance and an expected life of about 16 years when inflation is above 30 percent."[94] (Note also that the current inflation rate in Nigeria is between 64 and 80 per cent.) Przeworski et al. then conclude that "economic performance ... is crucially important for the survival of democracy in less-affluent countries. When the economy grows rapidly with a moderate rate of inflation, democracy is much more likely to last even in the poorest lands."[95] Therefore, to be able to build a stable and lasting democracy, Nigeria must embark on a serious and meaningful economic development capable of extricating its citizens from their economic quagmire, raising them above the poverty level and providing them with a better standard of living.

Economic development in a democracy means the creation or production of new wealth, by individuals and/or corporations, for the purpose - not of mere multiplication of products, nor of profit or dominion, but - of "the service of man, and indeed of the whole man, viewed in terms of his material needs and the demands of his intellectual, moral, spiritual, and religious life."[96] In short, it is for the enhancement of the quality of life of the individuals in the society. And it is best served by capitalism. As Boek argues,

> The economic system that, much more than any other, meets essential requirements of democracies is capitalism. Capitalists have beliefs about human activity that include continual striving to increase their income beyond that needed for the necessities of life. They do this by working hard to earn money and then by spending less than they earn. The money they save is used to obtain additional money by investing it in business or from interest for the use of it that is paid by banks who invest it. The objective of people who own business in capitalistic society is to increase the size or scope of their businesses with the profits from their endeavors rather than to spend it all on consumer goods and sevices.[97]

The emphasis then is more on investment and production than on consumption.

Moreover, in a democracy economic development demands economic freedom. This means that people should be "free to develop and operate their own enterprises as they see fit, to buy from and to sell to whomever they want to at whatever price they choose,"[98] without undue interference or control from the government or from any other group. As Boek has it, "the greatest error in the advancement of human societies has been restrictions placed on the procession of supply and demand. The most effective forces in economic development are free markets and free enterprise when these stretch across the boundaries of families, tribes, and nations, uninhibited by beliefs, ethnocentric loyalties, cutural biases, quotas, tariffs, subsidies, or taxes."[99] However, this does not mean that the government cannot control the possible excesses of the businesspersons - for example, to prevent them "from obtaining a monopoly by which they can burden consumers with prices for products and services that result in returns on the capital investments of the providers far beyond that which is considered normal."[100]

There has been much emphasis on "economic reform" if the developing economies must find their feet.[101] No doubt, economic reform is good and necessary for developing countries to rise from their poverty level. But what kind of economic reform? I am one of those strongly opposed to the type of reform - based on the structural adjustment programmes (SAPs) which emphasizes, inter alia, the devaluation of currency and removal of government subsidies - advocated and imposed by the World Bank and the International Monetary Fund (IMF). More often than not, as is the case in Nigeria, these structural adjustment programmes lack human face, and instead of ushering in economic reform, they bring about more suffering, poverty, and underdevelopment. I wonder if there is a country that has succeeded in its economic reform thanks to SAPs? Surely SAPs are not the best answer to our economic problems. Writing on "An Alternative for Africa," Adebayo Adedji (the executive director of the African Centre for Development and Strategic Studies, ACDESS, in Ijebu-Ode, Nigeria) comments:

> For more than three decades, Africa has been required to act as if the answer to its socioeconomic problems and the key to its future lay in the pursuit of economic growth based on expanded exports of primary commodities. Over the last 15 years, however, the structural adjustment programmes (SAPs) that the international lending institutions such as the World Bank and the International Monetary Fund (IMF) have offered to deeply indebted African countries on 'swallow-or-starve' terms have made Africa into a continent that can be molded at will to fit the needs of the global economy. Far from bringing about economic reform, these SAPs have severely eroded the development drive that has always been the best hope for stabilizing the precarious political structures that succeeded colonialism. Today, there is hardly a corner of Africa that is not affected by violence and on the verge of falling apart.
>
> The World Bank and IMF (whose policies approximate the collective will of the G-7 countries) have joined with their indigenous political-economic compradors to unravel many of the major achievements of the first decade of Africa's postcolonial history. The stringencies imposed by SAPs caused cuts in education and health care, in the provision of infrastructural facilities, and in the general enabling condi-

> tions needed for political stability and socioeconomic transformation. The cumulative result of making development an afterthought is now all too readily visible across Africa: hunger, misery, and despair are rampant.
> The orthodox development paradigm, which understands development in terms of increasing material wealth rather than in terms of the well-being of people, has badly failed Africa. Increases in national per-capita income, rather than in the sustainable quality of life, are at the centre of this approach, which dwells on such macroeconomic variables as GDP, saving rates, investment, foreign exchange, and the like. By chasing only material and quantifiable goals while neglecting people, and by relying on models derived from the experience of Western Europe and North America, development economics has only made it more difficult to unlock the dynamic forces that can fit underdeveloped economies out of the depths of poverty and injustice.[102]

Mr Adedeji goes on to point out that "the first fundamental flaw in the approach to the African condition favored by the dominant interests of the global North is the decision simply to ignore the continent's 500-year-long history of subjugation, slavery, colonialism, balkanization, and exploitation. While they readily recognize the instructive value of the past for the present and the future of their own countries and societies, citizens of the North seem to have a blind sport when it comes to Africa.... Unfortunately, those who today make decisions for Africa have no interest in developing strategies to overcome the colonial legacy of vulnerable and export-dependent economies that draw on Africa's own institutional, cultural, and political history. Were they to do so, they might find development approaches that could actually succeed."[103]

Definitely, Nigeria needs an alternative to SAPs. Its economic reform must go beyond SAPs' emphasis on short-term crisis management to long-term economic planning, with great emphasis on policy continuity and adherence by government officials to strict standards of public service and accountability. And, above all, its economic reform must be "premised on the primacy of the people and of human-capital development."[104] In this regard, Mr Adedeji calls for "long term, holistic restructuring" which "must reach beyond the economy and transform the polity and society as well. Its goal is to make the development process self-reliant, self-sustaining, and democratic. Such transformation policies would be possible 1) for domestic needs to determine the direction of development and the prevailing patterns of output and growth; 2) for domestic-factor inputs; 3) for popular participation to become an integral part of economic management; and 4) for mutually supportive and reinforcing structures to arise that would give the entire political and socioeconomic system an opportunity to unleash its own internal dynamics."[105] Nigeria therefore needs functional economic structures and policies.

4.1.3. 1.1. Functional economic structures and policies

Nigeria is blessed with good and fertile soil and with many natural resources. A country with these resources should be self-sufficient in food, have a good standard of living (with basic amenities of life and infrastructures in place), and have much for export. But this is not the case in Nigeria (as the discussion on "socio-economic factor" in part 2, 3.3., above shows).

Nigeria has not yet put to maximum utilisation its natural blessings. Some of these resources are yet to be tapped. Some of those tapped are not fully developed or are yet to be developed. Some of those developed are not functioning well or to full capacity. Consequently, many of these resources lie dormant while many others are wasted away. Think, for instances, of the many fruits, grains, vegetables and other food stuffs that rotten away - wasted - each year, because Nigeria lacks adequate preservation facilities. Again think of the huge amount of different gases burnt away each day at our oil-refineries, because Nigeria lacks petrochemical-allied industries to transform these gases into other valuable forms. Nigeria therefore needs functional economic structures that would encourage investment culture, provision of employment and just wages, and maintenance culture.

4.1.3.1.1.1. Investment culture.

Nigeria is known for its consumer rather than production oriented economy. Much money is spent on non- or less-income-yielding ventures: importation of consumer goods (like food stuffs, electronics), maintaining a splendiferous life style (like feasting, going for prestigious and flamboyant things), building individual and family edifices, supporting religious organisations and social gatherings lavishly, huge budgets on defence, financing government bureaucracies, expanding non-productive property holdings, and so on. It is true that some of these ventures do result in jobs and thus in income for people, none of them can produce growth in the number of jobs beyond those necessary to carry out the immediate tasks. For example, no matter how one may admire a luxurious home costing ten million naira, it is quite a different investment in terms of economic return to the country than a factory that produces farm machinery. "When the home is built, it does not produce income. The factory, however, can keep on producing income that can be used to expand it or build other factories for the next generation if it is carefully managed with a resulting improvement in the level of living of the people."[106] Therefore, to have a stable and healthy economy necessary for a stable and lasting democracy, Nigerians must stop squandering their money and instead invest it in profit-making ventures. In other words, they should transform their money into further means of production - invest it in productive sectors. And any money that they do not immediately need they should put in the bank to earn interest for them and at the same time make it possible for the bank to lend the money to business people.

Special emphasis should be on capital-oriented investments, especially in agriculture and industries.

1) **Investment in agriculture**

Agriculture in Nigeria is a sick baby; it is a depressed and neglected sector. (See part 2, 3.3.1.) The pitiable position of agricultural sector in Nigeria today fits in well in the observation made in 1981 by Pope John Paul II, viz.:

> Agricultural work involves considerable difficulties, including unremitting and sometimes *exhausting physical effort* and *lack of appreciation on the part of society*, to the point of making agricultural people feel that they are social outcasts and speeding up the phenomenon of their mass exodus from the countryside to the cities and unfortunately to still more dehumanizing living conditions. Added to this are the *lack of adequate professional training and of proper equipment*, the spread of certain individualism, and also objectively unjust situations. In certain developing countries, millions of people are forced to cultivate the land belonging to others and *are exploited* by the big landowners, without any hope of ever being able to gain possession of even a small piece of land of their own. There is a *lack of forms of legal protection* for the agricultural workers themselves and for their families in case of old age, sickness or unemployment. Long days of hard work are *paid miserably*. Land which could be cultivated is left abandoned by the owners. Legal titles to possession of a small portion of land that someone has personally cultivated for years are disregarded or left defenseless against the 'land hunger' of more powerful individuals or groups....[107]

Because of this neglect of the agricultural sector, "many farmers have abandoned their rural birthplace, and seek out either the more populous centres of the cities themselves"[108] - so too the youths who would have taken to agriculture, after their parents - because of "the desire to escape from a confined environment offering no prospect of a more comfortable life; the wish ... to undertake new activities and to acquire new experiences; the attraction of quickly acquired goods and fortunes; a longing after a freer life, with the advantages that larger towns and cities usually provide. But there is no doubt about this point: rural dwellers leave the fields because nearly everywhere they see their affairs in a state of depression, both as regards labour productivity and the level of living of farm populations."[109] Hence something must be done to ameliorate this situation.

In the first place, "radical and urgent changes are ... needed in order to restore to agriculture - and to rural people - their just value as the basis of a healthy economy, within the social community's development as a whole. Thus it is necessary to proclaim and promote the dignity of work, of all work but especially of agricultural work, in which man so eloquently 'subdues' the earth he has received as a gift from God and affirms his 'dominion' in the visible world."[110] Hence,

Nigerians should stop regarding "farming" or agriculture as a field for the illiterates, and they should stop looking down on farmers, as if farmers were second class citizens. The farmers themselves should neither feel nor consider themselves inferior to others in the society; so too members of the farmers' families - so that a child should no longer be ashamed of acknowledging in public that his/her father is a farmer. Everybody should bear in mind therefore that no work is "infra dig"; every work, including farming, has its dignity and contributes to the general welfare of the society.

Secondly, the essential services which make life worth living - and the lack of which lure the people away from the rural areas to the cities or urban areas where such services are somehow available - should be provided at rural areas, and social welfare programmes extended also to the farmers. (See 4.1.3.2., below.)

Thirdly, the farmers should be exposed to new information and modern techniques in agriculture according to the dictates of the developments in science and technology. As Pope John XXIII would have it:

> Above all, it must be emphasized that enterprises and bodies of this sort, in order that they may survive and flourish, should be continuously adapted - both in their productive structure and in their operating mehtods - to new conditions of times. These new conditions constantly arise from advances in science and technology, or from changing consumer needs and preferences. It is especially appropriate that all this can be done by the craftsmen themselves and by the associates in the cooperatives.[111]
>
> In particular, care must be had that within the agricultural sector innovations are introduced as regards productive technology whether these relate to productive methods, or to cultivation of the fields, or to equipment for the rural enterprise, as far as the overall economy allows or requires. And all this should be done, as far as possible, in accordance with technical advances in industry and in the various services.[112]
>
> The family farm will be firm and stable only when it yields money income sufficient for decent and humane family living. To bring this about, it is very necessary that farmers generally receive instruction, be kept informed of new developments, and be technically assisted by trained men.[113]

Therefore, agriculture in Nigeria should become mechanised. Nigerian farmers should be helped to rise from the use of mainly manual labour (which consumes a lot of time and energy and yields very little output) to the use of modern equipment and instruments (which consumes less time and energy and yields much output).

To help better their lot, "it is also necessary that farmers form among themselves mutual-aid societies; that they establish professional associations; that they function efficiently in public life, that is, in various administrative bodies and in political affairs."[114] It is true that the various co-operative societies formed by the farmers in Nigeria are doing well in helping their members to get various assistance, for example loan, from the government, but the farmers have no strong unifying force that could help them press their points home to any government and to the public. It would therefore be of immense help to the farmers if they organised themselves into a strong association or trade union, at least for the purpose of defending the vital interests of their members.[115]

Other measures for the promotion of agricultural development in rural areas are given below, viz.: appropriate economic policy (in 4.1.3.1.1.1. 3)), and provision of essential public services and social welfare programmes (in 4.1.3.2.).

2) **Investment in industries**

Industries should be established to process, develop and preserve Nigeria's many agricultural and mineral resources. Nigeria exports mainly raw materials (which yields little income to the nation) and imports these back as finished products (which are very costly and which drain the nation's purse). Therefore, it is better for Nigeria to establish, or to get investors (native and foreign) to establish here in the country industries which can process and transform the raw materials into finished products for internal consumption and for exports. If this is done, Nigeria would definitely be saving a lot of money from what it would have expended on import and making a huge income from the increased export.

Nigeria should not concentrate its industries in the cities. It should rather embark on intensive rural industrialisation. The rural areas have got the land and the raw materials and even labour, and many of them have also rivers - all these make for good siting of industries. All that needs to be done is to build good and accessible roads and to provide electricity in these rural areas and then any industry can take off.

The advantages of rural industrialisation are many and well known. Suffice to say that **rural industrialisation**, over and above, makes for rural development which affords the people better standard of life and which, in turn, helps to reduce urban migration. Because the essential services are now available in the rural areas, many people who would have gone to the cities in search of these amenities would remain at home to contribute their own effort towards the development of these areas and also help to decongest the cities. Moreover, the cities are saved from environmental pollution, especially air pollution, due to the concentration of many industries in the cities.

Not only the big and multi-national industries count for developments, **small scale industries** are also very important; and both should be encouraged. But whether large scale or small scale, to accomplish the task of industrialisation the state must provide its enterprising citizens with sufficient government subsidy and commercial protection. (More on this below - 4.1.3.1.1.1. 3))

Like industries, **granarries** and other appropriate **storerooms** or **storehouses** should be built to take care of and preserve Nigeria's surplus agricultural produce (like grains and fruits) that would normally rot away or become spoilt during the harvest seasons. Such granarries and other storehouses would help make these produce available all the year round, as is the case in developed countries.

To make investment in industries further succeed, the industrialists, especially the rural ones, need a certain conducive economic, social and political atmosphere in order to function better. (See below: 4.1.3.1.1.1. 3) and 4.1.3.2.1..)

3) **Policies promoting economic investment**

To encourage economic growth - to achieve orderly progress in various sectors of economic life - especially in areas of investment and production (particularly in agriculture and industry), Nigerian government should devise appropriate economic policies regarding taxation, credit schemes, price protection, insurance schemes, essential services, and requisite business ethics and skills.

Taxation. Nigeria's rule of tax assessment is according to the ability to pay - "pay as you earn" (PAYE). By all standards, this is good and just. However, this system has a problem. It is very difficult to assess people who have no regular income and whose income is not a matter of public knowledge. For instance, the rural dwellers, mainly farmers, have no regular income and the much that accrues to them is not public. Therefore, "in determining taxes for rural dwellers, the general welfare requires public authorities to bear in mind that income in a rural economy is both delayed and subject to greater risk. Moreover, there is difficulty in finding capital so as to increase returns."[116]

To encourage investment, the government should grant tax-exemptions to those willing to invest their money in the development of the economy, and that is, for the period of establishing their enterprises. This implies that once their enterprises start production, so as to have income and make gains, these investors would no longer be exempt from tax. In the same vein, any material they import for the same enterprise should be duty-free. Moreover, "taxes that impose a handicap on the production and flow of products to consumers should be eliminated or reduced. Similarly, any government processing of essential permits, such as those for building facilities, storing supplies and processing or manufacturing products whether for health, safety or environmental reasons, should be sped up so that enterprising individuals will not be hampered by delays. The objective should be to make sure that the energy, inventiveness and management skills of people driven by profit motive are not hampered by government rules and processes."[117]

On the contrary, to discourage ostentatious and luxurious living and thereby further to encourage local investment, heavy tariffs or custom duties should be imposed on the importation of luxurious goods into the country.

Credit schemes. Investment requires much capital. Normally investors go to the banks to obtain loan (capital) at a certain interest for their business. But it is a common knowledge that bank loans are not easily available to most small businesspersons. Though they very much need credit to initiate their businesses and/or to keep them going, these small businesspersons lack the "collateral security" necessary for obtaining bank loans; and consequently, most banks are unwilling to take the risks of granting them loans. Therefore, there is much need for the government to establish supervised credit schemes for small businesses such as farming, processing, manufacturing, transportation, distribution and marketing. According to W. E. Boek,

> Since regulatory requirements generally do not permit banks to make high risks loans by themselves, governments need to establish programmes that insure loans to citizens who want to start or expand their own small businesses. To provide these loans, an insurance system may be established by the government that is financed by a small charge on every loan, such as one percent. The government should establish a reserve of funds to reimburse banks in the event that a businessperson is unable to pay back the loan to the bank. Along with credit, governments in the newer democracies should provide business management training for small businesspersons in order to increase their rate of success....
> Such a programme for small farmers was started during the depression of the 1930s in the United States.... The key to the success of this government program was supervision provided by experienced farmers. These supervisors would visit the farm before the loan was made and then frequently during the year to ensure that the plan was being carried out. Adjustments were made whenever the farmer faced unusual problems such as illness or weather damage to crops or buildings. The cost of supervision came from the interest paid by farmers on their loans.[118]

The emphasis is on *supervision*. Private banks will supply the credit, while people with practical experience who know the local situation will do the supervision.

Apart from the above system whereby the credit is supplied by private banks, the government can also establish banks that solely provide capital to small businesspersons. As Pope John XXIII puts it, "those with money to invest are more inclined to invest it in enterprises other than in the rural economy. And for the same reason, rural dwellers cannot pay high rates of interest. Nor are they generally able to pay prevailing market rates for capital wherewith to carry on and expand their operations. Wherefore, the general welfare requires that public authorities not merely make special provision for agricultural financing, but also for establishment of banks that provide capital to farmers at reasonable rates of interest."[119]

Meanwhile such banks established in Nigeria for rural investment and development have not met the goal for their establishment. Regretably these banks prefer to give out the loans meant for rural farmers/investors to business tycoons (who must have "greesed the bank-managers' hands with some bundles of Naira"), thereby depriving the right people of enough capital needed to develop the rural business. Therefore, it is not enough to establish such banks, the government must ensure that these banks play the game according to rules.

Price protection. Goods produced in rural areas can hardly compete favourably in the open market with goods from big factories or companies. For one thing, agricultural goods are seasonal. During the on-season the goods are so much that their prices fall; and during the off-season the goods are scarce that their prices go up. To protect the farmers (and even the society) from these fluctuation in the prices of agricultural goods, the government should introduce "price protection" to stabilise the prices of these goods. Pope John XXIII writes:

> Since agricultural products have special characteristics, it is fitting that their price be protected by methods worked out by economic experts. In this matter, although it is quite helpful that those whose interests are involved take steps to safeguard themselves, setting up, as it were, appropriate goals, public authorities cannot stand entirely aloof from the stabilization procedure.[120]
> Inasmuch as agricultural products are destined especially to satisfy the basic needs of men, it is necessary that their price be such that all can afford to buy them. Nevertheless, there is manifest injustice in placing a whole group of citizens, namely, the farmers, in an inferior economic and social status, with less purchasing power than required by a decent livelihood. This, indeed, is clearly contrary to the common good of the country.[121]

Insurance schemes. Every investor needs some security. This requires the "provision for a twofold insurance, one covering agricultural output, the other covering farmers and their families. Because, as experience shows, the income of individual farmers is, on the average, less than that of workers in industry and the services, it does not seem to be fully in accord with the norms of social justice and equity to provide farmers with insurance or social security benefits that are inferior to those of other classes of citizens. For those insurance plans or provisions that are established generally should not differ markedly one from another, whatever be the economic sector wherein the citizens work or from which they derive their income."[122] (For more on social welfare programmes, see 4.1.3.2.2., below.)

Provision of essential services: Government economic policies should include the provision of essential public services in the rural areas. According to Pope John XXIII: "In rural areas it is fitting that industries be fostered and common services be developed that are useful in preserving, processing, and finally, in transporting farm products."[123] Surely these essential services do promote agricultural and industrial development in rural areas. For instance, "there is a direct causative relationship between the success of the economic system and the ability of people to transport products, machinery and equipment to where they are needed and to communicate rapidly over long distances."[124] (For more on the provision of essential services, see below, 4.1.3.2.1.)

Business trust: Every business transaction has got its ethics. Every business transaction involves a relationship (of two or more persons) based on mutual trust: openness, sincerity, honesty and truth. For example, when A and B are involved in a business transaction - A and B could be individuals or corporate bodies - they trust that each would uphold fairness and justice in their business dealings. And any serious breach of this trust strains the relationship and eventually breaks up the business. Nigerian businesspersons must therefore cultivate and maintain the business ethics in their relationship with one another and with their customers (local and foreign).

The tendency in Nigeria for the sellers to cheat the buyers - by exploiting the their ignorance of the prevailing market prices (because the prices of goods are not fixed in the Nigerian markets except in departmental stores) and selling goods to them at higher prices; by selling inferior and/or adulterated goods to them as superior and/or genuine goods; by manipulating the measuring instruments, thereby making the buyers to go home with less stuff than they had paid for - must stop. This must stop if we are to have a free enterprise that promotes a lasting democracy. Free enterprise in a democracy demands a good, friendly and mutual relationship between buyers and sellers. Buyers and sellers are supposed to treat each other as friends and not as enemies that must be exploited and cheated. On the one hand, Nigerian businesspersons must therefore discard the haggling method and have the same price for each purchaser. They should see the buyers as customers and friends who deserve the best treatment and who should be told the truth about the quality and quantity of what they are buying. In this way, the sellers have a better chance of retaining their customers and of winning new ones. On the other hand, the buyers should also see the sellers as their friends who should not be assaulted and whose property should not be stolen or destroyed. Customers who think the prices are too high in one place should take their business somewhere else, without bitterness or rancour.

The government must do all in its power to eradicate cheating in its bigger dimension - a type of "scientific" duping: money swindling - known as "419" (named after the decree 419 promulgated to fight and eradicate the "disease"), which today pervades the whole of Nigerian society and even goes beyond its borders. It is "scientific" in that the "419ers" do a lot of "research and experiment" - they do a lot of paper works and contacts (by phone, fax and letter-writing); they dig information from computers and internets, and intercept people's mails and phone-calls; they steal official and/or classified documents and files, etc. - in order to know who is who, who has what, who is doing what, who is likely to fall for their "offer", what risks are involved, what gain is to be made, how to avoid the watching eyes of the law and how to escape from its punitive hands, and so on. These "419ers" always pose as genuine and honest businesspersons, leaving no doubts in the minds of their victims (most often foreigners or Nigerians living abroad) as to the genuineness of their business dealings with them. They present their victims with attractive business offers (meant to bring quick returns and profits to the latter). But no sooner had their victims fulfilled their parts of the contract, than the "419ers" disappeared (with the money) into thin air; and their victims would never be able to trace them because all the information they have about the "419ers" are false. Consequently, the "419ers" do much damage to the business relationship between Nigerian businesspersons and their foreign counterparts, thereby hindering foreign investments in Nigeria.

Nigerian businesspersons also have the tendency to create artificial scarcity (through hoarding of goods) in order to make higher profits. It has become a normalcy in Nigeria for prices of things (like petrol, cooking gas) to go up during festivals, like Christmas, because the dealers on these goods hoard them and sell them piecemeal at exorbitant prices to customers. The customers buy them at whatever prices the dealers set for them because they cannot do without these goods. (For example, vehicle owners need fuel to drive them. Therefore, they pay any price to buy some litres of fuel that would keep their vehicles on the road.) The high cost of petrol, for instance, results in high cost of transportation and consequently in high cost of goods, thereby making life miserable for the people. To have a lasting democracy based on free enterprise in Nigeria, hoarding - especially of essential goods - must be made illegal and thus criminal. Nigerian businesspersons should, instead of creating artificial scarcity, work very hard to have more goods in the market to meet the people's demands during festivals. By selling more goods (at the right prices) they are bound to make more gains. This is the case in developed countries. In Germany, for example, more goods are produced during festivals to meet up with the many demands, so that prices do not rise but remain more or less the same.

4.1.3.1.1.2. Employment and Just Wages.

Investments should be capital intensive: geared towards production, which creates opportunities for jobs, and, consequently, makes it possible for workers to receive wages without which their life would be miserable. Fundamental human rights underline the right to gainful employment: opportunity to work, good working conditions, and just wages. Pope John XXIII writes on the economic rights of man thus:

> it is clear that man has a right by natural law not only to an opportunity to work, but also to go about his work without coercion.
> To these rights is certainly joined the right to demand working conditions in which physical health is not endangered, morals are safeguarded, and young people's normal development is not impaired. Women have the right to working conditions in accordance with their requirements and their duties as wives and mothers.
> From the dignity of the human person, there also arises the right to carry on economic activities according to the degree of responsibility of which one is capable. Furthermore ... the worker has a right to a wage determined according to criterions of justice, and sufficient, therefore, in proportion to available resources, to give the worker and his family a standard of living in keeping with the dignity of the human person.[125]

1) **Employment opportunities**[126]

Unemployment is growing at an alarming rate today in Nigeria. There are very little job opportunities for the millions of job-seekers. Therefore, the Nigerian government must create and secure job opportunities for its citizens. It should also encourage more investments in the country, and through subsidies encourage individuals and corporations to establish more rural enterprises and industries - in order create more jobs. Moreover, the Nigerian government should provide unemployment benefits which are indispensable for the subsistence of unemployed workers and their families. This is "a duty springing from the fundamental principle of moral order in this sphere, namely the principle of the common use of goods or, to put it in another and still simpler way, the right to life and subsistence."[127]

2) **Just Wages**

The biblical saying, "the labourer deserves his wage,"[128] still holds much water today. According to Pope John Paul II,

> Whether the work is done in a system of private ownership of the means of production or in a system where ownership has undergone a certain 'socialization', the relationship between the employer ... and the worker is resolved on the basis of the wage, that is, through just remuneration of the work done.... In every system, regardless of the fundamental relationships within it between capital and labour, wages, that is to say remuneration for work, are still a practice means whereby the vast majority of people can have access to those goods which are intended for common use: both the goods of nature and manufactured goods. Both kinds of goods become accessible to the worker through the wage which he receives as remuneration for his work. Hence in every case a just wage is the concrete means of verifying the justice of the whole socioeconomic system and, in any case, of checking that it is functioning justly. It is not the only means of checking, but it is a particularly important one and in a sense the key one.
>
> This means of checking concerns above all the family. Just remuneration for the work of an adult who is responsible for a family means remuneration which will suffice for establishing and properly maintaining a family and for providing security for the future. Such remuneration can be given either what is called a family wage - that is, a single salary given to the head of the family for his work, sufficient for the needs of the family without the spouse having to take up gainful employment outside the home - or through other social measures such as family allowances or grants to mothers devoting themselves exclusively to their families. These grants should correspond to the actual needs, that is, to the number of dependents for as long as they are not in a position to assume proper responsibility for their own lives.[129]

Going by this standard, Nigeria's socio-economic system is everything but just. There is much exploitation of workers in Nigeria. In a government sponsored study of labour and productivity in the mid-1970s, "the result obtained did show that labour was under-compensated relative to its productivity in seven out of ten selected industries.... The evidence was that in most industries, wage rates did not advance as fast as productivity and cost of living increases. In fact in some industries the average wage rate was below the subsistence wage."[130] Moreover, Nigeria has no such social measures as family allowances or grants to mothers devoting themselves exclusively to their families.

Nigeria therefore needs a reform as to the "minimum wage" any worker (whether in private or public sector) should be paid. According to Pope Pius XI: "the wage paid to the workingman should be sufficient for the support of himself and of his family.... Every effort must therefore be made that fathers of families receive a sufficient wage adequate to meet ordinary domestic needs. If in the present state of society this is not always feasible, social justice demands that reforms be introduced without delay which will guarantee every adult workingman just such a wage."[131] This reform is very necessary because Nigeria's salary structure, based on the current minimum wage and considering the present harsh economic situation, is not realistic. Such a reform should leave the salary structure flexible: always in line with the current economic realities, and always making sure that a worker's wage is such as would be enough to support him/her and his/her family "in reasonable and frugal comfort." In making such a reform, while allowing free agreements between workers and employers (in private sectors) to determine wages, the government should fix the minimum wage for all, so that, as a matter of law, no employer (not even the churches that are known for underpaying their workers) would pay any worker anything less than the minimum wage. This agrees with Pope Leo XIII's writing, thus:

> Let it be granted, then, that, as a rule, workman and employer should make free agreements, and in particular should freely agree as to wages; nevertheless, there is a dictate of nature more impetuous and more ancient than any bargain between man and man, that the remuneration must be enough to support the wage earner in reasonable and frugal comfort. If through necessity or fear of worse evil, the workman accepts harder conditions because an employer or contractor will give him no better, he is the victim of force and injustice.[132]

4.1.3.1.1.3. Maintenance Culture

Nigerians like and always go for "the new" and "the modern". This in its face value is not bad; if anything, it is good to be up-to-date with the trends of events, especially with scientific and technological developments. But then Nigeria lacks the maintenance culture: it does not maintain its structures and equipment. This accounts for the many dilapidated structures (like buildings, furniture, bridges, and roads) found everywhere today in Nigeria. It accounts for the many abandoned government vehicles that are rusting away under the vagaries of weather. When a vehicle breaks down, it is abandoned instead of its being repaired and a new one bought. It accounts also for the constant abandonment of government projects. When a part of the machinery for a project breaks down, it is never repaired; and if a new machine is difficult to procure (to replace the spoilt one), the project is abandoned. Many a time such abandoned vehicles and projects, apart from losing value due to depreciation, are plundered by some "unknown" vandals. The same applies to the roads which are left unmaintained until they totally break up and become impassable and death-traps and eventually closed to the public.

Nigeria needs and must develop a maintenance culture. Things should not be abandoned but repaired as soon as they spoil or break down. The saying, "a stitch in time saves nine" should be taken to heart by all Nigerians. This practice will definitely save much money for the country. To help make this practice more effective, a department or ministry should be established at all government levels to take charge of repairs and maintenance of public properties (like roads, buildings, etc.). Moreover, people should be specially trained to man and maintain any new and/or complex equipment.

One could add to maintenance culture the **recycling** industries. Here and there are littered with papers, bodies and parts of bodies of vehicles, old wheels and tyres, cans and bottles, and so on. At best these materials are gathered up and burnt or are dumped in a marked out areas. These methods of disposal do not help environmental cleanliness, neither do they save money for nor yield income to the state. Nigeria should build recycling industries to take care of all recyclable materials. Such industries would help minimise environmental pollution, save money for and yield income to the state, and help to reduce unemployment.

4.1.3.2. Social development

The provision of essential public services and social welfare programmes will be the centre of this discussion on social development. Man has right to life and a worthy standard of living. A worthy standard of living is measured by the provision of essential public services (like food, good water supply, housing, medical services, highway construction, transport services, communications, marketing facilities, education, things requisite for religion and for recreation) and of social welfare programmes (like insurance systems, whereby in case of misfortune or increased family responsibilities, no person will be without the necessary means to maintain a decent standard of living).[133]

Nigeria is lagging very much behind in the provision of essential services and in social welfare programmes. (See part 2, 3.3.2.2., above). Although Nigeria provides its citizens - mainly those living in the cities and urban areas - with some measure of the essential services, it is failing totally in the provision of social welfare programmes. Nigerians do not have the security in cases of sickness, inability to work, widowhood, old age, unemployment, or in any other case in which they are deprived of the means of subsistence through no fault of their own. It is therefore of paramount importance that the standard of living of Nigerians be raised and improved upon through the provision of essential services and social welfare programmes.

Before considering in detail the provision of essential services and social welfare programmes, it is important to note that these essential provisions are no luxuries but basic necessities of life. They are not meant for the rich and the powerful alone, nor are they meant for only those living in the cities and urban areas. They are needed by all - rich or poor, ruler or ruled, in the city or in the village - for a worthy standard of life. There is no doubting the fact that the provision of these essentials of life in rural areas will, among other things, drastically reduce, if not stop, the mass exodus of the rural population to urban areas, something that has become a daily occurrence in Nigeria.[134]

4.1.3.2.1. Essential public services

On the area of essential services, the already existing ones should be improved upon and new ones provided. Such public services that must be provided include roads, public transportation, good water, electricity, hospitals and health centres, schools, shelter, communication systems, recreational facilities and means of practising one's religion.

Roads. Good and durable tarred roads should be constructed to link up the rural areas with one another, the cities with one another, and the rural areas with the cities. Without good network of roads transportation is made difficult. According to Mr Boek: "These needs were recognized in countries like the United States where 'farm to market' all weather roads were constructed with federal and state funds allocated to local governments. These roads were built from the villages to the farms, most with a gravel or crushed stone foundation topped by an asphalt mixture."[135] Nigeria should construct these types of roads in the rural areas. Moreover, these roads should have good drainage system. It makes no sense to build roads without gutters for example. And every effort should be made to check the menace of erosion on our roads.

It is not enough to build roads. People's safety on such roads must be guaranteed by the provision of all relevant roads signs and information, speed limits, traffic lights, well marked out sidewalks and bicyclist zones (where possible). Everybody's right to use the roads must also be guaranteed and respected. The bicyclists, for example, have the right to share the road, travelling in the same direction as vehicles (where there are no special bicyclists' zone), and drivers of vehicles must yield the right-of-way to a bicyclist just as they would to another vehicle. All drivers, regardless of the rules of the road or right-of-way, must exercise great care to avoid striking pedestrians; and they should remember that pedestrians legally crossing at intersections *always* have the right-of-way. The handicapped, for example blind pedestrians, crossing the road must *always* be given the right-of-way, even if the traffic signals or other right-of-way rules are not in their favour. To implement the road-safety

Public transportation. Variety of means of transportation - buses, taxis, trams, trains, etc. - should be provided in the cities as well as in the rural areas: to link the rural areas with each other, the cities with each other, and the rural areas with the cities. This should be the affair of the government as well as private individuals and organisations. With the availability of such variety and well organised public transportation system, people would have the choice as to which means to take, and they would travel at regular intervals with maximum ease and comfort. The heavy traffic jams in the cities would vanish. The trauma of travelling long distances on foot by the rural populace would be a thing of the past. And there is no over-stressing the fact that well organised transportation system does help in boosting the economy and social life of the people.

Good water supply. Water - good water - is a basic necessity of life. Therefore, Nigerians should have constant supply of good water - in their homes and in public places. It is the primary duty of the government to make sure that its citizens, no matter where they are located, are provided with the necessities of life, including potable water. The government's bore-hole projects in the rural areas are commendable. But it is not just enough to sink the bore-holes, without connecting them to the people. The government must also make sure that water from these bore-holes is constantly available to the people, even to their very doors. The availability of potable water to the people would, among other things, reduce the sufferings of those people who have no rivers and/or springs and who must thus go long distances in search of drinking water, and also help to eradicate waterborne diseases which people get from the use of bad water.

Electricity. Every home should be able to enjoy constant supply of electricity. It is no luxury but a necessity of life. According to Dr Nwafor Orizu, "Africa has great rivers to be harnessed in order that electricity may be utilized in domestic life and the burdens of the African housewife lightened. There is a need for electric lights to take the place of candles and oil lamps in poor African homes. Women and house boys in the kitchen in poor homes should be able to heat their kettles, oven, and grill by the turn of a switch. Tropical cotton wear will iron more quickly with electricity. Hand-brooms must give place to vacuum cleaners so that the knees of the housewife can be saved. Without electricity the industrial society ... would not come into being. Without electricity radio cannot be a success, and all other avenues to free movement and communication would be closed. Political democracy in Africa must, therefore, plan for the electrification of life if true progress is to be possible."[136] To help make this possible, the rural electrification programme, which is already on in the country, should be intensified, so that electricity would reach every nook and corner of Nigeria. Moreover, NEPA (the body in-charge with electric power in the country) should be re-organized and sanitsed to make it more efficient and less corrupt, so that electric power would be available to the people all the time. Obviously, this would help to boost industrialisation and rural development, and thus economic growth.

Hospitals and **health-centres**. The government, private organisations and individuals should embark on the building of more hospitals and health-centres in rural and urban areas, with adequate facilities and drugs and many qualified personnel, to take care of the people's health problems. And these should be within the reach of the common man.

Schools. Primary, secondary and tertiary institutions, with enough qualified teachers and adequate facilities, should be within the reach of every citizen. And the government should make sure that the teachers are well paid and that they receive their salaries and allowances as when due, to enable them pay full attention to their teaching work.

Shelter. This is a necessity of life. Everybody needs adequate and comfortable shelter. Therefore, housing development should be intensified - especially in the cities where it is very difficult for low-income people to get an apartment and where the landlords demand "a pound of flesh"[137] from people for the few available ones. This will also enable those Nigerians who are not able to build their own houses to rent or buy a flat or an apartment or a house to shelter themselves and their families. Apart from the government's low income housing development, individuals should be granted loans to build or buy their own houses. The government should encourage private organisations and individuals (who can afford it) to embark on low-income housing constructions. The building of *condo-minium* - a building containing flats which are individually owned - should be encouraged. It is important that such houses meet certain approved standards, with all the basic facilities like bathroom, toilet, kitchen, fire-safety equipment and exit, and so on. Moreover, the government should set a limit to the various rents (in line with prevailing economic realities) beyond which the landlords must not go. This will help to stop the current incessant exploitation of tenants by landlords.

Communication systems. Post offices, postal agencies, telephones, faxes, newspapers, radios, televisions, and so on, should be available to the people for easy and constant communication within and without the country. These communication systems should be well organised and well managed as to make them very functional, efficient and cheaper. To make this a reality, NITEL (the sole body in-charge of telecommunications in Nigeria) should be privatised and competition allowed in the telecommunication market.

To essential public services should be added **recreational facilities** and **the means of practicing one's religion**. Recreational facilities should be provided and people encouraged to utilise them. The saying, "a healthy mind in a sound body," should be taken to heart. With regard to the means of practicing one's religion, the government should see to it that the freedom of religion is respected and protected without its inclining to any one religion.

4.1.3.2.2. Social welfare programmes

Concerning social welfare programmes, Nigeria has not yet started. But now is the time to begin if Nigeria is to have a stable and lasting democracy. Apart from providing the essential services as discussed above, Nigeria must also strive to achieve social security for its citizens. Therefore, the government must make **insurance systems** "available to the citizens, so that, in case of misfortune or increased family responsibilities, no person will be without the necessary means to maintain a decent standard of living."[138] This is the only way the nation can secure the welfare of any of its citizens in case of sickness, inability to work, widowhood, old age, unemployment, or in any other case in which one is deprived of the means of subsistence through no fault of his/her own. In providing its citizens with social securities, Nigeria must avoid the system in the USA whereby healthy and able-bodied persons live on "social welfare". Such people should rather be offered employment to enable them cater for themselves and their dependents or they could be provided welfare assistance in exchange for work.

Nigeria also needs to introduce some social measures in the form of allowances or grants to mothers devoting themselves exclusively to their families and for the unemployed or jobless in order to alleviate the sufferings of the many housewives and of the jobless in our society. First, with regard to mothers, the government should realise and acknowledge that the task of rearing children is an enormous one and very vital to the society, with the result that mothers who devote themselves exclusively to this task deserve to receive assistance from the government. In the words of Pope John Paul II:

> Experience confirms that there must be a social re-evaluation of the mother's role, of the toil connected with it and of the need that children have for care, love and affection in order that they may develop into responsible, morally and religiously mature and psychologically stable persons. It will redound to the credit of society to make it possible for a mother - to devote herself to taking care of her children and educating them in accordance with their needs, which vary with age. Having to abandon these tasks in order to take up paid work outside the home is wrong from the point of view of the good of society and of the family when it contradicts or hinders these primary goals of the mission of a mother.[139]

The system in Nigeria whereby a working mother "abandons" her baby three months after birth to resume her work is not to the best interest either of the new baby or of the mother or of the society. The government should therefore make adequate provisions for the care of mothers.

Second, with regard to the jobless - those who could not find job (after graduation from school or training) and those who lost their job due to no fault of their own - Nigeria should introduce a system whereby they would receive some help. The jobless should be required to register with the ministry of works and employment whose duty it would be to secure jobs for them and to grant them "unemployment benefits" for the duration of their joblessness. When this ministry finds a job for someone and one refuses the job for no genuine reason, then one automatically loses one's entitlement to unemployment benefits.

4.1.3.2.3. Disabled persons and work

The case of the disabled in Nigeria is a special one, a pitiable one. This accounts for why I am devoting a special heading to it. The disabled persons are very much neglected in Nigeria. For example, majority of the lame crawl on the ground (muddy or dusty) to get to their destinations and majority of the blind are left best as beggers. In short, to be handicapped in Nigeria is to be a "perpetual nobody". This is unlike in the developed countries where the law is on the side of the handicapped: they have special provisions which enable them to enjoy all the rights and privileges due to a citizen, and to be, more or less, self-reliant. Therefore, Nigeria should borrow a leaf from the developed countries, especially from the USA and Germany, with regard to the appropriate care of its disabled citizens. It should also always keep in mind the golden words of Pope John Paul II about disabled persons:

> They too are fully human subjects with corresponding innate, sacred, and inviolable rights, and, in spite of the limitations and sufferings affecting their bodies and faculties, they point up more clearly the dignity and greatness of man. Since disabled people are subjects with all their rights, they should be helped to participate in the life of society in all its aspects and at all levels accessible to their capacities. The disabled person is one of us and participates fully in the same humanity that we possess. It would be radically unworthy of man, and a denial of our common humanity, to admit to the life of the community, and thus admit to work, only those who are fully functional. To do so would be to practise a serious form of discrimination, that of the strong and healthy against the weak and sick. Work in the objective sense should be subordinated, in this circumstance too, to the dignity of man, to the subject of work and not to economic advantage.
> The various bodies ... should therefore foster the right of disabled people to professional training and work, so that they can be given a productive activity suited to them. Many practical problems arise at this point, as well as legal and economic ones; but the community, that is to say, the public authorities, associations and intermediate groups, business enterprises, and the disabled themselves should pull their ideas and resources so as to attain this goal that must not be shirked: that disabled people may be offered work according to their capabilities, for this is demanded by their dignity as persons and as subjects of work. Each community will be able to set up suitable structures for finding and creating jobs for such people both in the usual public or private enterprises, by offering them ordinary or suitably adapted jobs, and in what are called 'protected' enterprises and surroundings.
> Careful attention must be devoted to the physical and psychological working conditions of disabled people - as for all workers - to their just remuneration, to the possibility of their promotion, and to the elimination of various obstacles. Without hiding the fact this is a complex and difficult task, it is to be hoped that a correct concept of labour in the subjective sense will produce a situation which will make it possible for disabled people to feel that they are not cut off from the working

world or dependent upon society, but that they are full-scale subjects of work, useful, respected for their human dignity and called to contribute to the progress and welfare of their families and of the community according to their particular capacities.[140]

4.1.4. Cultural-Moral Development

Human development is not merely a political or an economic matter, but also, and essentially, a moral one. According to Pope John Paul II, to limit development to its economic aspect leads to the subordination of the human person to "the demands of economic planning and selfish profit."[141] Such development then must be brought about within the framework of *solidarity* and *freedom*, because there is a paramount need for any project of human development to be built around respect: respect for the individual person and respect for the cultural identity of whole communities. Thus the cultural-moral values could be regarded as the *vitamins* of all human and social developments, which, if cultivated would usher Nigeria onto a platform of a democratically developed country, and if omitted, then all our efforts at becoming a democratically developed country would be in shambles. Therefore, it is the aim of this section to call the attention of all Nigerians to the importance of the common good and its allies, solidarity and subsidiarity, in the democratic development of Nigeria.

4.1.4.1. Common Good: Basis for social justice and national unity[142]

It is not easy to define the term "common good". It could be described as a *string* which holds all the members of a community together, as one entity, and without which the community falls apart. Because the members of the community are bound together by this *string*, no member could remove himself or herself or could be removed from "the bundle" without loosening or damaging the *string* - an act which is detrimental to the community. This implies that every member of the community (no matter his/her tribe, tongue, religion, gender, or status) is important and has rights (to draw life from the community) and duties (to respect the being of each member of the community and to preserve the entity of the community). From this analogy three conclusions could be made about the common good. One, the common good "embraces the sum total of those conditions of social living whereby men are enabled more fully and more readily, to achieve their own perfection."[143] Two, it "is chiefly guaranteed when personal rights and duties are maintained. The chief concern of civil authorities must therefore be to insure that these rights are acknowledged, respected, co-ordinated with other rights, defended and promoted, so that in this way each one may more easily carry out his duties."[144] And three, it is the affair of every member of the community to promote and work for the common good. According to Pope John XXIII,

"Individual citizens and intermediate groups are obliged to make their specific contributions to the common welfare. One of the chief consequences of this is that they must bring their own interests into harmony with the needs of the community, and must contribute their goods and their services as civic authorities have prescribed, in accord with the norms of justice and within the limits of their competence."[145]

The common good has its essentials. These are well brought out by Pope John XXIII in his *Pacem in Terris*:

> Assuredly, the ethnic characteristics of the various human groups are to be respected as constituent elements of the common good, but these values and characteristics by no means exhaust the content of the common good. For the common good since it is intimately bound up with human nature cannot therefore exist fully and completely unless the human person is taken into consideration and the essential nature and realization of the common good be kept in mind.
>
> In the second place, the very nature of the common good requires that all members of the state be entitled to share in it, although in different ways according to each one's tasks, merits and circumstances. For this reason, every civil authority must take pains to promote the common good of all, without preference for any single citizen or civic group.... Considerations of justice and equity, however, can at times demand that those involved in civil government give more attention to the less fortunate members of the community, since they are less able to defend their rights and to assert their legitimate claims.
>
> In this context, we judge that attention should be called to the fact that the common good touches the whole man, the needs both of his body and of his soul. Hence it follows that the civil authorities must undertake to effect the common goods by ways and means that are proper to them; that is, while respecting the hierarchy of values, they should promote simultaneously both the material and the spiritual welfare of the citizens.[146]

Then the essence of the common good is to cater for, protect and promote the well-being, dignity, and development of each human person, especially the weaker members of the community, and thus to build a humane society not only for the present but also for the future generation. Again we read from Pope John XXIII:

> Considering the common good at the national level, the following points are relevant and should not be overlooked: to provide employment for as many workers as possible; to take care lest privileged groups arise even among the workers themselves; to maintain a balance between wages and prices; to make accessible the goods and services for a better life for as many persons as possible; either to eliminate or to keep within bounds the inequalities that exist between different sectors of the economy - that is, between agriculture, industry and services; to balance properly any increases in output with advances in services provided to citizens, especially by public authority; to adjust, as far as possible, the means of production to the progress of science and technology; finally, to ensure the advantages of a more humane way of existence not merely subserve the present generation but have regard for future generations as well.[147]

Apart from every member of the community contributing to the upkeep of the common good, it is the primary duty of the public authorities to safeguard the common good through appropriate laws that are in themselves not in any way harmful to the ideals of the common good. In the words of Pope John XXIII: "since the whole reason for the existence of civil authorities is the realization of the common good, it is clearly necessary that, in pursuing this objective, they should respect its essential elements, and at the same time conform their laws to the circumstances of the day."[148]

The problem of national unity in Nigeria (see part 2, 2.1. above) is due to the lack of the spirit of the common good among Nigerians. People are so individualistic that they do not care about the rights of others nor about the welfare of the society at large. Therefore, to overcome our differences and then build a united Nigeria, all Nigerians must be educated on the principles of the common good; they must allow these principles to be part of their lives; and they must come together, talk together and work together.

4.1.4.2. Solidarity[149]

Solidarity is a *virtue*, an enabling power that provides the capacity to respect one another as persons. In his encyclical, "On Social Concern" (1987), Pope John Paul II writes:

> The exercise of solidarity *within each society* is valid when its members recognise one another as persons. Those who are more influential, because they have a greater share of goods and common services, should feel *responsible* for the weaker and be ready to share with them all they possess. Those who are weaker, for their part, in the same spirit of *solidarity*, should not adopt a purely *passive* attitude or one that is *destructive* of the social fabric, but, while claiming their legitimate rights, should do what they can for the good of all. The intermediate groups, in their turn, should not selfishly insist on their particular interests, but respect the interests of others.
>
> ....
>
> Solidarity helps us to see the 'other' - whether a person, people, or nation - not just as some kind of instrument with a work capacity and physical strength to be exploited at low cost and then discarded when no longer useful, but as our "neighbour," a "helper" (see Gen. 2: 18-20), to be made a sharer, on a par with ourselves, in the banquet of life to which all are equally invited by God.[150]

Solidarity, within a country, transforms the *interpersonal relationships* of individuals with the persons around them, thereby enabling them to overcome distrust and to collaborate with one another. Thus solidarity is the correct moral response to the fact of interdependence, because people live within a system that determines how they relate to one another in the economic, cultural, political, and religious spheres. It evokes in one "a firm and persevering determination to commit oneself to the common good" - an attitude of commitment to the good of one's neighbour, coupled with a readiness to sacrifice oneself in the service of the other.[151]

Nigeria needs the spirit of solidarity to be able to overcome its problem of disunity. Every sincere and well-informed Nigerian knows that the disunity among Nigerians, be it ethnic or religious, though very deep, is man-made. It is a product of bias and prejudice. Each ethnic group or religious body has a long nurtured prejudice - an opinion formed without taking the time or care to judge others fairly. The Hausas, the Yorubas and the Igbos, the moslems and the christians, the catholics and the protestants, all have wrong opinions about each other. In many cases this prejudice has given birth to unfair, abusive, or even violent treatment of one another. Therefore, to overcome the differences and make for one nation, ways must be found to eliminate the unnecessary ethnic and religious biases and prejudices. True and mutual knowledge of each other is necessary to avoid prejudices and unhealthy rivalries. To achieve this, "an interactional equilibrium between them has to be established that is satisfactory to both."[152] And in order to arrive at this "interaction equilibrium," which resolves or prevents the conflicts between the differing people or groups, Boek suggests that:

> 1) people will get along better if they get to know one another better; 2) children and adults should learn to be tolerant of one another; 3) people should improve their negotiating skills; 4) individuals must adjust their goals in respect for those of others; 5) people should be cognizant of results of their bitterness toward others and amend their ways to reduce conflict; and 6) those who tend to dominate while conversing or in their actions need to realize the negative affect it has on most people and stop doing it. These adjustments have and are being made by some people, and conflicts have been and are being reduced because of them.[153]

In this regard I consider the "Constitutional Conference" inaugurated in 1994 by President S. Abacha as a first and good step toward bridging the gap between the differing groups. For the first time in the history of Nigeria, people from the various cultural, ethnic and religious backgrounds came together to debate the future the country. Such dialogue should not end at the constitutional drafting project. Other ways must be found to continue this dialogue and interaction between the different cultures, languages and religions in Nigeria, at local and national levels.

One other way of enhancing the consciousness of the common good and of national unity in the country is to avoid discriminatory policies, policies founded on exclusion. For example, admission into schools and colleges, offer of employment, award of government contracts, and so on, should never be based on the "place of origin" but solely on merit and qualification. Why, for instance, should the government of "X" part of Nigeria have a policy of free education only for children of "X" parentage while they impose school fees on other children of non-"X" parentage, even when these other children are born in "X" part of Nigeria and their parents live and work in "X" part of Nigeria and pay their taxes to the government of "X" part of Nigeria? This makes nonsense of the Nigerian citizenship. No, a child of "Y" parentage, born in "X" part of Nigeria, should have the same rights - the right to free education inclusive - as the children of "X" parentage. In the same line, every Nigerian should be able to get employment in any part of the country; every Nigerian should be granted contract appointment in any part of the country; every Nigerian should be able to buy land in any part of Nigeria; every Nigerian should be able to exercise his/her political rights in any part of the nation. Therefore, there should be "mutual acceptance of one another's full citizenship of Nigeria and the paramountcy of the status of Nigerian citizen,"[154] so that nobody would feel like or be a stranger in his/her own country. E. Odumegwu-Ojukwu writes: "The Nigerian citizenship should suffer no diminution in any part of Nigeria. A citizen of Nigeria has the same right, political or otherwise, wherever he might find himself within the territorial confines of Nigeria. As citizens of Nigeria, we should be residents of any state of our choice."[155]

It must be pointed out, at this juncture, that the "coming together" of the various groups does not imply the obliteration of ethnic or cultural or religious or any other differences nor does it imply an imposition of one culture or religion on others. It implies rather "unity in diversity". This is so because solidarity means taking seriously the different value systems of the various cultures,[156] for the sake of the common good.[157] As Pope Pius XI puts it: "Order, as the Angelic Doctor well defines, is unity arising from the apt arrangement of a plurality of objects; hence, true and genuine social order demands various members of society, joined together by a common bond. Such a bond of union is provided on the one hand by the common effort to employers and employees of one and the same "group" joining forces to produce goods or give service; on the other hand, by the common good which all "groups" should unite to promote, each in its own sphere, with friendly harmony...."[158] Therefore, the new Nigerian nation to emerge is one, using the words of Sir Abubakar, "where now instead of cutting heads they are cracking tribal jokes," and where "there will be no question of Hausa, Ibo, and Yoruba. We will belong to our tribal groups but we will feel that Nigeria is more than anything to us.... We must feel always for our tribe but the unity of Nigeria must be paramount."[159]

Such coming together to foster national unity demands, in the words of Alhaji Shagari (Nigeria's president in the second republic), "a dedicated leadership and citizenry imbued with faith to cultivate a widespread national feeling for 'One Nigeria',"[160] who would always work to eliminate the things that divide us and encourage and promote the things that unite us. According to Pope Pius XI: "Now this is a major and pressing duty of the state and of all good citizens: to get rid of conflict between "classes" with divergent interests, and to foster and promote harmony between the various "ranks" or groupings of society."[161] And Dr Orizu agrees: "... people must not live just as mere individuals interested in 'I' and in nothing else.... The first duty of democracy, then, is to train men to know that they are men first - but that men, in their individual capacities, must embrace the total human family in their affection. There must be deep-seated belief in the *Unity* and *Interdependence* of that family - reflecting the Unity of God.... In short, African democracy demands a community of interdependent men and women, in which each person regards himself as a guarantor responsible for others within the community...."[162] Therefore, every hand must be on deck to make sure that the yawning gap between individuals, between one ethnic group and another and between one religious denomination and another is bridged. In every activity, each individual, each ethnic group and each religious denomination should always ask this one question: "If 'right' or 'good' means what is for me, how does that fit in with what is good for persons around me, whose needs often seem (at least at first sight) to be in competition with me?"[163]

4.1.4.3. The self and the common good[164]

This topic "the self and the common good" is here discussed against the back drop of bribery and corruption that infest the Nigerian society. This is so because behind every act of bribery and corruption is the manifestation of egoism and of lack of concern for the common good.

As noted above (part 2, 3.5.2.), corruption has become so widespread in Nigeria that many people have come to accept it as an unavoidable fact and way of life. Corruption hinders the advance of democracy and economic growth, and gives rise to the erosion of national consciousness and patriotism among Nigerians. This manifests itself in the prevailing notion of most Nigerians that the country exists to be exploited rather than developed. As corruption negates the principle of the common good, every effort must be made to eradicate it in the country, if Nigeria is to become democratically developed.

Combatting corruption, especially in a country like Nigeria is an uphill task. Peter Eigen writes:

> coping with corruption is usually not a simple matter enforcement, for the casualties of corruption often include the integrity system itself. A society may be plagued by corrupt judges, lawyers, and prosecutors; corrupt police officers and investigators; corrupt auditors; and, above all, corrupt political leaders who see the juridical system not as a check on their own power, but as a tool for perpetuating it. Even if a given country's judicial system is not corrupt, laws may be widely flouted with near impunity. Most countries have laws prohibiting bribery - with severe penalties prescribed for infractions by corrupt politicians and officials - and clear guidelines for how public servants should behave. Yet their effect is often minimal.[165]

Yet combatting corruption is a task that must be done. Some suggestions are already proffered on how to fight corruption. (See part 2, 4.1.2.3., above - under the integrity and accountability of leadership.) Here emphasis is laid on self discipline and reform in social habits and behaviours as a major step toward resolving the issue of bribery and corruption in Nigeria. Following the thoughts of P. Eigen, "in any attempt at reform, three truths must be kept in mind: First, the mere passage of legislation is unlikely to be effective unless it is accompanied by a raft of practical measures that maximize accountability and transparency, and minimize situations in which corruption is prone to occur. Second, the overall objective must be to change the general perception of corruption from a 'low-risk, high-profit' activity to a 'high-risk, low-profit' activity. Third, reform of anti-corruption measures - like reform in all other areas - should be undertaken in ways that conform to international human rights standards, particularly with regard to due process and fair trials."[166]

Nigeria is known to have introduced certain measures aimed at combatting corruption, call them anti-corruption drives, like "war against indiscipline" (WAI), "war against indiscipline and corruption" (WAIC), and so on. These measures have not worked because they lack an implementable legal framework and a range of other administrative measures that should support them, and because they are rarely directed to the personalities in government, especially those in the military, who are the perpetrators of the various acts of corruption. Nigeria therefore needs an effective reform in its anti-corruption measures. Such reform must be based on implementable legal framework aimed primarily at limiting the opportunity for corruption to occur, and, secondarily (but also very important), at prosecuting and punishing the culprits, no matter one's position in the society. According to Peter Eigen,

> effective reform, then, requires a legal framework that can and will be implemented, and a range of administrative measures in support of the overall process. Experience shows that corruption can be curbed by limiting the opportunity for it to occur, by bolstering outside monitoring by independent agents, and by reducing the benefits that corrupt behavior yields to both recipients and payers of bribes. The overall strategy, in other words, must be one of prevention, with prosecution and punishment eventually coming to play supporting rather than leading roles.[167]

Such an anti-corruption reform, Mr Eigen goes on, "must include the following: 1) a clear and demonstrable commitment on the part of political leaders to the eradication of corruption, from whatever source; 2) the adoption of comprehensive anticorruption legislation and its enforcement by a strong and independent agency of manifest integrity; 3) the identification of the areas of governmental activity most prone to corruption, and a review of relevant procedures; 4) a comprehensive review to ensure that salaries of civil servants and political leaders are commensurate with the responsibilities of their posts and are as comparable with salaries in the private sector; and 5) a review of legal procedures and remedies to ensure that they constitute an effective deterrent (for example, contracts induced by corruption should be rendered null and void)."[168]

This arduous all-side-war against corruption is the duty of every member of the civil society, not just that of the government. The general public should be educated on what constitutes corruption, and it should always report anybody involved in corrupt practices to the appropriate quarters. The press should be educating the public on the preventive measures against corruption as well as expose specific cases of corruption, no matter whose ox is gored. And then the government must make sure that everyone involved in corrupt practice(s) is prosecuted, and, if convicted, made to refund the ill-gotten wealth and then sent to jail.

4.1.4.4. Subsidiarity

Subsidiarity underlines three basic points: 1) the state should not usurp the economic, cultural and social duties which individuals and groups can resonably accomplish; 2) centralized authority should be avoided; and 3) the state should above all protect the fundamental rights and freedoms of the individuals and the families. The principle of subsidiarity, therefore, broadly speaking, is concerned with the limits of the right and duty of the public authority to intervene in social and economic life of the people. This implies that, for example, "in economic affairs first place is to be given to the private initiative of individual men who, either working by themselves, or with others in one fashion or another, pursue their common interests."[169] The public authorities should undertake only those tasks that cannot be done by individuals or private organisations (such as building of roads). This matter is well explained by Pope Pius XI thus:

> It is a fundamental principle of social philosophy, fixed and unchangeable, that one should not withdraw from individuals and commit to the community what they can accomplish by their own enterprise and industry. So, too, it is an injustice and at the same time a grave evil and a disturbance of right order to transfer to the larger and higher collectivity functions which can be performed and provided for by lesser and subordinate bodies. Inasmuch as every social activity should, by its very nature, prove a help to members of the body social, it should never destroy or absorb them.
>
> The State authorities should leave to other bodies the care and expediting of business and activities of lesser moment , which otherwise become for it a source of great distraction. It then will perform with greater freedom, vigour, and effectiveness, the tasks belonging properly to it, and which it alone can accomplish, directing, supervising, encouraging, restraining, as circumstances suggest or necessity demands.[170]

Public authorities, however, can intervene in the social and economic life of the people in order to promote and safeguard the common good. This implies that "whenever the general interest of any particular class suffers, or is threatened with, evils which can in no other way be met, the public authority must step in to meet them."[171] For example, a government should get itself involved in economic affairs in order "to increase output of goods and to further social progress for the benefit of all citizens."[172] However, its intervention "must be determined by the nature of the occasion which calls for the law's interference - the principle being this, that the law must not undertake more, nor go further, than is required for the remedy of the evil or the removal of the danger."[173]

The principle of subsidiarity, therefore, calls for less government and emphasizes self-help (individually and communally). Meanwhile many communities in Nigeria, especially among the Igbos, have embraced this principle of self-help. Every two or three or five years (as the case may be - depending on the people concerned), the various communities or towns have what is called a *mass return*, during which all their members (home and abroad) gather together to discuss about and raise fund for rural development. Through such self-help or self-development programmes, many communities or towns have embarked on such worthwhile ventures as rural electrification, rural water supply, building of roads, schools, hospitals, markets, churches, post offices, recreational facilities, and so on. However, many people in Northern Nigeria are yet to embrace this community-self-help principle. Therefore, instead of doing everything for them (at the negligence of other communities), the government should encourage and urge them to embark on self-help projects.

Nigerian government is often known to involve itself in those tasks which could better be left for individuals and private organisations. And the result has always been a sorry story: the businesspersons and private organisations always fare better than the government (which very often reckons with loss); and government-run services tend to be less responsive to actual needs of those people, businesses and other organizations for which they are provided. This is not healthy in a democracy. As E. Lindeman points out, "when in any society all primary functions are performed by the government and no room is left for private initiative and action democracy will already have ceased to exist. When all basic activities are controlled and regulated by governmental agencies it becomes impossible to retain those fundamental freedoms upon which the democratic ideal rests, and without freedom it is meaningless to speak as though democracy existed. This does not mean that there will not be a steady increase in governmental operations and controls, but it does mean that a democratic government will always stop short of complete control."[174] Therefore, a change is called for. And Nigeria should do well to follow the advice of Mr Boek:

> Almost all essential services such as communication systems whether they be telephone, radio, television or computerized information gathering, storage, retrieval and transmission must be privately owned and operated. The owners and operators should be citizens of the country they serve. Businesses supplying electricity to residences as well as natural gas, where it is available, also should be privately owned and operated. The government's role should be to determine the best way to enhance development of such services by private businesspeople through minimizing government restrictions and bureaucratic controls and stimulating private businesses with credit guarantees, temporary subsidies and tax limitations. The government should make providing utilities needed by all sections of the economy attractive to entrepreneurs.[175]

The government should even privatise its businesses which would constitute no harm to public welfare if undertaken by individuals.

However, the Nigerian government should intensify its duty to intervene whenever the need arises, as it very often does. In this regard, it should borrow a leaf from what the United States government did recently when the country witnessed a sudden rise in prices of petrol ("gas" in America) which brought much hardship to the people. The government set up a panel to find out the cause of the sudden rise in the prices of "gas" (whether it was caused by economic factors or by the greed of the "gas dealers"). In the main time, it released "gas" from the government reserves into the market to force the high prices down and thus to alleviate the people's suffering.

4.2. Democracy as a Way of Life

There is no genuine democracy which does not springs from the way of life of a people. Unless a given people can think, talk and act democratically, especially in the way they relate to one another, their democracy cannot be deep-rooted. And such shallow democracy can be easily wrecked by any socio-economic and religio-political storm. Therefore, to have a genuine, stable and lasting democracy in Nigeria, the way the people relate to one another in the family, in the community, at school, at the place of work and in the society at large ought to be democratic. It then follows that the family, the community, the school, the religious bodies, the state, the mass media, each has a special role to play towards the building of a stable and lasting democracy in Nigeria.

4.2.1. The role of the family: Democracy begins in the home[176]

The family has an important role, indeed a primary role, to play in the building and development of any country. Therefore, much time will be devoted here to the role of the family in the building of a stable and lasting democracy in Nigeria.

Democracy begins in the home.[177] Put in another way, "the family is the cradle of democratic living, that there appreciation of and loyalty to democratic ideals may be nurtured or destroyed. This belief implies not that individual families alone are responsible for the cultivation of democracy in society, but that families collectively in their reciprocal relationships are a most powerful force in moulding the concept of democracy by which individuals conduct their lives. "[178] It is in the home that the foundation for the child's future is laid. "Each and every one of us has been distinctly influenced by the relationships we experienced in our family. Those relationships, those experiences, to greater or lesser degree, continue to operate in our adult lives."[179] Fiction writers, sociologists, anthropologists, educational philosophers and many others attest this fact. For example, Jan Struther writes:

> Democracy begins at home; and it begins very early in the morning - not at breakfast, but when the first reluctant eye is opened by the first devilish trill of the alarm clock and when everybody thinks that everybody else takes much too long in the bath. The home, and not a college of political science, is the place to learn democracy - but it's no good for us grown-ups to try to teach it to our children unless we teach it to ourselves as well - and oh my! we've certainly got a lot to learn.... every family unit that manages to turn itself into a true democracy in miniature is a direct help toward the creation of that new world which is going to be, we most deeply hope, a democracy at large.[180]

From the viewpoint of sociology we have Una Bernard Sait and M. F. Nimkoff. According to Sait,

> Consideration for others and willingness to cooperate are fundamental social attitudes. They are best secured through an orderly home routine, designed in such a way that, as early as possible, the child begins to help himself and to engage in communal tasks, ...[181]
>
> If we would have peace and progress, we must develop social institutions which liberate capacity, promote good habits of thinking, and, above all, foster sentiments and attitudes necessary to effective cooperation. And of all social institutions, none possess a fraction of the potential power of the family.[182]

And Nimkoff points out that:

> Science has established two facts meaningful for human welfare: first, the foundation of the structure of human personality is laid down in early childhood; and second, the chief engineer in charge of this is the Family.[183]

On her part, Margaret Mead, a well known anthropologist, recognises the influence of the family in the building of the democratic culture. She writes: "Unless we democratize the family life it is idle to talk of democracy."[184] Then H. Gordon Hullfish, an educator, says that "the family is probably the first place in which to begin the growth of democratic understanding."[185] This agrees with the view that:

> Of all the institutions of society which exert an influence on individuals, determine the values they hold for their own lives, and set patterns of relationships in groups which influence all other group relationships, the family holds a place of unparalleled importance.
>
> In a democracy which is dependent upon the optimum development of each individual, it is vitally important therefore for the family to transmit democratic ideals and practices. A democratic experience in living in the family is a powerful influence in developing citizens who use democratic procedures.[186]

Therefore the family is very important in the cultivation of the democratic ideals and practices in its members that "if the home fails in its job, the schools have no machinery which can possibly be expected to undo the harm already done. In well-organized family the child learns by example and by daily practice that there is a balance between privileges and responsibilities in life."[187]

Nigerian parents therefore must take seriously the democratic education of their children. They must become conscious of what qualities and practices in the family living are democratic and foster and increase them. According to Mr Boek,

> It also is the responsibility of adults to claim their children for their democracy from the time they are born through childhood. To do this, parents must provide the security-giving relationships essential for children to develop into productive members of their societies. An effective democracy requires that its members have respect - respect for each other and the rights of others, respect for cultural variations in personalities of individuals and how people live in groups, respect for law and order and democratic principles, respect for property and respect for flora and fauna of the natural environment. Successful parents impart their values to their children, which influences how they react to events and people throughout their lives. Parents transfer their beliefs through language and by their actions.[188]

4.2.1.1. How democratic are the Nigerian families?

But how democratic are the Nigerian families? To answer this question, we must know what a democratic family is. A look at three different families will be of help here.[189] First, the Hauyorigbo family. Mr Hauyorigbo stands no nonsense from any of the children. When they were small, he was not one to spare the rod. Now he says, "As long as you live under my roof, you'll do what I say." A short time ago he decided that he would buy a new house and move the family into it. Everything was decided including the moving date before any of the rest of the family knew what was in the wind. The children have learnt that any suggestions or ideas they have are best kept to themselves.

Second, the Johnson family. Mr Johnson remembers how his stern parents made life miserable. When the Johnson children were born, Mr Johnson swore they would have a different sort of home life than he had. But most of his friends think that he has swung to the opposite extreme. The children "rule the roost." The entire household revolves around them. Both parents do everything possible to make life pleasant for the children. The youngsters are never asked to help with household chores. Mr and Mrs Johnson go without many things that they need so that the youngsters can have the best in toys, in clothes, and in good times.

Third, the Jaska family. Friends are struck with the spirit of give and take between parents and children. Recently the Jaskas bought a new car. Everyone in the family, from four-year-old Joy to Dad, helped decide what kind of car it would be. And what fun they had going over descriptive literature and talking to the different salesmen! It's a joy, too, say their friends, to see how all of them pitch into cleaning up the house or yard. Somehow or other they seem to have a good time with whatever they do.

There is no doubt that the above three families differ very much in their ways of life. There is also no doubt that these contrasting patterns of family life will have some effect on the kinds of persons that the children in the three families will become. There is stern authority in the Hauyorigbo family. Call it authoritarianism. Such family "is likely to develop individuals who either are resentful of all authority or who accept it passively and uncritically. They are the ones who in community matters will either take a 'Let George do it' attitude or be obstructively critical of all community leaders."[190] On its part, the Johnson family is too liberal. Call it liberalism. Such family is likely to develop "spoilt children", "individuals uninterested and uninvolved in what is going on around them except as they are directly touched. Without experience in taking responsibility, they will rarely feel any inclination to play a part in the improvement of community conditions. The self-centered existence they have led in their family will lead them to expect from others in their adult experiences a similar kind of feather-bed treatment."[191] Coming to the Jaska family, it is a balanced family, a family in which there is respect for every individual. Call it democracy. Such family is likely to develop truly democratic personalities. "Such persons have found deep satisfaction in cooperative activity. They had learned consideration for others through practice. Making intelligent choices - a part of their daily experience in the early years - tends to continue later. They have confidence that good can come through group thinking and group planning."[192]

Surely, there is no clear-cut pictures of family relationship as we have above. There are rather variations or mixtures of the different family patterns. A family may have more in common with say the Jaska family than with the other two. Then it is said to be like Jaska family. Following this pattern of thought, I must say that, in Nigeria, majority of the families are like the Hauyorigbo family. Very few families, if any, are like the Johnson family, while a few are like the Jaska family. This observation shows that majority of the Nigerian families are inclined to authoritarianism. In a normal Nigerian family, the parents wield so much power that the children do not have much say in major decisions of the family. A change in the family living - a change from autocratic to democratic family living - is, therefore, needed in Nigeria to enable the country build a stable and lasting democracy. This change is not going to be very easy but it is achievable with more enlightenment and education.

4.2.1.2. Essential learning processes in democracy in the family

A family can be said to live democratically when authority in this family is located in the total family group rather than in one or both parents. Four attitudes characterise democratic family living[193]: the freedom given a child to make progressively more significant decisions concerning his own welfare; the respect shown for his uniqueness; the understanding of his particular needs and how they may be fulfilled; and co-operative effort in seeking the individual and mutual satisfaction both parents and children desire. These attitudes in democratic family living, however, do not call for a uniform pattern for every family. "Democracy, as a way of life, may be expressed quite differently in different families. What is important is that the spirit of democracy - of cooperative sharing, of consideration for the rights of each in the group - is expressed through whatever is done."[194]

With regard to discipline, many Nigeria parents feel and act as though they own their children. Thus they expect unquestioning obedience from their children. Some parents say to their children: "As long as you live with us, you'll do what we say!" or "I'm not interested in that. It doesn't make any difference what other parents do. I'm your father and I know what is best for you!" Some parents require their children to go out at certain time and to come back before certain time; it does not matter what their colleagues and friends are doing. This is military, more than democratic, discipline. Democratic discipline is more on the side of self-direction than on the side of master-direction.

Also many parents want their children to behave or act in a certain way, as set for them. In this regard, E. G. Osborne writes: "Anxious to have our youngsters be and do their best, we may compare them unfavorably with brothers, sisters, or friends in the hope that they will improve their conduct or achieve more. This, too, is discipline. But most youngsters to hear over and over again, 'Why don't you keep yourself as neat as Suzanne?' or 'Johnny got all A's. Why can't you?' is defeating. As one youngster said, 'Johnny is Johnny and I'm I. Why do you think we should be the same?' Comparison with others is a kind of discipline - but it's a poor kind. It does not take individual differences or uniqueness of personality into account. In the democratically functioning family, there will be a minimum of it."[195] Parents should therefore bear in mind that no two individuals are the same, even when from the same parents: each person is unique. As Mr Osborne points out: "We assume that because our children have the same father and mother and were given the same opportunities that they should be alike. It is not easy to accept the fact our youngsters may be born with many real differences.... Even in the same family, no two children really live in the same family situation.... In all sorts of ways, children in the same family differ from one another. It is important that as parents we take this into account and that we help brothers and sisters accept this fact. It may be quite unfair and unjust to expect good grades in school from one child as from his brother.... In a democracy, whether a political democracy or a family, each person has his place. Happiness and success come far more effectively when we recognize differences and accept them rather than pushing all into the same mold."[196]

Added to the above is the fact that many Nigerian parents try to make their children over. Some parents expect certain things from their children, like having the same interest as their parents. Think of a father who is interested in football and expects his boy to be a star in the school football team while the boy is much more interested in playing by himself, in reading, and in drawing. Think also of the parents who may want their child to go into a certain profession which they consider the finest in the world (say, medicine or the priesthood) while the child's interest is in something else (say, farming or music). Indeed, "it is hard for parents to keep from wanting their children to follow in their footsteps or to go into life work that they believe is socially and financially superior. Yet, if we really hold to the belief that respect for individuals, their needs, and interests is of primary importance, we must discipline ourselves. We must not push our youngsters into work in which they are uninterested and for which they may not have the qualification. Lucky those young people whose parents are interested in their plans, are willing to talk with them about such plans, but do not try to impose their own values. This kind of attitude can surely be labeled 'democratic'."[197]

This brings us to the question of choice and decision. Many Nigerian children are denied the opportunity for personal choices and decisions. For many Nigerian parents still "don't see how inexperienced youngsters can be expected to make decisions or choices. That's the job of experienced grown-ups."[198] But the fact remains that children, right from infancy, have innumerable opportunities for choices and decisions, and the parents would be doing well if only they could pay attention to the feelings of their children. According to E. G. Osborne,

> in the early months and the first years of life, the foundation of democratic practices may be laid down. The infant who is treated with consideration, the child whose basic needs are considered, develops into the well-adjusted, happy individual who can live effectively with others.
>
> As youngsters grow older, the opportunities for making choices increase. The two year old can decide whether she will wear the ruffled blue dress or the pink gingham one. Mrs. Hart asks three-year-old Denny, 'Would you rather have carrot sticks or spinach today?' She is giving him an experience in choice with little or no extra trouble to herself....
>
> Then come the school days! Teachers and other children become more and more important in the life of the child. No longer is it only, 'My daddy says.' The teacher's ideas, the way other children behave become a part of the value system of the child of five years old and up. A wide field of choice and decision spreads out for him....
>
> The ways in which we meet these 'problems' when our children move out into a bigger world are important. And there is no easy answer. The mere fact that our youngster's schoolmates dress differently and act differently does not mean that without question he should follow in their footsteps. Sometimes a child has to be helped to see that while other families have the right to permit their children to have candy between meals, to dress in dirty corduroys, or to stay up late to see favorite television shows, we have our own ways of doing things. Too much of this emphasis can make a child feel himself unfairly treated or may even build up an undesirable attitude of superiority, but some is needed.
>
> Children of this age are not too young to take a part in deciding just what adjustments are to be made. If they are free to let us know how they feel about being

> 'different' from others in dress or what is permitted them in the way of behavior, together we can arrive at reasonable decisions. In such matters it is important for parents to realize how much it means to children to be accepted by their age-mates. Unless truly moral issues are involved, it usually is wise to compromise on matters of taste in dress or in day-to-day behavior.[199]

Some restraint is therefore called for on the part of the parents. They should let their children find their own way in their day-to-day activities, unless where truly moral issues are involved. They should realise that their children are living in a different age from theirs.[200] Parents may not understand, for example, how a child can do his/her homework with radio or music blaring in his/her ear (even when this constitutes no hindrance to the child). Thus the parents need some discipline not to see situations only in the light of their own experience. Where possible, leeway in the methods a youngster uses to get jobs done should be permitted. There is no reason why they should force their child to follow the method they have found most successful for themselves. The child may even arrive at a better one. But even if it is not better in the sense of being more efficient, the fact that it is his "discovery" is reason enough to keep hands off.

As the children grow older (adolescents), the field of decision-making becomes broader and they "feel" more mature and wish to be allowed to do their things their own way. But many parents, as E. G. Osborne rightly observes, "are all too prone to think of these near-adults as still children. And seeing them as children, far too large a number of parents believe that they are incapable of making choices, of coming to decisions. The so-called adolescent revolt may very well be due to this more than to any other thing. Grown-ups consider the adolescent a child. He considers himself grown up most of the time. Quite naturally, then, he resents having his choice of friends criticised. In the matter of hours, clothing, and a dozen of other things, he objects to being treated as he was when he a child."[201]

Being human, youngsters are bound to make mistakes. It can be in their use of money, in the selection of friends, the choice of recreation, and so on. Very often the parents correct their children by scolding them and/or by imposing corporal punishment on them. This mode of correction instils fear into the child and, at times, hardens his/her heart, and distorts the child's healthy development. But the best way to correct a child is to help him learn from his/her mistakes. Mr Osborne rightly argues that "in many such instances, we more experienced parents could help the child avoid such mistakes if we 'took over.' But, though we have a legitimate role as advisers, it is unwise to substitute our experience too often for the child's judgment. Given the proper attitude at home, a child can learn much more from the mistakes he will inevitably make. The important thing is that parents stand by the child, helping him see how and why he made his mistakes and giving him encouragement of the kind that will help him face future situations with courage and confidence."[202] In this way the child gradually develops in him the potentialities for self judgement, self expression, which are essential for the democratic spirit.

Democracy in the home demands a cordial and friendly relationship among the members of the family. The way members of the family relate to each other and the way matters are discussed or talked about in the family do influence how the child relates to people outside his family. On the one hand, if the family does things together - living, working, playing, praying together - without discrimination, the child learns the virtue of unity (to which belong tolerance or acceptance of and peaceful co-existence with others). This is so, because "it is primarily through the family-centered projects that the greatest contribution is made to the democratic spirit. The give and take of planning and acting, the sharing in decisions and in activities, provide the framework in which qualities of cooperation, consideration for others, thoughtful choosing, and other essentials for democracy are formed."[203] But, on the other hand, if the family is a quarrelsome and discriminating type, then the child would be full of prejudices and intolerance, hatred and antagonism toward others outside the family. Writing on "the larger family", E. G. Osborne expresses the same view this way,

> it is in the family that we find the seedbed of attitude and behavior toward others - toward the larger family. The lift of the eyebrow when one of another race or religion is mentioned, the condescending tone or sneering comment all have their impact on the impressionable child. But fortunately so do the appreciative comment, the warm welcome, the lively interest shown toward individuals who differ in skin color, religious affiliation, or living habits.
>
> ....
>
> The family in which the youngsters are treated democratically is the family from which comes friendly, unprejudiced attitudes and relationships with out-of-family individuals.[204]

To help bring democracy to their family living, Nigerians should adopt what Osborne calls "the family council approach". He explains the basic idea behind this approach thus:

> The basic idea is simple enough. Any problems to be solved, any decisions to be made, if they have bearing on the whole family, are worked out by the whole group, not by majority vote, but by discussion, give-and-take, and general understanding.... Some families prefer to have a regularly scheduled meeting of the family.... In addition to talking over any family matters ..., they use their family council time for a 'gripe' session as well. If something has happened during the week which displeases young Bruce, he tells the rest of (the family) about it.... Any other member of the family who have 'gripes' - parents included - have the opportunity of expressing them. Usually, misunderstanding can be talked through satisfactorily.... Many families would prefer neither to have regularly organized family councils nor a 'gripe' session. And the outward form isn't important. But the chance to talk through problems, the opportunity to decide together on family matters affecting the entire family, are important. If this can be done informally at the time issues come up, well and good. But many a family today finds a more regular family

council meeting of great value in helping them to live happily and satisfactorily together.[205]

As soon as the Nigerian families begin to live democratically, democracy will be rooted in the country. The following litmus test will help Nigerian families to determine whether they are or have become democratic or not. Each family should ask herself these four relevant questions[206]: 1) "Does the way we live in the family give increasing freedom to the child to make decisions concerning his own and the family welfare?" 2) "Do we, parents and children alike, show respect for one another's individuality, and accept our differences?" 3) "Are we learning more and more effectively to work together for our mutual good?" 4) "Are we aware that it is in the 'little things,' the daily give and take of family experience, that such qualities may develop?" If her answers to these questions are in the affirmative, then the family is democratic, but if her answers are in the negative, then she is not democratic.

Before going to another section, it is necessary to emphasise the importance of moral upbringing and character-formation of children in the home through worthy examples from parents. It is a fact that some parents, due to out-of-home engagements or due to sheer recklessness, have little or no time for the home-upbringing of their children. Some relegate their duties to home-care-centres or to baby-sitters, thereby denying their children the much needed parental care and love. It is not enough to have children and to provide them with food and drink, clothing, toys, send them to school, pay their school fees, and so on. The children's character-formation and moral upbringing are also very important. Therefore, parents should devote more time and attention to the upbringing of their children, so that their children would enjoy the security and love of the home.

The parents should bear the following points in mind: firstly, the family is the first school for the children and the parents their first teachers. The parents are the first persons responsible for the education of their children, in human as well as in spiritual matters. This task calls for prudence, understanding, a capacity to love and a concern for giving good examples. Secondly, the family is the foundation of all societies and the children are the tomorrow's leaders. The type of leaders the children will become, good or bad, depends very much on their family upbringing. Thirdly, the parents should bear in mind that children learn more and better by seeing than by listening to talks. They like to emulate what they see. Therefore, parents should teach their children mainly by examples. What a child looks for in a father or mother is not only a certain amount of knowledge or some more or less effective advice, but primarily something more important: a proof of the value and meaning of life, shown through the life of a specific person, and confirmed in the different situations and circumstances that occur over a period of time. And fourthly, "if the parents have not implanted their basic values solidly in the minds of their children, the youths' beliefs and actions may be transformed into anti-family and anti-society beliefs as well activities distasteful to the parents and destructive to their community and country. If, on the other hand, the parents have implanted their values well in the minds of their children by serving as positive examples and through relationships with them based on friendship, love and respect, they will successfully resist the pressures of other children in their schools and communities with different values as well as the forces of change from adults, including teachers and professors."[207]

4.2.2. The role of the community

The community has a great role to play in the building of a stable and lasting democracy. The extended family system in Nigeria makes family of the community.The family is very important because it defines the individual and makes him/her what he/she is. For example, among the Igbos "a person is thought of first of all as a member of a particular family, kindred, clan or tribe. Even today in an Igbo village, one is rarely asked, 'who are you?', but rather 'whose son are you?', and 'what lineage or clan do you belong to?' Thus one learns from an early age, that 'I am because I belong'. An individual without a family is an anomaly. The family makes the man. The family is made up of not only one's living relatives at the widest possible scope, but also the dead members and those yet to be born. The bond which links the family community is not only a socio-biological bond but also ontologico-spiritual."[208] This bond is reflected in the solidarity which exists among the members of the extended families. According to L. U. Ejiofor: "Solidarity prevails among all the members and component units of the extended family. Developments in one are accepted for others. Affluence or poverty, honour or shame, gain or loss, reflects on the entire image of the extended family. All the members are ... children of 'the same mother'"[209] - they are "brothers and sisters".

This principle of solidarity - of love and care for one another - found within the extended family system is a great democratic virtue which, if cultivated and extended to others from other clans, communities, local government areas, regions, and states, would help to make Nigeria a democratically developed country. It is a pity that tribalism, ethnicism and religious-divide - all based on prejudices - have prevented Nigerians from seeing each other as members - brothers and sisters - of one extended family. Therefore, something must be done to remedy this situation.

One way to remedy this situation is through education and public enlightenment in the schools, through community adult education, and through the mass media. Community adult education is our concern here. (The roles of the school and of the mass media will be treated later, in 4.2.3. and 4.2.6. respectively.) There is much need for adult education programme in Nigeria. This programme, as its name indicates, is meant to educate adults who are no longer enrolled in a school or college in the promotion of democracy in home and family life in a community. It has three major tasks:

> (1) to arouse the interest of a considerable number of the adults in the re-examination of their practices and relationships in family living; (2) to aid the adults to reinterpret for themselves the meaning of democracy in family life; and (3) to aid each person in reconstructing his own behavior as a family member so that he becomes continually more willing and able to share with other adults and with the younger members of the family in the ongoing experience of working for the common good.[210]

Obviously such a programme would "help adults to attain a broader and more consistent vision of the relationships of family members to each other and to those outside the family if human values are put first, if the possibilities of enriching personality through working and thinking with others are recognized, and if the method of intelligence is applied to choice of the ends and the means of family living."[211]

What more, the people should be actively involved in the political processes and activities, especially at the grass-root levels - at the ward and local government levels. This would create in them political awareness and alertness, and enable them to take active part in the political life of their states and nation.

4.2.3. The role of the school[212]

Political education is very paramount in the building of a stable and lasting democracy in Nigeria. This is so because "political education - the cultivation of the virtues, knowledge, and skills necessary for political participation - has moral primacy over other purposes of public education in a democratic society. Political education prepares citizens to participate in consciously reproducing their society, and conscious social reproduction is the ideal not only of democratic education but also of democratic politics."[213] Political education could be formal (in the school) or informal (outside the school). We are concerned here with formal education, in the primary, secondary, and tertiary institutions of learning.

Formal education is very important for the internalisation of democratic virtues, because "it is in the schools then that every type of person comes together to live, learn, work and play for long and definite periods of time. Schools thus serve as a sort of rallying ground or clearing house for all varying backgrounds, views, tastes and interests that make them the best kind of laboratory for democracy"[214] and because "schools are the great storehouses of knowledge and beauty"[215] and "the conservatories and experimental garden beds of the mind. There you should find the sunlight, the soil and the nourishment to produce the best mental flowering of which you are capable. In such a mental garden your mind should be free to expand and grow, checked and tested against other minds, and always sympathetically but firmly guided by the 'gardener' (teacher)."[216]

Nigeria's approach to education merits some attention if its dream to build a sustainable democracy is to be realised. Its approach to education would fit into A. Armstrong's description of the same situation in America in the early 1960s:

> Education is often too material, too mechanical, too lifeless. We think of jobs and hours and salaries, and assignments and tests, and standards and 'grounds to be covered'....
> We don't think nearly enough about young human beings - what motivates them, the backgrounds they come from, how to locate and train whatever talent or capacity they might have, how to create the kind of environment in which they will develop best. Rather than starting from these considerations we begin with a predetermined body of knowledge that stands more or less immutable and changeless, expecting everyone to master it in more or less the same way in more or less the same length of time and more or less through the same methods. Where these practices are followed slavishly, they breed only the qualities most desired in a dictatorship - obedience, conformity and thoroughness. Not that these qualities are undesirable in a democracy, but they are not *primary*.... (D)emocracy is concerned mostly with the development of each unique human being, creating in so far as possible an individuality out of an individual, a personality out of a person. This calls for cultivating and preserving natural curiosity, the inquiring and questioning mind. It is perhaps more important to question why 2 and 2 makes 4, and to get what help may be necessary to demonstrate that fact, than simply to memorize it and glibly repeat it.[217]

Some factors are responsible for this approach. One, Nigerian teachers, especially in primary and secondary schools, do not know enough about human behaviour. Many of these teachers are products of "crash programmes" which, as the word "crash" implies, are hurriedly and poorly done educational trainings. Two, in almost every school, especially in rural places, classes are simply too large - the pupils or students very much outnumber the teachers - giving rise to pressure of numbers, which has made our education a mass-production process. This mass-production process could be termed a "forcing" process: it lacks personal touch ("pupil/student-teacher" approach), emphasises "book learning", and neglects the fact that people have different aptitudes for different types of learning. It is thus undemocratic and unscientific. Three, we could add the fact that the Nigerian teachers are not always sure of their salaries at the end of each month. This makes for less devotion and dedication to teaching as the teachers worry more about how to "make ends meet" than about the welfare of their pupils or students.

These factors call for urgent attention from the government. Much more widespread and improved work in the field of guidance and teacher training than we have today is very necessary. It is most democratic to give young people the type of training most suitable to their individual abilities, and which thus should be the most satisfying for them.

Added to the above factors is the fact that some people believe that the chief reason for going to school is to get a good job. Because many school leavers do not easily get jobs, while their counterparts in businesses which require little or no education make exceedingly large incomes, some parents and some students do not see the need for furthering one's education (from primary to secondary school or from the latter to a higher institution). This accounts for one of the major reasons why many students join the "business world" as soon as they finish from the secondary school. This also explains why some students pursue some courses that will yield them better jobs and more income, even though they lack the aptitude and interest for such jobs or professions. But it must be emphasised here that "education is not primarily to make money nor is it even the best way to make money. Education in democracy is to learn to participate as fully as possible in those aspects of life that give us lasting satisfaction. One of the greatest losses any society suffers is the terrific loss from people doing work in which they have no real interest."[218]

Opportunities for *democratic* experiences and training in all studies and organised activities, particularly in social studies, should be provided in all schools. Rather than theoretical education, education for democracy should concern itself with ways of attacking problems. Call it "learning by doing". Out-of-class activities - such as control of students by students, activities that are of service to the school or of help to one another, building school morale or "spirit", recreational and social activities, and student organisations - are very helpful here. In these activities, it is desirable that the way be left open for the students to take more and more responsibility for their conduct, so that in the end most of them will be more self-reliant. As the saying goes: the best way to keep a youngster from tracking mud over a newly cleaned floor is to make him clean the floor. A. Armstrong argues that if youngsters were encouraged to beautify their school and its grounds, to make some of its equipment and to help maintain some of its services, they would not be so likely to harm or destroy things. And he asks the following questions (addressed to students): "And wouldn't your class in art be more interesting if it picked some of the best work to decorate the school or some of your drab public buildings, or send some of it to other countries through Junior Red Cross, so that thousands of other boys and girls could picture what kind of life you live? Why shouldn't the woodshops make some of the small furniture and gadgets needed ...; the home crafts or physics classes study and help maintain water, electricity and gas systems of the school, plus may be the public address system, movie equipment, and so on, or the cooking classes play as big a part as possible in the school cafeteria or lunchroom; the botany class do what it could toward improving and maintaining the school landscaping; the English and public speaking classes help handle the library, make announcements, care for the bulletin board, or develop a speaker's bureau to publicize your school to the community or explain some of its problems?"[219]

This reminds me of when I was the Vice-Rector of St. Augustine's Seminary, Ezzamgbo, Abakaliki, (1984-90). As soon as "Introductory Technology" was introduced into secondary school curriculum, we built a technology workshop, got and installed the designed equipment from the state Ministry of Education, employed well-qualified teachers for the different branches of the course (like building construction, wood work, metal work, electricity, creative arts, etc.). The junior secondary students were got deeply interested and involved in the course. They were allowed to use their initiatives, under the supervision of their teachers. After some time, the students were able to do a lot on their own. They could mould and lay blocks, draw house-plans and build small and uncomplicated houses and wire them. (The poultry house, external bathrooms and toilets, extensions of classrooms and dormitories that one sees today in this seminary speak for themselves.) They also made simple furniture like stools and tables, do some drawings and paintings, and so on. (One student even made a standard wooden xylophone.) The result was indeed immensely good, fascinating and rewarding - not only to the students, but also to their parents and to the seminary. The students took pride to show the world what they were capable of. Their parents benefited from what their children were able to do at home during the holidays (like moulding of blocks, fixing spoilt house furniture, making simple things like stools, doing simple electric wiring, and so on). And our seminary became a reference point (from the state Ministry of Education) for other schools. Even in the field of agriculture, we let each student have a portion of the school's farmland where he could do some experiments (the records of which were available to the public), grow his own crops and, during the harvest, contribute to the common food.

I would not like to bother you with the details of the recreational and social activities in our seminary (like sports, dramatics, debating society, science club, cultural club, geography society, school of journalism, photography, scout movement, etc.). It is enough to that these activities offered our students so much freedom, so much variety, and so much chance to give expression to their special interests and hobbies, to show initiative and prove their own worth. They also helped to build school morale and to enhance the spirit of living and doing things together.

It is therefore very necessary for school authorities in Nigeria to provide their students with varieties of recreational and social activities and to encourage the students to take active part in them. Obviously, such social activities in the schools, sports in particular, help to eliminate the differences (tribal, religious, social status, etc.) among the students. They also help the students to be tolerant of one another, to be honest, fair and just in their dealings with one another, to respect the freedom of others, and to promote the common good.

Lastly, educational programmes in Nigeria should be such as would help the student develop his/her talents and enable him/her grow into a good, reliable, respectable and hardworking citizen. Mr Boek advises that "leaders in developing nations striving to improve the formal education for children must make sure they do not follow advice from professional educators in the older democracies that has caused the decline in the quality of instruction and learning in those countries. For effective formal education at the elementary and secondary school levels, the curriculum needs to be a combination of courses that are useful to the students in their communities, and courses that prepare them for a technologically advancing society. They must have courses that help them become knowledgeable and effective participants in their democratic government and free market, capitalistic economy. Children must be taught to think effectively and to solve problems."[220] And our educational programmes should also be such as would encourage the spirit of community-living based on the primary virtues of love, justice, tolerance, and honesty.

4.2.4. The role of the state

The state has the duty of legislation and administration of justice through the enactment of laws and through the application of sanctions when necessary. In doing this, the state must uphold and defend the rights of all citizens, maintain public order and tranquility, and promote the common welfare. It has also the duty of promoting socio-economic welfare and public health: care for economic growth, social progress and hygienic conditions of the nation. It is also the state's duty to care for the cultural and moral values: the general instruction and schooling, the cultivation of sciences and arts, and the fostering of good morals.

Top in Nigeria's agenda, if the nation is to have a sustainable democracy, must be to make sure that the laws and institutions, the general character and administration of the commonwealth, are such as to produce of themselves public well-being and private prosperity - with special regard for the poor. As Pope Leo XIII points out, "a State chiefly prospers and flourishes by morality, well-regulated family life, by respect for religion and justice, by moderation and equal distribution of public burdens, by the progress of the arts and of trade, by the abundant yield of the land - by everything which makes the citizens better and happier. Here, then, it is in the power of a ruler to benefit every order of the State, and among the rest to promote in the highest degree the interest of the poor; this by virtue of his office, and without being exposed to any suspicion of undue interference - for it is the province of the commonwealth to consult for the common good."[221]

The Nigerian state must maintain justice toward all, irrespective of rank or status. So writes Pope Leo XIII: "To the State the interest of all are equal whether high or low. The poor are members of the national community equally with the rich; they are real component parts, living parts, which make up, through the family, the living body.... It would be irrational to neglect one portion of the citizens and to favour another; and therefore the public administration must duly and solicitously provide for the welfare and comfort of the working people, or else that law of justice will be violated which ordains that each shall have his due.... Among the many and grave duties of rulers who would do their best for their people, the first and chief is to act with strict justice ... toward each and every class."[222]

It has also the paramount duty to promote and safeguard the rights of individuals in order to help them carry out their duties. In the words of Pope John XXIII, "the chief concern of civil authorities must therefore be to ensure that these rights are acknowledged, respected, coordinated with other rights, defended and promoted, so that in this way each one may more easily carry out his duties.... This means that, if any government does not acknowledge the rights of man or violates them, it not only fails in its duty, but its orders completely lack juridical force."[223] In doing this, the state should "coordinate social relations in such fashion that the exercise of one man's rights does not threaten others in the exercise of their own rights nor hinder them in the fulfilment of their duties."[224] Therefore, "the rights of all should be effectively safeguarded and, if they have been violated, completely restored."[225]

Added to the above is the duty of the state "to bring about a situation in which individual citizens can easily exercise their rights and fulfil their duties as well. For experience has taught us that, unless these authorities take suitable action with regard to economic, political and cultural matters, inequalities between the citizens tend to become more widespread, especially in the modern world, and as a result human rights are rendered totally ineffective and the fulfilment of duties is compromised."[226] Therefore, the Nigerian state must pay adequate attention to the social and economic progress of its citizens especially in the areas of essential services, insurance systems, employment opportunities accompanied by just wages, and so on.

Finally, for the Nigerian state to perform its duties more efficiently, its various organs - the legislature, the executive and the judiciary - must have the public well-being as the determining factor in all their actions. The primary question that should govern all their decisions and activities is: Is it good for the Nigerian people? "This requires that, in constantly changing conditions, the legislators never forget the norms of morality, or constitutional provisions, or the common good. Moreover, executive authorities must coordinate the activities of society with discretion, with a full knowledge of the law and after a careful consideration of circumstances, and the courts must administer justice impartially and without being influenced by favouritism or pressure."[227] Therefore, the fear of God should be the foundation upon which the Nigerian state is built - like the American "In God we trust". For unless the Lord builds a house, they labour in vain who do so; and unless the Lord watches over the city, the labour in vain those who keep vigil (Psalm 127).

4.2.5. The role of religious bodies

I would have treated here the role of the Church in Nigeria. But since Nigeria has three fundamental religions - namely Christianity (with many denominations or churches), Islam, and traditional religions - I have chosen rather to consider the role of all religions (especially Christianity and Islam), in their different colours, as one toward the building of a stable and lasting democracy in the country. Hence my use of the term "religious bodies" to denote Christianity and Islam.

Just as the state is the society instituted for the universal establishment of the secular common weal, so are the different religions instituted for the universal promotion of the spiritual and religious weal of mankind: to imbue everyday activity of men with a deeper meaning and to serve as a leaven and as a kind of soul for human society, with the goal to transform it into God's family.[228]

The religious bodies in Nigeria should emphasise, and educate their members on the importance of brotherly love and on the unity of all in the country, irrespective of one's religious inclinations. The habit of seeing everything, especially elections, political posts, siting of certain amenities/structures, as a struggle between Moslems and Christians on the one hand, and between Catholics and non-Catholics on the other hand, must be checked and stopped.

The primary tasks of all religions are not only spiritual but also temporal. Thus the religious bodies in Nigeria should cater for the body and soul of their members. They should be known and seen as defenders of the poor, and thus help the poor to "rise above poverty and wretchedness, and ... better their condition in life."[229] Then they should be propagators of social justice. When there is social injustice and deprivation in the community, apart from speaking out against such evils, the religious leaders should take concrete actions against such issues.

Added to this, the leaders of each religious body should organise themselves well at local, state, and national levels, so that they would be able to take unanimous decisions on issues affecting the moral and social life of the people, and so that their voices on these issues would be heard and known everywhere. The Nigerian Catholic Bishops are in the fore-front in this area.[230] Moreover, all the religious bodies in the country should have a "common force" to fight the social ills of the country, and to be able to defuse the religious tensions and acrimony prevalent among the different religions.

To maintain the unity of the country, all religious bodies must uphold and maintain the secular nature of the Nigerian state - that is, the separation of state and religion. No mosque and no church should be used for political gatherings. They should be strictly used for what they are - the places of prayer and worship. In the same vein, the religious bodies or their leaders should not identify themselves with the political community, nor should they be inclined toward any political party. Here the view of the Fathers of the second Vatican Council on "Politics and the Church" could apply to any religious body in Nigeria:

> It is highly important, especially in pluralistic societies, that a proper view exists of the relation between the political community and the Church. Thus the faithful will be able to make a clear distinction between what a Christian conscience leads them to do in their own name as citizens, whether as individuals or in association, and what they do in the name of the Church....
> The role and competence of the Church being what it is, she must in no way be confused with the political community, nor bound to any political system. For she is at once a sign and a safeguard of the transcendence of the human person.
> In their proper spheres, the political community and the Church are mutually independent and self-governing. Yet, by a different title, each serves the personal and social vocation of the same human beings....[231]

Therefore, instead of being partisan, the religious bodies should be there for all without discrimination.

On the whole, each religious body should urge and encourage its members to live a godly life in whatever state they find themselves. And the religious leaders should co-operate and work together in order to make sure that God remains the head of every family, including the civil family. They should keep a watchful eye on the politicians to make sure they are not being bereft of morality (a danger to the commonweal), knowing that politics cannot work without ethics and that "if the Lord does not build the house, in vain do its builders labour; if the Lord does not watch over the city, in vain does the watchman keep vigil" (psalm 127). And they should always be on the side of the poor, the oppressed, and the downtrodden.[232]

4.2.6. The role of the mass media

As already stated (in part 2, 3.6.), the mass media in Nigeria are hardly free because they are under the chain of their proprietors. This makes them partisan. News is slanted to suit particular interests. Consequently, professional ethics and standards as well as objectivity are sacrificed. And the public is misinformed, fed with truncated news, lies, and, at best, with half-truths.

For many Nigerians, news from the press is "a gospel truth" that must be believed. These people place tremendous amount of faith and trust in the ability of the press to feed the public with the truth and nothing but the truth. This is why it is very immoral for the press to misinform the people. Therefore, the Nigerian press needs much reformation and change. The freedom of the press should be respected by all and sundry, especially by those in public authority. The press should stop being partisan. It should be objective in their news reports and stop peddling rumours and falsehood. In short, the mass media should maintain, with all seriousness and sincerity, its all important role as "a watch dog" - educating and informing the public and correcting public ills. And it will do us much good to pay attention to the advice of Pope Paul VI,

> We do not wish to forget to emphasize the growing role being assumed by the media of social communication and their influence on the transformation of mentalities, of knowledge, of organizations, and of society itself. Certainly they have many positive aspects. Thanks to them news from the entire world reaches us practically in an instant, establishing contacts which supersede distances and creating elements of unity among all men. A great spread of education and culture is becoming possible. Nevertheless, by their very action the media of social communication are reaching the point of representing as it were a new power. One cannot but ask about those who really hold this power, the aims that they pursue and the means they use, and finally, about the effect of their activity on the exercise of individual liberty, both in the political and ideological spheres and in social, economic, and cultural life. The men who hold this power have grave moral responsibility with respect to the truth of the information that they spread, the needs and the reactions that they generate, and the values which they put forward.[233]

News reporting should be positive. The press should bear in mind that the youths are very much influenced by what they see, hear and read from radio and television programmes, movies, performances by popular musicians, and books and articles glamourizing individuals with bizarre ways of behaving. As Mr Boek rightly points out: "Mass media coverage of a person who has murdered another, can impress youth with the prominence of the murderer even though society regards the murderer as repugnant. The negative effect on youth of the message from the media may be enhanced further if a trial leads to a sentence of death that is followed by numerous widely publicized appeals during the many years they may take before the execution.... Because of the free press in democracies, some publishers like to print stories about murders because they think people want to read about them and will buy their papers. Those publishers concerned about the negative effect of such news items, minimize the importance of murders by placing items about them on inside pages of the paper instead of keeping them on the front page. Most newspaper editors, however, favor negative stories rather than positive ones. Although they might not want to admit it, this should be brought to their attention with the hope that they would consider changing their approach to news reporting."[234] Therefore, the Nigerian should not relegate, but intensify, its role of educating, informing and entertaining the people.

The mass media also has an important role to play in the political education of the masses. As is well known, politics has become a mass media affair. According to Judith Lichtenberg, "The press today - the mass media in particular - is one of the primary actors on the political scene, capable of making or breaking political careers and issues."[235] The Nigeria press should help educate the people on their political rights and duties, thereby helping and urging them to take active part in the political life of the country. It should inform the people about the options available to them - for example, information about the different political parties and their manifestoes; information about the candidates vying for elections; information about voting rules and procedures; and so on - and thus help the people to organise themselves and to build up their minds on different issues. And through its objective criticisms and reporting, the ills of the society are corrected, thereby helping the people to cultivate the democratic virtues of justice and fair-play. This helps to keep the government officers on the alert, and to make them more conscious of their duties, since these officers know that every of their utterances and actions are being critically watched.

Therefore, if the men and women of the press do their jobs well, going by the all important roles of the press and by its unwieldy influence on the society at large, then Nigerian society will be all the better for it.

4.3. Conclusion: A Call to Patriotism

From all we have discussed above, Nigerian democracy, to be stable and lasting, must be based on political, socio-economic and moral-cultural development of the human person. Such development is something of a lifetime - a way of life - from the cradle (in the family), through various stages of maturation (in the community, in the school, and in the society at large), to the grave. But such development is impossible unless Nigerians have love for their fatherland and stop involving themselves in plans and actions that are counter-productive and contrary to the national interests. Hence a call to patriotism.

Our study has shown that one of the greatest problems Nigeria has is lack of national unity. (See part 2, 3.1.) Certainly "every kingdom divided against itself is heading for ruin, and a household divided against itself collapses."[236] So too with Nigeria. If this country is divided against itself - with its component parts divided against each other (on ethnic and/or religious basis), each to itself - with tribal loyalties stronger than national loyalty - with everybody thinking of himself or herself alone - with nobody interested in the common good, how can its kingdom stand?[237] And so true is the saying: "Divided we fall, united we stand." Therefore, every Nigerian should work toward breaking down the barriers of prejudice which keep the country apart. Nigerians should avoid all divisive thoughts, words and actions and go always for those things that will unite and promote national integration.

One of the consequences of lack of national conciousness is the urge in Nigerians, from top to bottom, to loot the national treasury, often tagged "sharing of the national cake". (See part 2, 3.5.2. above.) "This lack of national consciousness," writes Dr T. A. Imobighe, "is manifested in the prevailing attitude of most Nigerians that the country exists to be exploited to aggrandize self and close associates rather than an entity to be developed. A nation whose citizens lack a national consciousness and patriotism is a nation that has lost its soul. Such a nation falls easy prey to internal disruptions and external violations. The situation in the country is particularly serious in that the lack of national consciousness and patriotism has permeated all sectors of public life, be they the security enforcement sector or the strategic resource management sector."[238] Surely this is not the way to love the fatherland. This is killing Nigeria! Therefore, "every Nigerian should take it as his responsibility to defend the interests and integrity of this country.... They should reject the now popular slogan that it is the time of those in power to chop, implying that one will ultimately have one's own turn to chop. They should instead uphold and defend the universal theory that public functionaries are servants of the people who should serve their masters faithfully and not loot what belongs to the people."[239]

Every government costs money to run. Taxes are the main source of revenue for any country. Government raises most of its funds with which it operates and caters for the needs of its citizens from the various taxes which it imposes on citizens: property taxes, income taxes, business taxes, sales taxes, fuel taxes, road use taxes, franchise taxes, luxury taxes, and so no. Nigeria loses much of its revenue due to tax evasion by its citizens. According to Major-General Oluleye: "It was observed that many rich individuals and corporate organizations neglect their civic duties as far as payment of taxes was concerned. To fault-proof tax evasion and tax avoidance, the production of TAX Clearance Certificates was made compulsory to have access to foreign exchange approvals. The production of TCC was equally made compulsory for contract dealings with the Federal and State Ministries and their parastatals. Total tax evasion was over-come but tax avoidance, as an age long practice remains unsolved."[240] Obviously this is not the way to love one's fatherland. Nigerians should therefore stop evading their civic duty of contributing their dues for the upkeep of the society.

Nigerians have a strong inclination - a type of fanatic attraction - toward anything "foreign". For many Nigerians, anything "foreign" is better than anything "Nigerian". With regard to goods, "foreign made" is always the best. Nigerians can spend a huge amount of money on one "foreign item", even when the same amount would have fetched them more of the same good ("Nigerian made").[241] Not only that, many Nigerians are copying the "western lifestyle", especially the American. To this could be added the obnoxious practice by some affluent Nigerians, mostly by politicians and those in government, of carting away our national wealth for investment in foreign countries. This is sabotage, pure and simple, against Nigeria's economy and development. According to Dr Imobighe: "Looting the country's treasury is bad enough for national security, but taking the fruits of that loot away from the country to stimulate the economies of other countries is a double tragedy. And this is the plight Nigeria is presently facing."[242] What all these boil down to is *satrapism*, the denial of one's culture and identity, the aping of external culture which is considered superior, and self-subordination to foreign values. Again this is killing Nigeria rather than loving one's fatherland. Nigerians should therefore be proud of their culture and identity, and of their abilities and capabilities. They should take to heart the golden words of Prof. E. A. Ayandele:

> Borrowed ideas, customs, and institutions have their values, but only to the extent that they are adapted or adaptable, to the indigenous milieu in which they are being adopted. To miss this point is to miss one's bearings, to cease to know oneself.

> History is yet to reveal genuine nations born out of cultural womb completely alien to it. It is a law of nature that the pride of any people is found in those customs and institutions peculiarly their own. Not that these customs and institutions are fixed, immutable entities, but they cannot reasonably be changed or wished away overnight, just as they did not come into existence overnight. The process of their being changed is necessarily gradual. The extent to which a people ignores this fact and turns it back on its culture is the extent to which it is inviting humiliation and effeteness.[243]

Nigerians should also pay attention to the advice of General Olusegun Obasanjo urging them to liberate themselves "from the bondage of our colonial past and our experience and wholesale importation of foreign ideas and beliefs that are irrelevant if not inimical to our situation and progress...."[244] They should patronise their home-made goods and invest their capital in the country to help develop and boost the country's economy.

At this juncture, I urge Nigerian producers of goods to improve the quality of their products, to bring them to the same standard as those produced overseas. This will make those who go for "foreign goods" because of their superior quality change their minds and begin to patronise home-made goods. In the same vein, the Nigerian government should make life in the country worth living for all, through the provision of essential services and social justice and security. This will obviously make citizens to be proud of their country and to identify themselves with its aspirations and yearnings, instead of migrating to other countries in search of a better life. According to Pope Leo XIII, "men would cling to the country in which they were born; for no one would exchange his country for a foreign land if his own afforded him the means of living a tolerable and happy life."[245]

All said and done, Nigerians should not compromise their citizenship, no matter what. To borrow Christ's pattern of thought,[246] he/she who - in his/her thoughts, words and actions - is not with Nigeria (in its goals and aspiration) is against Nigeria; and he/she who does not gather with Nigeria scatters. No matter where we find ourselves, we should love, cherish, nurture, protect and project the good image of our dear country. If anything, using Prof. Eya Ita's thought-pattern: "The love of (Nigeria) must consume us. The zeal for her emancipation must be our food and drink. We are either (Nigerians) or nothing. To the degree in which (Nigeria) is saved to that degree shall we be saved...."[247] And it should be the aim of all leaders - traditional, religious, political, and so on - to inculcate in the minds of their followers, borrowing the wordings of one of the aims of the 1951 Northern People's Congress, "a genuine love for (Nigeria) and all that is (Nigerian), and a special reverence for Religion, Laws and Order and the preservation of good customs and traditions, and the feeling that the sorrow of one (Nigerian) shall be the sorrow of all and that the happiness of one is also the the happiness of all."[248]

Finally, every Nigerian should memorise our national anthem and harking to its call to patriotism:

Arise, O compatriots
Nigeria's call obey
To serve our Fatherland
With love and strength and faith;
The labour of our heroes past
Shall never be in vain.
To serve with heart and mind
One nation bound in freedom, peace and unity.

And every Nigerian should also memorise and live out, to the letter, our national pledge:

> I pledge to Nigeria my Country: To be faithful, loyal and honest; To serve Nigeria with all my strength; To defend her unity and Uphold her honour and glory. So help me God.

Once we do these, then the zeal of our fatherland would always urge us on, and we shall never do anything that is not in the interest of the Nigerian nation.

Now bringing this study to an end, I have no doubt that if the fruit of this research is taken seriously by all Nigerians: if we see and appreciate democracy, in its political, socio-economic and moral-cultural dimensions, as a way of life, and if we love our fatherland, then we will be able to build a stable and lasting democracy in country. Then Nigeria will be a disciplined, fair, just and humane society where everybody will live with every other person in freedom, peace and unity.

However, it must be pointed out that the realisation of such a democracy, such a society, as we have in mind is not something of overnight. It takes time, quite some long time, to materialise. According to Olin Robinson: "The effort to foster democracy is necessarily a long-range project. In most cases, results will not be attained quickly but will require long years of steady, persistent work."[249] S. G. Ikoku agrees:

> America had nearly a hundred years of concensus government before the present two party system blossomed. In Britain, the transition from absolute monarchy to a sovereign parliament with a constitutional monarch and a fully fledged multy-party system needed a near-dictatorship for about half a century. In France, a democratic republic with a multy-party system came into being nearly a century after the Revolution in 1789.
>
> The point I am trying to make is that the democratic system we strive so hard to copy only blossomed after a considerable period of non-democratic government - non-democratic, that is, in institutional terms. It seems to me that a concensus government that accurately reflects the will of the people and the yearnings of a nation but lacking the beautiful paraphernalia of modern democracy has been a historical pre-requisite for the establishment of working democracy in its modern connotation. Do we think that Nigeria can circumvent this necessary stage of political evolution?[250]

Nigeria must undergo different stages of development - with its trials and errors, its pains and glories - before it will arrive at a stage in which it will be recognised as developed. The fact is that Nigeria, as a nation, is still very young - thirty-six years old. And being young, one would expect it to falter and to make mistakes in her democratic experiences and practices. However, nobody would expect it to remain in its mistakes. Instead, Nigeria is expected to learn from its mistakes, past and present, and to keep forging ahead, showing steady and visible improvements, toward its goal of becoming a democratically developed state.

Nigeria is a country in a haste. It is too much in a hurry and too impatient. It wants to be like America overnight without undergoing the long processes which America went through. But the truth remains that "Rome was not built in a day!" Nigeria's development must be gradual, yet marching on steadily. The country must first of all lay deep and solid foundations for development, and then begin to build upon these foundations. This calls for patience, perseverance, hard work, dedication, singleness of purpose, strict adherence to the rule of law and social justice - all based on love of God and of neighbour. In this way Nigeria's dream of becoming a democratically developed nation will become a reality.

NOTES

1 Seymour Martin Lipset rightly points out that "the technologically advanced and wealthy democracies cannot impose their vision of democracy on the developing world. But they can create an international, political, and economic climate, and a structure of linkages and ties, that strengthen democratic leaders and groups in the Third World and so increase their chances of succeeding in building and sustaining democracy in their own nations." (See his "Building Democratic Institutions," in: **The Challenge of democracy: proceedings of a conference on efforts underway to advance the cause of democracy throughout the world**, sponsored by the National Endowment for Democracy (Washington, DC: The Endowment, 1987), p. 90.)

2 Charles Wright Ferguson, **A little democracy is a dangerous thing** (New York: Association Press, 1948).

3 Dr A. A. Nwafor Orizu expressed the same view thus: "Democracy is a principle of living; it is not a particular culture. Democracy adapts itself to particular cultures; it does not destroy them. For example, in political democracy there are essential basic principles which make any country politically democratic, though other differences may be seen in its practice which may depend on cultural differences.... In that sense, both America and England are democracies in principle, both their political culture and practices in some measure are not the same...." See the chapter on "The Democracy We Want," in his book: **Without Bitterness** (Enugu, Nigeria: Nwamife Publishers Ltd., 1980), pp. 214-215.

4 Dan Agbese, "Paths to Democracy," in: **Newswatch**, May 15, 1995, p. 10.

5 Adebayo Adedeji, "An Alternative for Africa," in: L. Diamond and M. F. Plattner, eds., **Economic Reform and Democracy** (Baltimore and London: The Johns Hopkins University Press, 1995), p. 134.

6 A. A. Nwafor Orizu, op. cit., p. 212.

7 Giovanni Sartori writes: "There is no doubt that the theory and practice of liberal democracy are a Western product rooted in Western history and culture. Thus as democracy is exported from the West to other areas and cultures we hear references made to 'cultural imperialism' and to a 'biased, Western-centric model.' But I do not think that ideas should be rejected on the basis of where they originated. That democracy is a Western invention does not entail that it is a bad invention, or a product suitable only for Western consumption.... I do recognize, however, that the prescription of democracy for non-Western areas confronts us with 'traveling issues.' First, can democracy be exported to any place, regardless of 'import conditions,' that is, of conditions in the importing countries? Second, can and should democracy be exported in *toto* and in its most advanced (Western) formulation, or should we first break the concept of liberal democracy down into its *necessary* (defining) and *contingent* (variable) elements?...." (See his "How far can free Government travel?" in: **Journal of Democracy**, vol. 6, no. 3, July 1995 (Baltimore: The John Hopkins University Press), p. 101.)

8 Cf. Boyd Henry Bode, **Democracy as a way of life** (New York: The Macmillan Company, 1937).

9 Quoted in A. A, Nwafor Orizu, op. cit., pp. 215f..

10 Cf. John Arkas Hawgood, **The Citizen and Government** (London: Nicholson & Watson, 1947), pp. 11-13.

11 Michael Novak, "Democracy and Human Rights," in: Peter L. Berger and Michael Novak, **Speaking to the Third World: Essays on Democracy and Development** (Washington, D.C.: American Enterprise Institute for Public Policy Research, c1985), pp. 43-44.

12 Ibid., p. 31.

13 Ibid., pp. 31f.

14 Cf. David Braybrooke, **Three Tests for Democracy: personal rights, human welfare, collective preference** (New York: Random House, 1968).

15 Cf. Anton Rauscher (Prof. Dr.), "Der Mensch ist Person", in his book: **Kirche in der Welt**, vol. 1, (Würzburg: Echter Verlag, 1988), p. 259; the same article could be found in the booklet **Katholische Soziallehre in Text und Kommentar**, vol. 1, (Köln: J. P. Bachem Verlag GmbH, 1975), p. 7.

16 Cf. R. Heckel, S.J., presenter, **The Social Teaching of John Paul II (Oct: 1978 - Nov. 1979): The Human Person and Social Structures** (Vatican City: Pontifical Commission "Iustitia et Pax," 1981 edition).

17 Ibid., p. 1.

18 Cf. Paul VI (Pope), Encyclical **Populorum Progressio** ("On the Development of Peoples"), 1967, No. 14, in: David J. O'Brien & Thomas A. Shannon, ed., **Catholic Social Thought: The Documentary Heritage** (Maryknoll, New York: Orbis Books, 1992), p. 243.

19 John Paul II (Pope), Encyclical **Sollicitudo Rei Socialis** ("On Social Concern"), 1987, No. 27, in: ibid., pp. 411-412.

20 The Gospel of St. Luke, 12: 15.

21 John Paul II, **Sollicitudo Rei Socialis**, No. 33, in: ibid., pp. 417-418. See also his address to the president and government leaders of Nigeria during his historic

visit to the country in 1982. He enjoined "all those entrusted with the well-being of their fellowman to make the human person the true criterion of all development efforts;" adding that development projects "cannot be reduced to a purely materialistic or economic endeavour," since "progress can therefore not be separated from the dignity of the human person nor from the respect of his or her fundamental rights." (See **L'Osservatore Romano**, March-April 1982, pp. 6-7.)

22 Arthrur Armstrong, **What do you know about Democracy? A guide for young people** (New York: Exposition Press, 1963), p. 48.

23 Ibid.

24 Mary Stewart Lyle, **Adult Education for Democracy in Family Life** (Ames, Iowa: The Collegiate Press, Inc., 1944), p. 3.

25 G. H. Sabine & T. L. Thorson, op. cit., pp. 68-69.

26 John XXIII (Pope), Encyclical **Pacem in Terris** ("Peace on Earth"), 1963, no. 13, in: David J. O'Brien & Thomas A. Shannon, ed., op. cit., p. 133.

27 Cf. G. H. Sabine & T. L. Thorson, op. cit., p. 103 (for Aristotle) and pp. 68-69 (for Plato).

28 Augustus Adebayo, op. cit., p. 27.

29 Prof. Sanya Onabamiro was (in 1979) the Chairman of the Implementation Committee, National Policy on Education. His suggestions were made in his article, "The Place and Role of Education in the Evolution of an Egalitarian Society," published in: **Report of Seminar on Nigeria in Transition** (Lagos: Federal Ministry of Education, 1980?), p. 96. His article as a whole is worth reading - pp. 89-96.

30 Ibid., pp. 93-94.

31 Vatican Council II, Pastoral Constitution **Gaudium et Spes** ("The Church in the Modern World"), 1965, no. 74, in: D. J. O'Brien & T. A. Shannon, ed., op. cit., p. 216.

32 Ibid.

33 Edward Schillebeeckx's book, **Weil Politk nicht alles ist - Von Gott reden in einer gefährdeten Welt** ("Because politics is not everything - Speaking about God in an endangered world") (Freiburg . Basel . Wien: Herder, 1987), is worth reading.

34 Michael Novak, op. cit., p. 43.

35 Vatican Council II, **Guadium et Spes**, no. 75, in: O'Brien and Shannon, ed., op. cit., p. 217.

36 Ibid., p. 218.

37 Cf. Felix Uche Onwukike, "True Leadership," in his unpublished bachelor's degree project in Theology: **Authority In Romans 13:1-7: An Exegetical Analysis** (Enugu, Nigeria: Bigard Memorial Seminary, 1984), pp. 61-65.

38 The Gospel of St. Matthew, 20: 24-28; cf. Mk. 10: 41-45 and Lk. 22: 24-27.

39 The Gospel of St. Mark, 9: 35, but read 9: 33-37.

40 The Gospel of St. John, 13: 12-15.

41 Cf. Emeka Odumegwu-Ojukwu, op. cit., pp. 56, 143-144.

42 Walter E. Boek, op. cit., p. 117.

43 See **Newswatch**, Oct. 10, 1994, p. 37.

44 See Eddie Iroh, "Worthy of the title," in: **Newswatch**, Feb. 15, 1993, p. 6.

45 See "America's changing of baton" in: **Newswatch**, Feb. 15, 1993, p. 42; cf. **Newswatch**, Nov. 16, 1992, p. 6. (Nigerian leaders should also borrow a leaf from the Bible: the encouragement from the outgoing Moses to the incoming Joshua, in Dt. 3: 23-29.)

46 To cite two examples from Germany: Jürgen Möllemann, Germany's Economic Minister, resigned on Jan. 3, 1993, because of abuse of office - the famous "Biefbogen Affäre". (Cf. **Augsburger Allgemeine**, Jan. 4, 1993, pp. 1 & 3.) And on accusation of misuse of public fund, the German Transport Minister, Günther Kraus, resigned from office on Thursday, May 6, 1993.

47 Felix Uche Onwukike, op. cit., pp. 46-51.

48 This injunction is biblical: "Be subject for the Lord's sake to every human institution, whether it be to the emperor as supreme, or to governors as sent by him to punish those who do wrong and to praise those who do right" (I Pet. 2: 13f.); "One must be subject, not only to avoid God's wrath but also for the sake of conscience" (Rom. 13: 2-5); and St. Paul admonishes theCchristians to pray "for kings and all who are in high positions" (I Tim. 2: 2); cf. **Gaudium et Spes**, no. 74.

49 **Gaudium et Spes**, no. 74.

50 **Joint Pastoral Letter of the Nigerian Catholic Bishops**, February 10, 1979, no. 9, pp. 5-6.

51 Quoted in: Peter Williamson and Kevin Perrotta, ed., **Christianity Confronts Modernity** (Michigan, U.S.A.: Servant Books, 1981), p. 206.

52 Mokwugo Okoye, **A Letter to Dr. Nnamdi Azikiwe** (Enugu, Nigeria: Fourth Dimension Pub. Co. Ltd., 1979), p. 79. (My brackets.)

53 Emeka Odumegwu-Ojukwu, op. cit., p. 91.

54 This is a lecture delivered by Nwafor Orizu at the Emy Cinema Hall, Aba, on Feb. 22, 1959, and published into a pamphlet in 1993 by the Nnewi-based Horizontal Publishers. But our source is **Newswatch**, March 29, 1993, pp. 14-15.

55 Emeka Odumegwu-Ojukwu, op. cit., pp. 91-93.

56 A. A. Nwafor Orizu, op. cit., pp. 221f..

57 I have treated earlier on the rule of law as one of the major principles of democracy. See part I, 3.5. of this work.

58 L. Stapleton, op. cit., p. 77.

59 Ibid.

60 W. E. Boek, op. cit., p. 123.

61 Ibid., pp. 234-135.

62 Ibid., p. 138.

63 L. Stapleton, op. cit., p. 96.

64 S. K. Padover, on "Presidential Statements On Law and Equality," op. cit., p. 13.

65 A. M. Bingham, op. cit., p. 44.

66 Nigerian government must do something to redeem the battered image of the Nigerian police. The police are so bad and corrupt that they have constituted themselves into a fear-and-terror-engendering-force rather a peacekeeping force. They extort money from the people; they brutalise the people; and some of them are even involved in armed robbery. You cannot just go to the police for help when you need one.

The government therefore must take immediate actions to redeem the image of the police force in Nigeria. First, the police force must be sanitised and purged of all bad eggs. The hand of the law should be used to discipline any policeman or policewoman who violates the rights of the people and/or who violates the law. Second, the police should be well paid. Till date, the salaries paid the Nigerian police is unsatisfactory. And third, much discipline should be introduced in the training of the Nigerian police; and then, once commissioned, they should be constantly and carefully supervised to make sure that the required discipline is maintained.

67 See my treatment of the judiciary as a necessary institution of democracy in part I, 4.4.

68 **The Federalist**, no. 47.

69 S. K. Padover, op. cit., p. xix.

70 It is a pity that in many countries the appointment of judges is done on political considerations and loyalties. Let us cite the US and the Great Britain as examples. J. R. Lewis writes: "while politics plays little or no part in the selection of Federal judges in the United States, this is not the case with the selection of state judges;" and in Britain, "though the judges are deemed to hold no political opinions in their official capacities, and should not allow political considerations to cloud their impartiality, the head of the judiciary in England is in fact the Lord Chancellor, a man who is appointed for his political leanings, and a man who will become an ex-Lord Chancellor when his party loses office, to be superseded by another." (J. R. Lewis, op. cit., p. 85.)

71 T. Roosevelt, **A Charter of Democracy** (Washington Govt. Print. Off., 1919), p. 19.

72 Ibid., pp. 83-84. Cf. T. L. Thorson, on the influence of environmental factors on the judges, in: H. M. Bishop et al., op. cit., pp. 87-88.

73 Egbuna Onyeagwa, "Ways Forward," in: **Newswatch**, Dec. 28, 1992, p. 4.

74 W. E. Boek, op. cit., p. 282.

75 Egbuna Onyeagwa, "Ways Forward," in: **Newswatch**, Dec. 28, 1992, p. 4.

76 W. E. Boek, op. cit., pp. 282f. (My brackets.)

77 Emeka Odumegwu-Ojukwu, op. cit., p. 11.

78 From General Sani Abacha's inauguration speech, "Insuring Democracy's Steady Growth," on June 27, 1994, during the inauguration of the Constitutional Conference. See "Country Profile/Advertisement: Nigeria" in: **Time**, No. 48, 28. Nov., 1994.

79 Ibid.

80 Cf. **Newswatch**, Dec. 14, 1992, pp. 14-18.

81 Ibid., p. 15. Dr Azikiwe's view is that "there should not be an immediate transfer of power to complete civilian rule, rather a *modus operandi* should be devised for a combined civilian and military government that should rule this country, on a democratic basis, for five years, after which period the continuation of such a regime should be reviewed in the light of experience and reason."

82 Ibid.

83 Ibid., pp. 15-16.

84 Niyi Osundare, "'No-Go' Legislators", in: **Newswatch**, Feb. 8, 1993, p. 34.

85 Olu Onuagoruwa, a constitutional lawyer, is opposed to diarchy because it is "an implicit acknowledgment that the military have a right to rule" and because "under constitu-

tional history, the military is a servant of the people (which) cannot govern and cannot share sovereign equality with the people." See **Newswatch**, Dec. 14, 1992, p. 17.

86 Emeka Odumegwu-Ojukwu, op. cit., p. 50.

87 Cf. Walter E. Boek (with the assistance of Hatten S. Yoder, Jr. ... et al.), **How to establish a democracy or improve the one you now have: A practical guide for developing essential government and business structures and personal systems of values** (Arlington, Va.: College of Democracy of National Graduate University, 1993), pp. 43-59.

88 The article, "Armed Forces and Democracy: Reforming Civil-Military Relations," by Samuel P. Huntington (Eaton Professor of the Science of Government and director of the John M. Olin Institute of Strategic Studies at Harvard University) is worth reading. See **Journal of Democracy**, Vol. 6, No. 4, Oct. 1995, pp. 9-17.

89 Walter E. Boek, op. cit., p. 58.

90 Vatican Council II, **Gaudium et Spes**, no. 63, in: O'Brien and Shannon, ed., op. cit., p. 208.

91 Cf. Jagdish Bhagwati, "The New Thinking on Development," in: **Journal of Democracy**, vol. 6, no. 4, Oct. 1995, pp. 50-64; Adam Przeworski, et al., "What makes democracies endure," in: **Journal of Democracy**, vol. 7, no. 1, Jan. 1996, pp. 39-55. Good articles in this regard are also found in: L. Diamond and M. F. Plattner, eds., **Economic Reform and Democracy** (Baltimore, U.S.A.: The Johns Hopkins University Press, 1995).

92 Adam Przeworski, et al., "What makes democracies endure," in: **Journal of Democracy**, vol. 7, no. 1, Jan. 1996, p. 41.

93 Larry Diamond and Juan Linz, "Introduction: Politics, Democracy, and Society in Latin America," in: Diamond, Linz; and Lipset, eds., **Democracy in Developing Countries: Latin America** (Boulder, Colo: Lynne Rienner, 1989).

94 Adam Przeworski, et al., op. cit., p. 42.

95 Ibid..

96 Vatican Council II, **Gaudium et Spes**, no. 64.

97 Walter E. Boek, op. cit., p. 28.

98 Ibid., p. 27.

99 Ibid., p. 36.

100 Ibid., p. 40.

101 For some interesting articles on "economic reform," see L. Diamond & M. F. Plattner, eds., **Economic Reform and Democracy** (Baltimore and London: John Hopkins University Press, 1995).

102 Adebayo Adedeji, "An Alternative for Africa," in: L. Diamond & M. F. Plattner, eds., **Economic Reform and Democracy** (Baltimore and London: John Hopkins University Press, 1995), pp. 126-127. Cf. Patricia Adams, "The World Bank and the IMF in sub-Saharan Africa: Undermining Development and Environmental Sustainability," in: **Journal of International Affairs**, vol. 46, no. 1, Summer 1992, pp. 97-118; and Richard Jeffries, "The State, Structural Adjustment and Good Government in Africa," in: **Journal of Commonwealth & Comparative Politics**, vol. 31, no. 1, (March 1993), pp. 20-35.

103 Ibid., p. 128.

104 Ibid., p. 127.

105 Ibid., p. 131.

106 Walter E. Boek, op. cit., p. 31.

107 John Paul II, Pope, the Encyclical **Laborem Exercens**, ("On Human Work"), 1981, no. 21. (My italics.)

108 John XXIII, Pope, **Mater et Magistra**, ("Christianity and Social Progress"), 1961, no. 123.

109 Ibid., no. 124.

110 John Paul II, Pope, **Laborem Exercens**, no. 21.

111 John XXIII, Pope, **Mater et Magistra**, no. 87.

112 Ibid., no. 128.

113 Ibid., no. 143.

114 Ibid.

115 Pope John Paul II's writing on the "Importance of Unions" is worth reading: see his Encyclical **Laborem Exercens**, no. 20; cf. Leo XIII, Pope, **Rerum Novarum**, ("On the Condition of Labour"), 1891, nos. 36, 38 and 42.

116 John XXIII, Pope, **Mater et Magistra**, no. 133.

117 W. E. Boek, op. cit., pp. 319f.

118 Ibid., pp. 331-333.

119 John XXIII, Pope, **Mater et Magistra**, no. 134.

120 Ibid., no. 137.

121 Ibid., no. 140.

122 Ibid., no. 135.

123 Ibid., no. 141.

124 W. E. Boek, op. cit., p. 347.

125 John XXIII, Pope, the Encyclical **Pacem in Terris**, nos. 18-20.

126 Two articles by Prof. Dr Anton Rauscher with regard to unemployment problems in Germany are worth reading: 1) "Arbeit für alle" ("Work for all") and "Die Arbeitsplätze sind der Schlüssel" ("Jobs are the key") in the booklet: **Kirche und Gesellschaft**, no. 207 and no. 226 respectively, edited by "Katholische Sozialwissenschaftlichen Zentralstelle Mönchengladbach (Köln: J. P. Bachem Verlag GmbH, 1994 and 1996 respectively).

127 John Paul II, Pope, the Encyclical **Laborem Exercens**, no. 18.

128 The Gospel of St. Luke, 10: 7.

129 John Paul II, Pope, **Laborem Exercens**, no. 19.

130 **Economic and Financial Review**, Vol. 13, No. 1, C.B.N., June, 1975, p. 13; cf. A. R. Mustapha, "Repression and the Nigerian Political Economy," in: A. S. Mohammed & T. Edoh, eds., op. cit., pp. 33-34.

131 Pius XI, Pope, the Encyclical **Quadragesimo Anno**, no. 71; cf. John XXIII, Pope, the Encyclical **Mater et Magistra**, nos. 68-72.

132 Leo XIII, Pope, the Encyclical **Rereum Novarum**, no. 34.

133 Cf. John XXIII, **Pacem in Terris**, nos. 11 & 64, and **Mater et Magistra**, no. 127.

134 Pope John XXIII writes: "Where these requirements for a dignified farm life are lacking to rural dwellers, economic and social progress does not occur at all, or else very slowly. Under such conditions, nothing can be done to keep men from deserting the fields, nor can anyone readily estimate their number." (See **Pacem in Terris**, nos. 11 & 64, and **Mater et Magistra**, no. 127.)

135 W. E. Boek, op. cit., p. 347.

136 Dr. A. A. Nwafor Orizu, op. cit., p. 219.

137 While the government stpulated maximum rent for rentage of three bedroom flat or apartment is N500.00 per month, the landlords charge between N1,000.00 and N2,000.00 per month. Not only this, the landlords demand that one pays this huge amount for two years in advance - plus other charges, like the payment of N2,000.00 "extra charge" to the association of landlords - ("cash down") before one could get the flat. Only one God knows how a civil servant with family, posted to work in the city, could cough out N48,000.00 + N2,000.00 (= N50,000.00) before he/she could get an apartment. There are many other ways in which the landlords misuse their rights and thus abuse the rights of their tenants: like ejecting the tenants without notice or without enough time to get another accommodation - both, without the tenants contravening any law; or like demanding some months rent (in advance) in one month because the landlord needs money to accomplish some business (within or without the premise). Therefore, as a matter of urgency, the government must step in to check and stop the many abuses of the "Shylock-landlords" and thereby protect the rights of the common man.

138 John XXIII, Pope, **Pacem in Terris**, no. 64.

139 John Paul II, Pope, **Laborem Exercens**, no. 19.

140 John Paul II, Pope, the Encyclical **Laborem Exercens**, no. 22.

141 John Paul II, Pope, Encyclical **Sollicitudo Rei Socialis**, no. 33.

142 The following two books are very good for the treatment of the common good: **Reconstructing the Common Good: Theology and the Social Order**, by Gary J. Dorrien (Maryknoll, New York: Orbis Books, 1992) and **Selbstinteresse und Gemeinwohl: Beiträge zur Ordnung der Wirtschaftsgesellschaft**, Soziale Orientierung Band 5, edited by Anton Rauscher (Berlin: Duncker & Humblot, 1985).

143 John XXIII, Pope, **Mater et Magistra**, no. 65.

144 John XXIII, Pope, **Pacem in Terris**, no. 60.

145 Ibid., no. 53; cf. his **Mater et Magistra**, no. 147.

146 John XXIII, Pope, **Pacem in Terris**, nos. 55-57.

147 John XXIII, Pope, **Mater et Magistra**, no. 79.

148 John XXIII, Pope, **Pacem in Terris**, no. 54.

149 **The Logic of Solidarity: Commentaries on Pope John Paul II's Encyclical "On Social Concern,"** edited by Gregory Baum and Robert Ellsberg (Maryknoll, New York: Orbis Books, 1989) is very good for the treatment of our subject.

150 John Paul II, Pope, **Sollicitudo Rei Socialis**, no. 39.

151 Cf. Ibid., no. 38.

152 W. E. Boek, op. cit., pp. 228-229.

153 Ibid., p. 232.

154 Emeka Odumegwu-Ojukwu, op. cit., p. xvi.

155 Ibid., p.24.

156 Cf. John Paul II, Pope, **Sollicitudo Rei Socialis**, no. 14.

157 Cf. Pius XI, Pope, **Quadrogesimo Anno**, no. 85: "... in these associations the common interest of the whole "group" must dominate: and among these interests the most important is the directing of the activities of the group to the common good...."

158 Ibid., no. 84.

159 J. O. Ojiako, op. cit., p. 180.

160 Ibid., p. 322.

161 Pius XI, Pope, **Quadragesimo Anno**, no. 81.

162 A. A. Nwafor Orizu, op. cit., pp. 213-214.

163 Donal Dorr, "Solidarity and Integral Human Development," in: Gregory Baum and Robert Ellsberg, eds., **The Logic of Solidarity: Commentaries on Pope John Paul II's Encyclical "On Social Concern"** (Maryknoll, New York: Orbis Books, 1989), pp. 146f.

164 Cf. Anton Rauscher, ed., **Selbstinteresse und Gemeinwohl: Beiträge zur Ordnung der Wirtschaftsgesellschaft**, Soziale Orientierung Band 5 (Berlin: Duncker & Humblot, 1985).

165 Peter Eigen, "Combatting Corruption around the World," in: **Journal of Democracy**, vol. 7, no. 1, Jan. 1996 (Baltimore: John Hopkins University Press), p. 161.

166 Ibid., pp. 161-162.

167 Ibid., p. 162.

168 Ibid..

169 John XXIII, Pope, **Mater et Magistra**, no. 51.

170 Pius XI, Pope, **Quadragesimo Anno**, nos. 79-80; cf. John XXIII, Pope, **Mater et Magistra**, no. 53.

171 Leo XIII, Pope, **Rerum Novarum**, no. 28.

172 John XXIII, Pope, **Mater et Magistra**, no. 52.

173 Leo XIII, Pope, **Rerum Novarum**, no. 29.

174 Stephen Brookfield, **Learning democracy: Eduard Lindeman on adult education and social change** (London; Wolfeboro, N.H.: Croom Helm, c1987), p. 166.

175 W. E. Boek, op. cit., p. 350.

176 For details, see Ernest Glenn Osborne, **Democracy begins in the Home** (New York: Public Affairs Committee, 1953); Christine Beasley, **Democracy in the Home** (New York: Association Press, 1954); David Gray Davis, **Parents and Democracy** (Toronto: The Ryerson Press, 1941); Mary Stewart Lyle, **Adult Education for Democracy in Family Life** (Ames, Iowa: The Collegiate Press, Inc., 1944). Walter E. Boek, **How to establish a Democracy or Improve the One You Now Have: A Practical Guide for Developing Essential Government and Business Structures and Personal Systems of Values** (Arlington, Va.: College of Democracy of National

Graduate University, 1993); Arthur Armstrong, **What do you know about democracy? A guide for young people** (New York: Exposition Press, 1963).

177 Cf. Arthur Armstrong, **What do you know about democracy? A guide for young people** (New York: Exposition Press, 1963), pp. 97-107.

178 Mary Stewart Lyle, **Adult Education for Democracy in Family Life** (Ames, Iowa: The Collegiate Press, Inc., 1944), p. 1.

179 Ernest Glenn Osborne, **Democracy begins in the Home** (New York: Public Affairs Committee, 1953), p. 4.

180 Jan Struther, "Democracy Begins at Home," in: **Adult Education Journal**, vol. I, no. 3 (July, 1942), p. 118.

181 Una Bernard Sait, **New Horizon for the Family**, p. 687.

182 Ibid., p. 745.

183 M. F. Nimkoff, **The Family**, p. ix.

184 Margaret Mead, "The Comparative Study of Culture and the Purposive Cultivation of Democratic Values," in: **Science, Philosophy and Religion**, p. 63.

185 H. Gordon Hullfish, "Education and Post War Economics," in: **Educational Research Bulletin**, XXI (Jan. 14, 1942), p. 4.

186 **Family Living and Our Schools**. Joint Yearbook, p. v.

187 Paul Popewor (of the American Institute of Family Relations), recommending E. Osborne's book, "Democracy begins in the Home," to parents, in: Ernest G. Osborne, op. cit., p. i.

188 W. E. Boek, op. cit., p. 178.

189 These three examples are adapted from Ernest G. Osborne, op. cit., pp. 1-2.

190 E. G. Osborne, op. cit., p. 3.

191 Ibid.

192 Ibid.

193 These four attitudes were posited by Christine Beasley, in her study, *At Home With Democracy*, cited in: Ernest Osborne, op. cit., p. 4.

194 E. G. Osborne, op. cit., p. 5.

195 Ibid., pp. 7-8.

196 Ibid., pp. 19-20.

197 Ibid., pp. 21-23.

198 Ibid., p. 9.

199 Ibid., pp. 10-11.

200 Cf. W. E. Boek, op. cit., pp. 82f.: "There needs to be a recognition on the part of parents that youth in a democracy, because of their formal education and their associations outside their families, will differ from their parents in their knowledge and understanding of issues and ways of solving problems."

201 E. G. Osborne, op. cit., p. 13.

202 Ibid., pp. 17-18.

203 Ibid., pp. 24-26.

204 Ibid., p. 23.

205 Ibid., pp. 26-27. (My brackets.)

206 Cf. ibid., p. 28.

207 Walter E. Boek, op. cit., pp. 83-84.

208 Emefie I. Metuh, Prof., **African Religions In Western Conceptual Schemes: The Problems of Interpretation** (Jos, Nigeria: Ehindero (Nigeria) Limited, 1991 edition), pp. 113-114.

209 Lambert U. Ejiofor, **Dynamics of Igbo Democracy: A Behavioural Analysis of Igbo Politics in Aguinyi Clan** (Ibadan, Nigeria: University Press Limited, 1981), p. 39.

210 Mary Stewart Lyle, op. cit., p. 20.

211 Ibid., pp. 20f.

212 Cf. Arthur Armstrong, **What do you know about Democracy? A guide for young people** (New York: Exposition Press, 1963); Colin Wringe, **Democracy, Schooling, and Political Education** (London; Boston: G. Allen & Unwin, 1984); Philadelphia Public Schools, **Our Schools: Beginnings in Democracy** (Philadelphia, 1941); Anne L. McGregor, **Living Democracy in Secondary Schools ...** (Washington: US Govt. Print. Off., 1941); John Lund, **Practicing Democracy in the College ...** (Washington: US Govt. Print. Off., 1942); Robert S. Sigel and Marilyn Hoskin, eds., **Education for Democratic Citizenship: A Challenge for Multi-ethnic Societies** (Hillsdale, N.J.: Lawrence Erlbaum Associates, 1991).

213 Amy Gutmann, **Democratic Education** (Princeton, N.J.: Princeton University Press, c1987), p. 287.

214 Arthur Armstrong, op. cit., p. 49.

215 Ibid.

216 Ibid., p. 51.

217 Ibid., pp. 55-56.

218 Ibid., p. 59.

219 Ibid., p. 67.

220 W. E. Boek, op. cit., p. 190.

221 Leo XIII, Pope, **Rerum Novarum**, no. 26, also no. 29; cf. Pius XI, Pope, **Quadragesimo Anno**, no. 25.

222 Ibid., no. 27.

223 John XXIII, Pope, **Pacem in Terris**, nos. 60 & 61.

224 Ibid., no. 62.

225 Ibid..

226 Ibid., no. 63.

227 Ibid., no. 69.

228 Cf. Vatican II, **Gaudium et Spes**, no. 40.

229 Leo XIII, Pope, **Rerum Novarum**, no. 23.

230 See, for example, **The Church and the Nigerian social problems : Memorandum of the Catholic Bishops of Nigeria** (Lagos: Catholic Secretariat of Nigeria, 1972); and **Joint Pastoral Letter of the Nigerian Catholic Bishops**, Feb. 10, 1979, no. 9.

231 Vatican Council II, **Gaudium et Spes**, no. 76.

232 Cf. Donal Dorr, **Option for the Poor** (Maryknoll, New York: Orbis Books); see also his **The Social Justice Agenda : Justice, Ecology, Power and the Church** (Maryknoll, N.Y.: Orbis Books, 1991).

233 Paul VI, Pope, Encyclical **Octogesima Adveniens** ("A Call to Action on the Eightieth Anniversary of Rerum Novarum"), 1971, no. 20.

234 Walter E. Boek, op. cit., pp. 97-98.

235 Judith Lichtenberg, ed., **Democracy and the Mass Media** (Cambridge . New York . et al. : Cambridge University Press, 1990), p. 1.

236 The Gospel of St. Luke, 11: 17-18.

237 Note Tunji Olagunju's observation: "The demonstration of a Nigerian community and commitment to that community has been relatively minimal or at least uneasy. The experience before the war showed clearly that the large majority of the socially mobilised people was more willing to sacrifice the interests of the national community for those of the person and immediate groups. The history of political institutions in this country attests to the fact that the interests of individuals and groups have tended to take precedence over the interests of the country as a whole." (See his article, "Transition to the Second Experiment - Some Political Issues," in: Sam E. Oyovbaire, op. cit., pp. 35f.)

238 T. A. Imobighe, "Chasing the Shadow: The Illusory Battle for Law, Order and Security in Nigeria," in: A. S. Mohammed & T. Edoh, eds., op. cit., p. 55.

239 Ibid., p. 60.

240 J. J. Oluleye, Major-General, op. cit., pp. 211f.

241 This attitude has forced some Nigerian traders to resort to an unholy act of putting foreign labels on their home-made goods, in order to compel the foreign-good-fanatics to buy these goods.

242 T. A. Imobighe, op. cit., p. 42.

243 Prof. E. A. Ayandele, "Evolving the New Nigerian Society," in: **Report of the Seminar on Nigeria In Transition** (Lagos: Federal Ministry of Information, 1980?), p. 64.

244 General Olusegun Obasanjo, "The Demise of the Rule of Law in Nigeria under the Military: Another point of view," in: F. Shyllon and O. Obasanjo, op. cit., pp. 32-33.

245 Leo XIII, Pope, **Rerum Novarum**, no. 35.

246 Cf. The Gospel of St. Luke 11: 23.

247 Quoted in: J. O. Ojiako, op. cit., p. 11. (My brackets.)

248 Ibid., p. 17. (My brackets.)

249 Olin Robinson, in: **The Challenge of democracy: proceedings of a conference on efforts underway to advance the cause of democracy throughout the world**, sponsored by the National Endowment for Democracy (Washington, D.C.: The Endowment, 1987), p. 83.

250 S. G. Ikoku, "Party Politics in the New Nigeria," in: **Report of the Seminar on Nigeria In Transition** (Lagos: Federal Ministry of Information, 1980?), pp. 75-76.

BIBLIOGRAPHY

Books

Achebe C., **The Trouble with Nigeria** (Enugu, Nigeria: Fourth Dimension Publishing Co. Ltd., 1983).

Achike O., **Groundwork of Military Law and Military Rule in Nigeria** (Yugoslavia: Fourth Dimension Publishers, 1980).

Achu K., **Nigeria** (New York: Bookwright Press, 1992).

Adamolekun L, **Public Administration: A Nigerian and Comparative Perspective** (New York, USA: Longman Inc., 1986).

Ade J. F. & Ikara B., eds., **Evolution of Political Culture in Nigeria** (Ibadan: UPL and KSCAC, 1985).

Adebayo A., **Power in Politics** (Ibadan, Nigeria: Spectrum Books Limited, 1986).

Adedeji A., "An Alternative for Africa," in: L. Diamond & M. F. Plattner, eds., **Economic Reform and Democracy** (Baltimore and London: The Johns Hopkins University Press, 1995).

Ademoyega A., **Why We Struck** (Nigeria: Evan Brothers (Nigerian Publishers) Ltd., 1981).

Adigwe H., **Nigeria Joins the Organisation of Islamic Conference, O.I.C.: the Implications for Nigeria** (Onitsha, Nigeria: Archdiocesan Secretariat, Catholic Archdiocese of Onitsha, 1986).

Afigbo E. A., **The Warrant Chiefs: Indirect Rule in Southern Nigeria, 1891-1929** (London: Longmans, 1972).

Agbaje A. A. B., **The Nigerian Press, Hegemony, and the Social Construction of Legitimacy, 1960-1983** (Lewiston: E. Mellen Press, 1992).

Ajayi J. F. A. & Espie I., eds., **A Thousand Years of West African History**, (Ibadan, Nigeria: Ibadan University Press and Nelson, 1981).

Ajayi J. F. A., **The Problems of National Integration in Nigeria: A Historic Perspective** (Ibadan: Nigerian Institute of Social and Economic Research, 1984).

Ake C., "Rethinking African Democracy," in: L. Diamond & M. F. Plattner, eds., **The Global Resurgence of Democracy** (Baltimore and London: The Johns Hopkins University Press, 1993).

Akinyemi A. B., **Foreign Policy and Federalism** (Ibadan, Nigeria, 1974).

Akpan N. U., **The Struggle for Secession** (London: Frank Cass, 1972).

Aliyu A. Y., ed., **Return to Civilian Rule** (Zaria, Nigeria: The Institute of Administration, Ahmadu Bello University, Zaria, 1982).

Ambedka B. R., **Conditions Precedent For The Successful Working Of Democracy** (Nagpur: Y. M. Panchbhai, 1976).

Arendt H., **On The Human Condition** (Chicago: University of Chicago Press, 1958).

Arikpo A., **Who Are the Nigerians?** (Lagos, 1958).

Armijo L. E., et al., "The Problems of Simultaneous Transitions," in: L. Diamond and M. F. Plattner, eds., **Economic Reform and Democracy** (Baltimore and London: The Johns Hopkins University Press, 1995), p. 226-240.

Armstrong A., **What do you know about Democracy? A guide for young people** (New York: Exposition Press, 1963).

Atanda J. A. & Aliyu A. Y., eds., **Proceedings of the National Conference on Nigeria Since Independence**, vol. 1, (Zaria, Nigeria: Gaskiya Corporation Ltd., 1983).

Awolowo O., **Path to Nigerian Freedom** (London: Faber & Faber, 1947).

Awolowo O., **The People's Republic** (Ibadan: OUP, 1968).

Awolowo O., **The Problem of Africa: The Need for Ideological Reappraisal - Kwame Nkruma Memorial Lectures** (London: Macmillan for University of Cape Coast, 1977).

Awolowo O., **Voice of Reason: Selected Speeches of Chief Obafemi Awolowo, Vol. 1** (Akure, Nigeria: Fagbamigbe Publishers, 1981).

Awolowo O., **Voice of Courage: Selected Speeches of Chief Obafemi Awolowo, Vol. 2** (Akure, Nigeria: Fagbamigbe Publishers, 1981).

Awolowo O., **Voice of Wisdom: Selected Speeches of Chief Obafemi Awolowo, Vol. 3** (Akure, Nigeria: Fagbamigbe Publishers, 1981).

Ayandele E. A., **The Missionary Impact on Modern Nigeria 1842-1914: A Political and Social Analysis** (London: Longman, 1966).

Azikiwe N., **Political Blueprint of Nigeria** (Lagos, Nigeria, 1943).

Azikiwe N., **Development of Political Parties in Nigeria** (London, 1957).

Azikiwe N., **Zik: A Selection From the Speeches of** (London: CUP, 1961).

Babatope E., **Nigeria, "Elections 1979": The Betrayal of a Nation** (Ibadan, Nigeria: Deto Deni Productions, 1979).

Barker E., Sir, **Greek Political Theory, Plato And His Predecessors**, 5th. ed. (London: Metheien & Co. Ltd., 1977).

Barret L., **Danjuma: The Making of a General** (Enugu, Nigeria: Fourth Dimension Publishers Co. Ltd., 1979).

Bascom W. R. & Herskovits M. J., eds., **Continuity and Change in African Cultures** (Chicago: University of Chicago Press, 1958).

Basden G. T., **Niger Ibos** (London, 1968).

Baum G. & Ellsberg R., eds., **The Logic of Solidarity: Commentaries on Pope John Paul II's Encyclical "On Social Concern"** (Maryknoll, N.Y.: Orbis Books, 1989).

Baum G. & Coleman J., eds., **The Church and Christian Democracy** (Edinburgh: Concilium and T. & T. Clark Ltd., 1987).

Beasley C., **Democracy in the Home** (New York: Association Press, 1954).

Bechtold H. R., ed., **Aspects of Democracy** (Freeport, New York: Books for Libraries Press, 1968).

Bello A., Alhaji, **My Life** (London: Cambridge University Press, 1962).

Berger P. L. and Novak M., **Speaking to the Third World: Essays on Democracy and Development** (Washington, D.C.: American Enterprise Institute for Public Policy Research, c1985).

Bishop H. M. and Hendel S., eds., **Basic Issues of American Democracy: A Book of Readings**, 6th. ed., (New York: Appleton-Century Crofts, 1970).

Bode B. H., **Democracy as a way of life** (New York: The Macmillan Company, 1937).

Boek W. E., **How to Establish a Democracy or Improve the One You Now Have - A Practical Guide for Developing Essential Government and Business Structures and Personal Systems of Values** (Arlington, Va.: College of Democracy of National Graduate University, 1993).

Bossman W., **A New Accurate Description of the Coast of Guinea** (Translated from Dutch and printed in London, 1705).

Bottke W. & Rauscher A., eds., **Gerechtigkeit als Aufgabe: Interdisziplinäres Gespräch über ein zentrales Problem der Rechts-, Wirtschafts- und Sozialethik** (St. Ottilien: EOS Verlag Erzabtei, 1990).

Braybrooke D., **Three Tests for Democracy: personal rights, human welfare, collective preference** (New York: Random House, 1968).

Bryson L., et al., eds., **Aspects of Human Equality** (New York: Harper, 1956).

Buhari M., Major-Gen., **Text of an Address to a World Press Conference** (Lagos, Jan. 5, 1984).

Burns A., Sir, **History of Nigeria** (London, 1972).

Busia K. A., **Africa in search of Democracy** (London: Routledge & Kegan Paul, 1967).

Callaghy T., "Africa: Back to the Future?," in: L. Diamond & M. F. Plattner, eds., **Economic Reform and Democracy** (Baltimore and London: The Johns Hopkins University Press, 1995).

Cameron D., **Principles of Native Administration and their Application** (Lagos, Nigeria, 1934).

Carlyle R. W. & Carlyle A. J., **A Hisory of Medieval Political Theory In The West** (Edinburgh & London: William Blackwood & Sons Ltd., 1928), esp. vols. 5 & 6.

Carpenter A., **Nigeria** (Chicago: Children's Press, c1978).

Carrier H., S.J., **The Social Doctrine of the Church Revisited: A Guide for Study** (Vatican City: Pontificium Consilium de Iustitia et Pace, 1990).

Carrier H., **Gospel Message and Human Cultures from Leo XIII to John Paul II**, translated by John Drury (Pittsburg, Pennsylvania: Dusquesne University Press, 1989).

Carter L. B., **The Quiet Athenian** (Oxford: Clarendon Press, 1986).

Cervenka Z., **A History of the Nigerian War, 1967-1970** (Ibadan, Nigeria: Onibonoje Press, 1972).

Chabal P., ed., **Political Domination in Africa: Reflections on the Limits of Power** (Great Britain: Cambridge University Press, 1986)

Civil Liberties Organisation, **Executive Lawlessness in the Babangida Regime: A Report of the Civil Liberties Organistion** (Lagos, Nigeria: Civil Liberties Organisation, 1991).

Clark J. M., K.C. (President of the Royal Canadian Institute) in his work, **The Reign of Law** (Toronto: University of Toronto Press, 1918).

Cohen B., **The Press and Foreign Policy** (Princeton: Princeton University Press, 1963).

Coleman J. A., S.J., ed., **One Hundred Years of Catholic Social Thought: Celebration and Challenge** (Maryknoll, New York: Orbis Books, 1991).

Commager H. S., **Majority Rule and Minority Rights** (New York: P. Smith, 1950, c.1943).

Connor W. R., et al., eds., **Aspects Of Athenian Democracy**, with a preface by J. Rufus Fears (Copenhagen: Museum Tusculanum Press, 1990).

Corbett P., **Ideologies** (London: Hutchinson & Co. (Publishers) Ltd., 1970).

Cram R. A., **The Nemesis of Mediocrity** (Boston: Marshal Jones Company, 1919).

Crowder M., **The Story of Nigeria** (London: Faber and Faber, 1962).

Dahl R. A., **A Preface to Democratic Theory** (Chicago: University of Chicago Press, c1956).

Dahl R. A., **Democracy And Its Critics** (New Haven & London: Yale University Press, 1989).

Danopoulos C. P., ed., **Civilian Rule in the Developing World: Democracy on the march?** (Boulder: Westview Press, 1992).

Davis D. G., **Parents and Democracy** (Toronto: The Ryerson Press, 1941).

Diamond L. and Plattner M. F., eds., **Economic Reform and Democracy** (Baltimore and London: The Johns Hopkins University Press, 1995).

Diamond L. J., **Class, Ethnicity, and Democracy in Nigeria: The Failure of the First Republic** (Syracuse, N.Y.: Syracuse University Press, 1988).

Diamond L., "Nigeria's Perennial Struggle," in: L. Diamond & M. F. Plattner, eds., **The Global Resurgence of Democracy** (A Journal of Democracy Book. Baltimore and London: The John Hopkins University Press, 1993).

Dike K. O., **100 Years of British Rule in Nigeria, 1851-1951** (Lagos, 1957).

Dike K. O., **Trade and Politics in the Niger Delta, 1830-1885** (Oxford, 1962).

Dimock M. & Hyde H. K., **Bureaucracy and Trusteeship in Large Corporations** (T.N.E.C. monograph, 1940).

Directorate for Social Mobilisation, **Report of the Political Bureau, March 1987** (Abuja, Nigeria: Directorate for Social Mobilisation (MAMSER), Council Secretariat, 1987).

Directorate for Social Mobilisation, **Political Education Manual: Towards a Free and Democratic Society** (Abuja, Nigeria: Directorate for Social Mobilisation, 1989).

Dorr D., **The Social Justice Agenda: Justice, Ecology, Power and the Church** (Maryknoll, New York: Orbis Books, 1991).

Dorrien G. J., **Reconstucting the Common Good: Theology and the Social Order** (Maryknoll, New York: Orbis Books, 1992).

Durujaiye O. O., **Nigeria Tomorrow: My Vision and Mission** (Nigeria: O. O. Durujaiye, 1992).

Eddy W. H. C., ed., **Studies in Democracy** (Melbourne, Canberra, etc.: Cheshire, 1966).

Ejiofor L. U., **Dynamics of Igbo Democracy: A Behavioural Analysis of Igbo Politics in Aguinyi Clan** (Ibadan, Nigeria: University Press Limited, 1981).

Elias B., **Democracy and the Majority Principle** (Goteborg, Sweden: Akademiforlaget, 1965).

Ellwein T., **Politische Verhaltenslehre** (Stuttgart, 1964).

Enahoro P., **How to be a Nigerian** (Ibadan, Nigeria: The Caxton Press (West Africa) Ltd., 1981).

English M. C., **An Outline of Nigerian History** (London, 1959).

Ezera K., **Constitutional Developments in Nigeria** (London, 1960).

Falola T. & Ihonvbere J., **The Rise and Fall of Nigeria's Second Republic, 1979-84** (London: Zed Books Ltd., 1985).

Farrar C., **The Origins of Democratic Thinking: The Invention of Politics in Classical Athens** (Cambridge: Cambridge University Press, 1988).

Federal Government of Nigeria, **The Federal Government Guidelines on Local Government Reforms** (Kaduna: Government Printer, 1975).

Federal Ministry of Information, **Report of the Seminar on Nigeria in Transition: A Critical Examination of the main Political, Economic and Social Aspects of the Nigerian Society** (Lagos, Nigeria: Federal Ministry of Information, 1980).

Ferguson C. W., **A little democracy is a dagerous thing** (New York: Association Press, 1948).

Filibeck G., **The Social Teaching of John Paul II: Human Rights** (Vatican City: Pontifical Commission "Iustitia et Pax", 1983 edition).

Finley M. I., **Democracy: Ancient and Modern** (New Bruswick: Rutgers University Press, (1973) 1985).

Finley M. I., ed., **Studies in Ancient Society** (London and Boston, 1974).

Flannery A., O.P., ed., **Vatican Council II: The Conciliar and Post Conciliar Documents** (Northport, New York: Costello Publishing Company, 1987 edition).

Ford D. & Jones G. I., **The Ibo and Ibibio-speaking Peoples of South Eastern Nigeria** (London: International African Institute, 1950).

Frankel C., **The Democratic Prospect** (New York, 1962).
Friedrich C. J., **Der Verfassungsstaat der Neuzeit** (Berlin-Göttingen-Heidelberg, 1953).
Frisch M. J. & Stevens R. G., eds., **American Political Thought** (New York: Charles Scribner's Sons, 1971).
Gailey H. A., **The Road to Aba: A Study of British Administrative Policy in Eastern Nigeria** (New York: New York University Press, 1970).
Gante M., **§ 218 in der Diskussion: Meinungs- und Willensbilding 1945-1976** (Düsseldorf: Droste Verlag GmbH, 1991).
Gibbon P., et al., eds., **Authoritarianism, democracy, and adjustment: The politics of economic reform in Africa** (Uppsala: Scandinavian Institute of African Studies, 1992).
Gibbs J. L., ed., **Peoples of Africa** (New York: holt, Rinehart and Winston, 1965).
Giovani S., **The Theory of Democracy Revisited** (New Jersey: Chatham House Publishers, Inc., 1987).
Graham K., **The Battle of Democracy: Conflict, Consensus and Individual** (Great Britain: Wheatsheaf Books, 1986).
Green M. M., **Ibo Village Affairs** (London: Sidgwick & Jackson, 1947).
Gremillion J., **The Gospel of Peace and Justice: Catholic social teaching since Pope John** (Maryknoll, N.Y.: Orbis Books, c1976).
Gutmann A., **Democratic Education** (Princeton, N.J.: Princeton University Press, c1987).
Hailey L., **Native Administration in British African Territories,** 5 vols. (London, 1951).
Hansen M. H., **The Sovereignty of the People's Court in the Fourth Century B.C. and the Public Action against Unconstitutional Proposals** (Odense, 1974).
Hansen M. H., **The Athenian Ecclesia: A Collection of Articles, 1976-83** (Copenhagen: Museum Tusculum Press, 1983).
Hansen M. H., **The Athenian Democracy in the Age of Demosthenes: Structure, Principles and Ideology** (Oxford: Blackwell, 1991).
Hättich M., **Demokratie als Herrschaftsordnung** (Köln-Opladen, 1967).
Hawgood J. A., **The Citizen and Government** (London: Nicholson & Watson, 1947).
Heckel R., SJ, **The Social Teaching of John Paul II: The Human Person and the Social Structures** (Vat. City, Rome: Pontifical Commission "Iustitia et Pax", 1981 edition).
Held D., **Models Of Democracy** (UK: Polity Press, 1987).
Henriot P. J., et al., **Catholic Social Teaching: Our Best Kept Secret**, Centenary edition (Maryknoll, New York: Orbis Books, 1992).
Hobbes T., **Leviathan**, Introduction by A. D. Lindsay (N. Y.: Dulton & Co., 1950).

Hobbes T., **Thucydides' History**, ed. by Richard Schlatter (New Bruswick: Rutgers University Press, (1627) 1975).

Holden B., **The Nature of Democracy** (London: Nelson, 1974).

Holmes P., **Nigeria: Giant of Africa** (Lagos: National Oil and Chemical Marketing Co. of Nigeria, 1985).

Holt A. E., **Christian Roots of Democracy in America** (New York: Friendship Press, 1941).

Hume D., **Essays: Moral, Political, and Literary** (Oxford: Oxford University Press, 1963).

Ibekwe W., et al., eds., **The Great Debate (Nigerian Viewpoints on the Draft Constitution)** (Lagos, Nigeria: Daily Times of Nigeria, 1979?).

Ihonvbere J. O., **The 1983 Elections and the Buhari Coup in Nigeria: Contradictions in a (Semi-) Peripheral Political Economy** (Halifax, N.S., Canada: Centre for African Studies, Dalhousie University, 1985).

Ikoku S. G., **Nigeria's Fourth Coup d'etat: Options for Modern Statehood** (Enugu, Nigeria: Fourth Dimension Pub. Co. Ltd., 1985).

Institute for Religious and Social Studies, Jewish Theological Seminary of America, **Foundations of democracy**, (New York: Cooper Square Publishers, 1964).

Irving C., **Public Opinion, Polls, and Democracy** (Boulder, Colo: Westview Press, 1989).

Isichei E., **A History of the Igbo People** (London and Basingstoke: MacMillan Press Ltd., 1976).

Jemibewon D. M., **A Combatant in Government** (Nigeria: Heinemann Education Books (Nig.) Ltd., 1979).

John Paul II, Pope, **Crossing the Threshold of Hope**, ed. by Vittorio Messori (New York: Alfred A. Knopf, 1994).

Jones A. H. M., **Athenian Democracy** (Oxford: Basil Blackwell, 1975).

Jones G. H., **Christianity and world democracy** (New York, Cincinnati: The Methodist Book Concern, c1918).

Joseph R., "Africa: The Rebirth of Political Freedom," in: L. Diamond & M. F. Plattner, eds., **The Global Resurgence of Democracy** (A Journal of Democracy Book. Baltimore and London: The John Hopkins University Press, 1993).

Kagan D., **Pericles of Athens and the Birth of Democracy** (New York: The Free Press, 1991).

Katholische Arbeitnehmer-Bewegung (KAB) Deutschland, **Texte zur katholischen Soziallehre: Die sozialen Rundschreiben der Päpste und andere kirchliche Dokumente**, mit einer Einführung von Oswald von Nell-Breuning, S.J., 5. erweiterte Auflage (Kevelaer: Bercker, Graphischer Betrieb GmbH, 1982).

Kennedy G., **The Military in the Third World** (London: Gerald Duckworth & Co. Ltd., 1974).

Ketchum R. M., ed., **What is democracy?** - with an introduction by Grayson Kirk (New York: Dutton, 1968).

Kirk-Green A. H. M., **Lugard and the Amalgamation of Nigeria: Documentary Record** (London, 1968).

Kirk-Green A. H. M., **Crisis and Conflict in Nigeria: A Documentary Sourcebook 1966-1969**, vol. 1 (London. New York. Ibadan: OUP, 1971).

Kirk-Green A. H. M., **Crisis and Conflict in Nigeria,** vol. I (London: Oxford University Press, 1971).

Kirk-Greene A. H. M., **Crisis and Conflict in Nigeria,** vol. II (London: Oxford University Press, 1971).

Kreisberg A., **The ABC of Democracy** (New York: Philosophical Library Inc., 1943).

Kurfi A., **The Nigerian General Elections 1959 and 1979 and the aftermath** (Lagos, Nigeria:MacMillan Nigeria, 1983).

Larson J. A. O., **Representative Government In Greek And Roman History** (Berkeley & Los Angeles: University of California Press, 1966).

Laufer H., **Die demokratische Ordnung** (Stuttgart-Berlin-Köln-Mainz, 1966).

Lecheler H., **Das Subsidiaritätsprinzip: Strukturprinzip einer europäischen Union**, Soziale Orientierung, Band 8, herausgegeben von Anton Rauscher (Berlin: Duncker & Humblot, 1993).

Levy P. M., **Nigeria** (New York: Marshall Cavendish, c1993).

Lewis J. R., **Democracy: The Theory and Practice** (London: Allman, 1966).

Lichtenberg J., ed., **Democracy and the Mass Media - A collection of essays** (New York: Cambridge University Press, 1990).

Linsday A. D., **The Essentials of Democracy** (Philadelphia: University of Pennsylvania Press, 1929).

Lippmann W., **The Phantom Public** (New York: The Macmillan Co., 1927).

Locke J., **Two Treatises of Government** (New York: Mentor, 1965).

Löwenstein K., **Verfassungslehre** (Tübingen, 1959).

Luckham R., **The Nigerian Military: A Sociological Analysis of Authority and Revolt, 1960-67** (London: Cambridge University Press, 1971).

Lugard F. D., **Report on the Amalgamation of Northern and Southern Nigeria and Administration** (London, 1920).

Lund J., **Practical democracy in the college ...** (Washington: U.S. Govt. Print. Off., 1942).

Lyle M. S., **Adult Education for Democracy in Family Life** (Ames, Iowa: The Collegiate Press, Inc., 1944).

Macdonald J., **The Corner Stone of Democracy** (Toronto: The Ryerson Press, 1939).

MacIver R. M., **The Web of Government** (New York: The Macmillan Co., 1947).

MacIver R. M., **The Ramparts We Guard** (N. Y.: The Macmillan Co., 1950).

Macpherson C. B., **The Real World of Democracy** (Oxford: Clarendon Press, 1966).

McGregor A. L., **Living democracy in secondary schools ...** (Washington, D.C.: U.S. Govt. Print. Off., 1941).

Madiebo A. A., **The Nigerian Revolution and the Biafran War** (Enugu, Nigeria: Fourth Dimension Publishers Co. Ltd., 1980).

Maritain J., **Christianity And Democracy & The Right of Man And Natural Law**, trans. by Doris C. Anson (San Fracisco: Ignatius Press, 1986).

Messner J., **Der Staat**, in: **Politische-Theoretische Reihe**, Band 2, ed. by Leo Schütze and Konrad Bonkosch (Bonn: R + S-Verlag, 1978).

Metuh E. I., **African Religions In Western Conceptual Schemes: The Problems of Interpretation** (Jos, Nigeria: Ehindero (Nigeria) Limited, 1991).

Metz H. C., ed., **Nigeria: A Country Study** (Wahington, D.C., 1992).

Mgbeahurike R. E., **The Ethical Challenges of Constant Military Intervention in Nigerian Politics to Nigerian Politics - Studies in the Political Ethics of Nigeria from 1960-1989** (Roma: N. Domenici-Pe´cheux, 1989).

Mill J. S., **Essays on Politics and Society** (Toronto: University of Toronto Press, 1977).

Mill J. S., **Three Essays**, with an introduction by Richard Wollheim (Oxford . New York: Oxford University Press, 1989 edition).

Milton J., "Areopagitica" (1644), in: **Complete Prose Works** (New Haven, Conn.: Yale University Press, 1959), vol. 2.

Mitford W., **The History of Greece** (London: t. Cadell, Strand, (1829) 1838).

Mohammed A. S. & Edoh T., eds., **Nigeria: A Republic in Ruins** (Zaria, Nigeria: Dept. of Political Science, 1986).

Morel E. D., **Nigeria: Its people and Problems** (London, 1912).

Murphy W., Msgr., **The Social Teaching of John Paup II: The Person, the Nation and the State** (Vatican City: Pontifical Commission "Iustitia et Pax", 1982 edition).

National Endowment for Democracy, **The challenge of democracy: Proceedings of a conference on efforts underway to advance the cause of democracy throughout the world, Monday and Tuesday, May 18 and 19, 1987, Rayburn House Office Building, Washington, D.C.** (Washington, D.C.: The Endowment, 1987).

National Institute for Policy and Strategic Studies, Kuru, **Round-Table Meeting on Ethnicity in Nigeria: Implications for National Development** (Kuru, Nigeria: National Institute for Policy and Strategic Studies, 1983).

National Institute for Policy and Strategic Studies, Kuru, **Round-Table Meeting on the 1983 General Elections** (Kuru, Nigeria: National Institute for Policy and Strategic Studies, 1983).

Nearing S., **Democracy Is Not Enough** (New York: Island Workshop Press, 1945).

Ngwoke B. I., **Islam, the O.I.C. and Nigerian Unity** (Enugu, Nigeria: I. Ngwoke, 1986).

Niven C. R., **A Short History of Nigeria** (London, 1937).

Niven R., Sir, **The War of Nigerian Unity** (Nigeria: Evans Brothers (Nigeria Publishers) Ltd., 1970).

Njaka E. N., **Igbo Political Culture**(Evanston: Northwestern University Press, 1974).

Nnoli O., **Ethnic Politics in Nigeria** (Enugu, Nigeria: Fourth Dimension Publishers, 1978).

Nwabueze B. O., **Military Rule and Constitutionalism in Nigeria** (Ibadan. Owerri. Kaduna. Lagos: Spectrum Law Publishing, 1992).

Nwabueze B. O., **The Presidential Constitution of Nigeria** (London, UK: C. Hurst & Co. (Publishers) Ltd., in association with Nwamife Publishers Ltd., Enugu, Nigeria, 1982).

Nwankwo A., **Nigeria: The Challenge of Biafra** (London: Rex Collins, 1972).

Nwankwo A., **Retreat of Power: The Military in Nigeria's Third Republic** (Enugu, Nigeria: Fourth Dimension Publishing Co. Ltd., 1990).

Nwankwo A., **Nigeria. Political Danger Signals** (Enugu, Nigeria: Fourth Dimension Publishing Co. Ltd., 1991).

Nwankwo A. A., **Nigeria: The Political Transition and the Future of Democracy** (Enugu, Nigeria: Fourth Dimension Publishing Co. Ltd., 1993).

Nzimiro I., **Studies in Igbo Political System: Chieftaincy and Politics in 4 Niger States** (London, 1972).

Obasanjo O., **A March of Progress: Collected Speeches of His Excellency, Lt. General O. Obasanjo** (Lagos: Federal Ministry of Information, n.d.).

Obasanjo O., General, **My Command** (Nigeria: Heinemann Educational Books (Nig.) Ltd., 1980).

O'Brien D. J. & Shannon T. A., eds., **Catholic Social Thought: The Documentary Heritage** (Maryknoll, New York: Orbis Books, 1992).

Odinamadu B. O., **Politics and Igbo Elites** (Ibadan, 1979).

Odumegwu-Ojukwu E., **Because I am involved** (Ibadan. Owerri. Kaduna: Spectrum Books Ltd., 1989).

Ojiako J. O., **Nigeria: Yesterday, Today, And...** (Onitsha, Nigeria: African Educational Publishers (Nig.) Ltd., 1981).

Ojiako J. O., **First Four Years of Nigeria Executive Presidency: Success or Failure?** (1983).

Okoye M., **A Letter to Dr. Nnamdi Azikiwe** (Enugu, Nigeria: Fourth Dimension Pub. Co. Ltd., 1979).

Olukoshi A. O., ed., **The Politics of Structural Adjustment in Nigeria** (London: J. Currey; Ibadan: Portsmouth; N.H.: Heinemann, 1993).

Oluleye J. J., Major-Gen., **Military Leadership in Nigeria, 1966-1979** (Ibadan, Nigeria: University Press Limited, 1985).

Oniororo N., **Nigeria's Future: Revolution Not Reformation** (Lagos, Nigeria: Nigerian Council of National Awareness, 1980).

Onwubiko K. B. C., **School Certificate History of West Africa, AD 1000-1800,** Books One & Two (Onitsha, Nigeria: Africana-Fep Publishers Limited, c1985).

Onwukike F. U., **Authority In Romans 13:1-7: An Exegetical Analysis**, unpublished bachelor's degree project in Theology (Enugu, Nigeria: BMS, 1984).

Orizu Nwafor A. A, **Without Bitterness** (Enugu, Nigeria: Nwamife Publishers Ltd., 1980).

Osborne E. G., **Democracy begins in the Home** (New York: Public Affairs Committee, 1953).

Otite O., **Ethnic Pluralism and Ethnicity in Nigeria: With Comparative Materials** (Ibadan, Nigeria: Shaneson, 1990).

Oyediran O., ed., **The Nigerian 1979 Elections** (Illupeju, Lagos, Nigeria: Macmillan Nigeria, 1981).

Oyediran O., ed., **Nigerian Government and Politics under Military Rule, 1966 - 79** (London: Macmillan Publishers, 1984).

Oyejide T. A., et al., **Nigeria and the IMF** (Ibadan: Heinemann Educational Books (Nigeria), 1985).

Oyovbaire S. E., **Federalism in Nigeria: A study in the development of the Nigerian State** (London: Macmillan Publishers Ltd., 1985).

Oyovbaire S. E., ed., **Democratic Experiment in Nigeria: Interpretative Essays** (Benin City, Nigeria: Omega Publishers, c1987).

Padover S. K., ed., **The Complete Madison** (New York: Harper, 1953).

Padover S. K., **Sources of Democracy; Voices of freedom, hope and justice** (New York: McGraw-Hill Book Co., 1973).

Peil M., **Nigeian Politics: The People's View** (London: Cassell & Company Ltd., 1976).

Pennock J. R., **Democratic Political Theory** (New Jersey: Princeton University Press, 1979).

Perham M., **Native Administration in Nigeria** (London, 1937).

Philadelphia Public Schools, **Our schools: Beginning in democracy** (Philadelphia, 1941).

Pontifical Commission "Justitia et Pax", **The Church and Human Rights: Working Paper No. 1** (Vatican City: Pontifical Commission "Iustitia et Pax", 1978 edition).

Pontifical Council for Justice and Peace, **Human Rights and the Church: Historical and Theological Reflections** (Vatican City, 1990).

Ranney A. & Kendall W., **Democracy and the American Party System** (New York: Harcourt, Brace & World, Inc., 1956).

Rauscher A., ed., **Selbstinteresse und Gemeinwohl: Beiträge zur Ordnung der Wirtschaftsgesellschaft**, Soziale Orientierung, Band 5, (Berlin: Duncker & Humblot, 1985).

Rauscher A., **Kirche in der Welt**, vol. 1, (Würzburg: Echter Verlag, 1988).
Rauscher A., ed., **Mönchengladbacher Gespräche** (a publication by K.S.Z. Mönchengladbach), vol. 9, entitled **Mehrheitsprinzip und Minderheiten-recht**, (Köln: J. P. Bachem Verlag, 988).
Reiss H., ed., **Kant's Political Writings** (Cambridge: Cambridge University Press, 1970).
Rejai M., ed., **Democracy: The Contemporary Theories** (New York: Atherton Press, 1967).
Riley M., **Power, Politics and Voting Behaviour - An introduction to the Sociology of Politics** (London: Harvester . Wheatsheaf, 1988).
Ronen D., ed., **Democracy and pluralism in Africa** (Boulder, Colo.: L. Rienner; Sevenoaks, Kent: Hodder and Stoughton, 1986).
Roos L., **Demokratie als Lebensform** (München . Paderborn . Wien: Verlag Ferdinand Schöningh, 1969).
Roosevelt T., **The Right of the People to Rule** (Washington DC: Government Printing Office, 1919).
Roosevelt T., **A Charter of Democracy** (Washington DC: Government Printing Office, 1919).
Ross S., **African Woman: A Study of Igbo of Nigeria** (New York: Frederick Praeger Publishers, 1965).
Sabine G. H. & Smith S. B., **On the Commonwealth: Marcus Tullius Cicero** (Columbus, Ohio, 1929).
Sabine G. H. & Thorson T. L., **A History of Political Theory**, fourth edition (Chicago et al.: Holt, Rinehart and Winston, Inc., 1973).
Sanda A. O., ed., **Ethnic Relations in Nigeria: Problems and Prospects** (Nigeria: Dept. of Sociology, University of Ibadan, 1976).
Sartori G., **The Theory Of Democracy Revisited** (Chatham, New Jersey: Chatham House Publishers, Inc., 1987).
Sheldon G. W., **The History Of Political Theory: Ancient Greece To Modern America**, Series X, Pol. Science, vol. 21 (New York-Bern-Frankfurt am Main- Paris: Peter Lang, 1988).
Scheuner U., **Das Mehrheitsprinzip in der Demokratie** (Opladen 1973).
Schillebeeckx E., **Weil Politk nicht alles ist - Von Gott reden in einer gefährdeten Welt** (Freiburg . Basel . Wien: Herder, 1987).
Schumpeter J. A., **Capitalism, Socialism and Democracy**, 3rd. ed. (New York: Harper & Brothers, 1950).
Shaw T., **Nigeria: Its archaeology and early history** (London: Thames and Hudson, c 1978).
Shaw T. M. & Ihonvbere J. O., eds., **Nigeria** (Boulder: Western Press, 1992).
Shils E., **Political Development in New States** (The Hague: Mouton & Co., 1962).

Shyllon F. and Obasanjo O., **The Demise of the Rule of Law in Nigeria under the Military: Two Points of View** (Ibadan: Insitute of African Studies, University of Ibadan, 1980).
Sigel R. S. & Hoskin M., ed., **Education for democratic citizenship: A challenge for multi-ethnic societies** (Hillsdale, N.J.: Lawrence Erlbaum Associates, 1991).
Sinclair R. K., **Democracy and Participation in Athens** (G. Britain: Cambridge University Press, 1989).
Smith M., **The Development of European Law** (New York, 1928).
St. Jorre J. de, **The Nigerian Civil War** (Hodder and Stoughton, 1972).
Stahn E., **Mai's Weltführer Nr. 3: Nigeria: Reiseführer mit Landeskunde** (Mai's Reiseführer Verlag Buchschlag bei Frankfurt, 1990).
Stapleton L., **The Design of Democracy** (New York: Oxford University Press, 1949).
Stokke O., **Nigeria: An Introduction to the Politics, Economy and Social Setting of Modern Nigeria** (Sweden: Söderström & Finn, Uppsala, 1970).
Suberu R. T., "The Travails of Federalism in Nigeria," in: L. Diamond & M. F. Plattner, eds., **Nationalism, Ethnic Conflict, and Democracy** (Baltimore and London: The John Hopkins University Press, 1994).
Sutherland D. B., **Nigeria** (Chicago: Children's Press, c1995).
Tamuno T. N., **Nigeria: its people and its problems** (Lagos: Panel on Nigeria since Independence History Project, 1989).
Thorson T. L., **The Logic of Democracy** (New York: Holt, Rinehart & Winston, Inc., 1962).
Turner F., **The Greek Heritage in Victorian Britain** (New Haven: Yale University Press, 1981).
Uchendu P. K., **The Role of Nigerian Women in Politics, Past and Present** (Enugu, Nigeria: Fourth Dimension Publishing Co. Ltd., 1993).
Usman Y. B., **For the Liberation of Nigeria** (London: New Beacon Books Ltd., 1980).
Usman Y. B., **Political Repression in Nigeria** (Zaria, Nigeria: Gaskiya Corporation Ltd., 1982).
van de Walle N., "Crisis and Opportunity in Africa," in: L. Diamond & M. F. Plattner, eds., **Economic Reform and Democracy** (A Journal of Democracy Book. Baltimore and London: The John Hopkins University Press, 1995).
Vanhanen T., ed., **Strategies of democratization** (Washington: Crane Russak, c1992).
Webster D., **Writings and Speeches**, national ed., (Boston: Little, Brown & Co., 1903).
Wellesley D., **Sir George Goldie - Founder of Nigeria** (London, 1934).
Wesson R., **Democracy: A Worldwide Survey** (New York: Praeger, 1987).

Whitaker B., ed., **Minorities: A Question of Human Rights?** (Oxford, New York: Pergmon Press, 1984).

Whitaker C. S., Jr., **The Politics of Tradition: Continuity and Change in Northern Nigeria, 1946-1966** (Princeton, New Jersey: Princeton University Press, 1970).

Williamson P. and Perrotta K., ed., **Christianity Confronts Modernity** (Michigan, U.S.A.: Servant Books, 1981).

Wills G., **Lincoln at Gettysburg: The Words that Remade America** (New York: Simon and Schuster, 1992).

Wilson M. L., **Democracy Has Roots** (New York: Carrick & Evans, inc., c. 1939).

Wiseman H. V., **Political Systems** (London: Routledge & Kegan Paul, 1966).

Wraith R. and Simpkings E., **Corruption in Developing Countries** (London: George Allen and Unwin Ltd., 1963).

Wringe C., **Democracy, Schooling, and Political Education** (London; Boston: G. Allen & Unwin, 1984).

Yar'Adua S. M., Brigd., **'Forward' to the Federal Government Guidelines on the Local Government Reforms of 1976** (Kaduna: Government Printer, 1976).

Zimmern A., **The Greek Commonwealth** (Oxford: At the Clarendon Press, 1914).

Encyclopaediae/Lexicons/Constitutions

Aristotle, *The Politics*, VI. ii. or 1317a(40) - 1318a(3), in: **Great Books Of The Western World**, vol. 8, (Chicago, USA: Encyclopaedia Britannica, Inc., 2nd. edition, 1990).

Cohen C., *The Justification of Democracy*, in: **The Monist**, vol. 55, no. 1 (Jan. 1971), p. 12.

Jefferson T., *The Declaration of Independence*, in: **Great Books of the Western World**, vol. 40, (Chicago, USA: Encyclopaedia Britannica, Inc., 1991), p. 1.

Locke J., *Second Treatise of Government*, chap. 6, para. 54, in: **Great Books of the Western World**, vol. 33 (Chicago, USA: Encyclopaedia Britannica, Inc., 1991), p. 36.

Locke J., *Second Essay Concerning Civil Government*, in: **Great Books of the Western World**, vol. 33, (Chicago, USA: Encyclopaedia Britannica, Inc., 1991), pp. 29-30.

Montesquieu B. de, *The Spirit of Laws* (1750), Bk. XI, Chap. 6, in: **Great Books of the Western World**, vol. 35, (Chicago, USA: Encyclopaedia Britannica, Inc., 1991), pp. 69-75.

Mortimer J. Adler, ed., **Great Books of the Western World,** vol. 1: **The Syntopicon I** (Chicago, USA: Encyclopaedia Britannica, Inc., 1990), p. 241.

New Catholic Encyclopaedia, vol. 13, pp. 762-763.

Nigeria, in: **1994 Britannica Book of the Year: Events of 1993** (Chicago, USA: Encyclopaedia Britannica, Inc., 1994), p. 684.

Nigerian Year Book (1958).

Report of the Constitutional Conference, vol. 1: The Draft Constitution of the Federal Republic of Nigeria (1995).

Rousseau J. J., *On The Origin Of Inequality*, in: **Great Books Of the Western World**, vol. 35, (Chicago, USA: Encyclopaedia Britannica, Inc., 1991), p. 343.

Rousseau J. J., *The Social Contract*, Bk. I,Chap. 8, in: **Great Books Of the Western World**, vol. 35, (Chicago, USA: Encyclopaedia Britannica, Inc., 1991), p. 393.

Shakespeare W., *Julius Caesar*, Act I, Scene II in: **Great Books of the Western World**, vol. 24 (Chicago, USA: Encyclopaedia Britannica, Inc., 1991), p. 570.

The Constitution of the Federal Republic of Nigeria: 1979, sec. 10.

The Constitution of the Federal Republic of Nigeria (Promulgation) Decree 1989, No. 12, Part II. Chap. IV, Sec. 32-44.

The Federalist, nos. 10, 37, 47, 51, 71, in: **Great Books of the Western World**, vol. 40 (Chicago, USA: Encyclopaedia Britannica, Inc., 1991).

The New Encyclopaedia Britannica (15th edition, 1992): vol. 6, p. 341; vol. 9, p. 564; vol. 25, pp. 979, 1013, 1025-1031;

Tocqueville A. de, *Democracy in America*, bk. 2, pt. 2, chap. 1, tr. by George Lawrence, in: **Great Books of the Western World**, vol. 44, (Chicago, USA: Encyclopaedia Britannica, Inc., 1991 edition), pp. 269-271.

Thucydides, *The History Of The Peloponesian War* (tr. by R. Crawley and rev. by R. Feetham), bk. II, 37 & 40, in: **Great Books Of The Western World**, vol. 5, (Chicago, USA: Encyclopaedia Britannica, Inc., 1990).

Encyclicals & Pastoral Letters

Catholic Church. Catholic Bishops of Nigeria, **The Church and the Nigerian social problems : Memorandum of the Catholic Bishops of Nigeria** (Lagos: Catholic Secretariate of Nigeria, 1972).

Catholic Truth Society, **Rerum Novarum: Encyclical Letter of Pope Leo XIII on the condition of the working classes**, Centenary Study Edition: with introduction and notes by Joseph Kirwan (London: Ludo Press Ltd., 1991 edition).

John XXIII, Pope, **Mater et Magistra**, ("Christianity and Social Progress"), 1961, no. 51-53, 65, 68-72, 79, 87, 123, 124, 127, 128, 133-135, 137, 140, 141, 143, 147.

John XXIII, Pope, the Encyclical **Pacem in Terris** ("Peace on Earth"), 1963, nos. 11, 13, 18-20, 54-57, 60-63, 64, 69.

John Paul II, Pope, the Encyclical **Sollicitudo Rei Socialis** ("On Social Concern"), 1987, nos. 14, 27, 33, 38, 39.

John Paul II, Pope, the Encyclical **Laborem Exercens**, ("On Human Work"), 1981, nos. 18-21, 22.

Leo XIII, Pope, **Rerum Novarum**, ("On the Condition of Labour"), 1891, nos. 15-17, 23, 26, 28, 29, 34-36, 38, 42.

Paul VI, Pope, the Encyclical **Populorum Progressio** ("On the Development of Peoples"), 1967, no. 14.

Paul VI, Pope, Encyclical **Octogesima Adveniens** ("A Call to Action on the Eightieth Anniversary of Rerum Novarum"), 1971, no. 20.

Pius XI, Pope, the Encyclical **Quadragesimo Anno**, ("After Forty Years"), 1931, no. 25, 27, 71, 74, 79-80, 81, 84, 85.

Pius XII, Pope, **Benegnitas et Humanitas** (ActApS 37, 1945).

Joint Pastoral Letter of the Nigerian Catholic Bishops, Feb. 10, 1979, no. 9, pp. 5-6.

Vatican Council II, Pastoral Constitution **Gaudium et Spes** ("The Church in the Modern World"), 1965, nos. 40, 63, 64, 74-76 - ed. by Austin Flannery, O. P. (Northport, New York: Costello Publishing Company, 1988 ed.).

Vatican Council II, **Dignitatis Humanae** ("Declaration on Religious Liberty"), 1965, nos. 1-2, ed. by Austin Flannery, O. P. (Northport, New York: Costello Publishing Company, 1988 revised edition).

Journals/Manuals

Adams P., "The World Bank and the IMF in sub-Saharan Africa: Undermining Development and Envirnmental Sustainability," in: **Journal of International Affairs**, vol. 46, no. 1, Summer 1992, pp. 97-118.

African Contemporary Record, 1978-79, p. B739.

African Report, 11, 1 (January 1966), pp. 40-42; 35, 3, (July - August 1990), pp. 50-53.

Ake C., "The unique case of African democracy," in: **Journal of International Affairs**, vol. 69, no. 2, April 1993, pp. 293-244.

Austin D., "Reflections on African politics: Prospero, Ariel and Caliban," in: **Journal of International Affairs**, vol. 69, no. 2, April 1993, pp. 203- 222.

Bayart J-F., "The Historicity of African Societies," in: **Journal of International Affairs**, vol. 46, no. 1, Summer 1992, pp. 55-80.

Beckstein G., "Rechtsbewußtsein contra Gewaltbereitschaft" in: **Politische Studien**, Sonderheft 5/1993, herausg. von Hanns Seidel Stiftung eV (München: Atwerb-Verlag, 1993), p. 32.

Bellamy R., "Joeph A. Schumpeter and his contemporaries: Introduction," in: **European Journal of Political Research**, No. 2, Feb. 1993 (Netherlands: Kluwer Academy Publishers), pp. 117-219.

Berghofer-Weichner M., "Einheit von Demokratie und Rechtsstaat - eine ständige Herausforderung," in: **Politische Studien**, Sonderheft 5/1993, herausg. von Hanns Seidel Stiftung eV (München: Atwerb-Verlag, 1993), p. 5.

Bhagwati J., "The New Thinking on Development," in: **Journal of Democracy**, Oct. 1995, vol. 6, no. 4, (Baltimore: The John Hopkins University Press), pp. 50-64.

Chabal P, "Democracy and Daily Life in Black Africa," in: **Journal of International Affairs**, vol. 70, no. 1, Jan. 1994, pp. 83-92.

Centre for Democratic Studies, Abuja, **Module I: Training Programme for State and National Officials of NRC and SDP, Part 1, Jul.-Aug. 1990. Training Modules** (Benin City: Hima & Hima Ltd., 1990), pp. 10-11.

Clark M. T., "Realism Ancient and Modern: Thucydides and International Relations," in: **PS: Political Science & Politics**, vol. XXVI, no. 3, Sept. 1993, pp. 491-494.

Dallmayr F., "Postmetaphysics and Democracy," in: **Political Theory - An International Journal of Political Philosophy**, vol. 21, no. 1, pp. 101-127.

Downing L. A. & Thigpen R. B., "Virtue and the Common Good in Liberal Theory," in: **The Journal of Politics**, vol 55, no. 4, Nov. 1993, pp. 1046-1059.

Economic and Financial Review, vol. 13, no. 1 (Nigeria: C.B.N., June 1975), p. 13.

Eigen P., "Combating Corruption Around the World," in: **Journal of Democracy**, January 1996, vol. 7, no. 1, (Baltimore: The John Hopkins University Press), pp. 158-168.

Euben J. P., "Democracy Ancient and Modern," in: **PS: Political Science & Politics**, vol. XXVI, no. 3, Sept. 1993, pp. 478-480.

Gladdish K., "Choosinf an Electoral System: Thc Primacy of the Particular," in: **Journal of Democracy**, January 1993, vol. 4, no. 1, (Baltimore: The John Hopkins University Press), pp. 53-65.

Grofman B., "Lessons of Athenian Democracy: Editor's Introduction," in: **PS: Political Science & Politics**, vol. XXVI, no. 3, Sept. 1993, p. 471-474.

Gyimah-Boadi E., "Civil Society in Africa," in: **Journal of Democracy**, April 1996, vol. 7, no. 2, (Baltimore: The John Hopkins University Press), pp. 118-132.

Horowitz D. L., "Democracy in a Divided Society," in: **Journal of Democracy**, October 1993, vol. 4, no. 4, (Baltimore: The John Hopkins University Press), pp. 18-38.

Hufen F., "Bürgersinn und Rechtsbewusstsein," in: **Politische Studien**, Sonderheft 5/1993, herausg. von Hanns Seidel Stiftung eV (München: Atwerb-Verlag, 1993), pp. 38-39.

Hullfish H. G., "Education and Post War Economics," in: **Educational Research Bulletin**, XXI (Jan. 14, 1942), p. 4.

Huntington S. P., "Armed Forces and Democracy: Reforming Civil-Military Realations," in: **Journal of Democracy**, Oct. 1995, vol. 6, no. 4, (Baltimore: The John Hopkins University Press), pp. 9-17.

Huntington S. P., "Democracy for the Long Haul," in: **Journal of Democracy**, April 1996, vol. 7, no. 2, (Baltimore: The John Hopkins University Press), pp. 3-13.

Ibrahim J., "The Politics of Religion in Nigeria: The Parameters of the 1987 Crisis in Kaduna State," in: **Review of African Political Economy**; No. 45/46, Winter 1989, pp. 65-82.

Jaycox E. V. K., "Sub-Saharan Africa: Development Performance and Prospects," in: **Journal of International Affairs**, vol. 46, no. 1, Summer 1992, pp. 81-96.

Jeffries R., "The State, Structural Adjustment and Good Government in Africa," in: **Journal of Commonwealth & Comparative Politics**, vol. 31, no. 1, (March 1993), pp. 20-35.

Joseph R., "Political Parties and Ideology in Nigeria," in: **Review of African Political Economy**, No. 13, May-August, 1978.

Law Notes and Reviews (1970), No. 6, pp. 30-31.

Lewis P. M., "Political Transition and the Dilemma of Civil Society in Africa," in: **Journal of International Affairs**, vol. 46, no. 1, Summer 1992, pp. 31-54.

Lijphard A., "Democracies: Forms, performance, and constitutional engineering," in: **European Journal of Political Research**, vol. 25, 1994, p. 1.

Lipset S. M., "Reflections on Capitalism, Socialism & Democracy," in: **Journal of Democracy**, April 1993, vol. 4, no. 2, (Baltimore: The John Hopkins University Press), pp.43-55.

Mainwaring S., "Presidentialism Multipartism, and Democracy," in: **Comparative Political Studies - a quarterly journal**, vol. 26, no. 2, July 1993 (Newbury Park: Sage Periodicals Press), pp. 198-228.

McCombs M. & Shaw D., "The Agenda-Setting Function of the Press," in: **Public Opinion Quarterly** 39 (1972).

Merkl G., "Bürgersinn und Rechtsbewusstsein," in: **Politische Studien**, Sonderheft 5/1993, herausg. von Hanns Seidel Stiftung eV (München: Atwerb Verlag, 1993), p. 40.

Mitchel J., "Hobbes and the Equality of All Under the One," in: **Political Theory - An International Journal of Political Philosophy**, vol. 21, no. 1, Feb. 1993, pp. 78-100.

Ndue P. N., "Africa's Turn Toward Pluralism," in: **Journal of Democracy**, Jan. 1994, vol 5, no. 1, (Baltimore: The John Hopkins University Press), pp. 45-54.

Norris P., "The 1992 US Elections," in: **Government and Opposition**, vol 28, no. 1, winter 1993, pp. 51-68.

Ober J., "Public Speech and the Power of the People in Democratic Athens," in: **PS: Political Science & Politics**, vol. XXVI, no. 3, September 1993, pp. 481-485.

O'Donnell G., "Delegative Democracy," in: **Journal of Democracy**, Jan. 1994, vol 5, no. 1, (Baltimore: The John Hopkins University Press), pp. 55-69.

Onwuteaka J. C., "The Aba Riot of 1929 and Its Relation to the System of Indirect Rule," in: **The Nigerian Journal of Economics and Social Studies**, Nov. 1975.

Przeworski A., et al., "What Makes Democracies Endure," in: **Journal of Democracy**, Jan. 1996, vol 7, no. 1, (Baltimore: The John Hopkins University Press), pp. 39-55.

Scanlon T., "A Theory of Freedom of Expression," in: **Philosophy & Public Affairs 1** (1972).

Rauscher A., "Der Mensch ist Person," in: **Katholische Soziallehre in Text und Kommentar**, vol. 1, (Köln: J. P. Bachem Verlag GmbH, 1975), p. 7.

Rauscher A., "Arbeit für alle," in: **Kirche und Gesellschaft**, no. 207, edited by "Katholische Sozialwissenschaftlichen Zentralstelle Mönchengladbach (Köln: J. P. Bachem Verlag GmbH, 1994).

Rauscher A., "Die Arbeitsplätze sind der Schlüssel," in: **Kirche und Gesellschaft**, no. 226, edited by "Katholische Sozialwissenschaftlichen Zentralstelle Mönchengladbach (Köln: J. P. Bachem Verlag GmbH, 1996).

Roosevelt T., "Letter to American Bishops," in: **Catholic News** (USA, Jan. 17, 1942).

Satori G., "How Far Can Free Government Travel?," in: **Journal of Democracy**, July 1995, vol. 6, no. 3, (Baltimore: The John Hopkins University Press), pp. 101-111.

Saxonhouse A. W., "Athenian Democracy: Modern Mythmakers and Ancient Theorists," in: **PS: Political Science & Politcs**, vol. XXVI, no. 3, Sept. 1993, pp. 486-490.

Simhony A., "T.H. Green: The Common Good Society," in: **History of Political Thought**, vol. XIV, issue 2, summer 1993, pp. 225-247.

Struther J., "Democracy Begins at Home," in: **Adult Education Journal**, vol. I, no. 3 (July, 1942), p. 118.

Transition to Civil Rule Programme, vol. 1 (Lagos, Nigeria: Federal Government Printer, 1987).

Trenchard J. & Gordon T., "Of Freedom of Speech: That the same is inseparable from Publick Liberty" (1720), in: **Cato's Letters: Essays on Liberty,**

Civil and Religious, and Other Important Subjects (New York: Da Capo, 1971), vol. 1, p. 98.

Turner J. M., "Democracy in Administration," **American Political Science Review** (1923), p. 216.

van de Walle N., "Crisis and Opportunity in Africa," in: **Journal of Democracy**, April 1995, vol. 6, no. 2, (Baltimore: The John Hopkins University Press), pp. 128-141.

Verba S., *The 1993 James Madison Award Lecture: The Voice of the People*, in: **PS: Political Science & Politics**, vol. XXVI, no. 4, Dec. 1993, p. 677.

Wallace H. A., **The Price of Free World Victory**: Speech dilivered on May 8, 1942, before the Free World Association.

Würtenberger T., "Beständigkeit im Wandel, Unser Rechtsstaat und der Zeitgeist" in: **Politische Studien**, Sonderheft 5/1993, herausg. von Hanns Seidel Stiftung eV. (München: Atwerb-Verlag, 1993), p. 16.

Yahaya A. D., "Representation in Local Government - The Emirate Case," in: **Nigerian Journal of Public Affairs**, vol. 11, no. 1 (May 1976).

Newspapers/Magazines

Africa Now, 1993: **May** 30, pp. 14-16.

African Concord, 1991: **Sept.** 30, p. 38; 1993: **May** 10, p. 31; **July** 19, pp. 14-25.

Augsburger Allgemeine, 1993: **Jan**. 4, pp. 1 & 3.

Daily Star, 1992: **March** 21.

Daily Times, 1961: **June** 28 and 29 (Editorials); 1979: **Aug**. 17, p. 1; Aug. 18,

Frankfurter Allgemeine, 1992: 14. **April**, p. 7.

National Concord, 1983: **Aug**. 20 (Editorial); **Dec**. 21 & 25.

New Nigerian, 1966: **Jan**. 17; 1967: **March** 8; 1977: **June** 2, p. 1; **Sept**. 13, pp. 2 & 34; 1980: **Jan**. 22; 1992: **March** 20.

Newswatch (Nigeria's Weekly Newsmagazine), 1991: **April** 8, pp. 18-19; **Oct**. 7, pp. 12-18; Oct. 21, pp. 21-23; Oct. 28, pp. 9-13; **Nov**. 4, pp. 9-16; Nov. 11, pp. 11-12; **Dec**. 9, pp. 9-16; Dec. 23, pp. 27-35; Dec. 30, pp. 13-18, 25-27.

Newswatch, 1992: **June** 8, pp. 33-35; **July** 13, pp. 9-16; July 20, pp. 13-20; **Aug**. 3, pp. 9-15; Aug. 17, pp. 11-18; **Sept**. 14, pp. 28-30; Sept. 28, pp. 24-26; **Oct**. 5, pp. 46-49; Oct. 19, pp. 14-19; Oct. 26, pp. 10-17; **Nov**. 16, pp. 6, 9-16; Nov. 23, pp. 10, 36-37; Nov. 30, p. 8; **Dec**. 7, pp. 14-20; Dec. 14, pp. 14-18; Dec. 21, pp. 21-22; Dec. 28, pp. 4, 42.

Newswatch, 1993: **Jan**. 11, pp. 16-17, 39-40; **Feb**. 1, pp. 9, 16-17; Feb. 8, pp. 3, 34; Feb. 15, pp. 6, 42; Feb. 22, p. 21; **March** 1, pp. 16-18; March 8, pp. 8-15; March 29, pp. 6, 13-15; **April** 12, pp. 7, 9 & 19; April 19, pp. 16-21; April 26, pp. 15 & 17; **May** 17, pp. 7, 25; **June** 21, p. 10-18;

June 28, pp. 8-21; **July** 5, pp. 9-10, 14-18; July 12, p. 6; **Aug**. 2, pp. 9- 13; Aug. 9, pp. 10-14, 18-20; Aug. 16, pp. 13-14, 37; Aug. 23, pp. 11-15; Aug. 30, pp. 8-14, 26-32; **Sept**. 6, pp. 10-16; Sept. 20, pp. 10-15, 20-22; Sept. 27, pp. 32-37; **Oct**. 18, pp. 12-15; **Nov**. 15, pp. 12-17; Nov. 22, pp. 12-16; Nov. 29, pp. 9-14, 17-21; **Dec**. 6, pp. 6, 11-18.

Newswatch, 1994: **Jan**. 17, pp. 10-14; Jan. 31, pp. 14-15, 23-25; **Feb**. 28, pp. 10-15; **April** 4, pp. 10-13, 18 & 19; April 11, pp. 27-28; **May** 9, pp. 10-16; May 16, pp. 11-18; May 23, p. 23; May 30, pp. 10-16; **June** 6, pp. 9-18; June 13, pp. 10-15; June 20, pp. 11-15; June 27, pp. 8-12; **July** 4, pp. 9-15; July 11, pp. 11-16; July 18, pp. 9-16; July 25, pp. 10-15; **Aug**. 1, pp. 24-28; Aug. 8, pp. 8-10, 15-17; Aug. 15, pp. 10-16; Aug. 29, pp. 10-14; **Sept**. 12, pp. 8-13; Sept. 19, pp. 26-31; **Oct**. 10, pp. 7-8, 25-30, 33-38; Oct. 17, pp. 17-18; **Nov**. 7, pp. 8-11; Nov. 21, pp. 30-33, 36; Nov. 28, pp. 13-18; **Dec**. 19, pp. 12-16; Dec. 12, pp. 14-22.

Newswatch, 1995: **March** 13, pp. 10-18; March 27, pp. 10-14, 18; **May** 8, pp. 10-13, 17-19; May 15, p. 10, 28-29; **June** 12, pp. 17-18; **July** 10, pp. 8-13; July 31, pp. 8-19; **Aug**. 7, pp. 9-16, 18-29; Aug. 21, pp. 23-24; **Oct**. 9, pp. 13-18.

Nigerian Tribune, 1977: **Sept**. 17, 1977, p. 4; 1990: **April** 23, p. 1.

Sunday Sketch, 1983: **Dec**. 25, 1983; 1992: **Sept**. 11, p. 21.

Sunday Triumph, **Aug**. 21, 1983.

TELL, 1992: **Oct**. 12, pp. 16-18; 1993: **July** 26, pp. 14-20.

The Economist, 1996: **June** 8, p. 50.

The Guardian, 1983: **Sept**. 10; **Oct**. 18; **Dec**. 24 & 29; 1984: **Jan**. 22, p. 3; 1992: **March** 20.

The Punch (Lagos), 1981: **Sept**. 21, p. 5; 1983: **Oct**. 1.

TIME, 1994: No. 48, **Nov**. 28; 1995: **May** 15, pp. 34-35.

Times International, 1980: **Jan**. 14, 1980.

Vanguard Newspaper, 1995: **Dec**. 11, p. 11; Dec. 14, pp. 12-13; Dec. 18, p. 13; Dec. 19, p. 18.

West Africa, 1953: **Dec**. 22; 1978: **May** 8, p. 901; 1983: **Nov**. 21, p. 2674;

West African Pilot, 1960: **June** 17 (Editorial).

Peter Lang · Europäischer Verlag der Wissenschaften

Stephen Theron

Africa, Philosophy and the Western Tradition

An Essay in Self-Understanding

Frankfurt/M., Berlin, Bern, New York, Paris, Wien, 1995. 156 pp.
ISBN 3-631-48611-1 pb. DM 54.–*
US-ISBN 0-8204-2902-3

This book examines the notion of an African philosophy, beginning with a critique of the assumptions behind this phrase and of the existing debate about "African philosophy". This leads to enquiry about the rise, establishment and maintenance of philosophy. Relations between consent to a theory of truth presupposed to philosophy and Western truth-claims in science, religion and human rights are studied. The relation of this to successful technology as vital for African development, but calling for the corresponding mental approach, is insisted upon. The book ends with stress on the central role of analogy in philosophical science and as a point of contact with African mythical tradition.

Contents: African philosophy, the idea and debate about it · Ethnicity and philosophy · How philosophy in fact arose, became established and was maintained · Truth, truth-claims and Western tradition · Human rights and truth · Technology and tradition · Analogy and myth

Frankfurt/M · Berlin · Bern · New York · Paris · Wien
Distribution: Verlag Peter Lang AG
Jupiterstr. 15, CH-3000 Bern 15
Telefon (004131) 9402131
*includes value added tax
Prices are subject to change without notice